TRAVELS, TREKS & TROMPS

A COMPENDIUM OF GOTHIC, ATMOSPHERIC & JUST PLAIN STRANGE SNAPSHOTS

CINSEARAE S.

Travels, Treks & Tromps: A Compendium of Gothic, Atmospheric, and Just Plain Strange Snapshots

ISBN-13: 978-1541080287
ISBN-10: 1541080289

http://BloodTouch.webs.com Official author website
Find the author on Facebook, Pinterest, Instagram, Twitter and YouTube @ Cinsearae

Author's Note

You are now holding in your hands my second collection of photographs I've (quite impatiently!) culminated over the last four and a half years; my first collection being **Terra Mysteria,** *released in 2011.*

I never leave home without my camera—who knows what kinds of interesting things I'll come across-- and nature always proves to be my best subject to photograph.

As I'm positive that my list of my favorite subjects to photograph will never be exhausted, this second collection is just the start of more interesting images to come.

I commend those who continue to live their lives with an open mind, an explorative heart, and a courageous, non-judgmental soul; those who are unafraid think for themselves and refuse to become part of the collective 'sheep'. On that note, I hope you'll enjoy this collection of snapshots, while I work on building my next one. Until then...

C.S.---2016

Dolls, Skeletons, & Other Oddities

Anyone who knows me pretty well knows I have an affinity for vintage/antique dolls, as some have a sort of creepy-cuteness all their own. I also love skulls, and all sorts of odd and unique objects. Usually, I love haunting local flea markets to find such treasures.

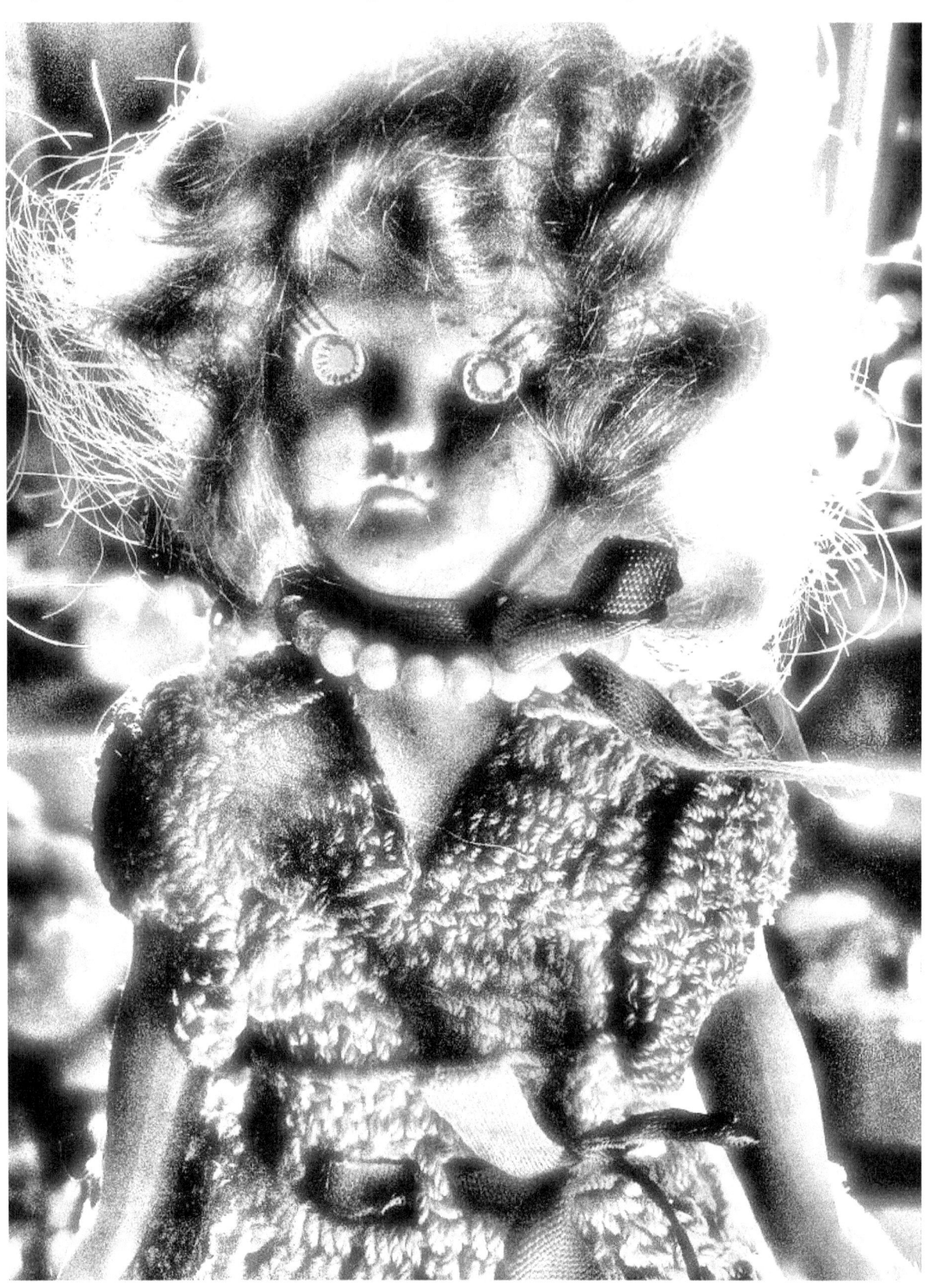

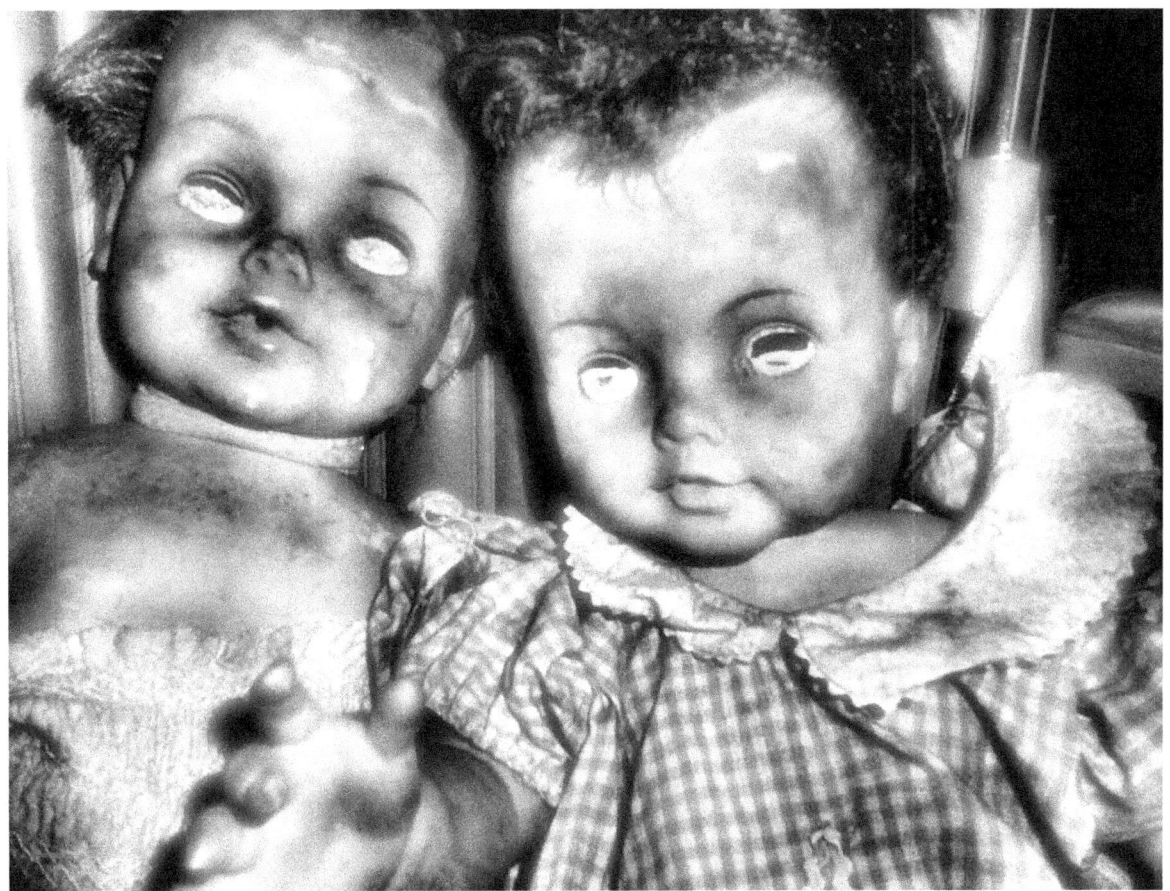

"Come play with us…."

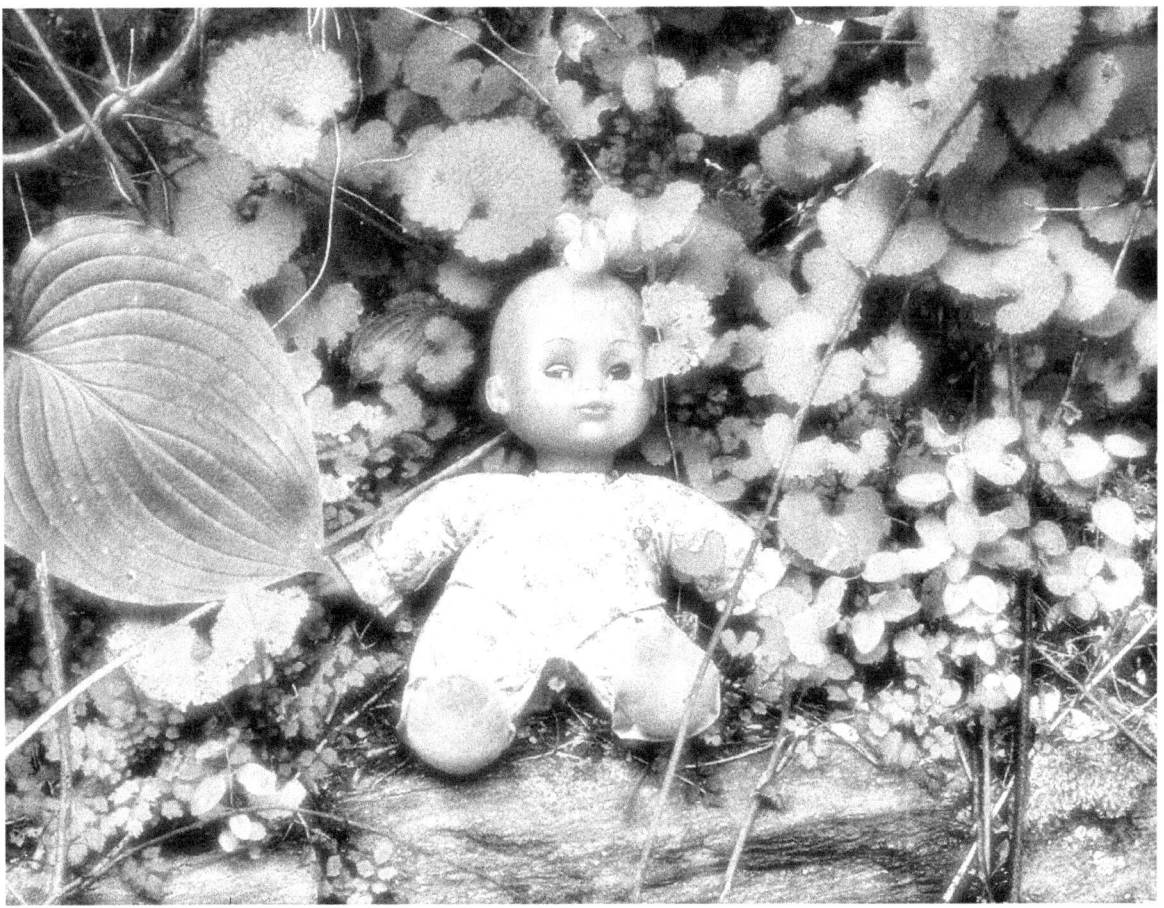

"I just woke up and found myself here…where am I??"

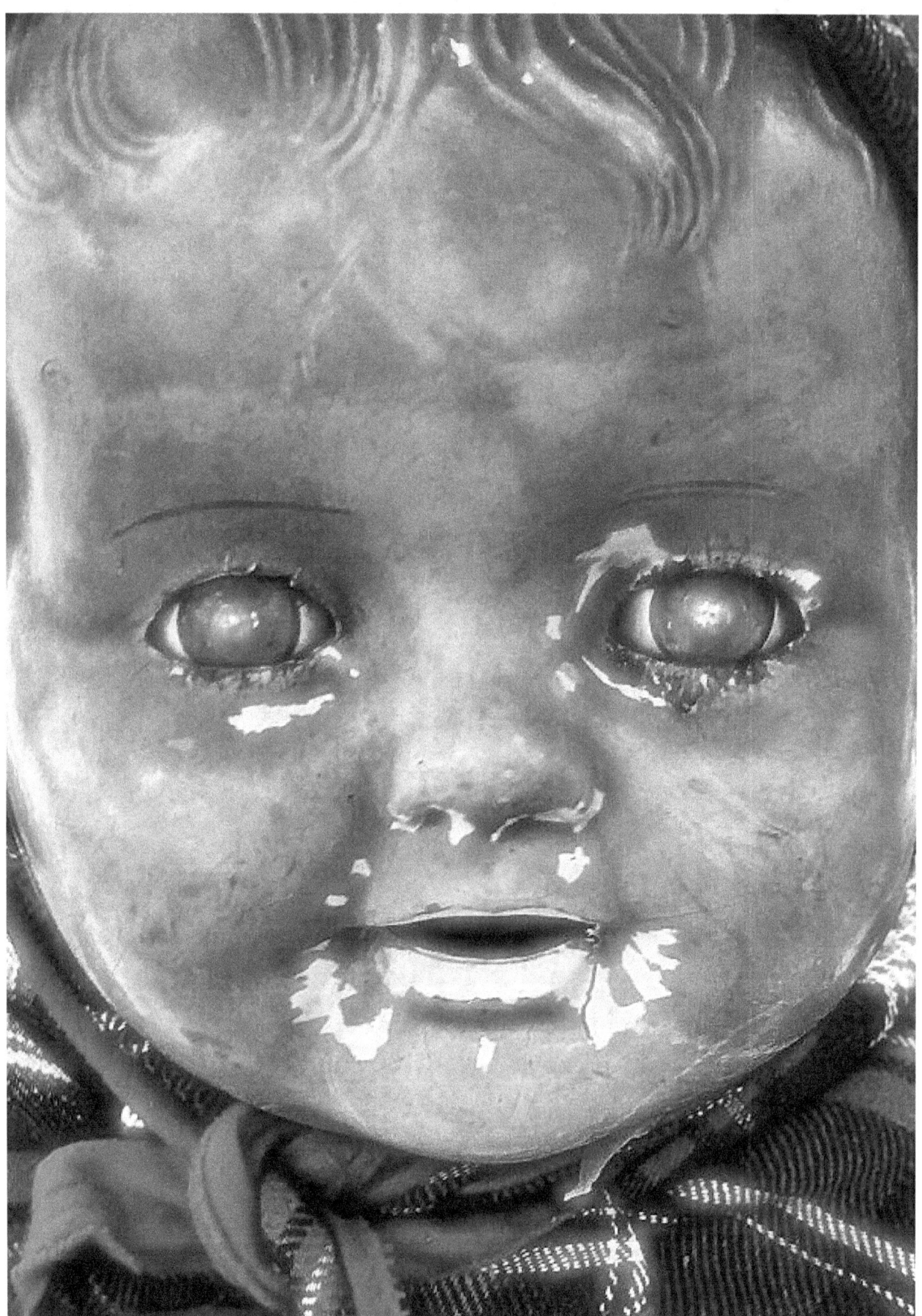

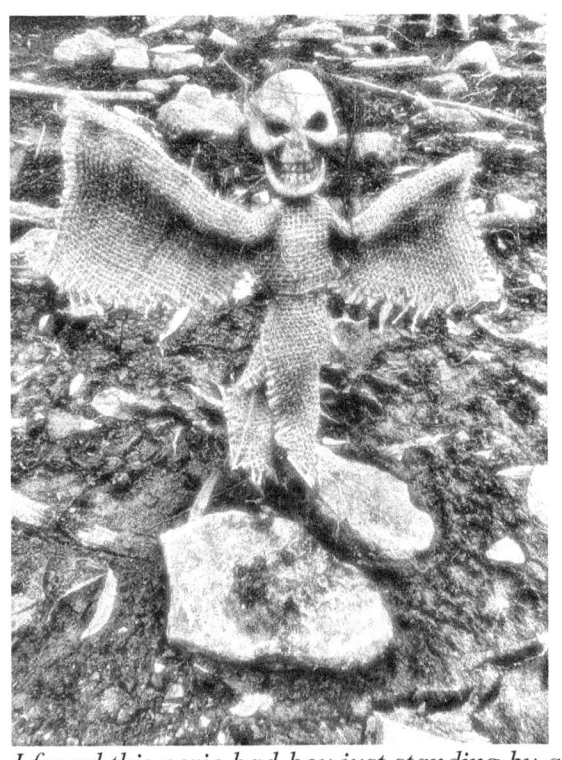

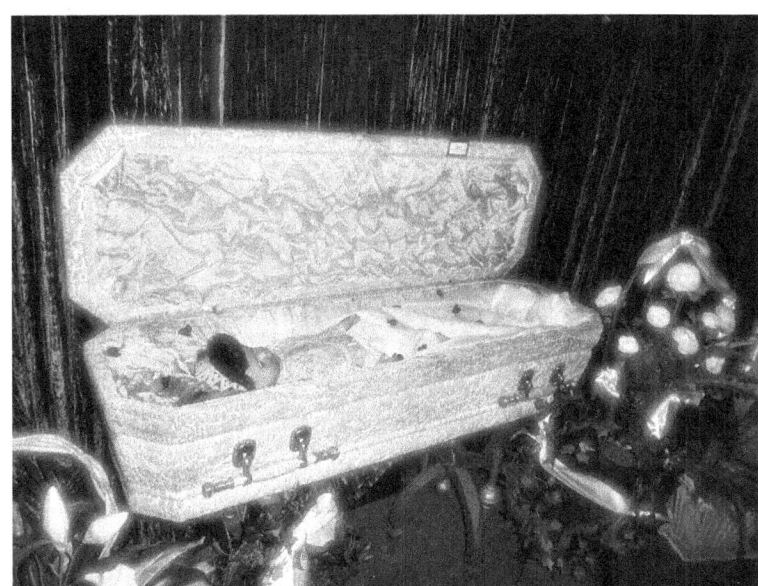

I found this eerie bad-boy just standing by a riverside. Needless to say, I left it right there.

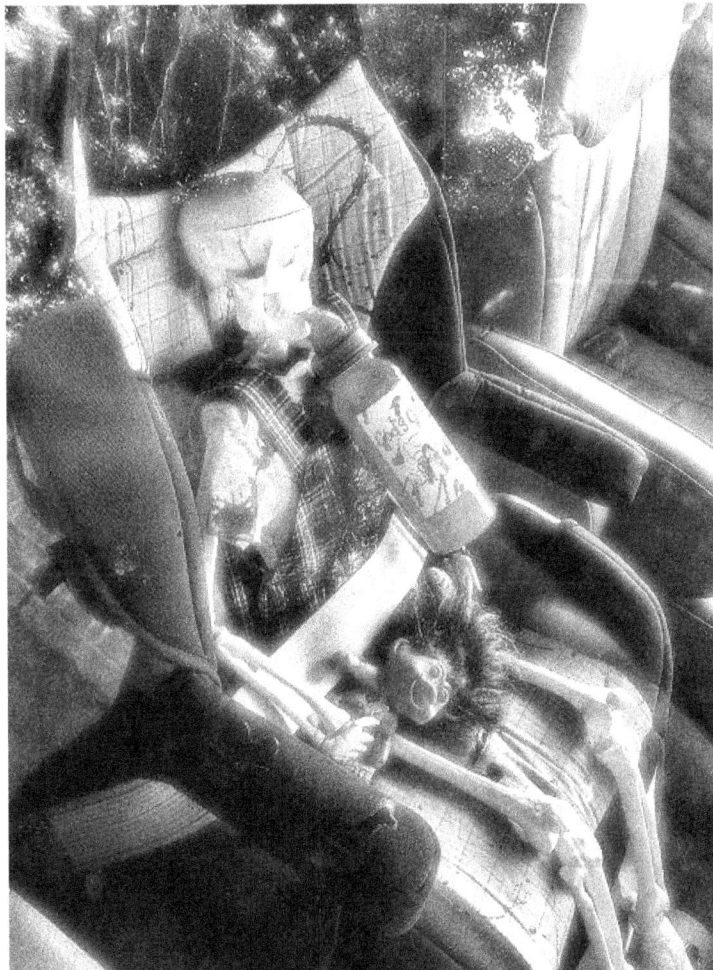

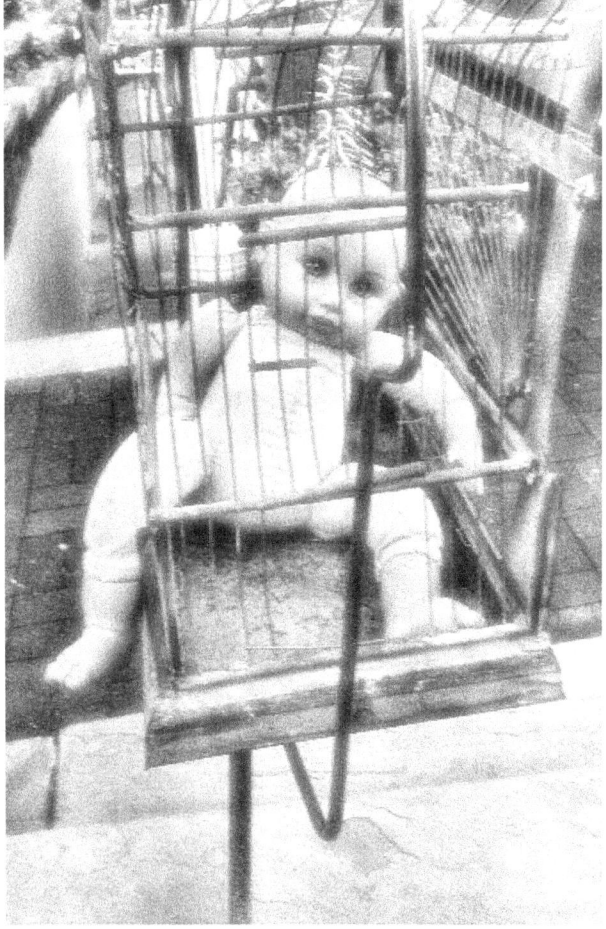

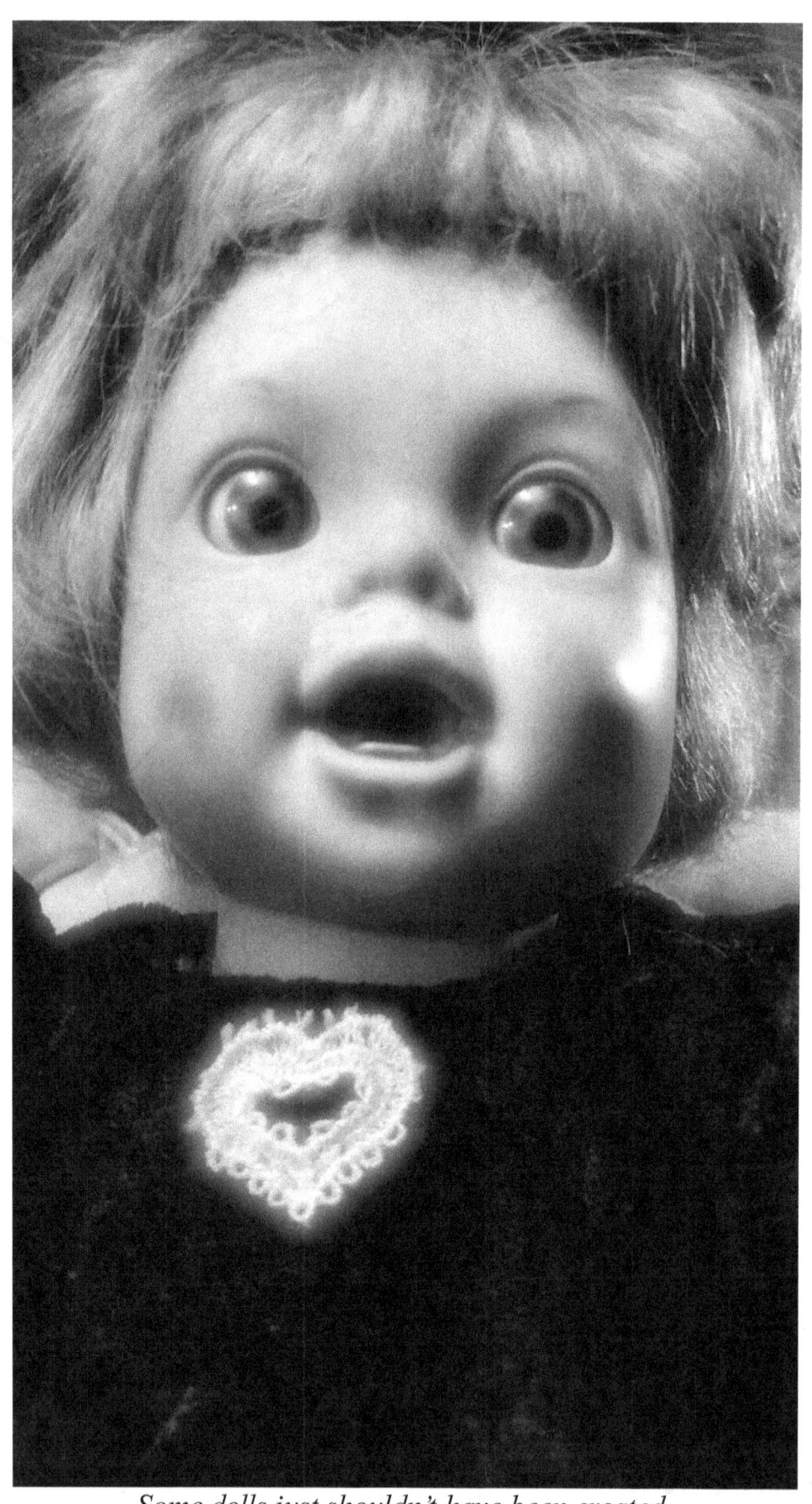

Some dolls just shouldn't have been created.

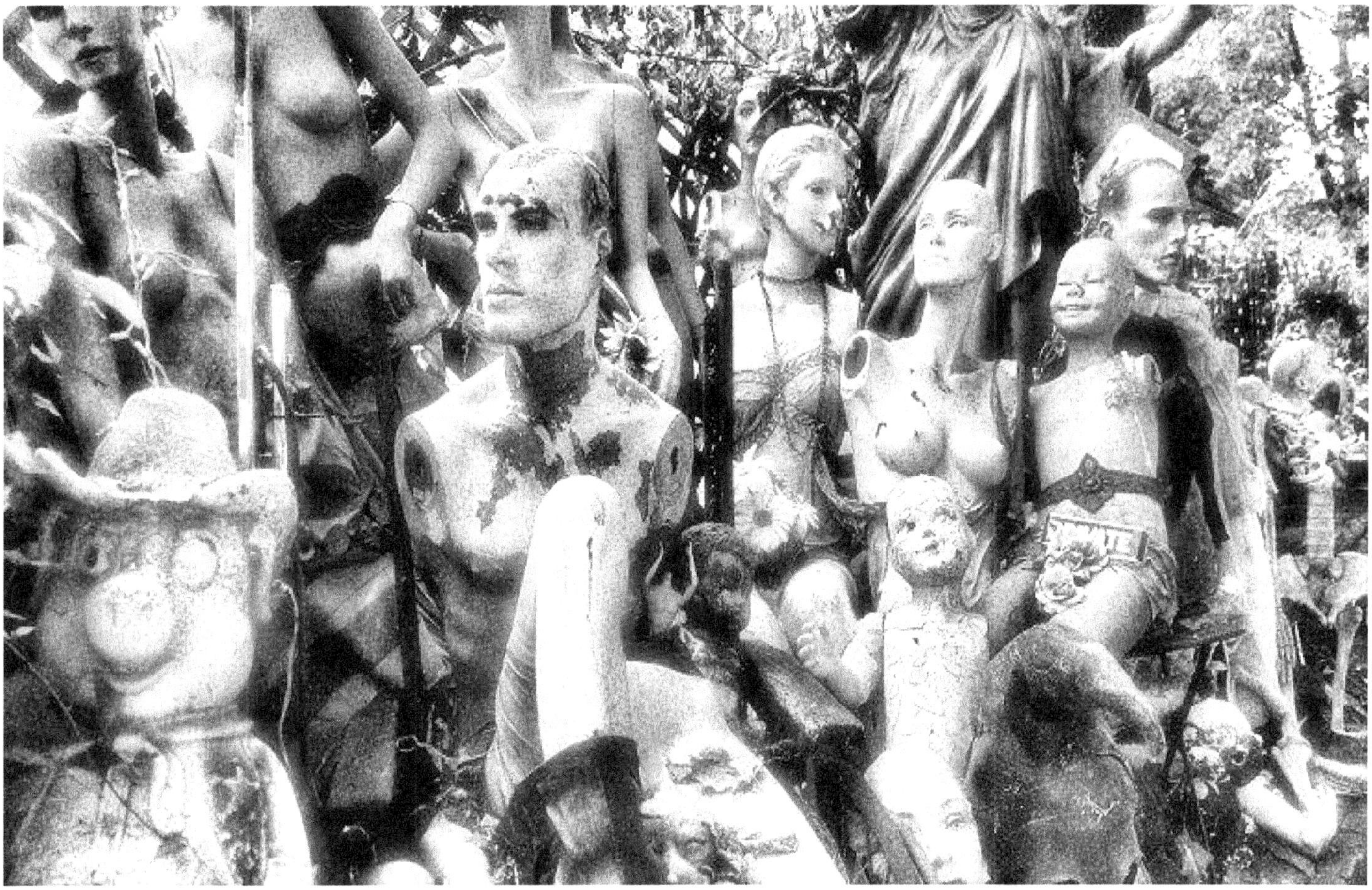

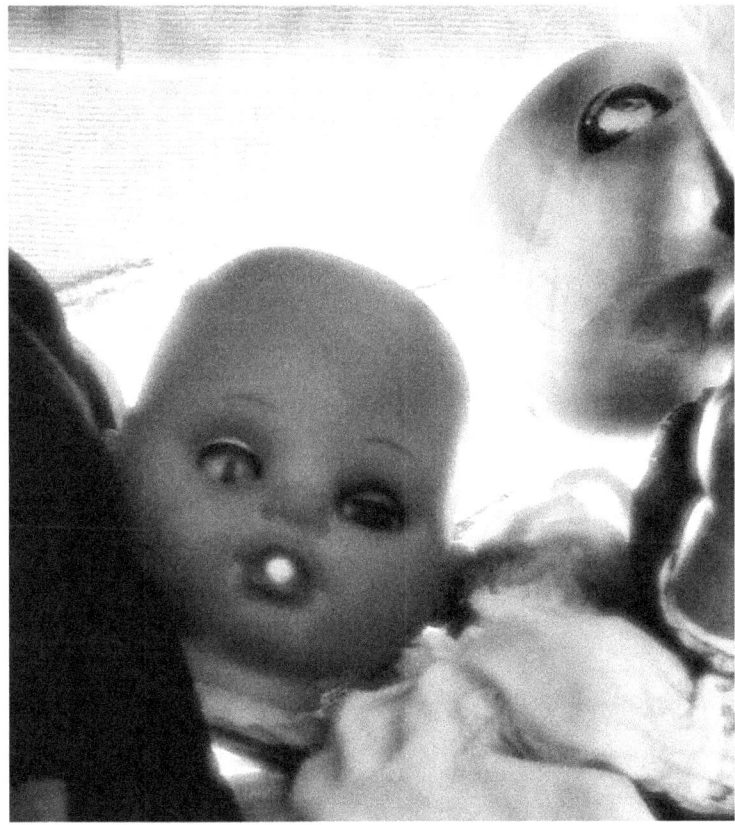
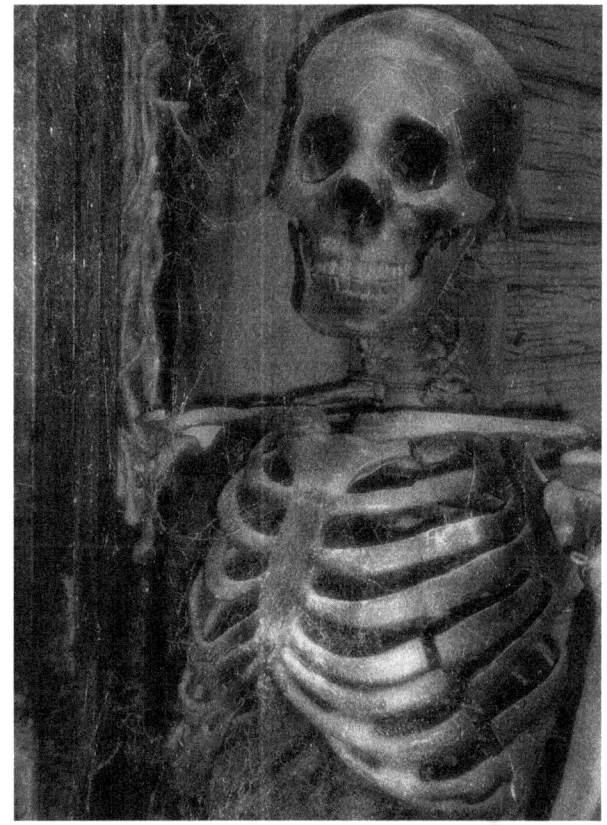

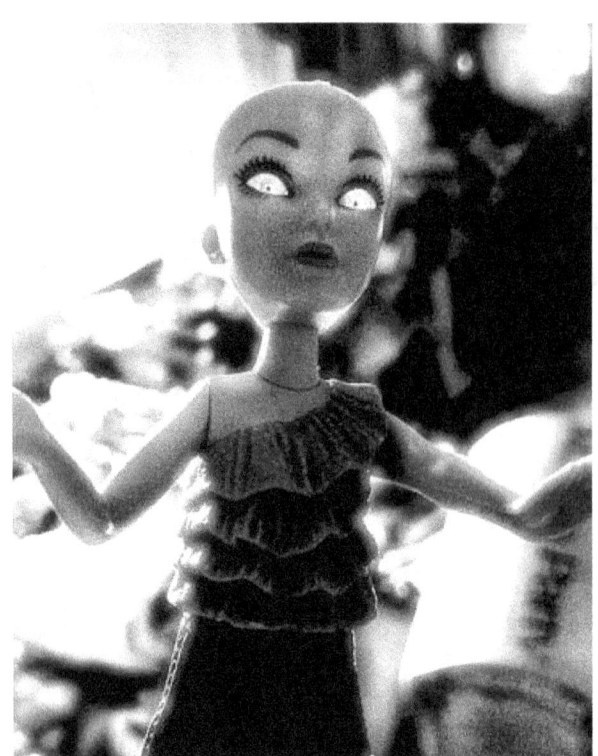
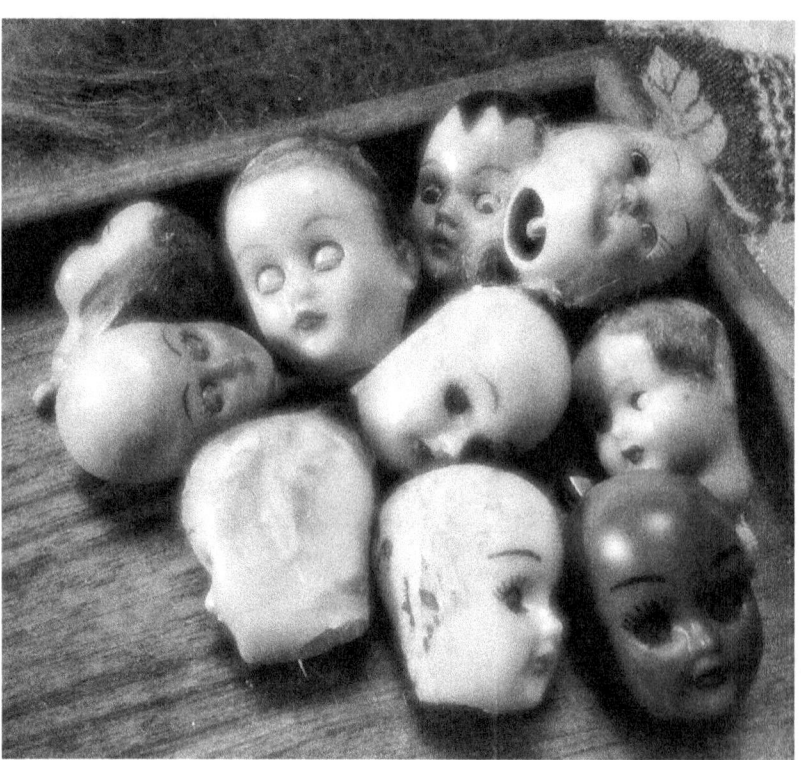
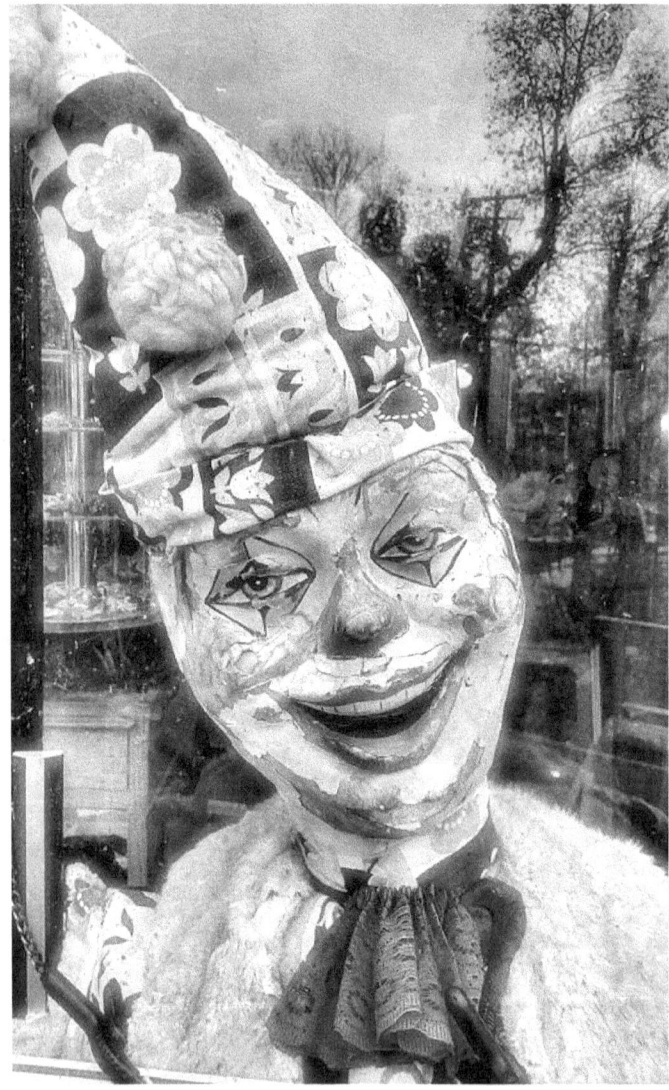
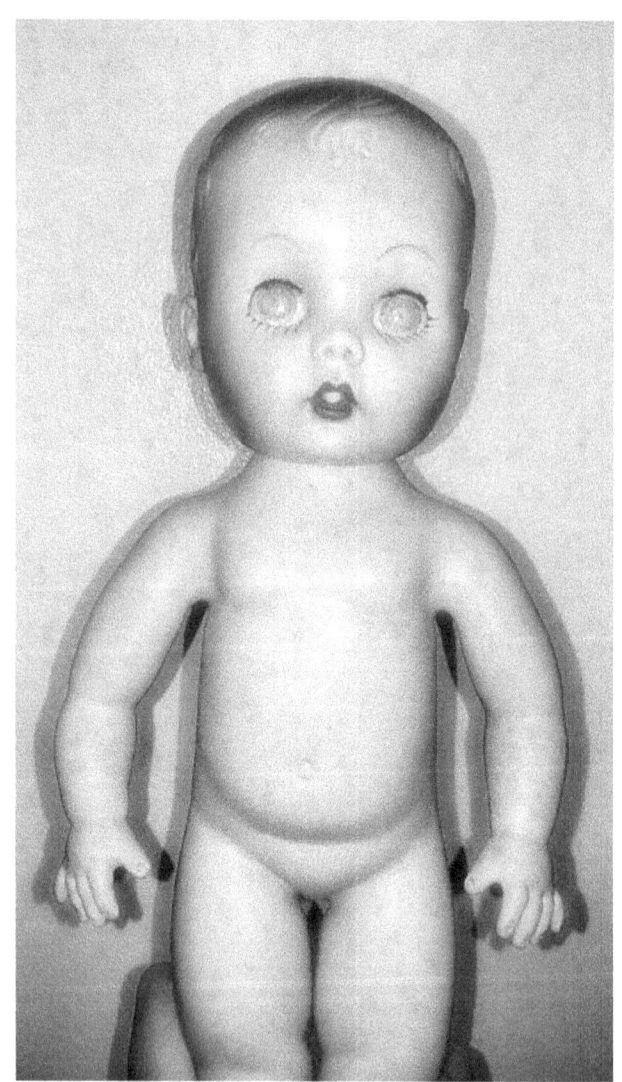

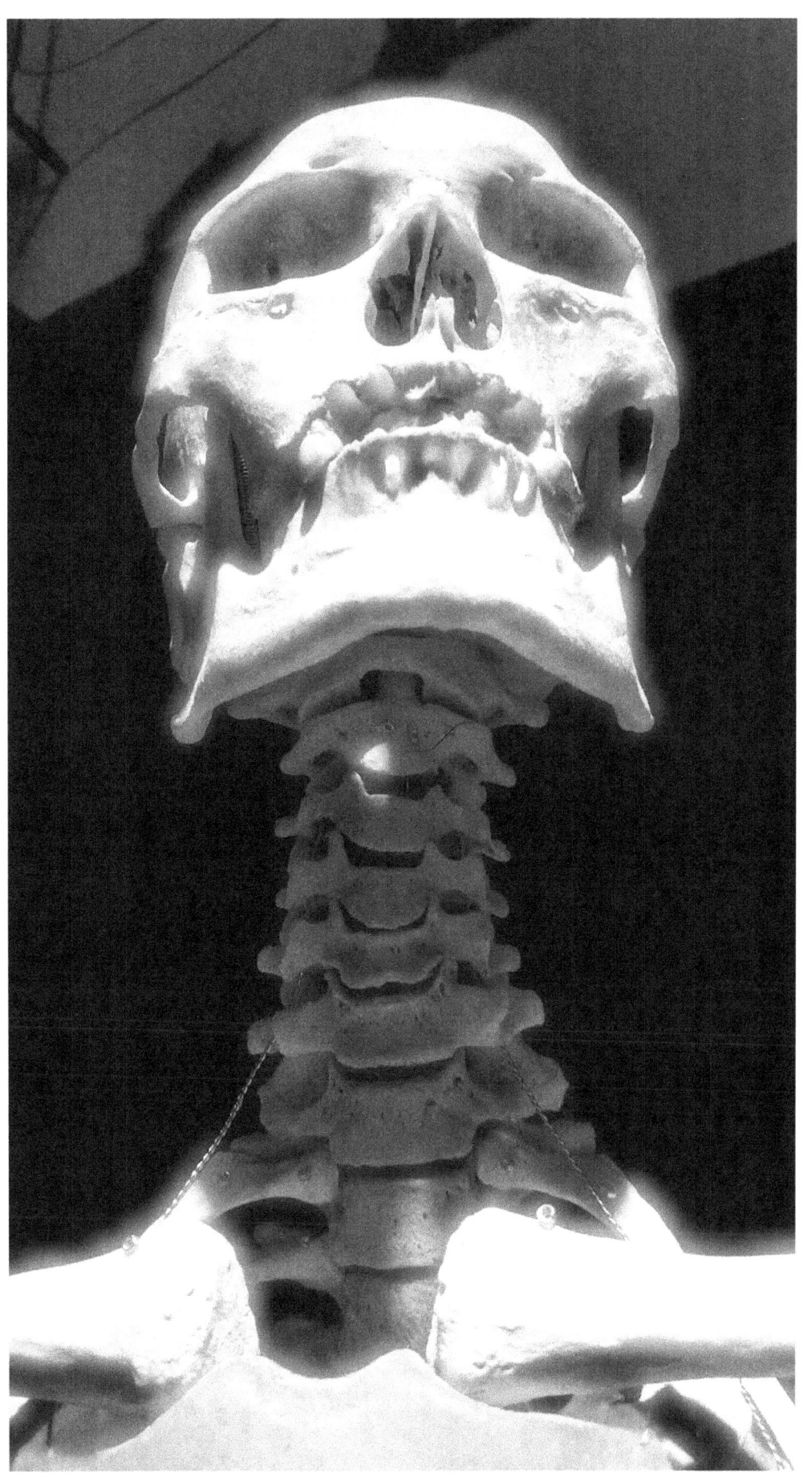

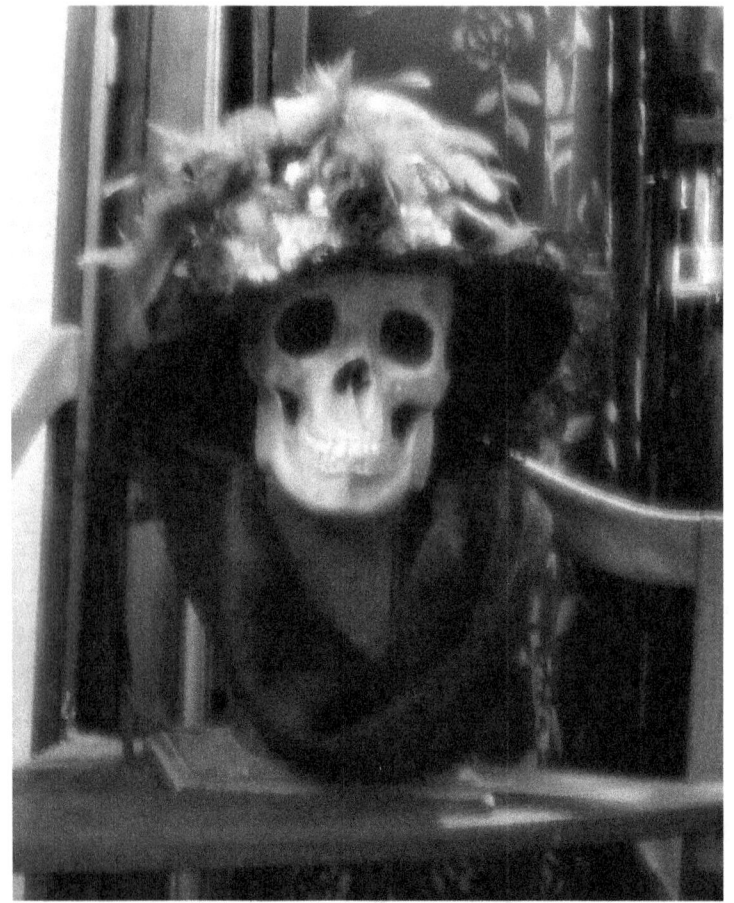

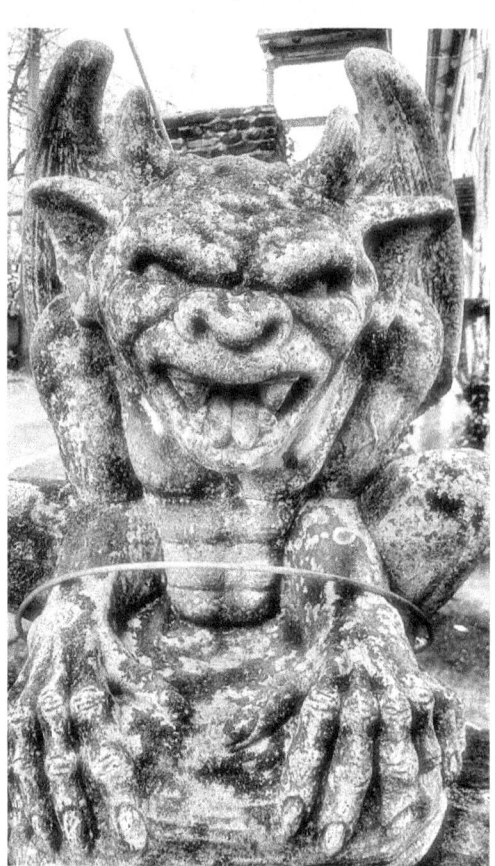

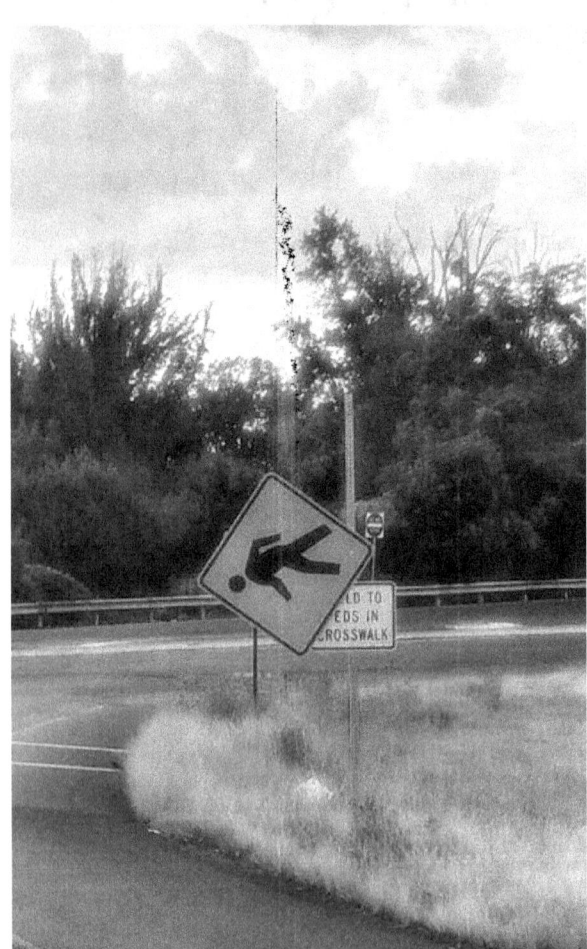

Perhaps this means: "This way to Hell"?

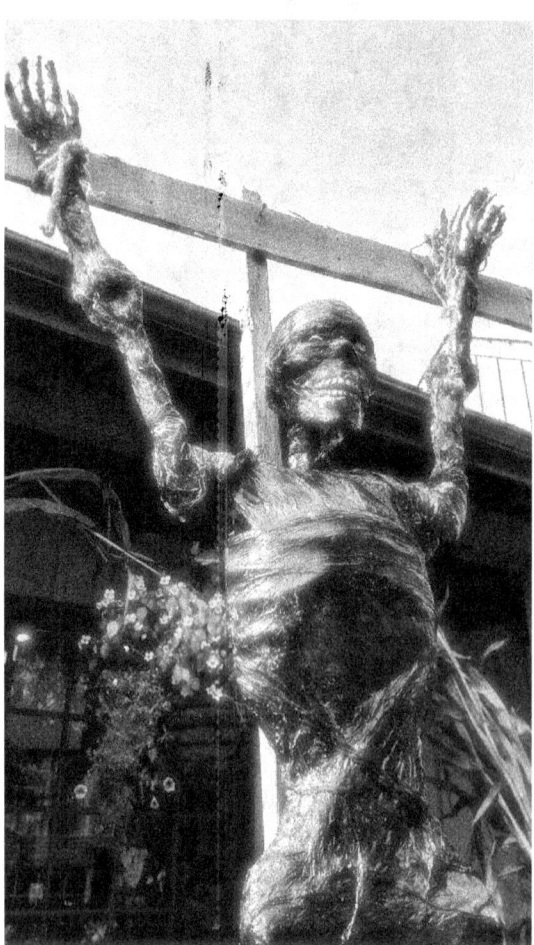

Just call him Mr. Crispy.

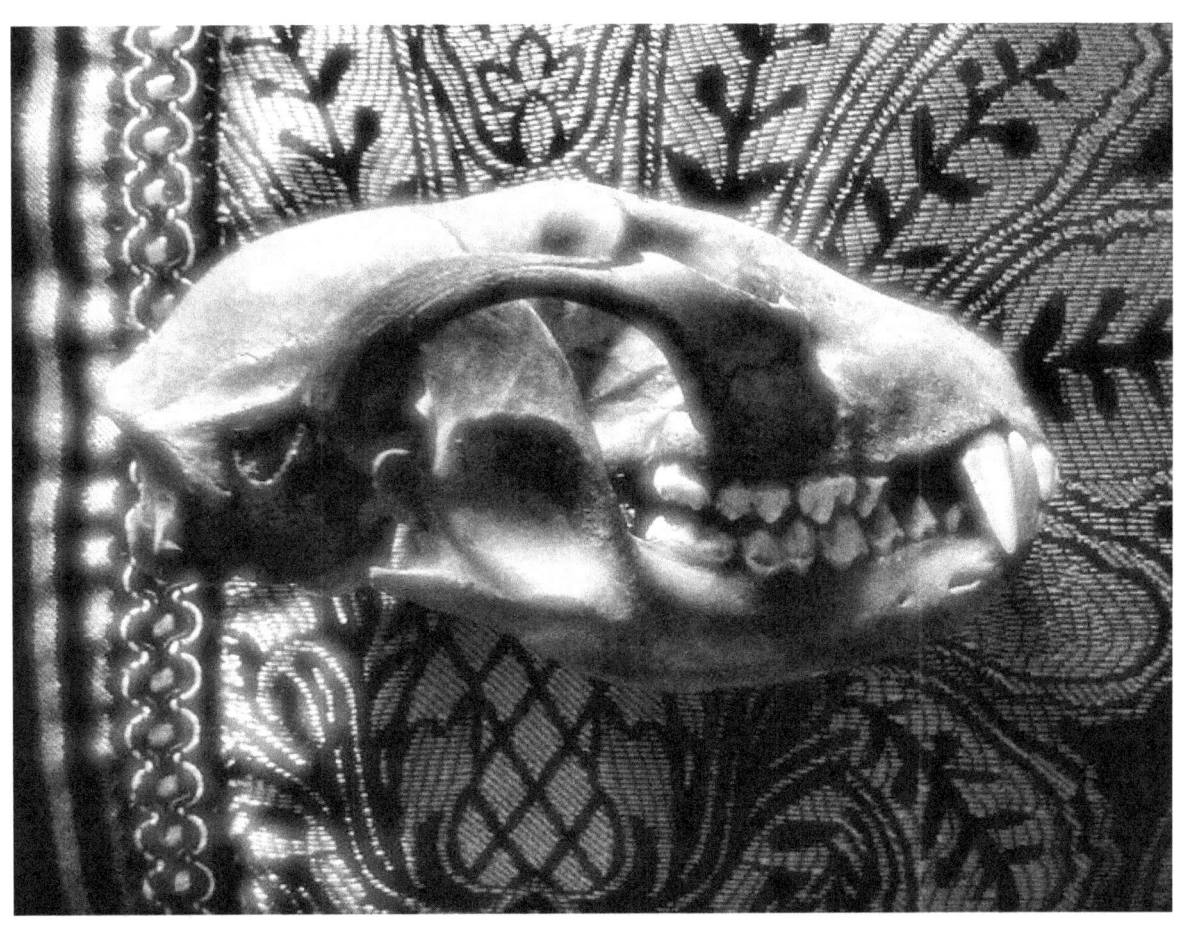

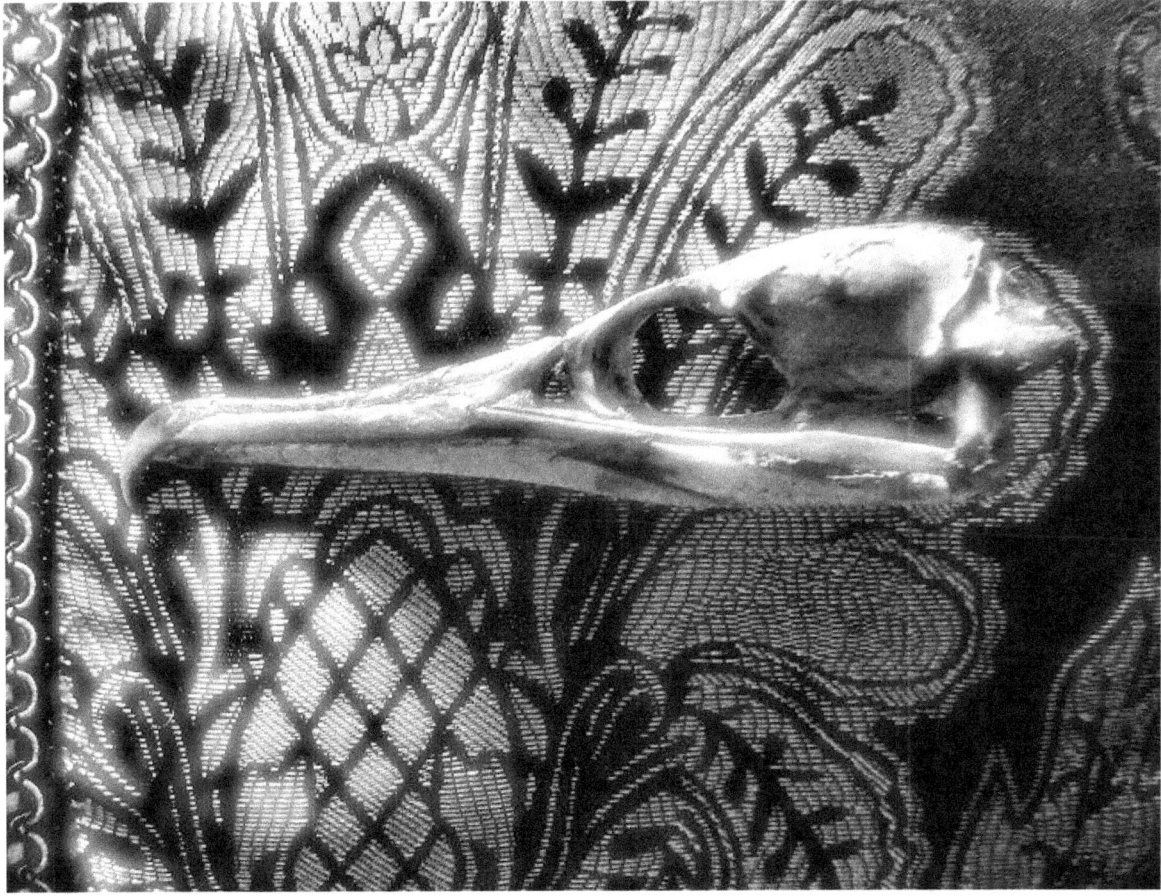

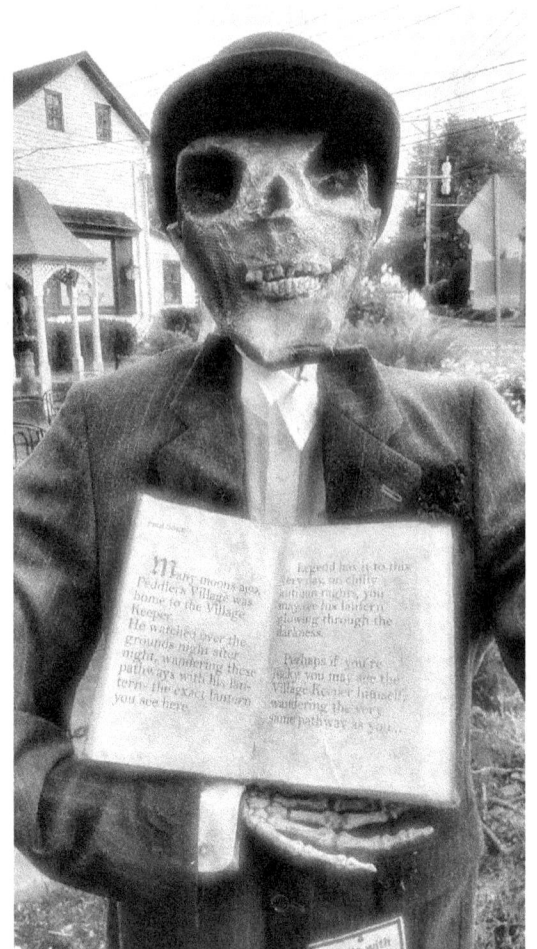

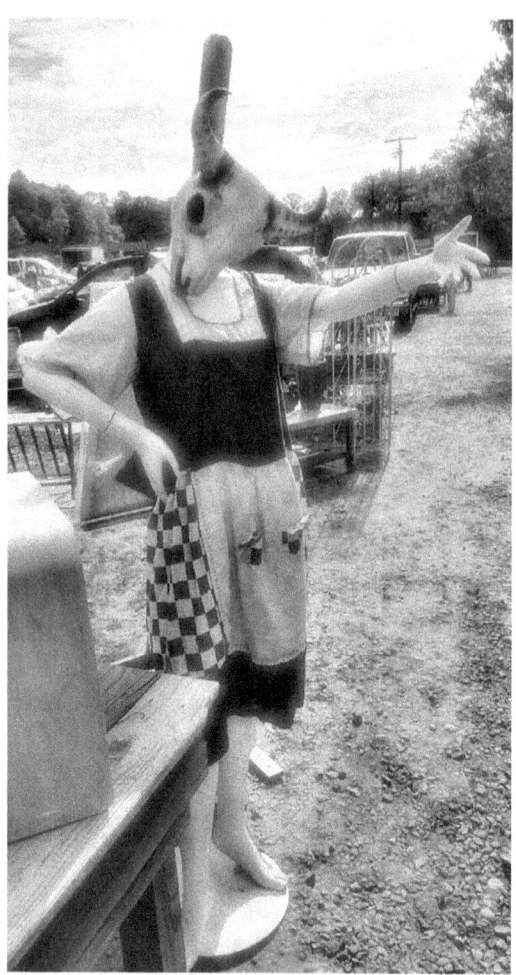

Interesting attention-getter at a flea market.

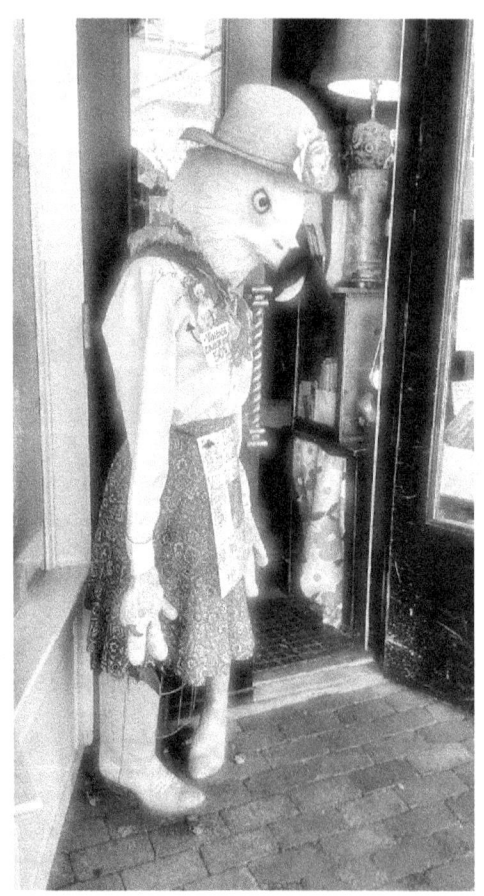

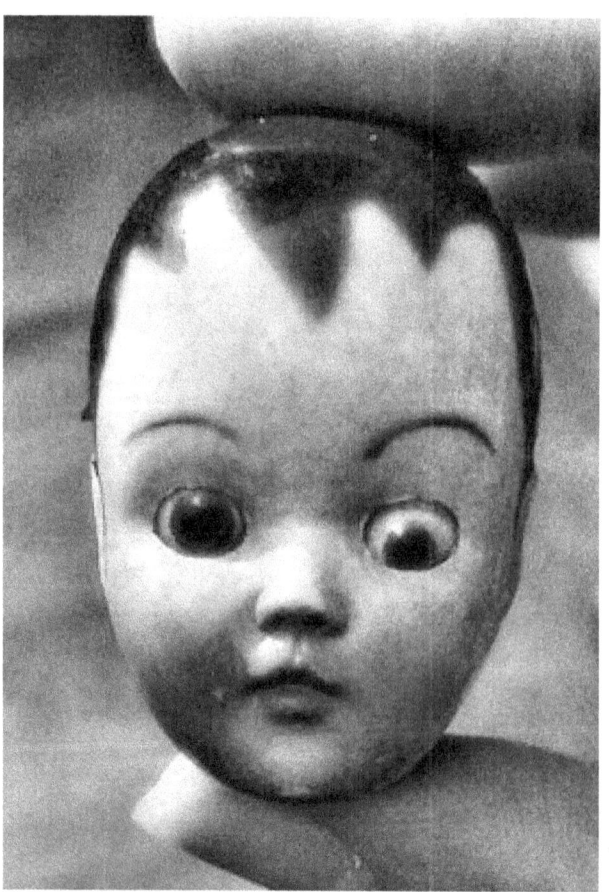

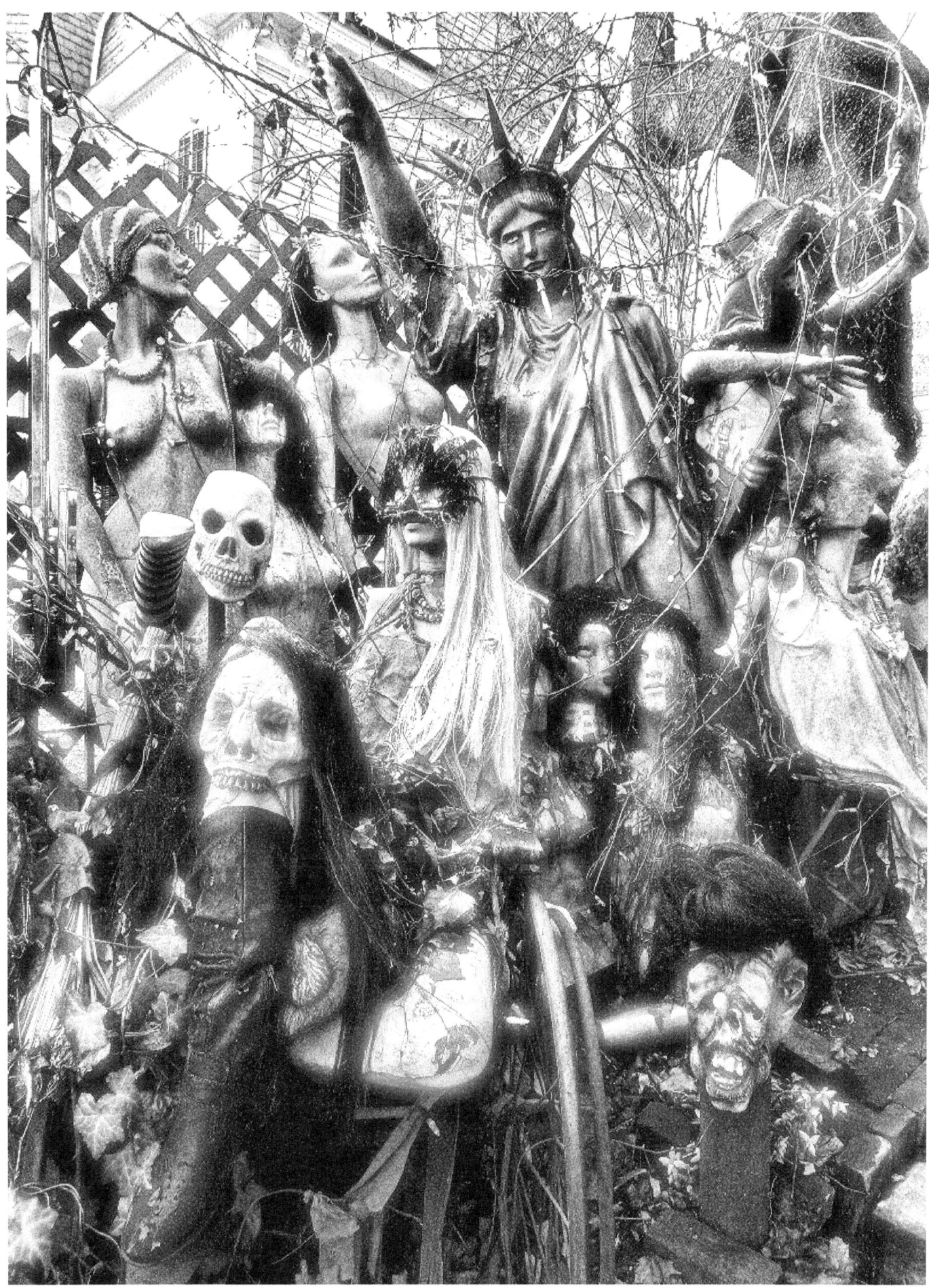

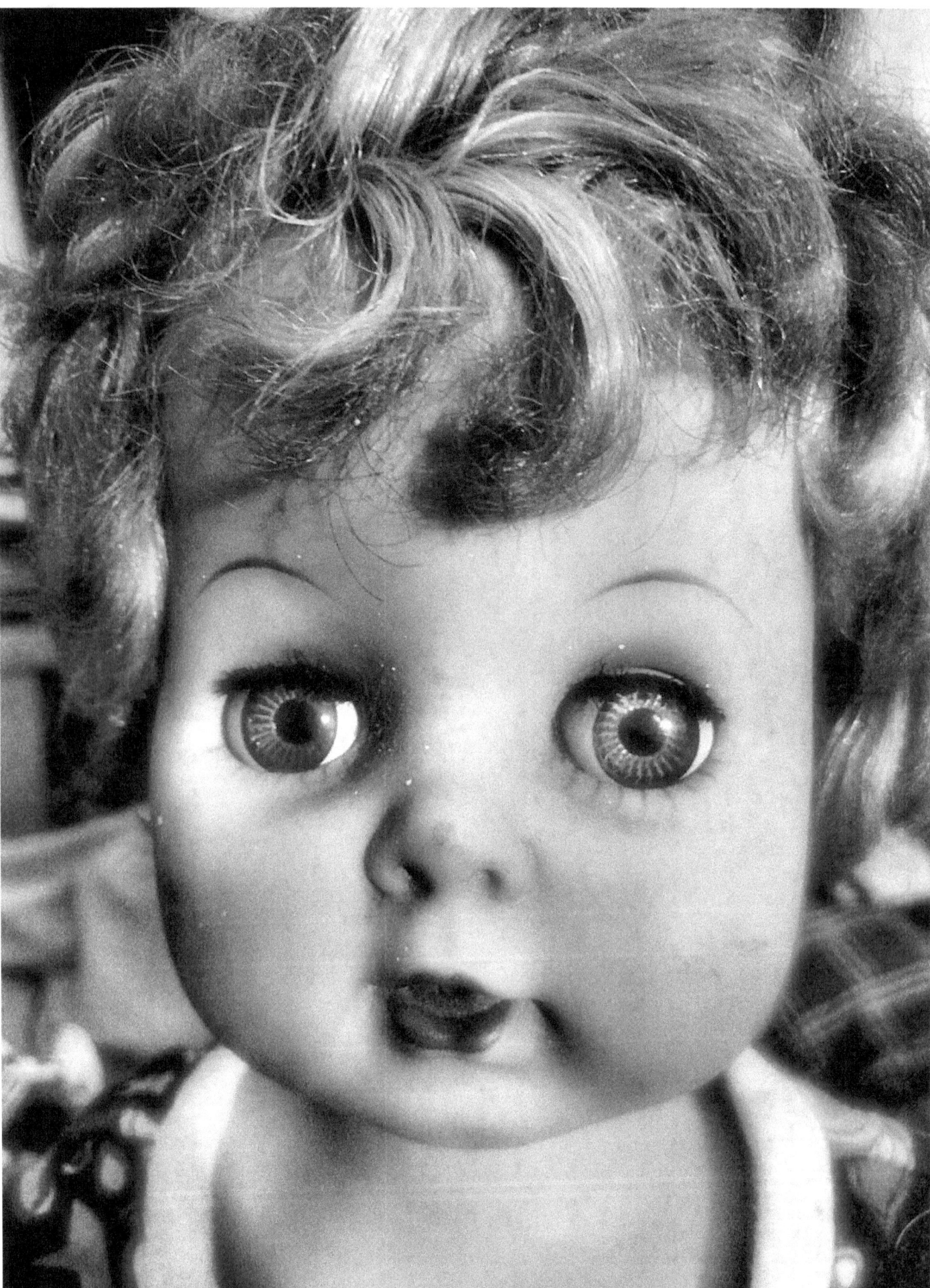

Nature in Her Grimness & Glory

Nature is both beautiful and horrific, yet peaceful and violent. There is serenity to be had on a quiet hike through the woods, or tragedy to be found when you encounter a situation of 'survival of the fittest'.

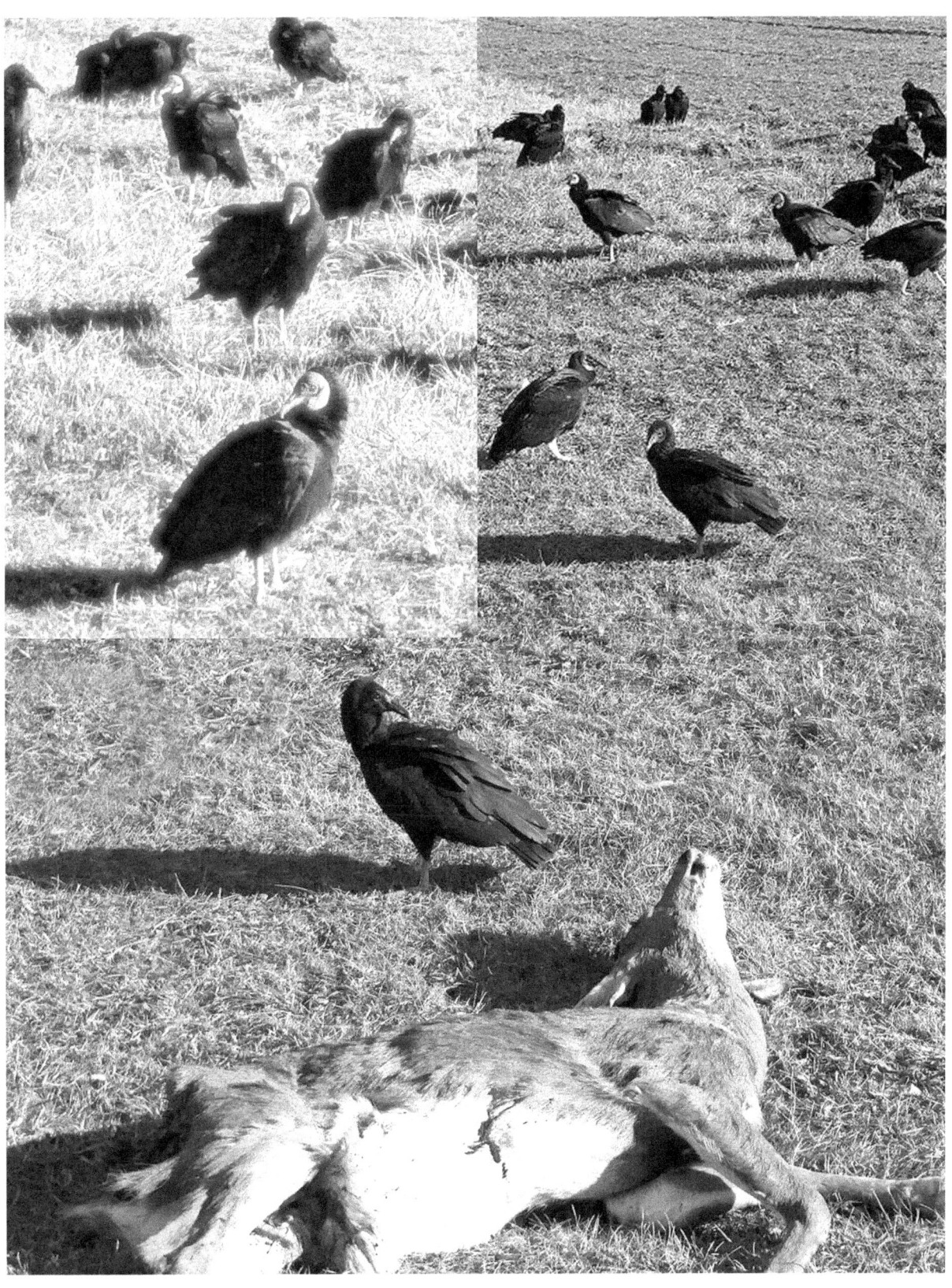

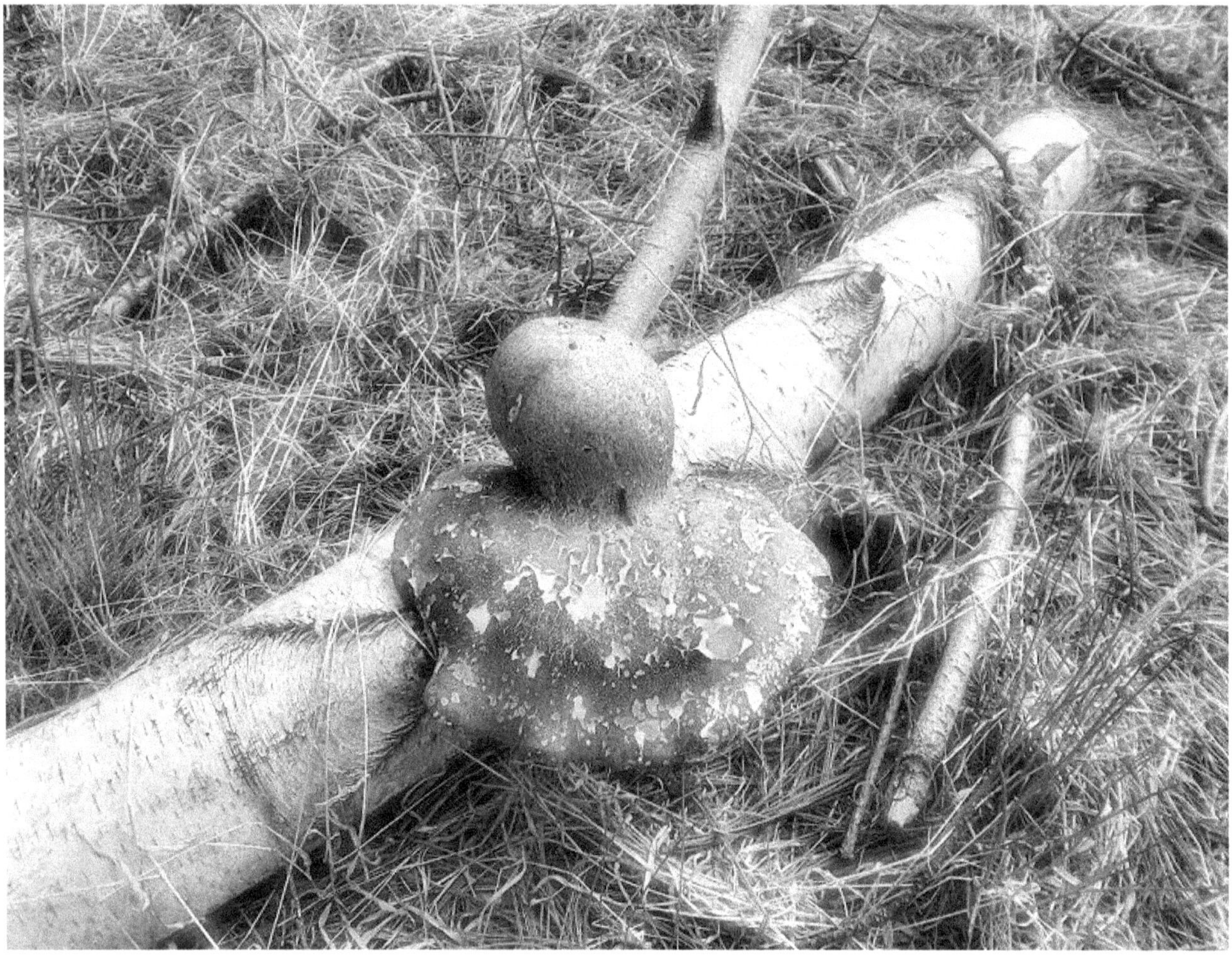

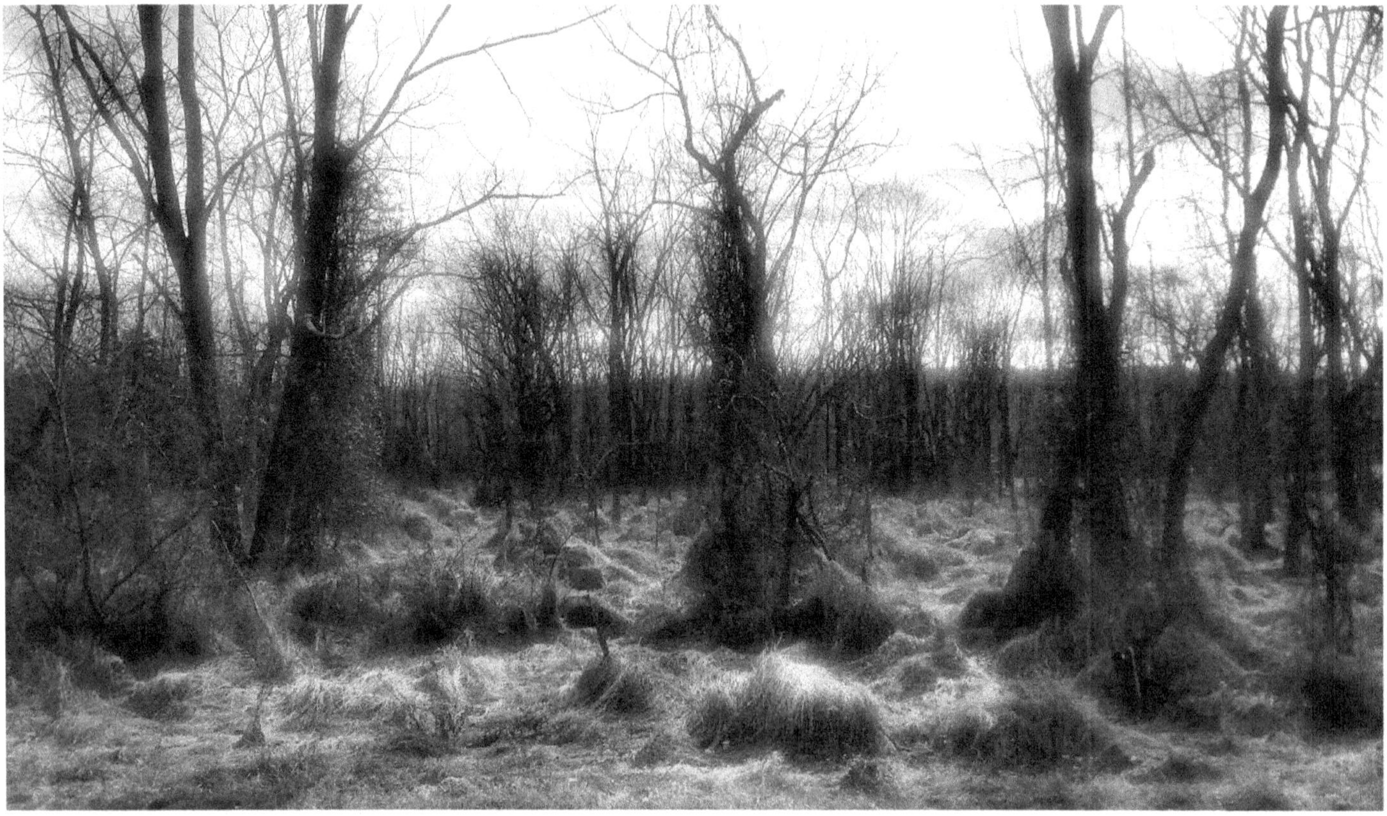

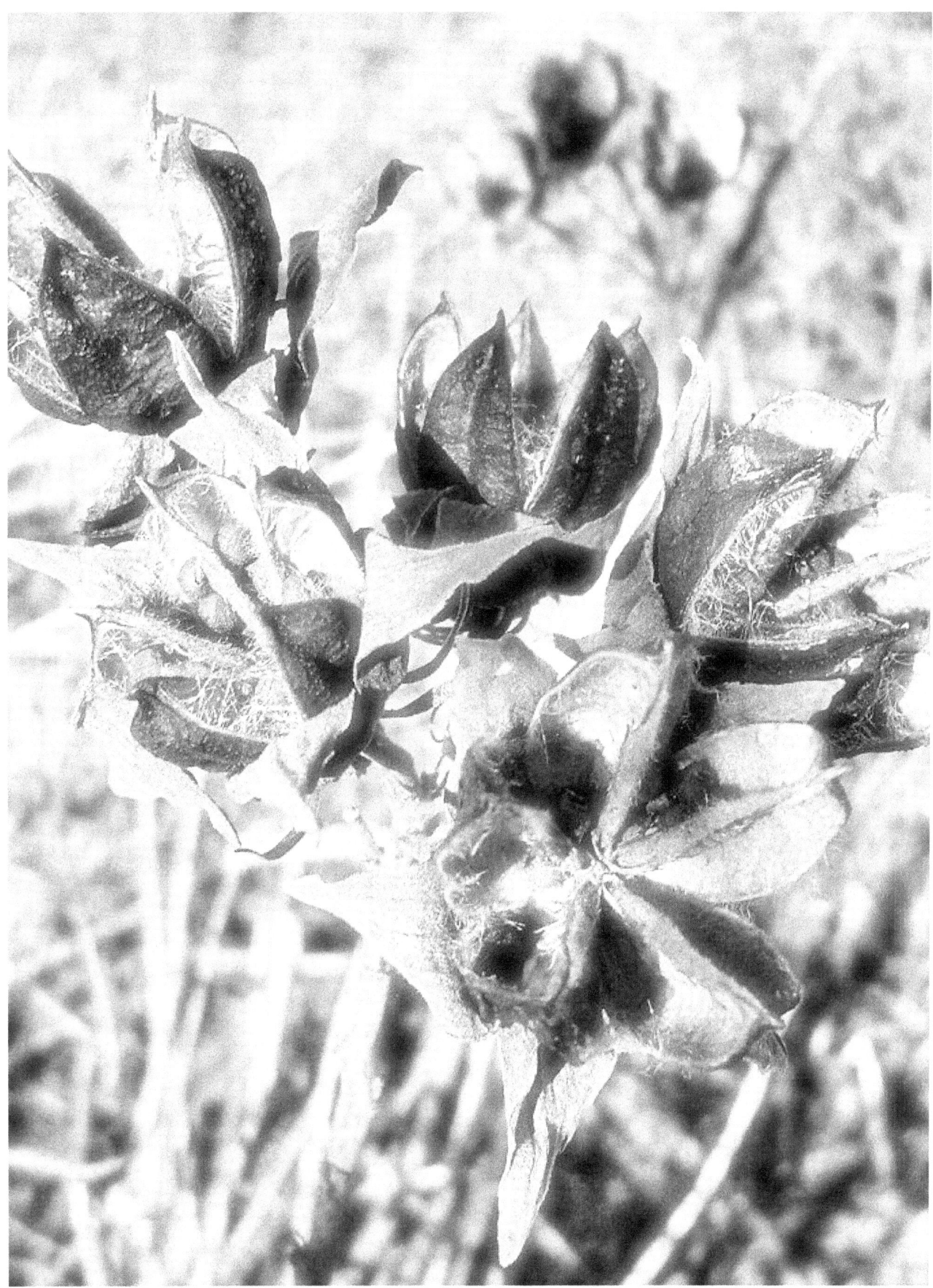

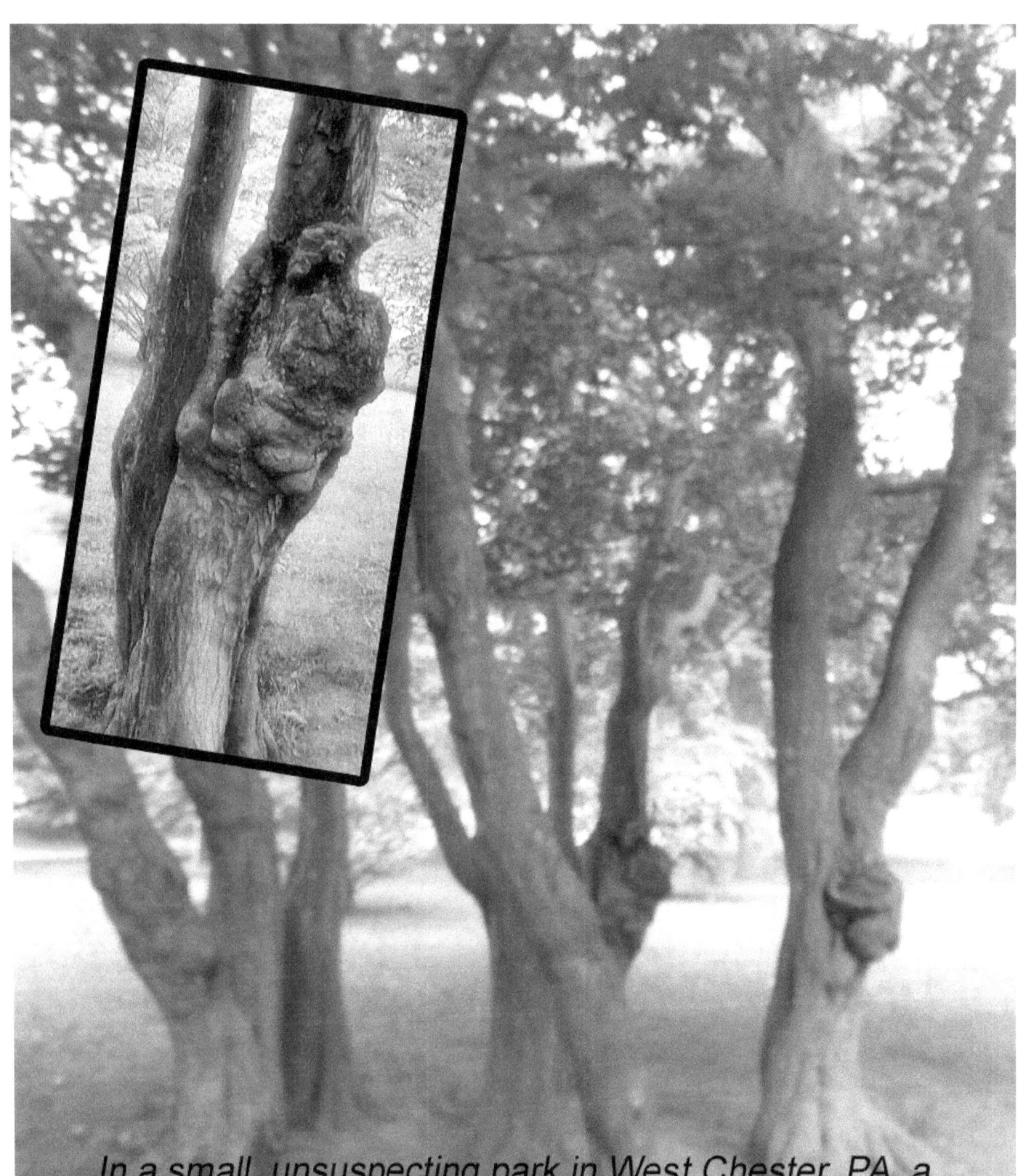

In a small, unsuspecting park in West Chester, PA, a peculiar ring of trees stand on open ground. Some believe dark magic was performed around them, and their twisted bodies reveal very demonlike shapes clinging to their trunks.

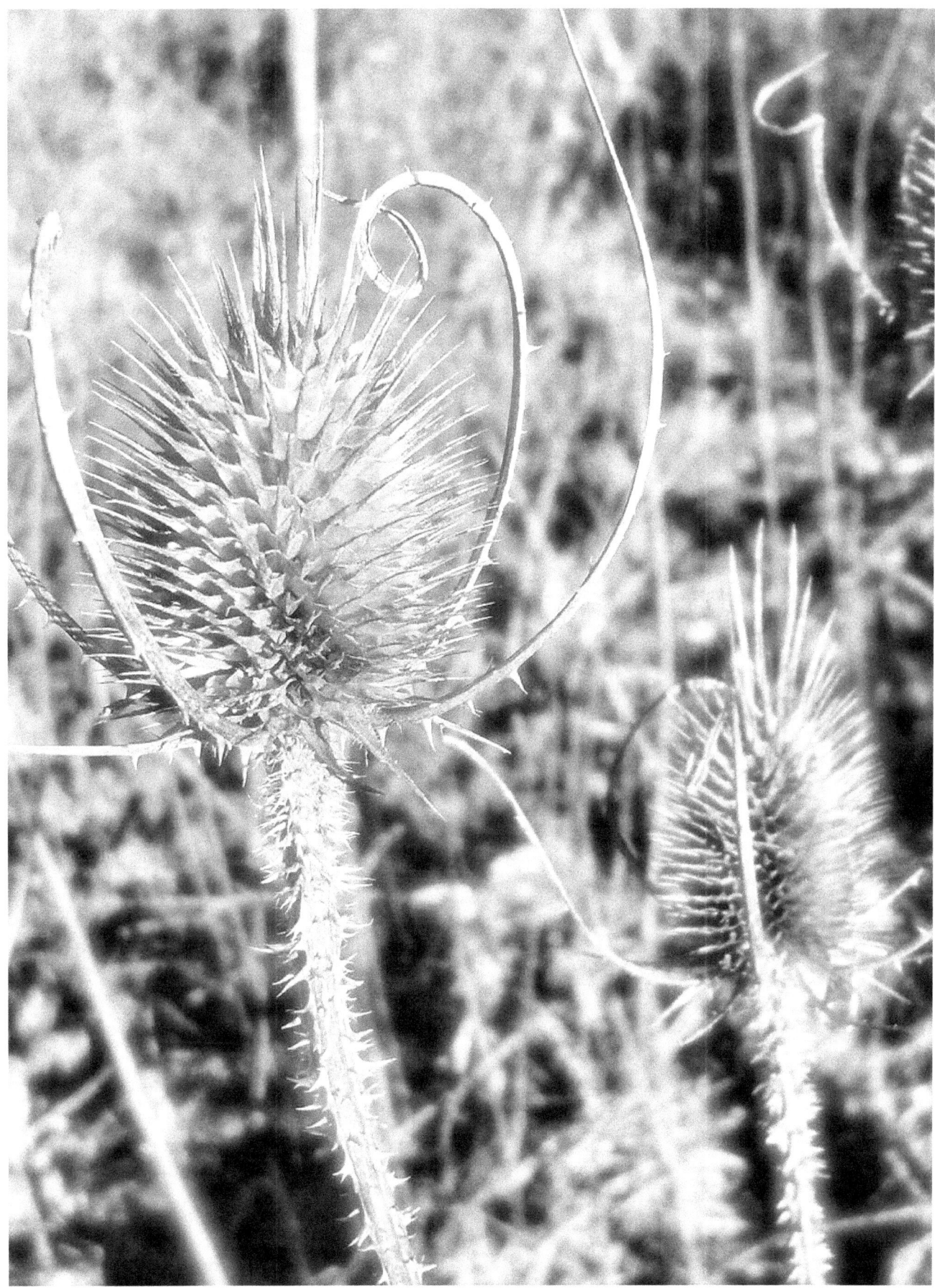

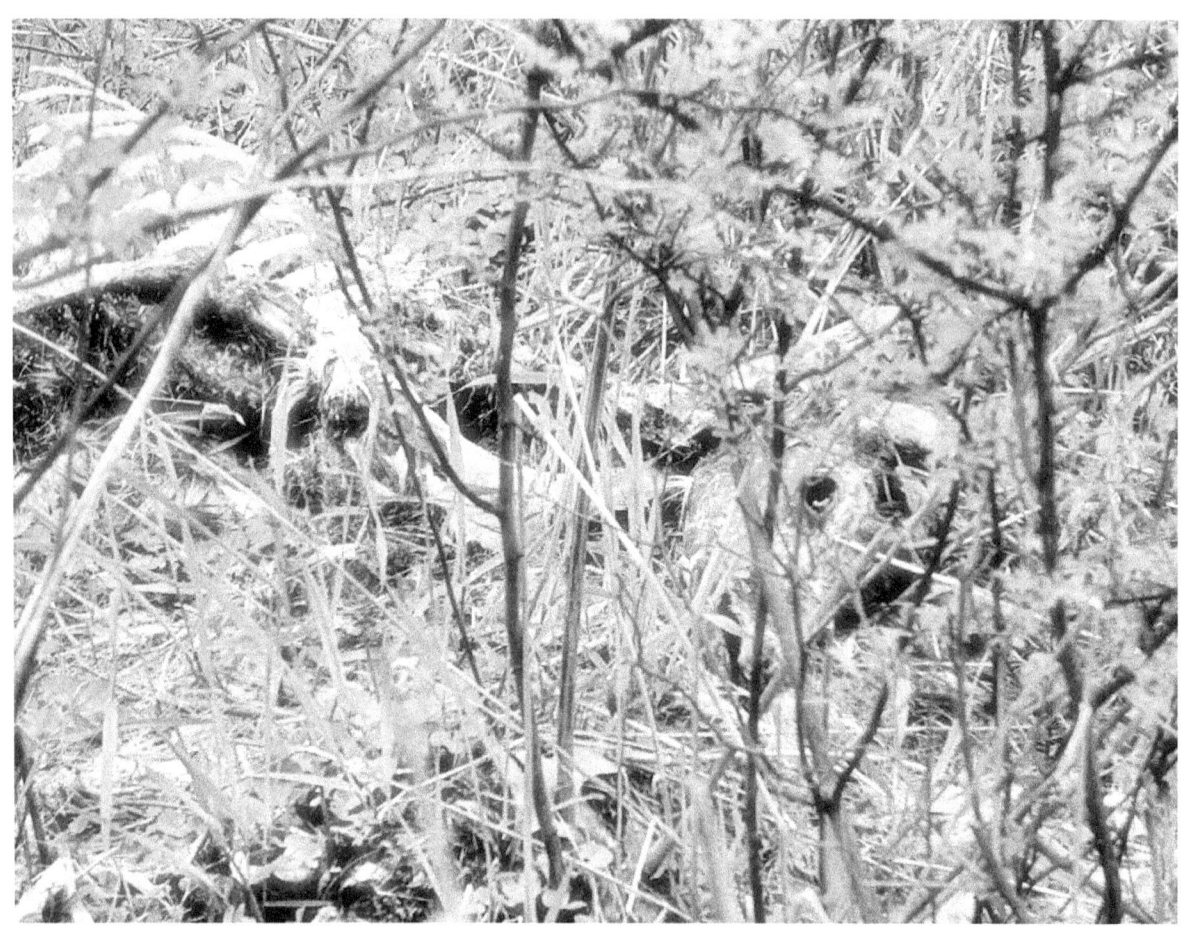

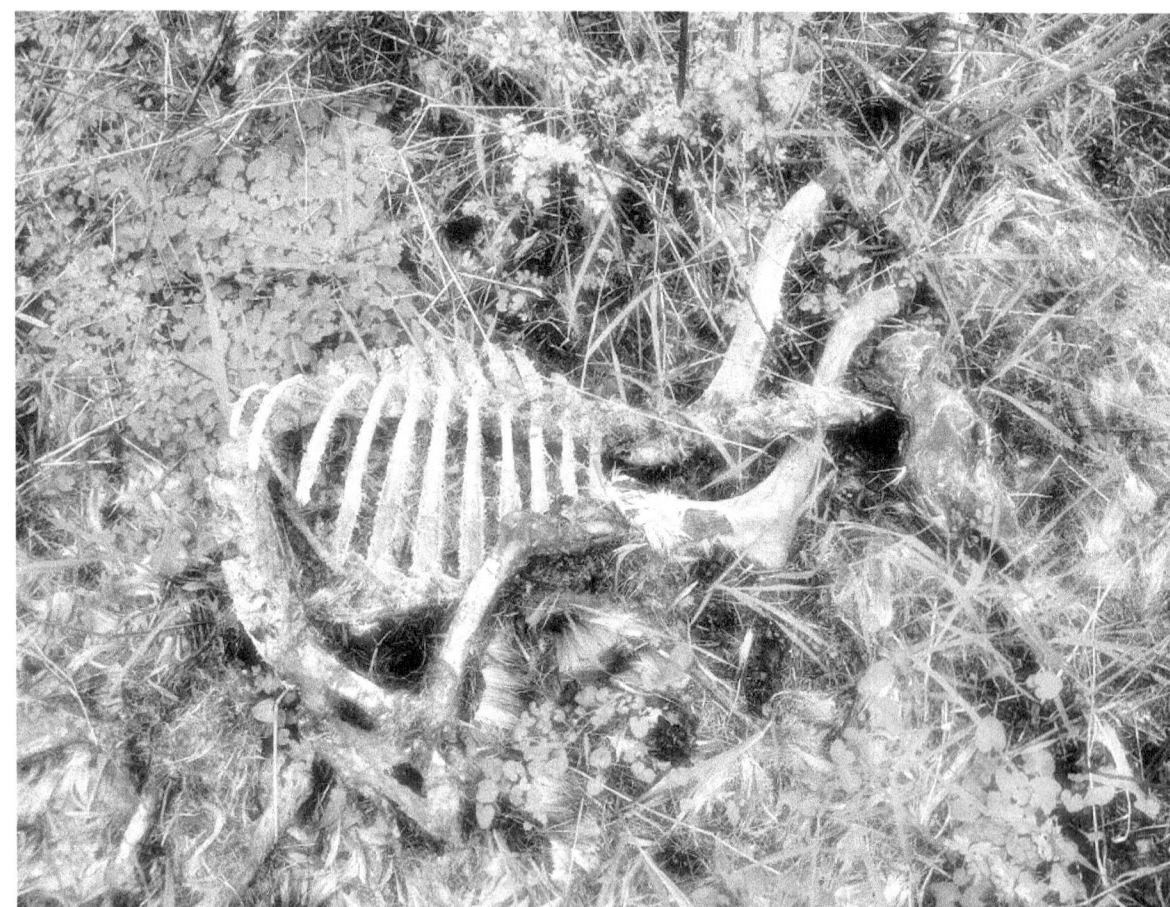

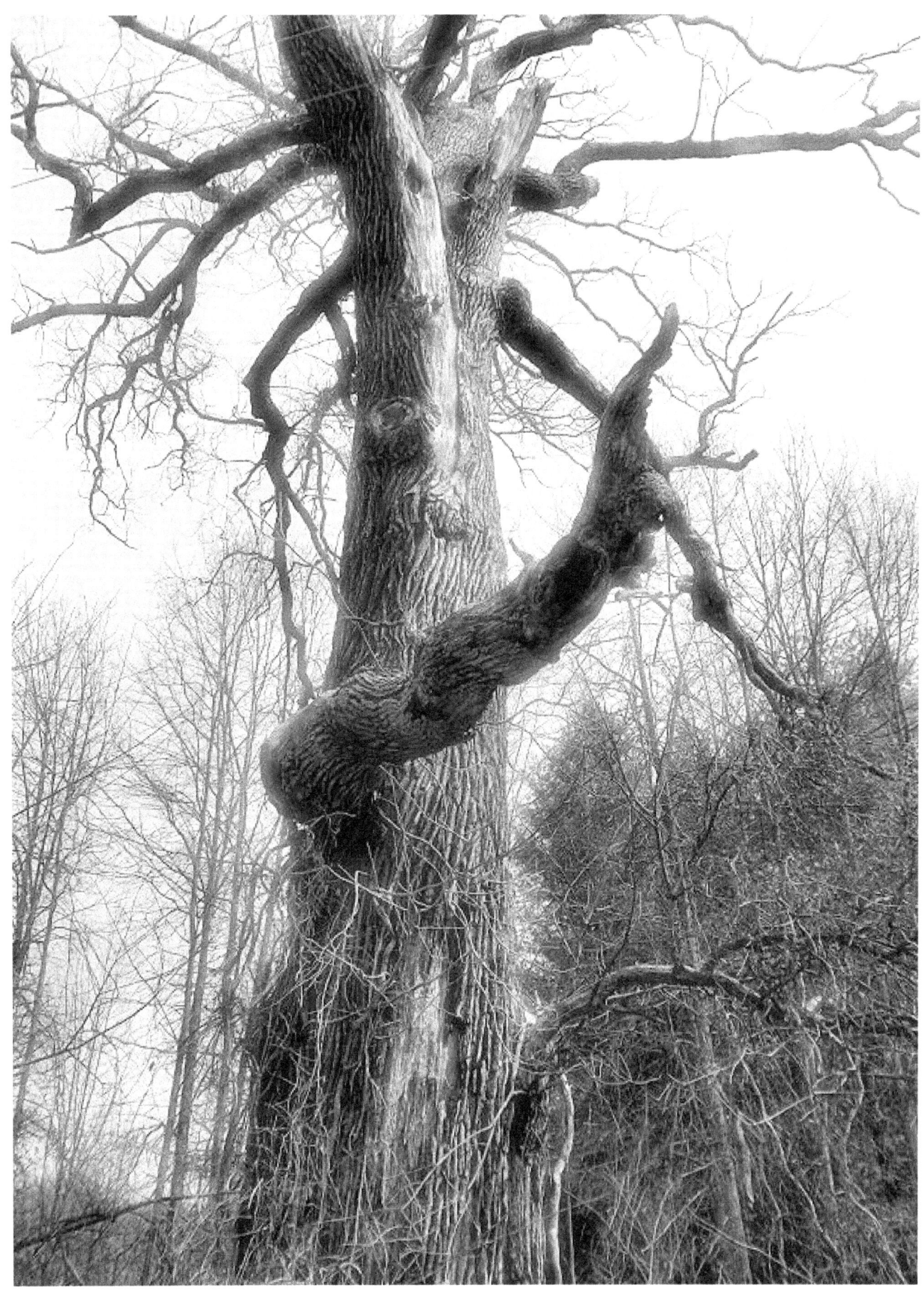

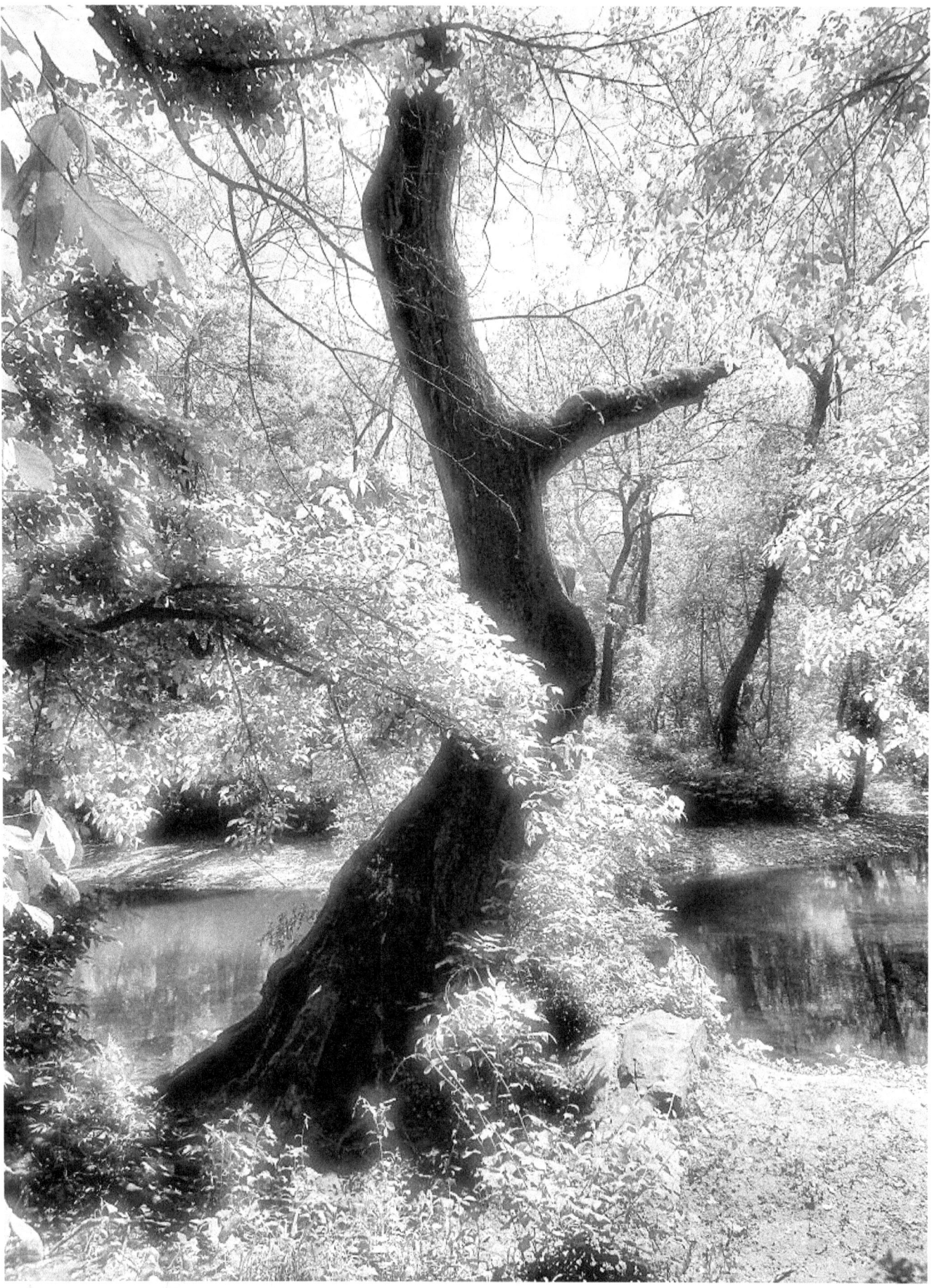

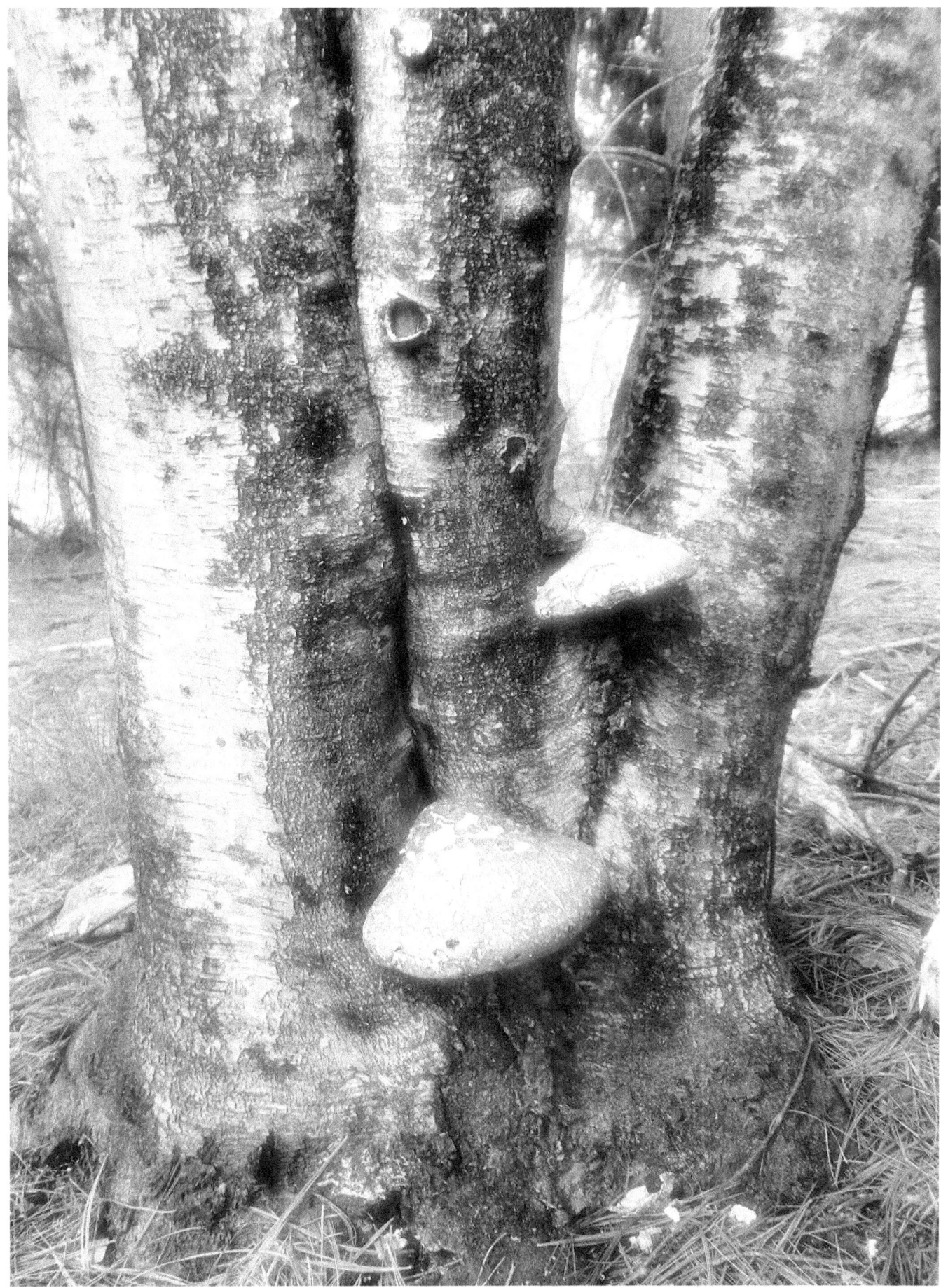

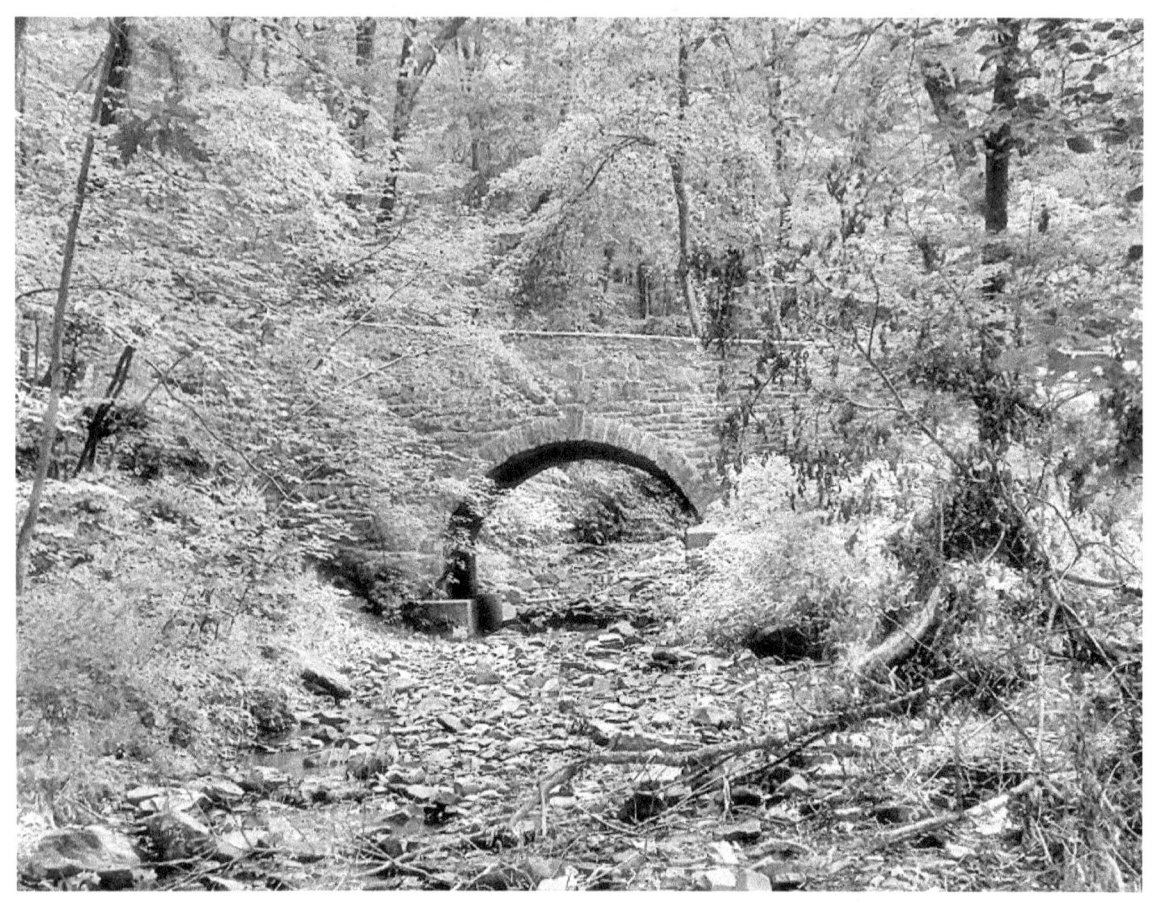

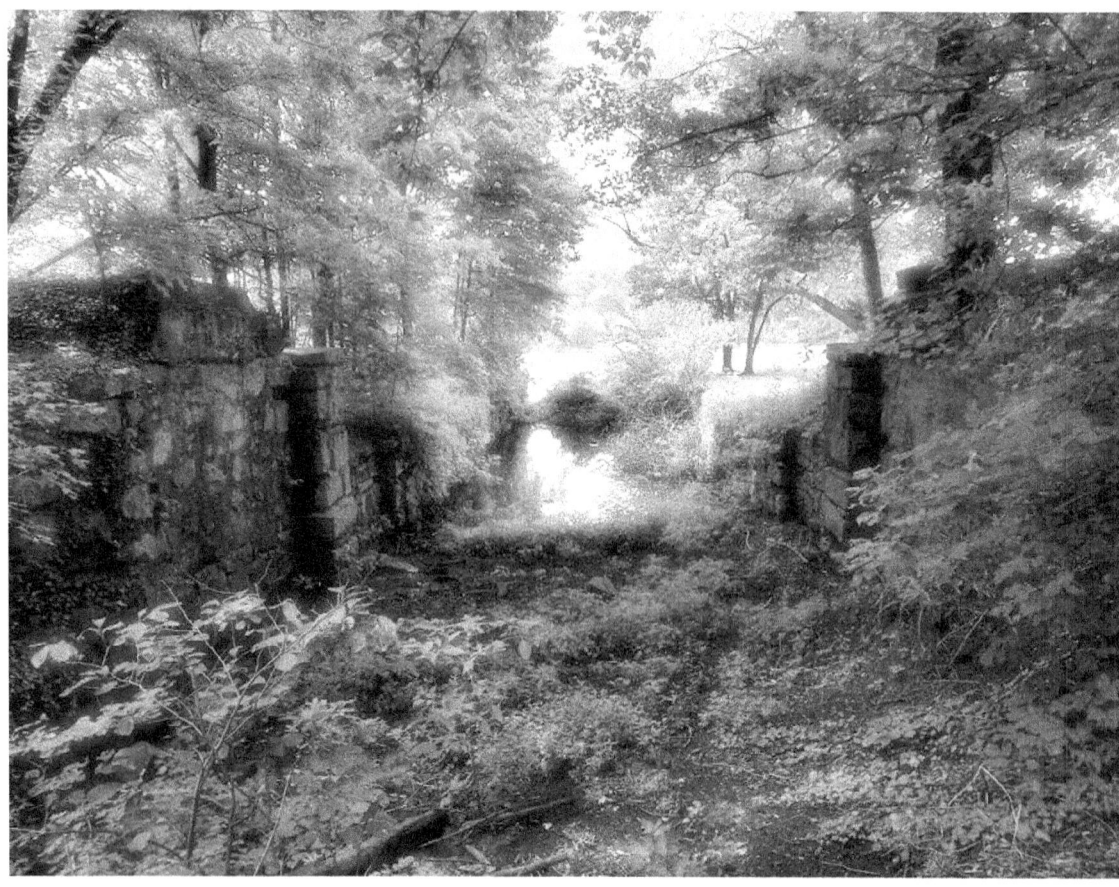

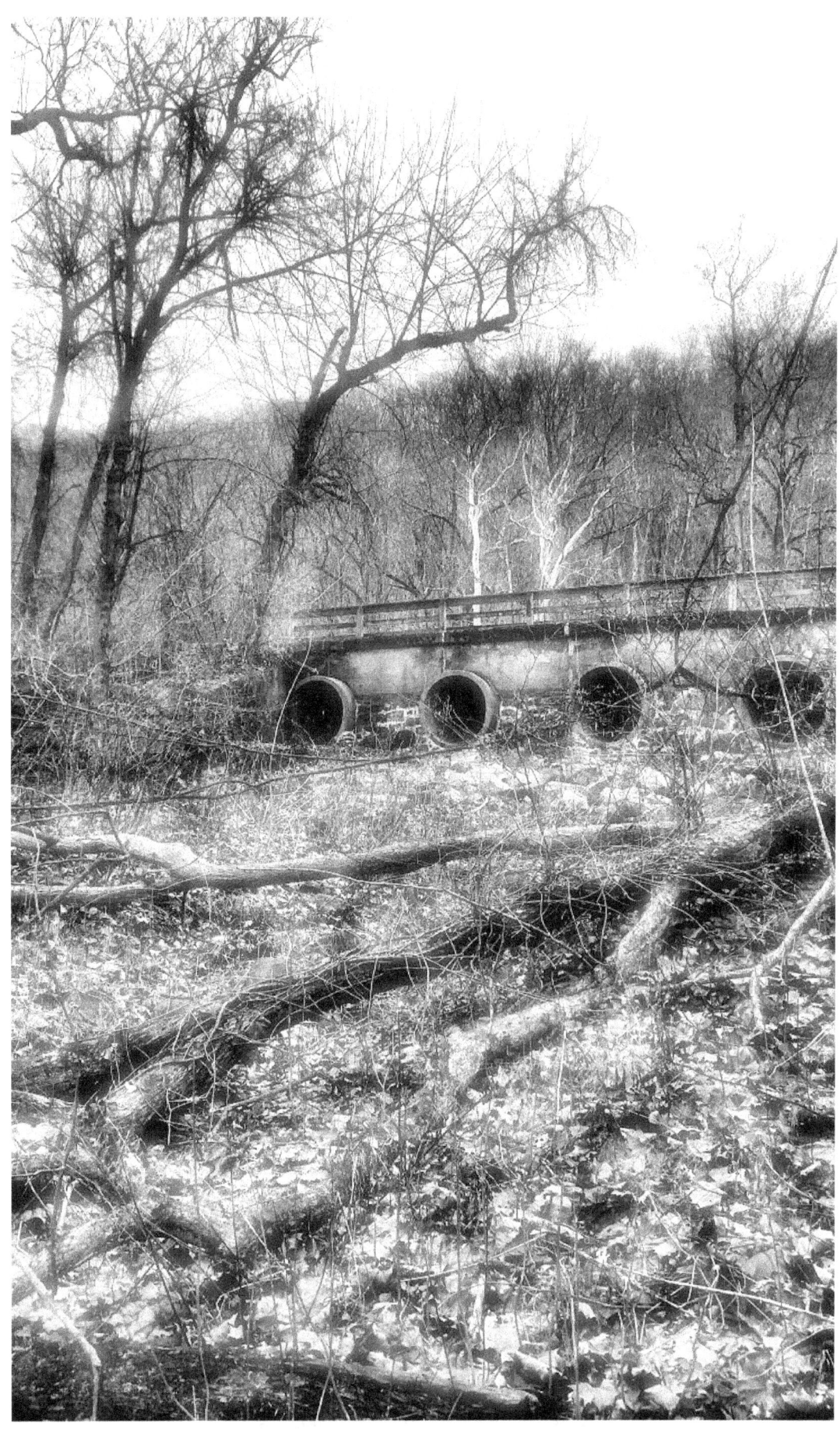

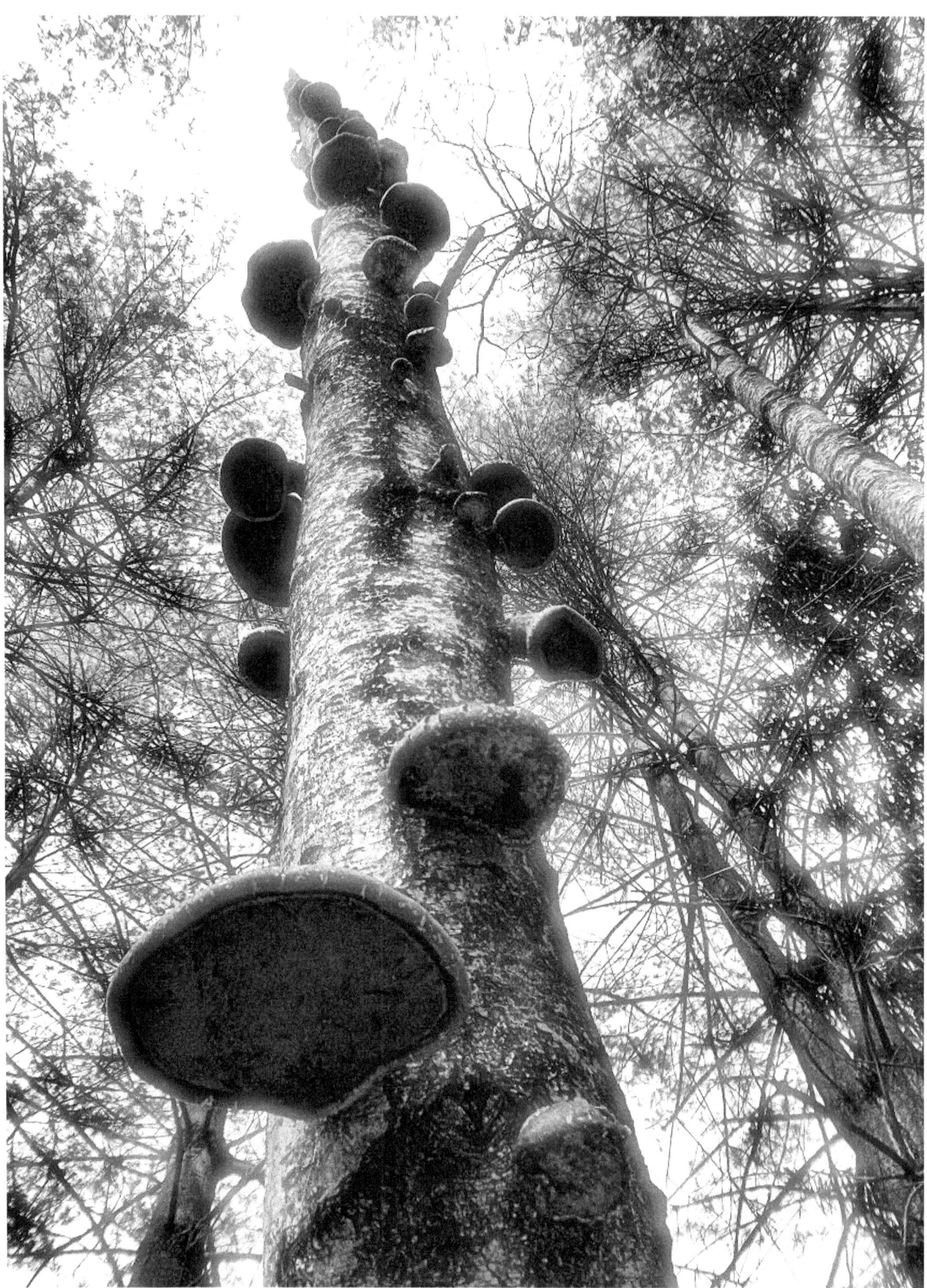

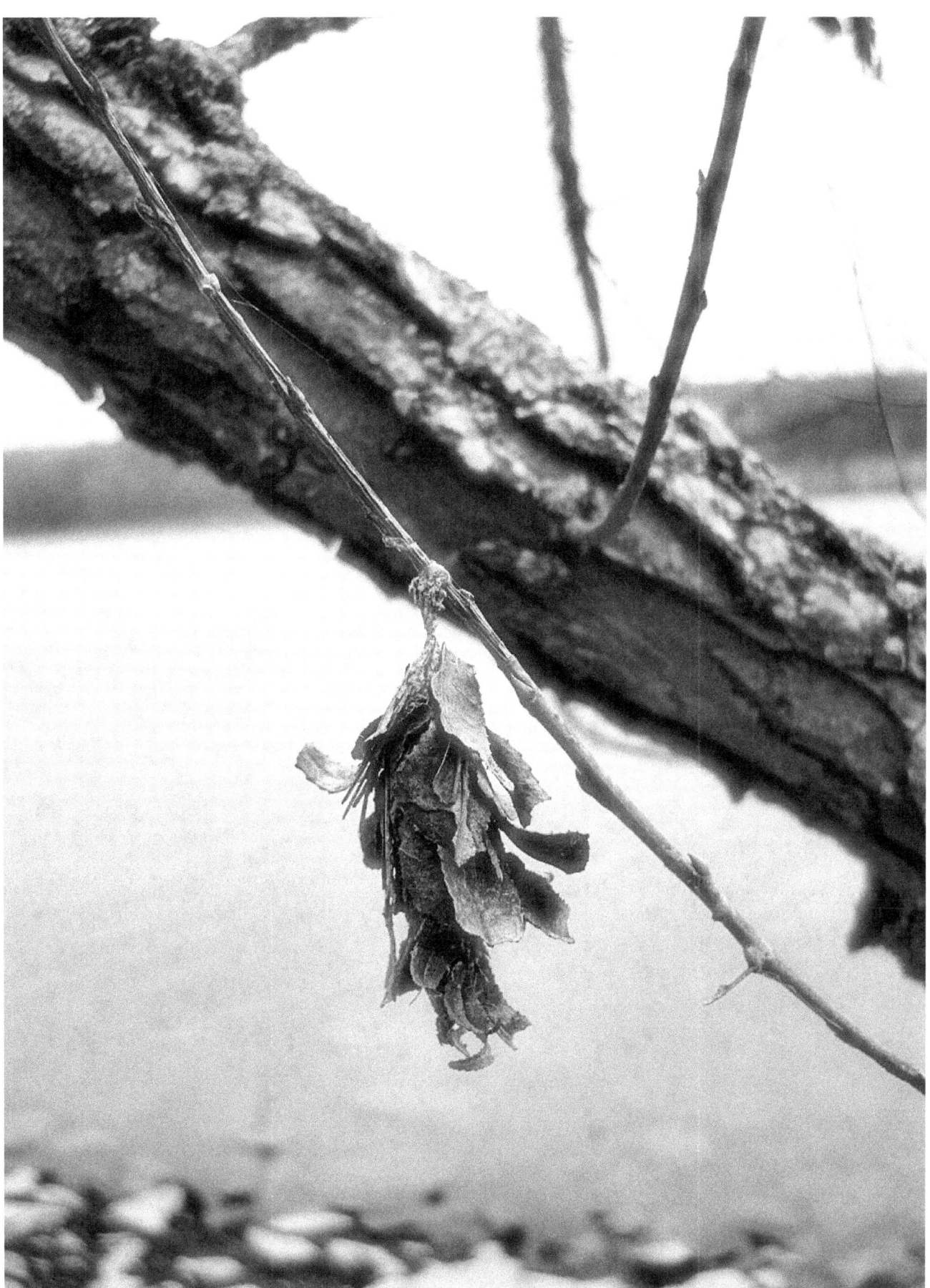

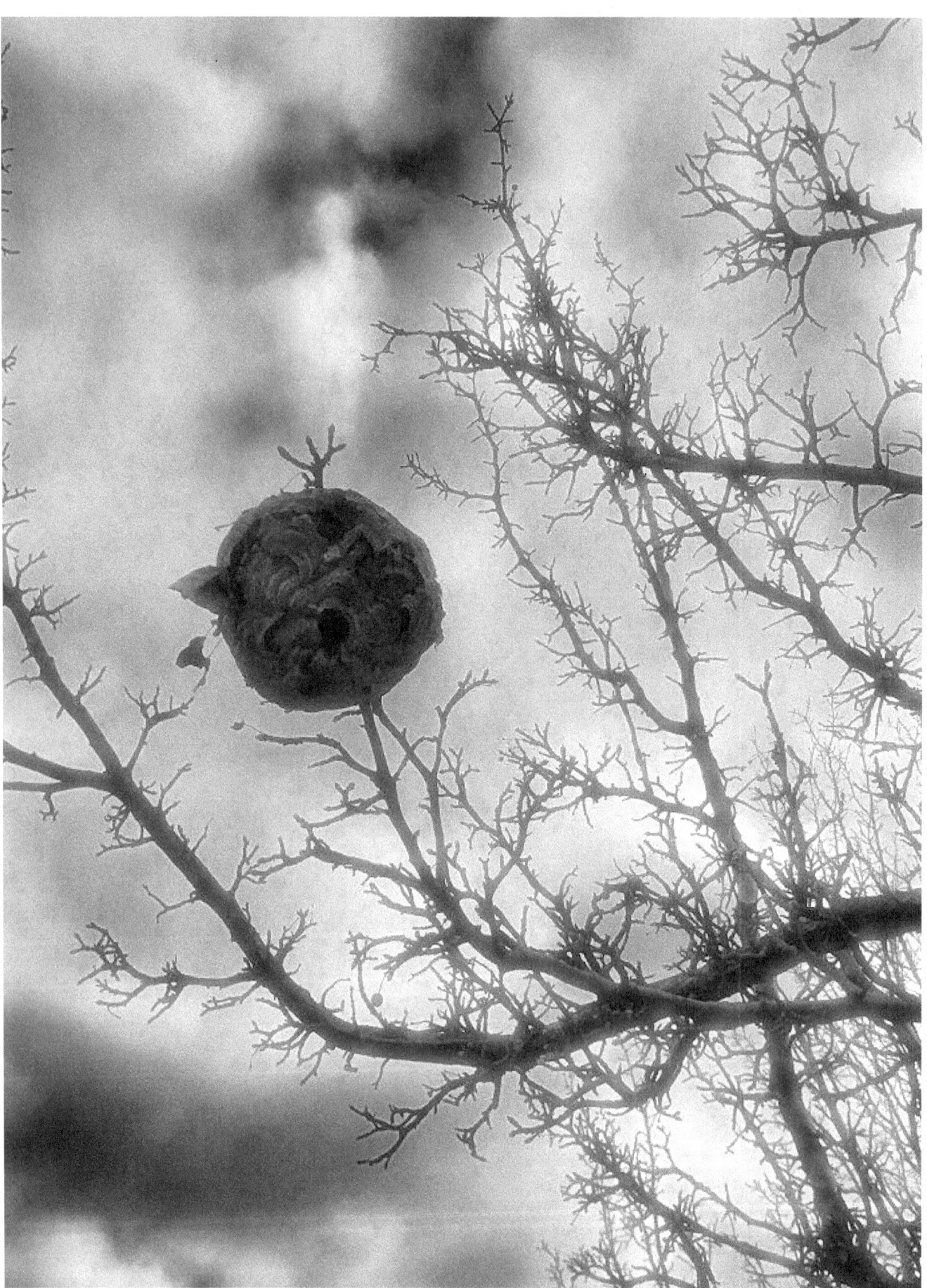

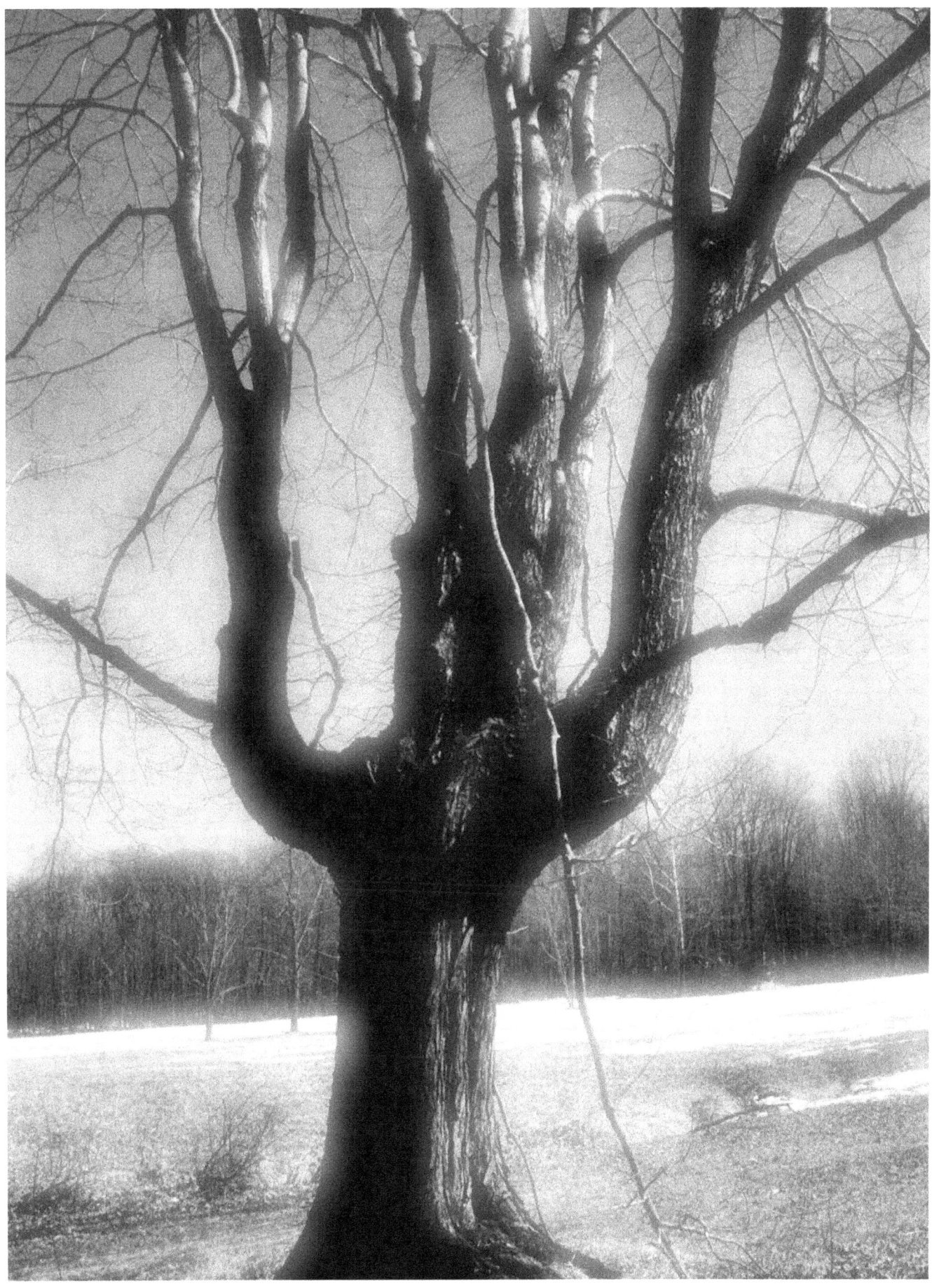

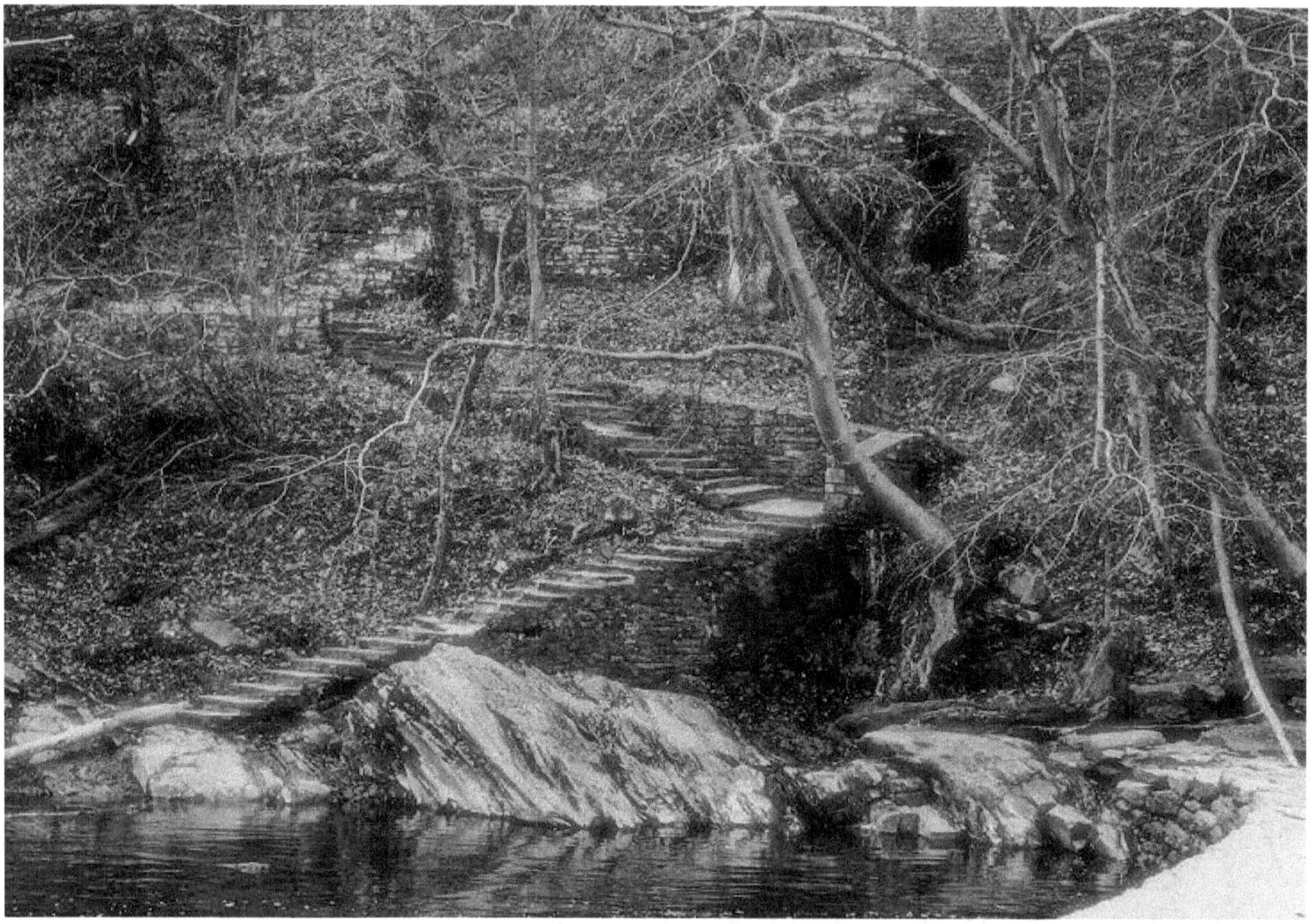

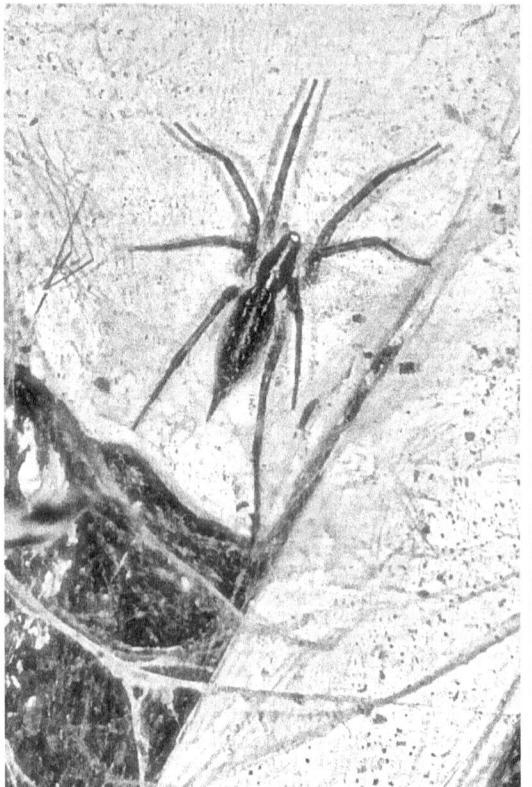

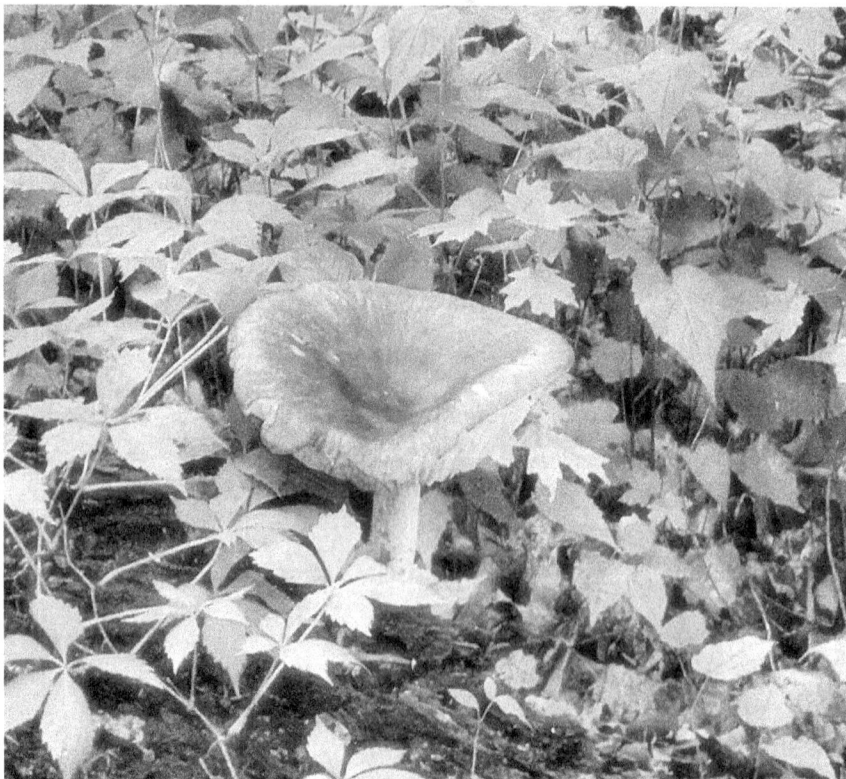

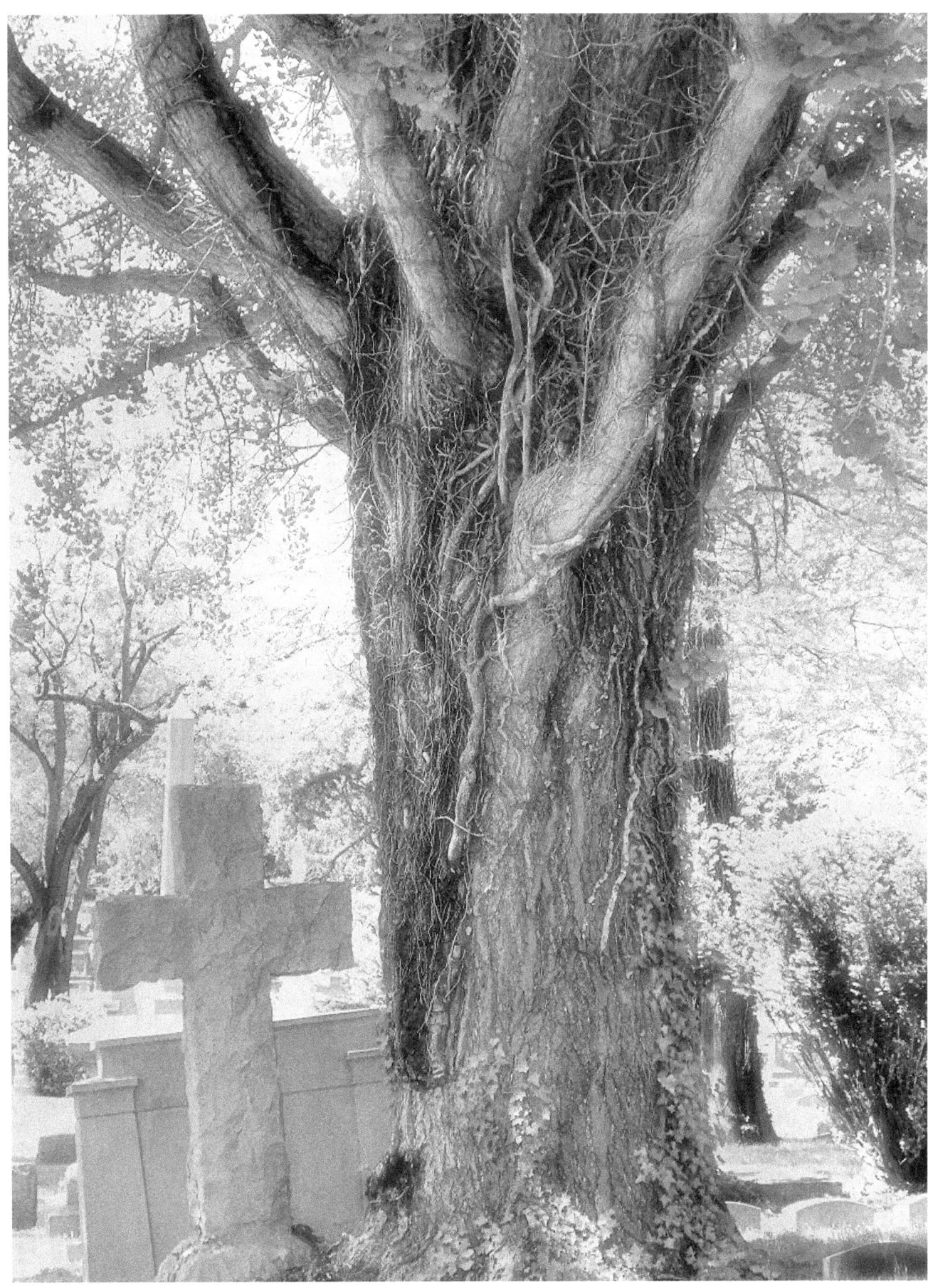

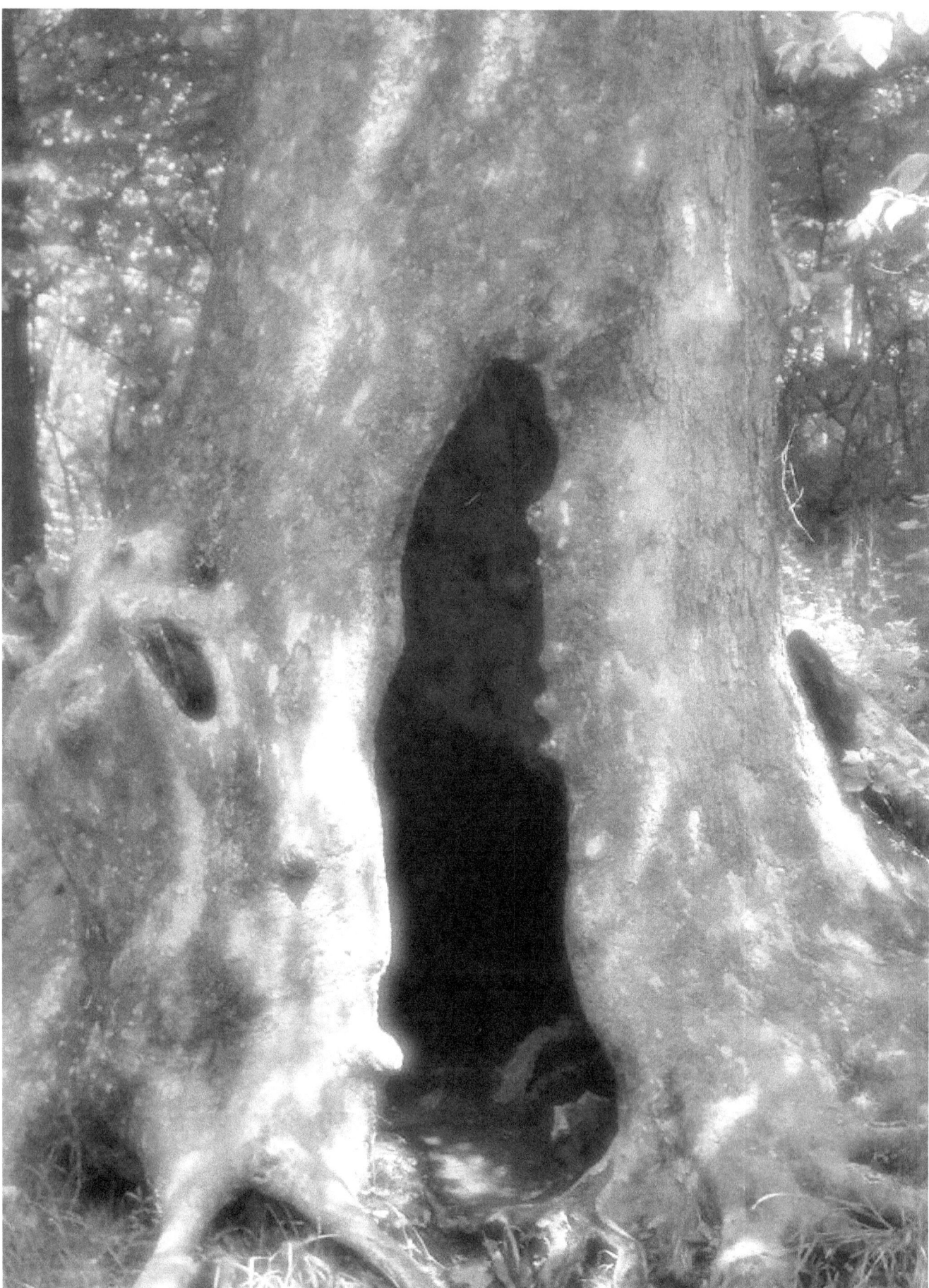

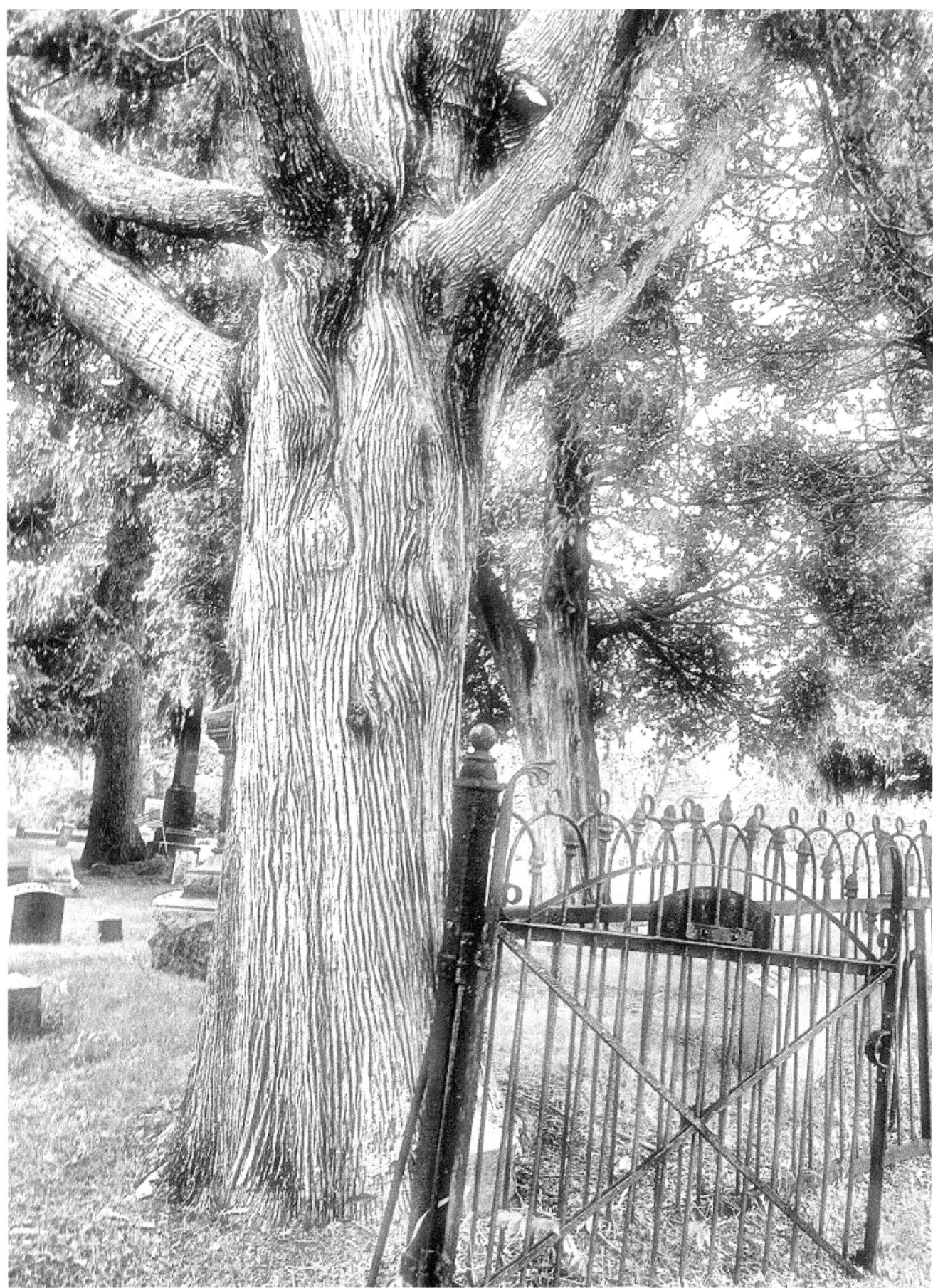

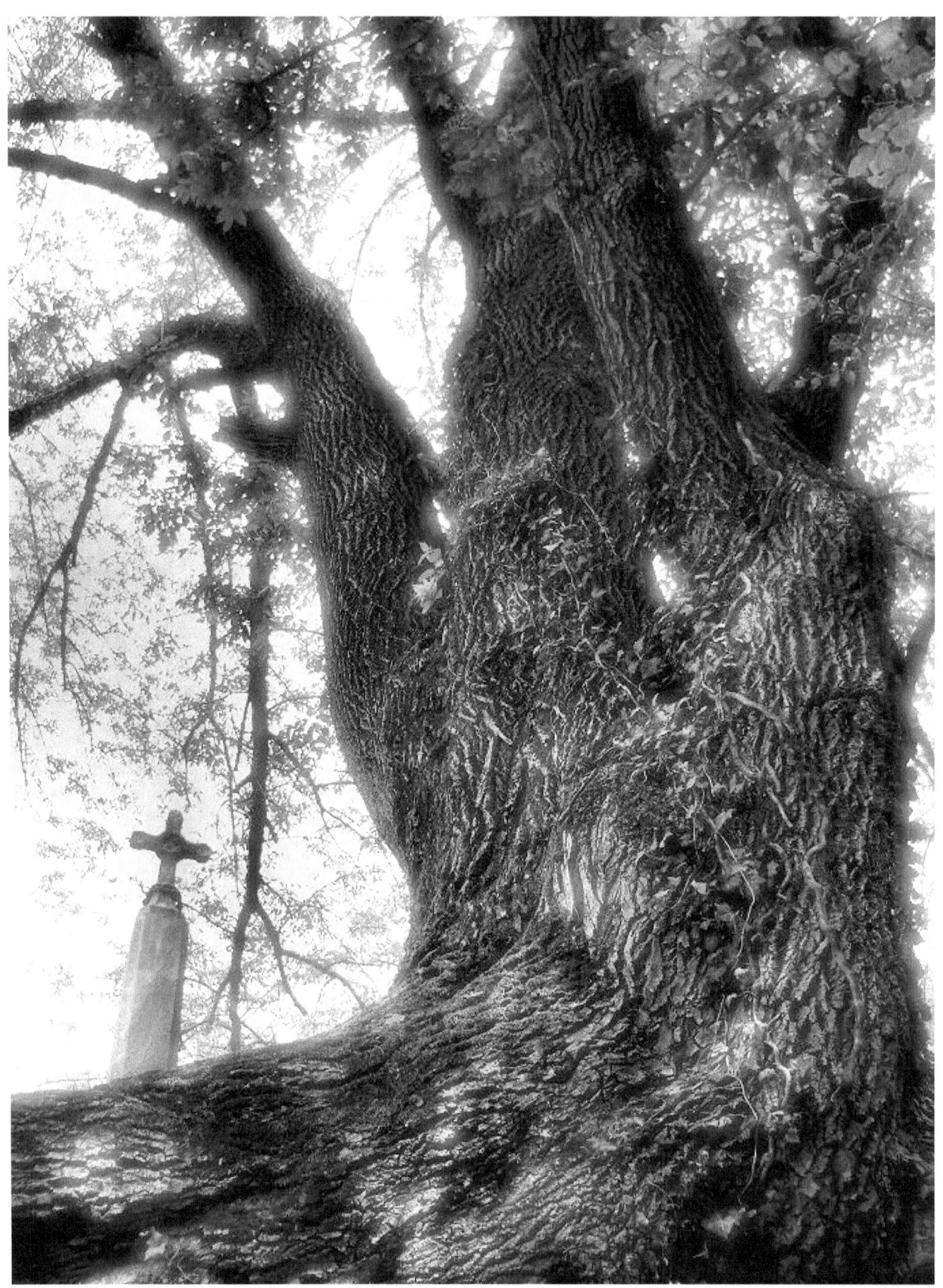

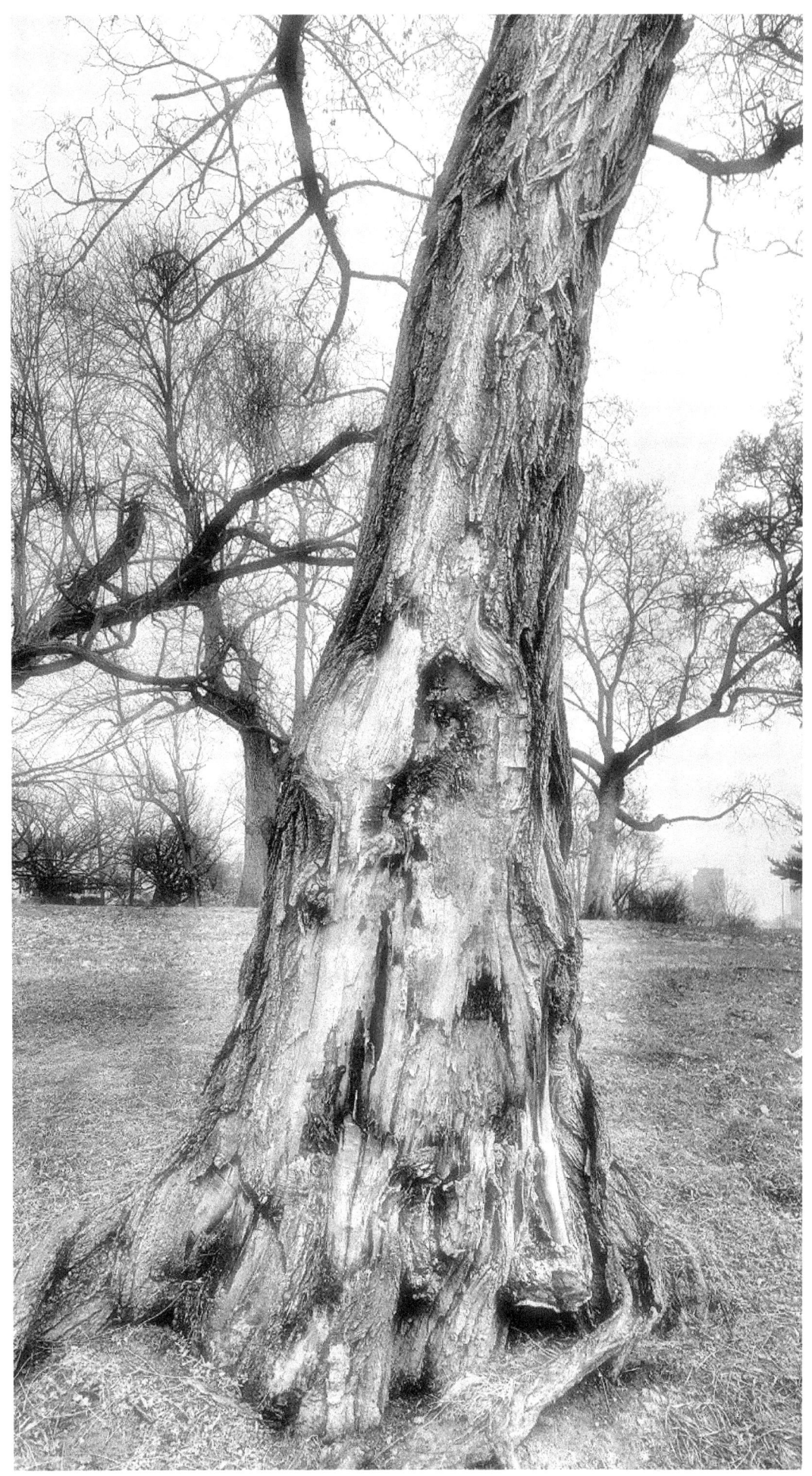

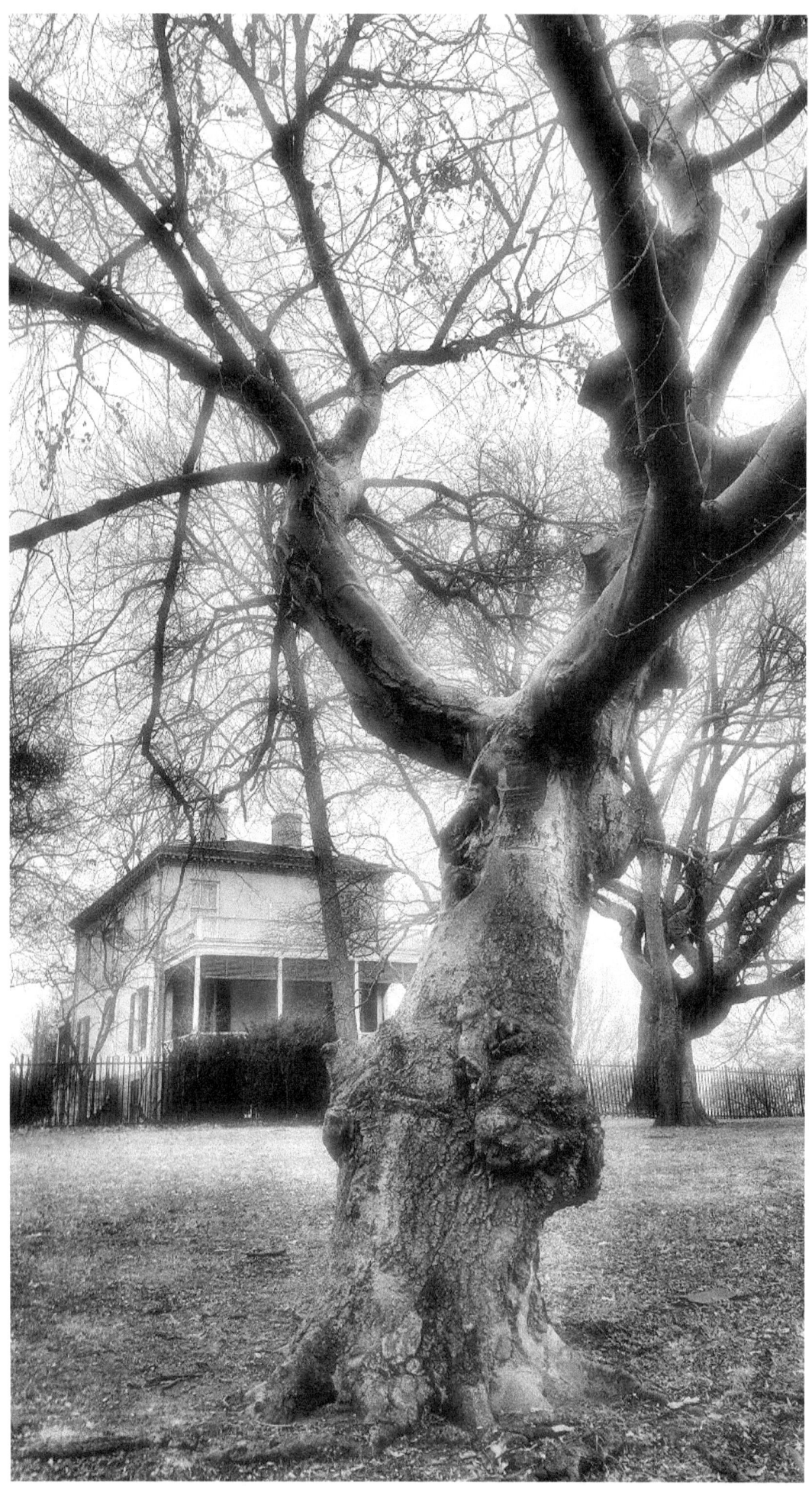

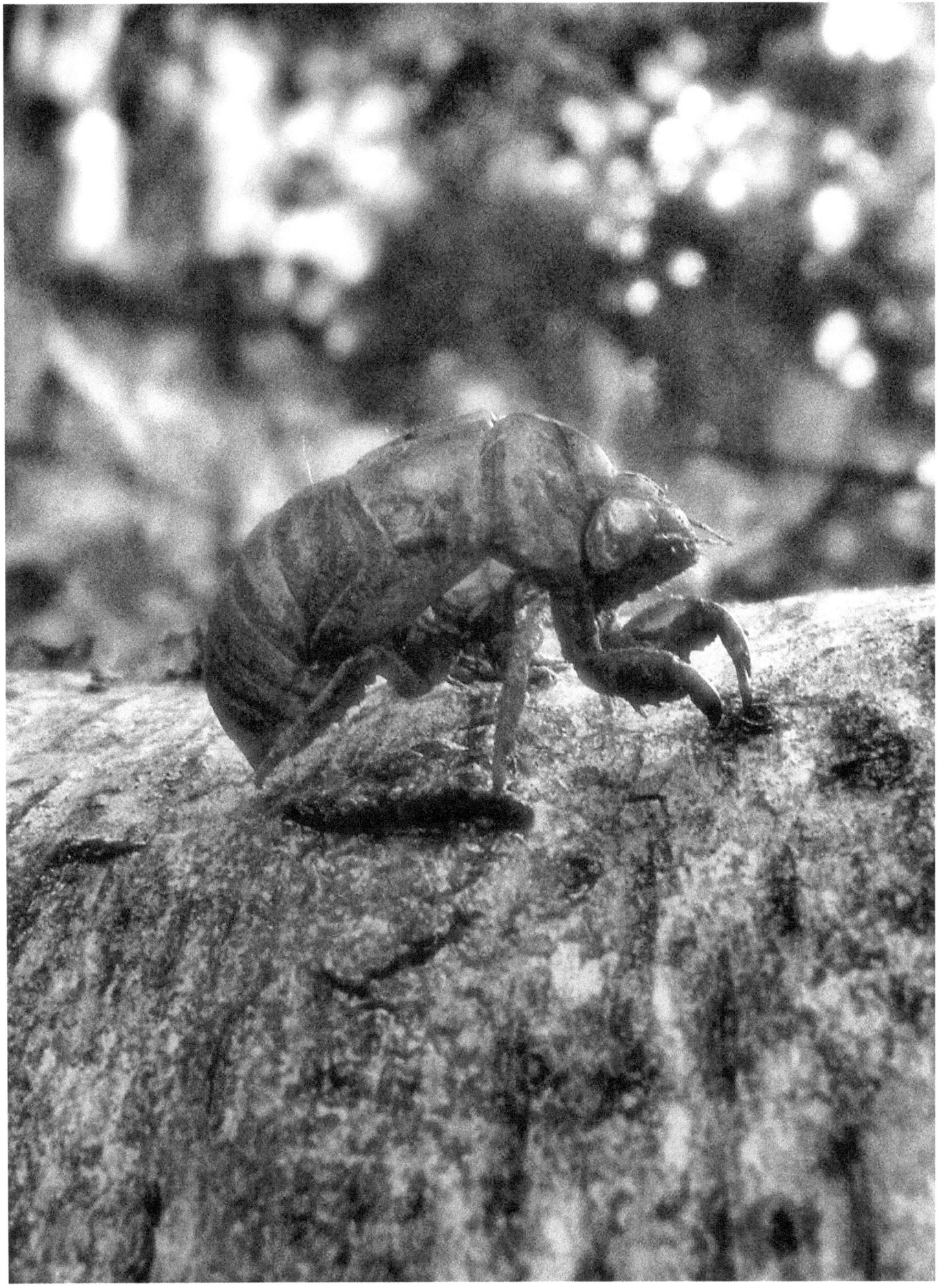

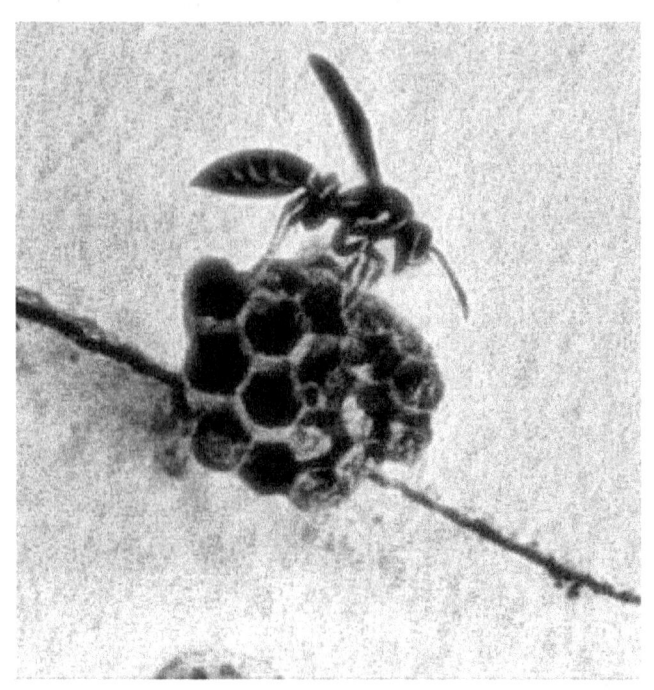

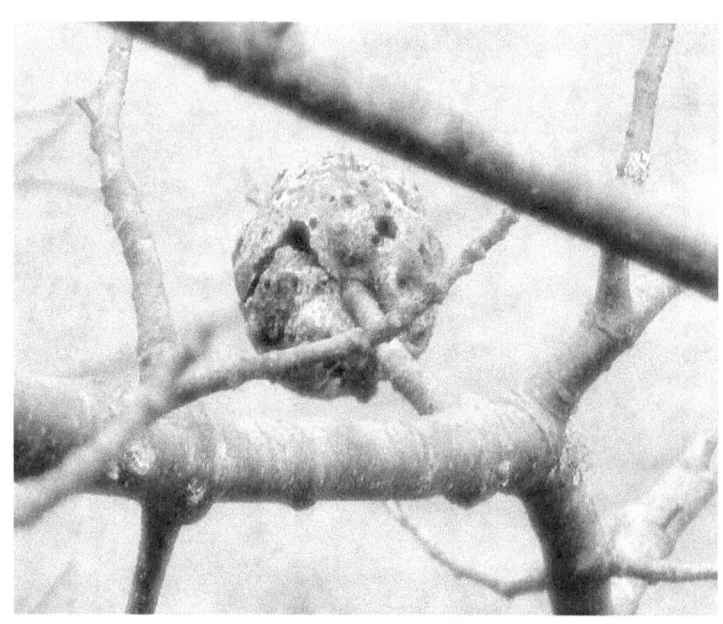

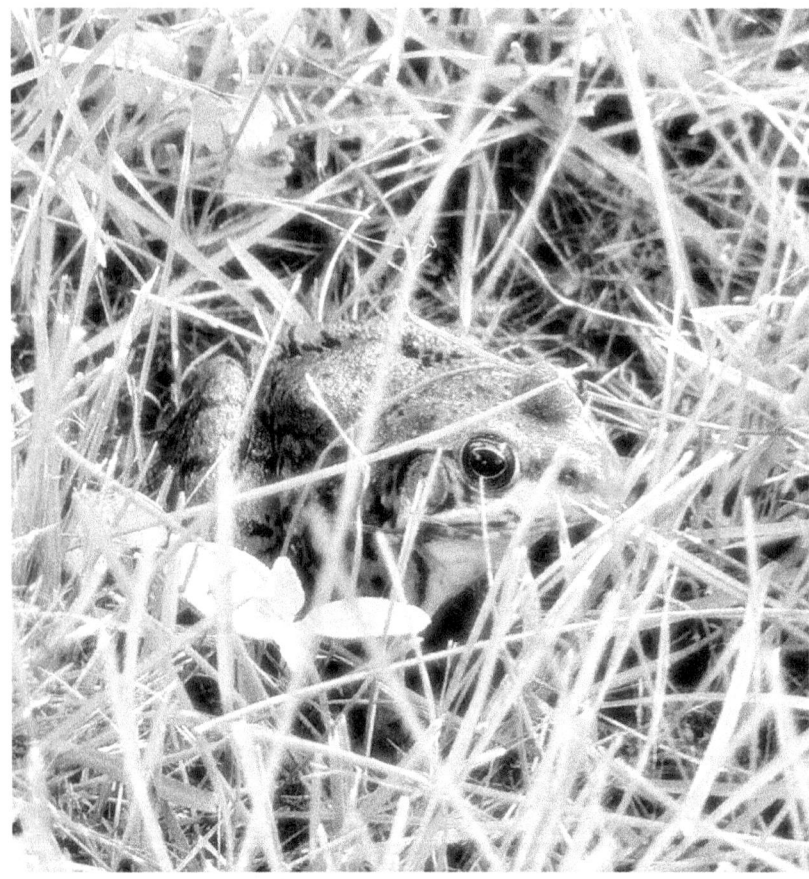

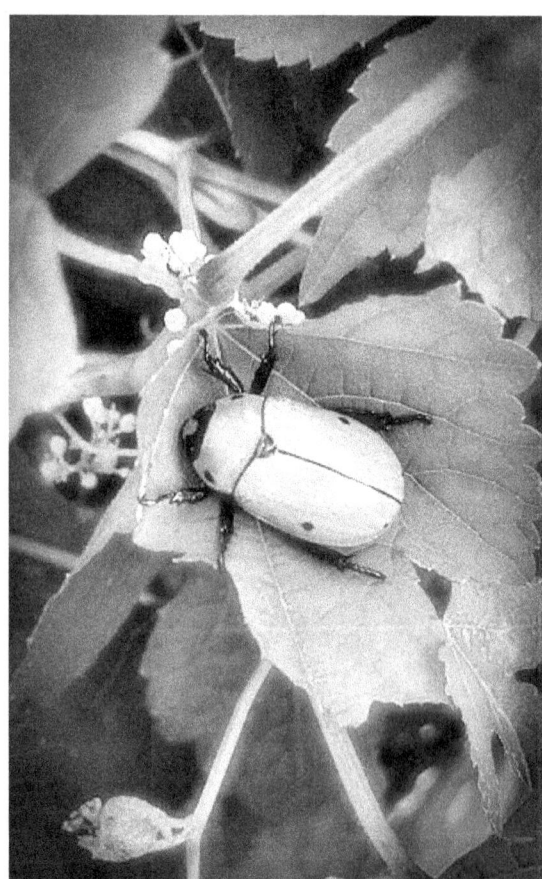

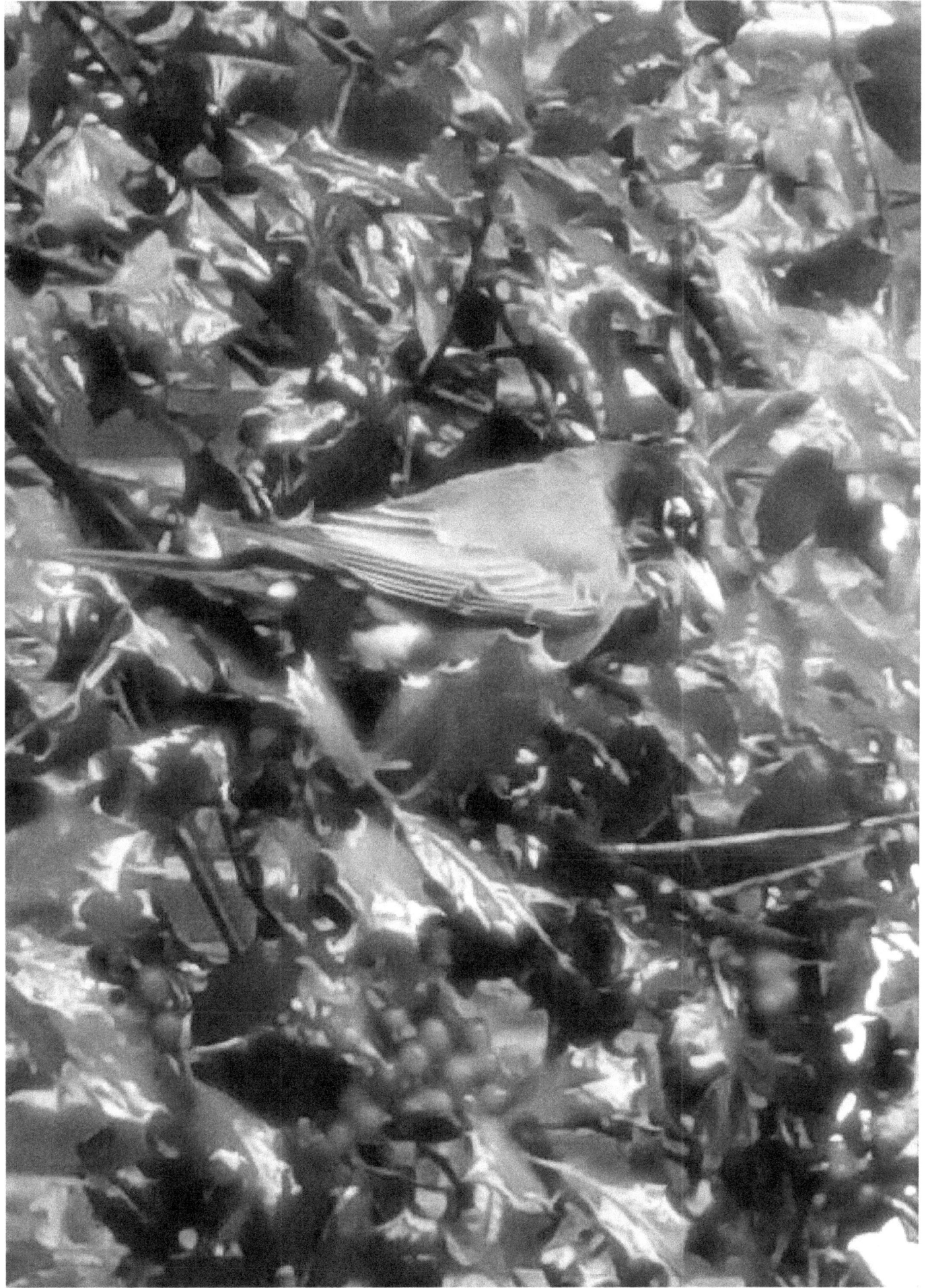

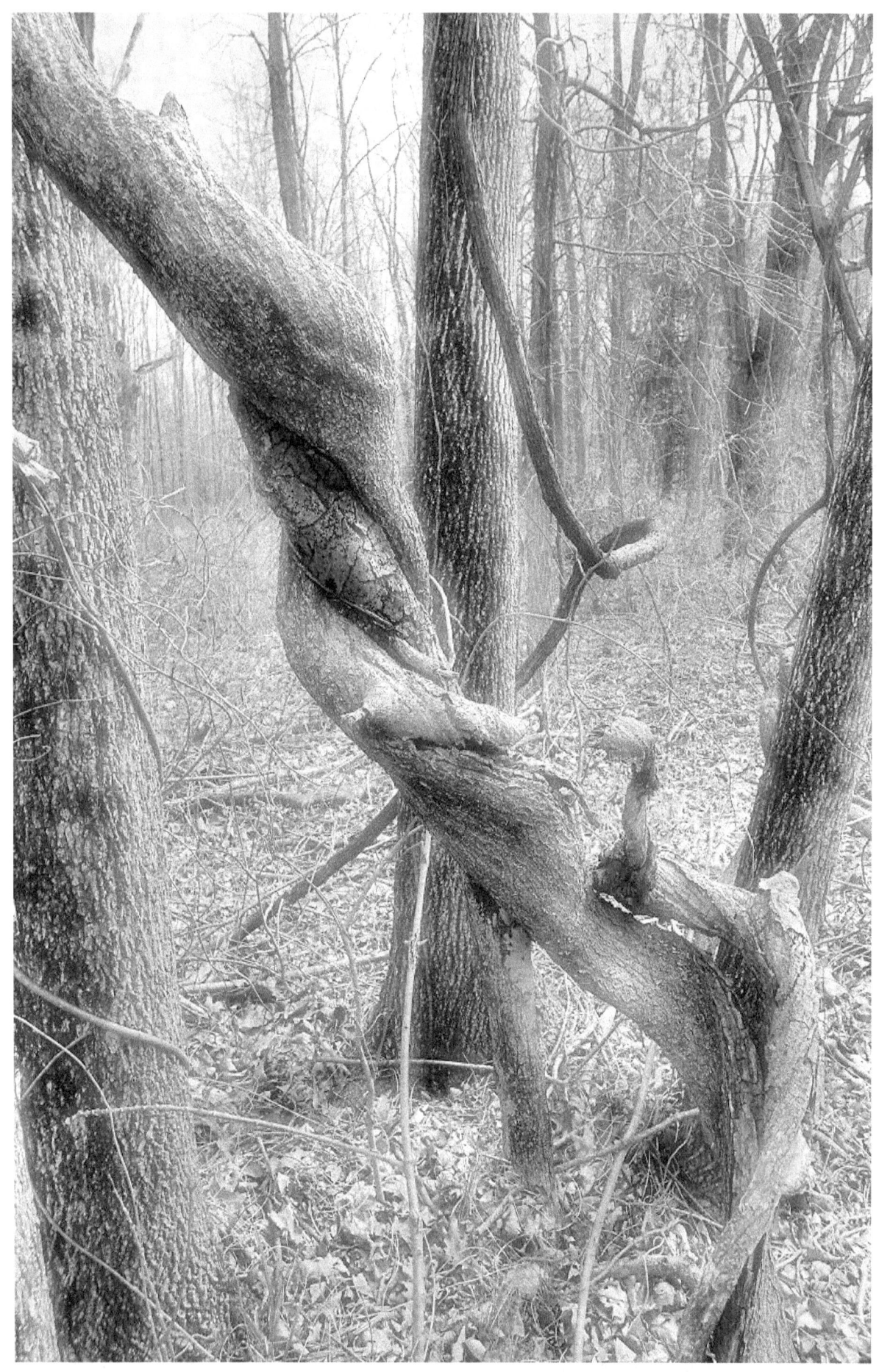

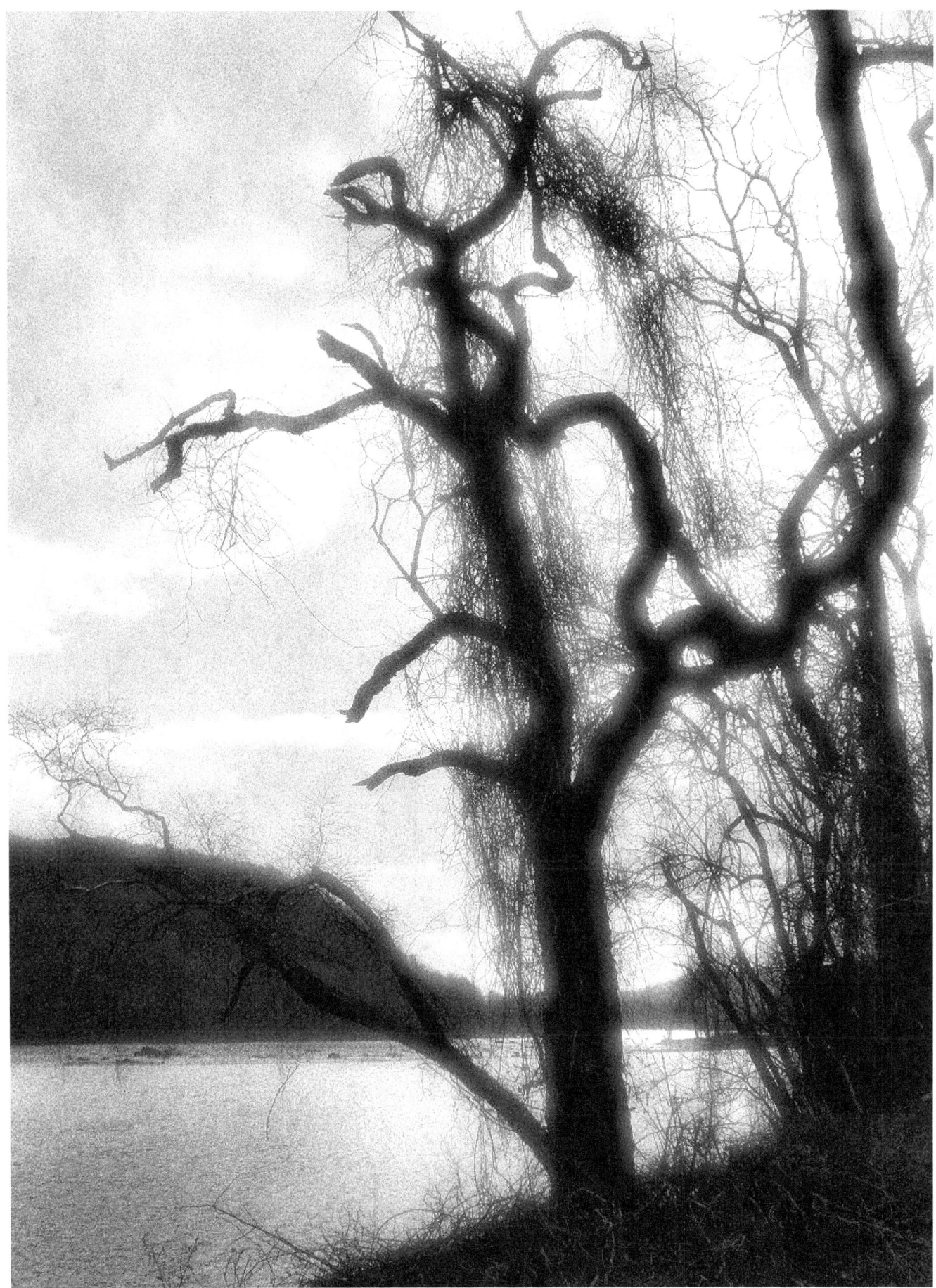

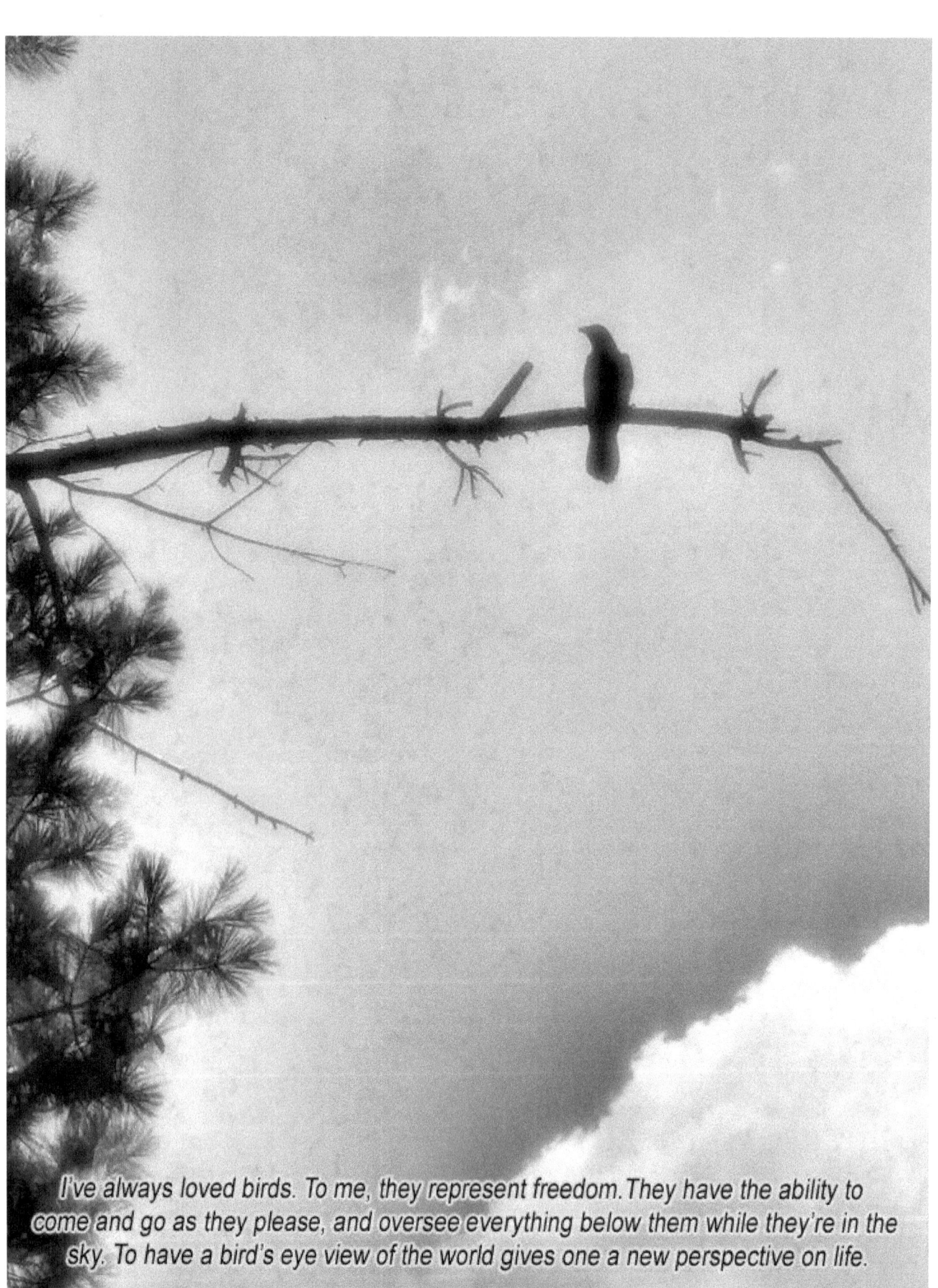

I've always loved birds. To me, they represent freedom. They have the ability to come and go as they please, and oversee everything below them while they're in the sky. To have a bird's eye view of the world gives one a new perspective on life.

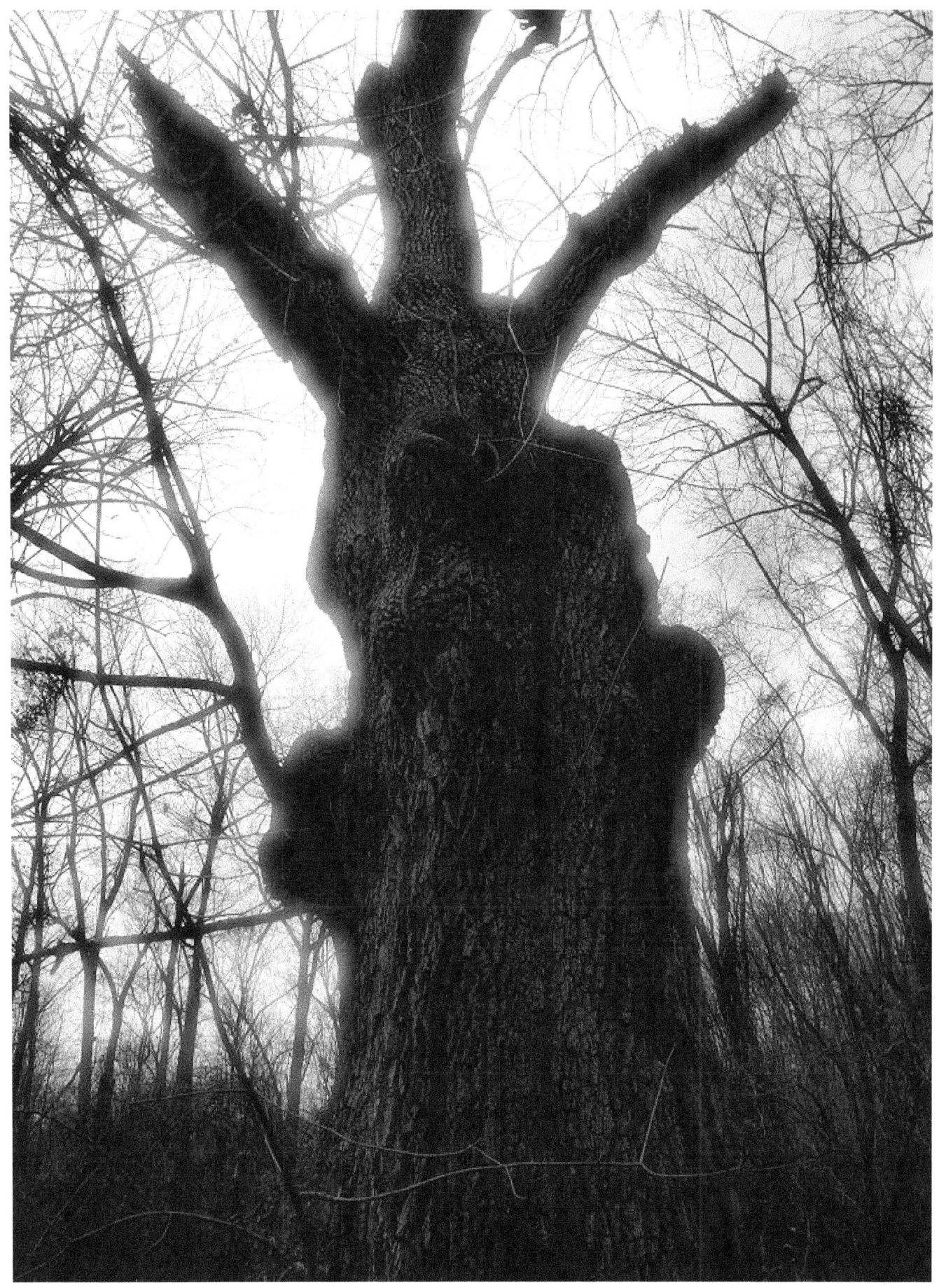

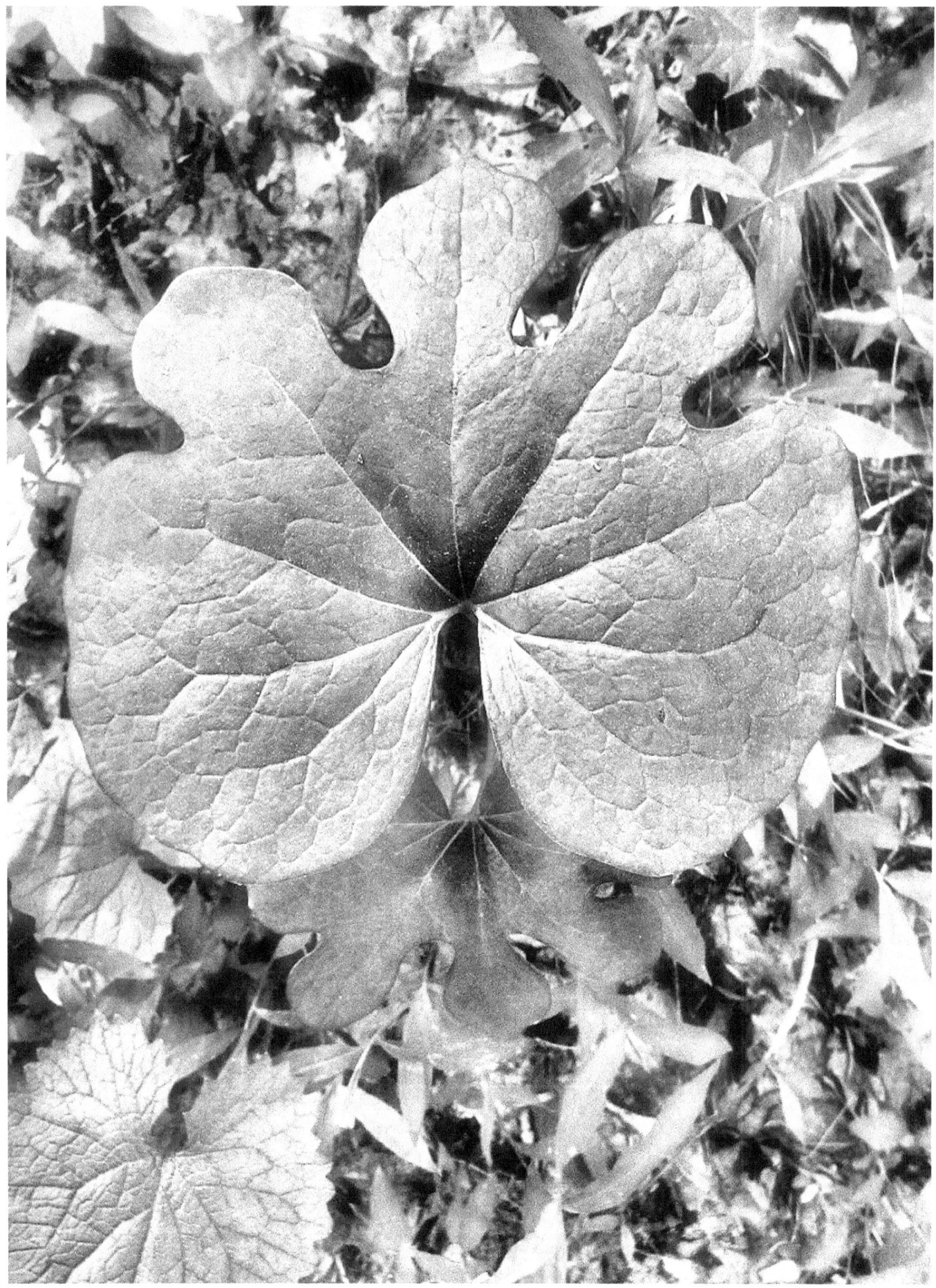

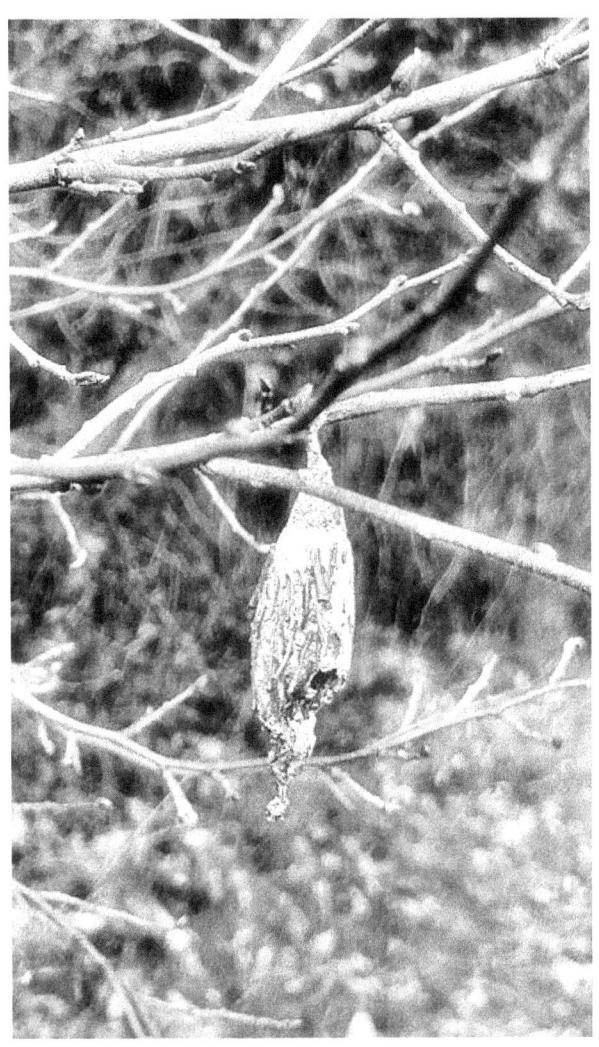

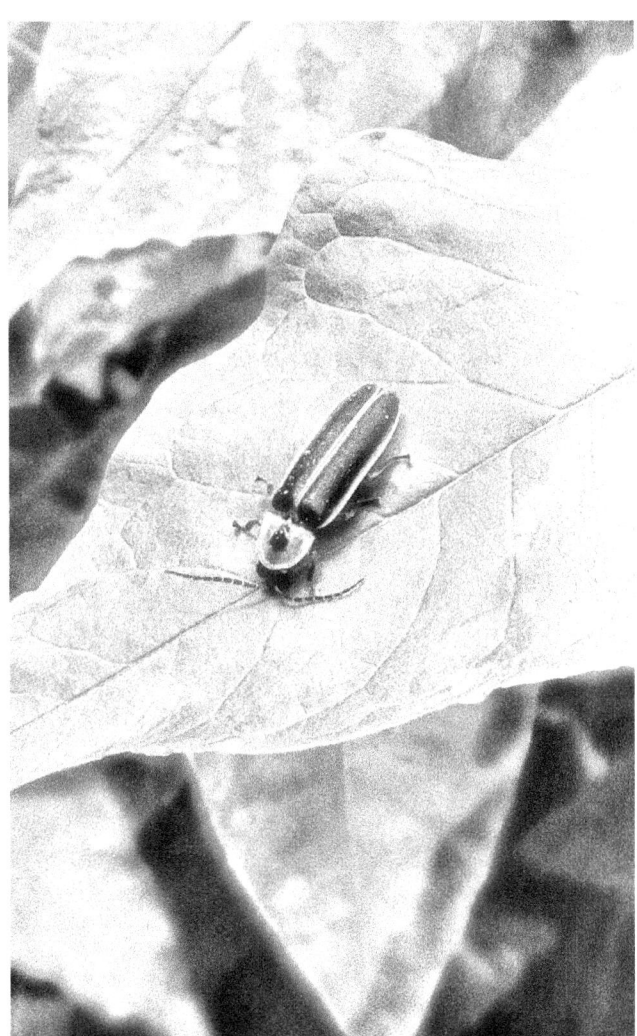

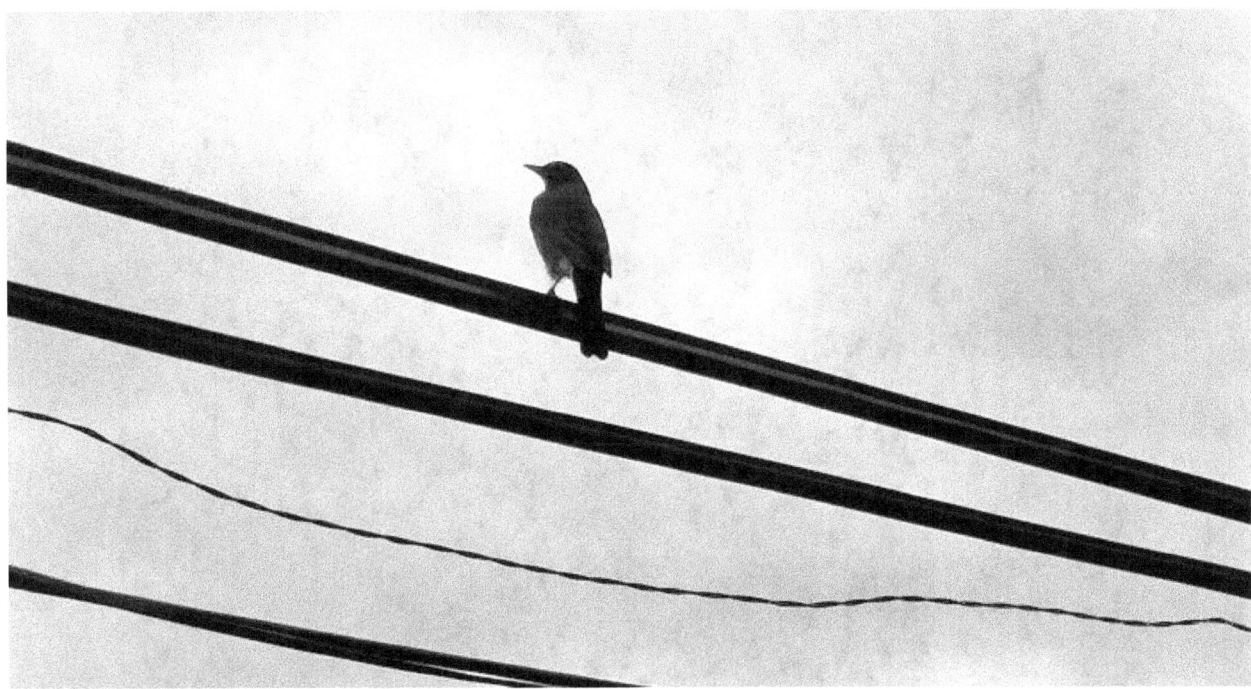

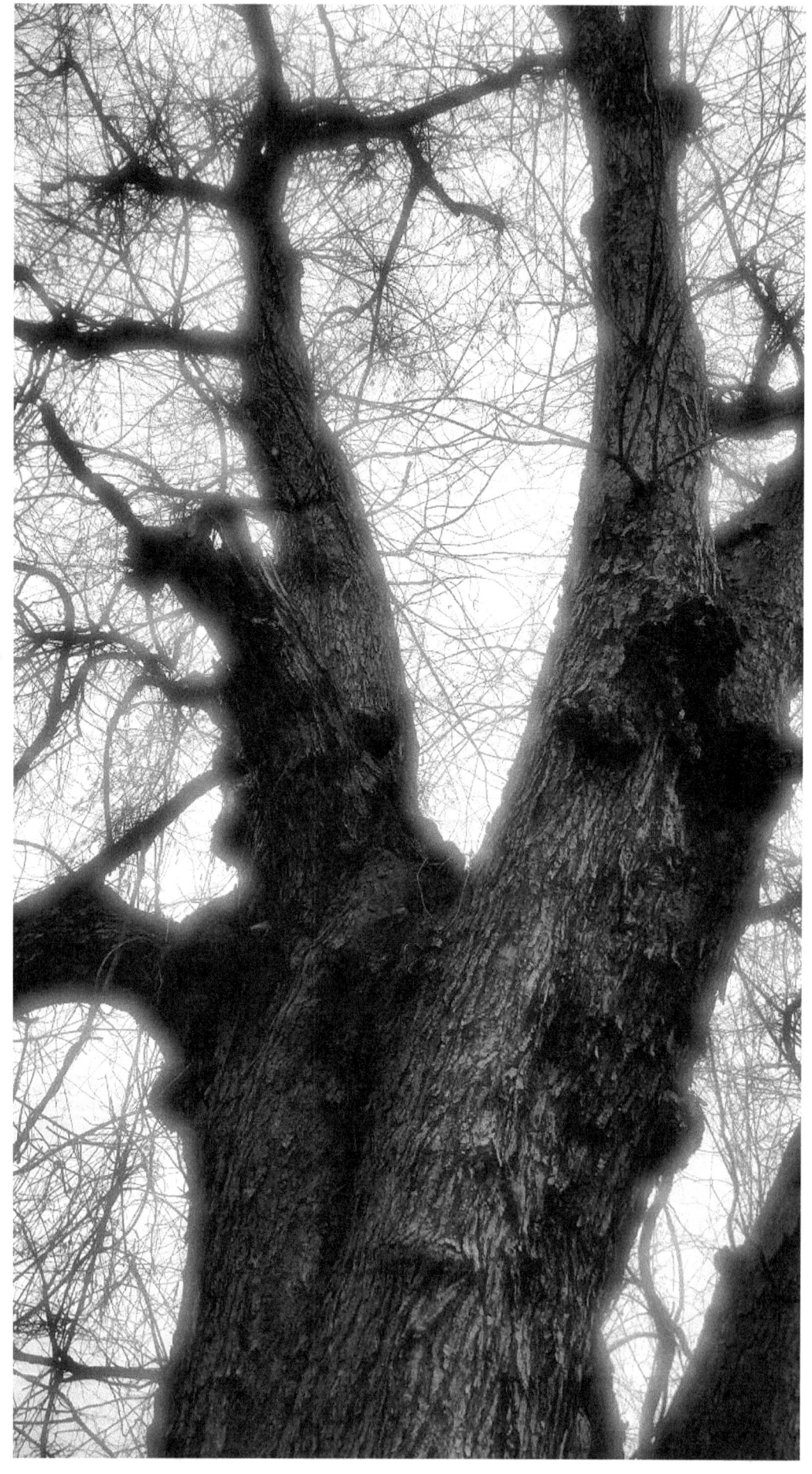

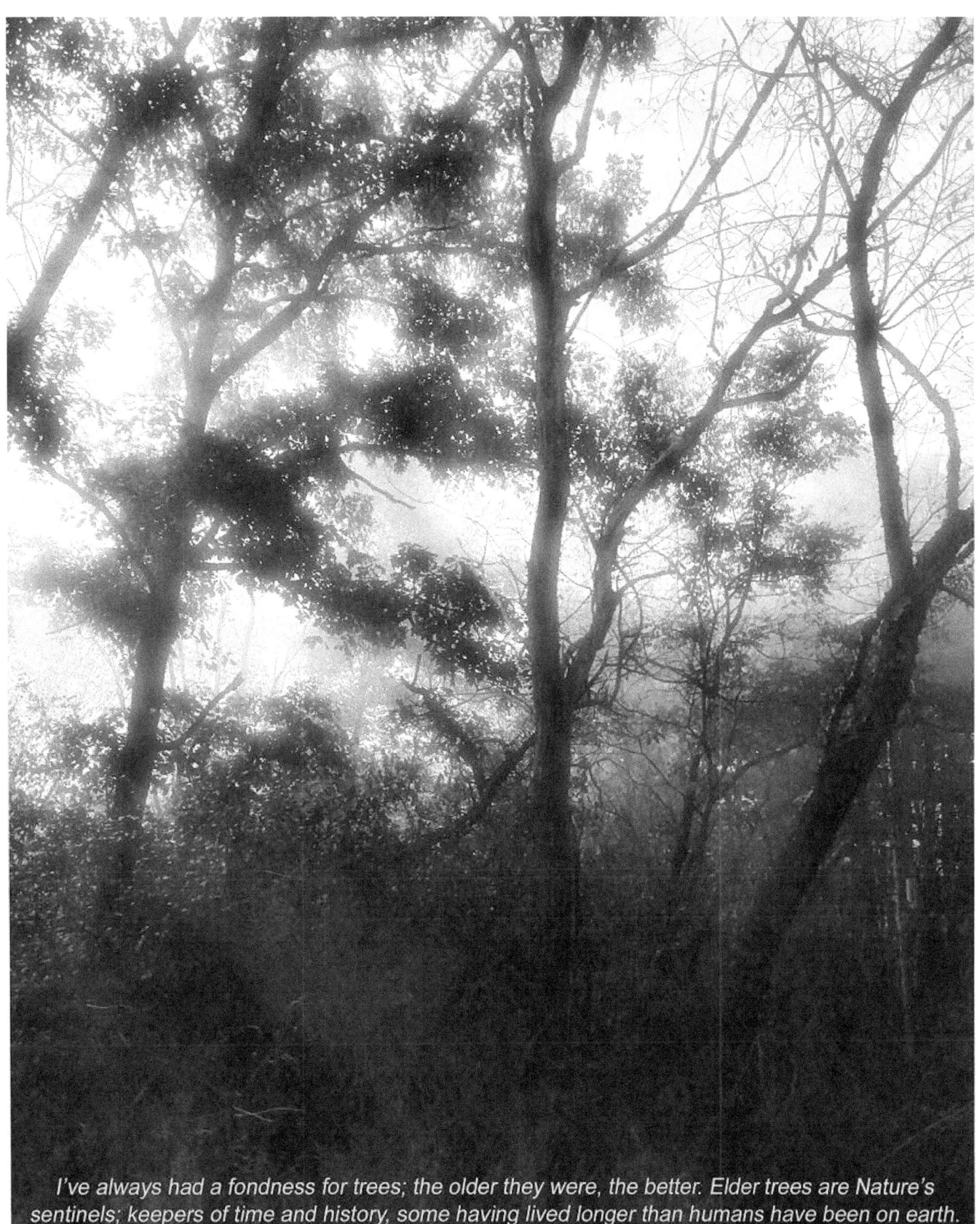

I've always had a fondness for trees; the older they were, the better. Elder trees are Nature's sentinels; keepers of time and history, some having lived longer than humans have been on earth. Their gnarled and twisted branches give them personalities of their own. Fog-enshrouded trees offer mystery and allure; enticing you to uncover secrets they may be hiding in their midsts.

Buildings, Cemeteries and Other Ruined Structures

More and more I seem to be encountering old, dilapidated buildings, making me wonder if it is a reflection of our crumbling society, or simply eras of history gone by. Either way, those weather-beaten and time-worn structures make for haunting imagery. Teetering and sinking headstones are yet another reminder of the passing of time, and that our time here on earth is limited, encouraging us to live our lives to the fullest.

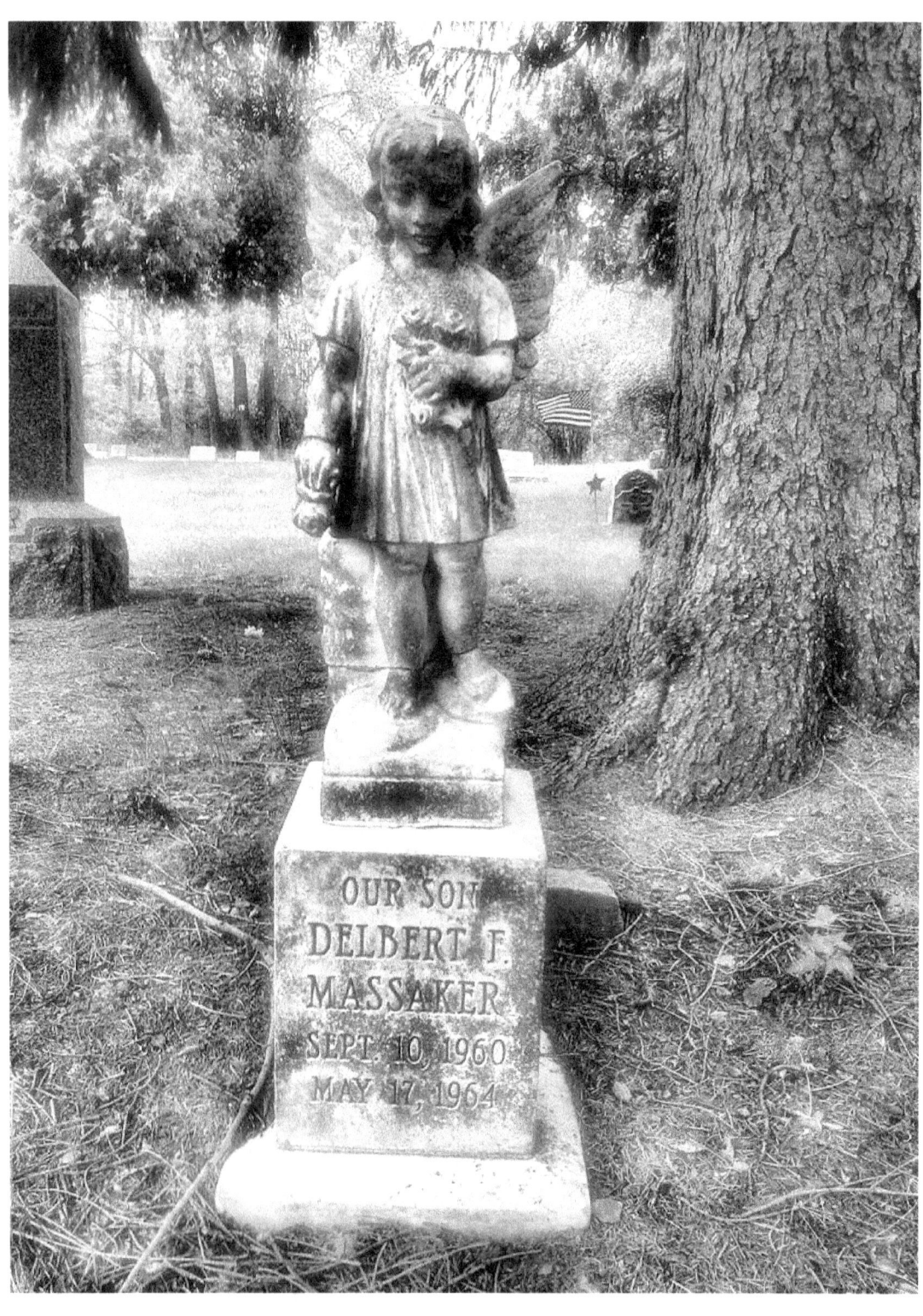

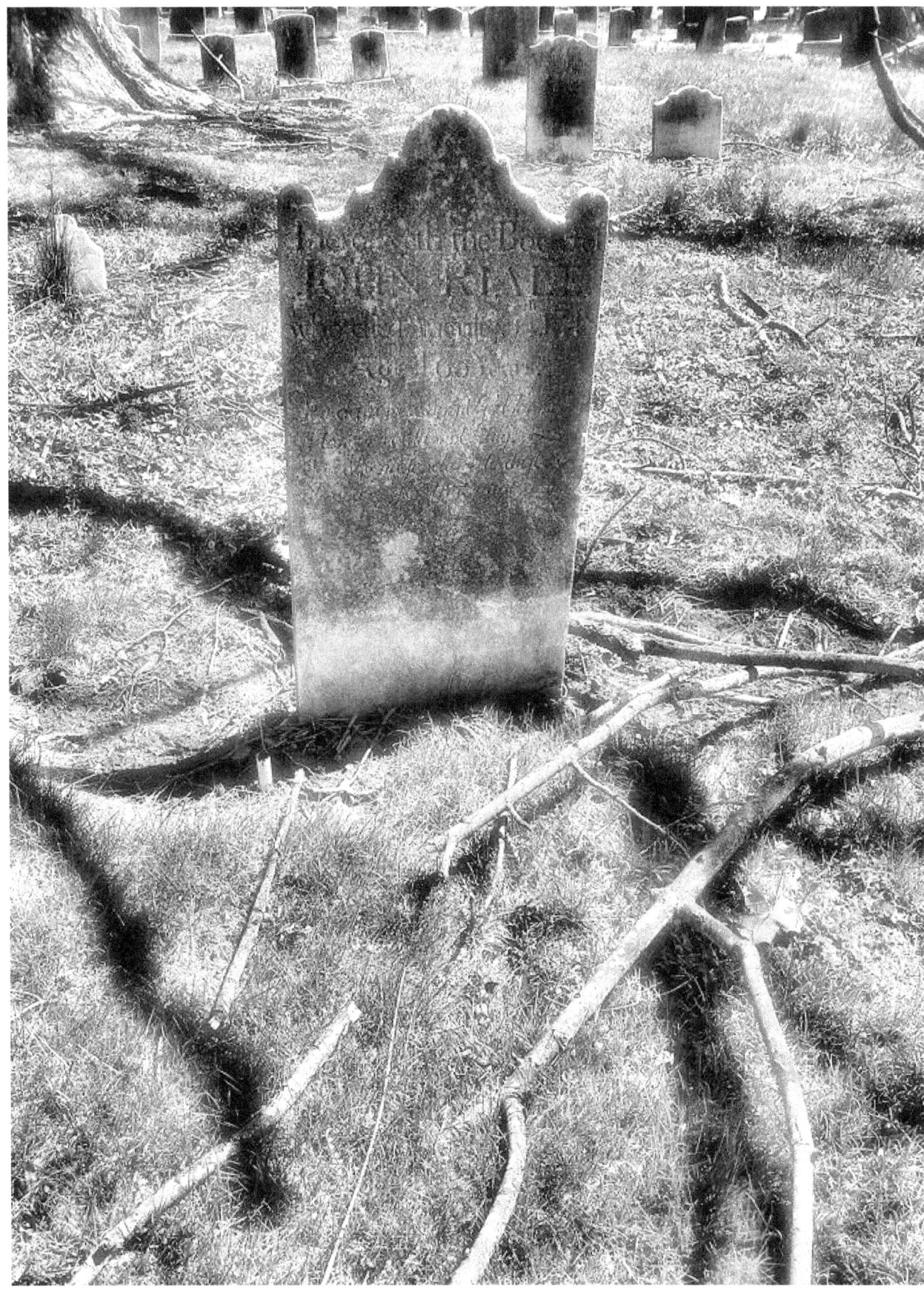

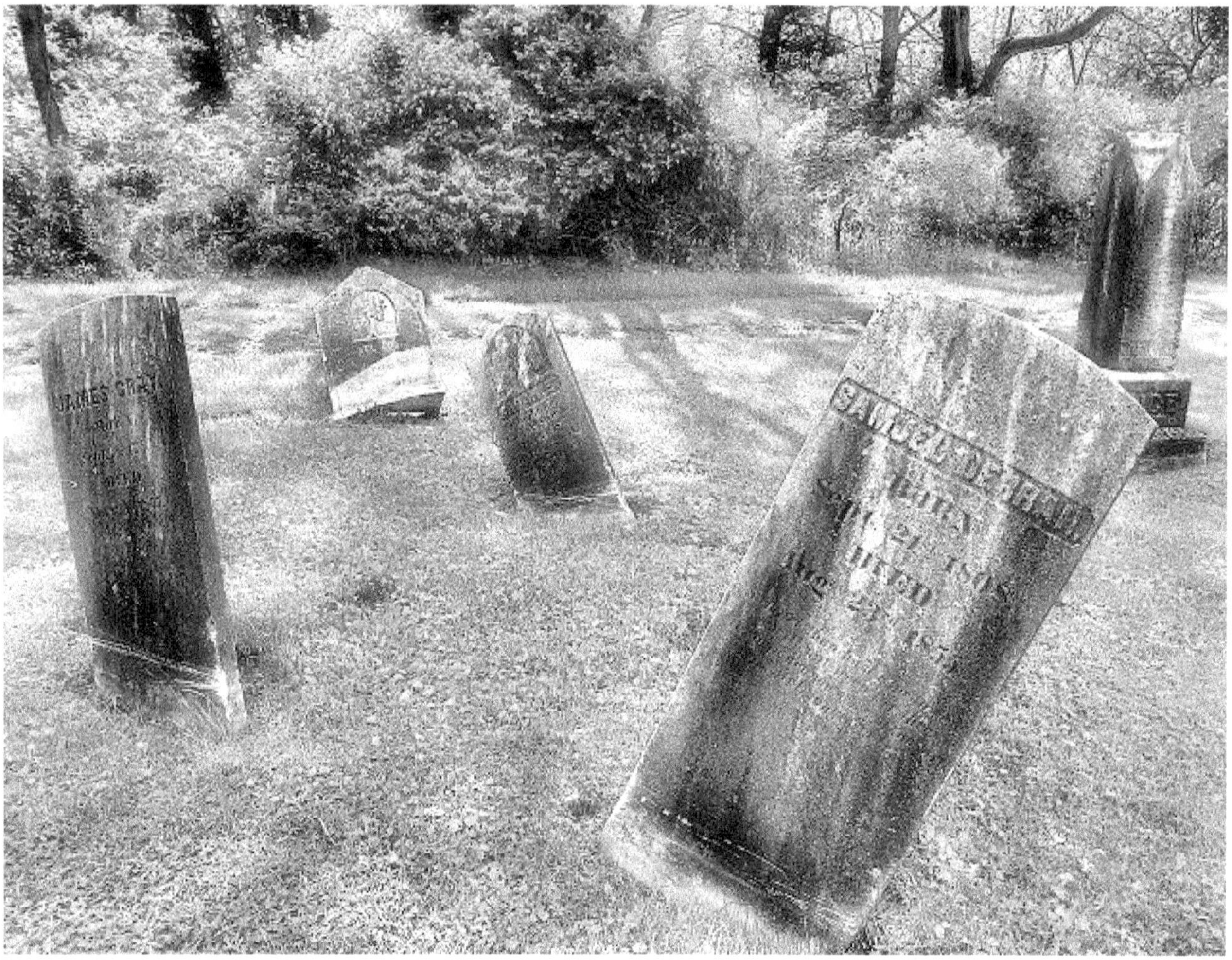

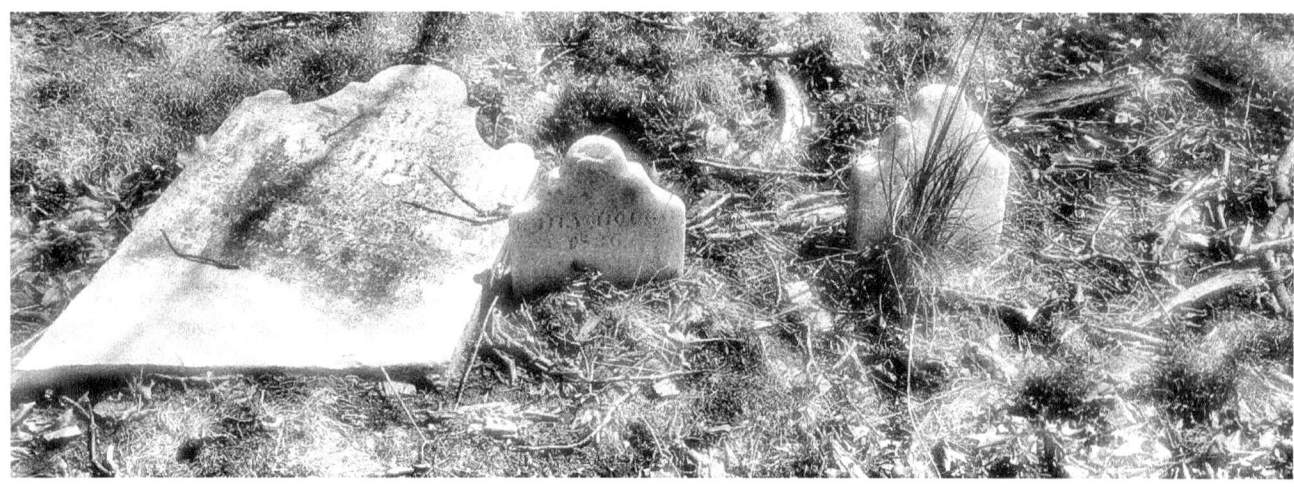

Never say goodbye, because saying goodbye means going away, and going away means forgetting." ---Peter Pan

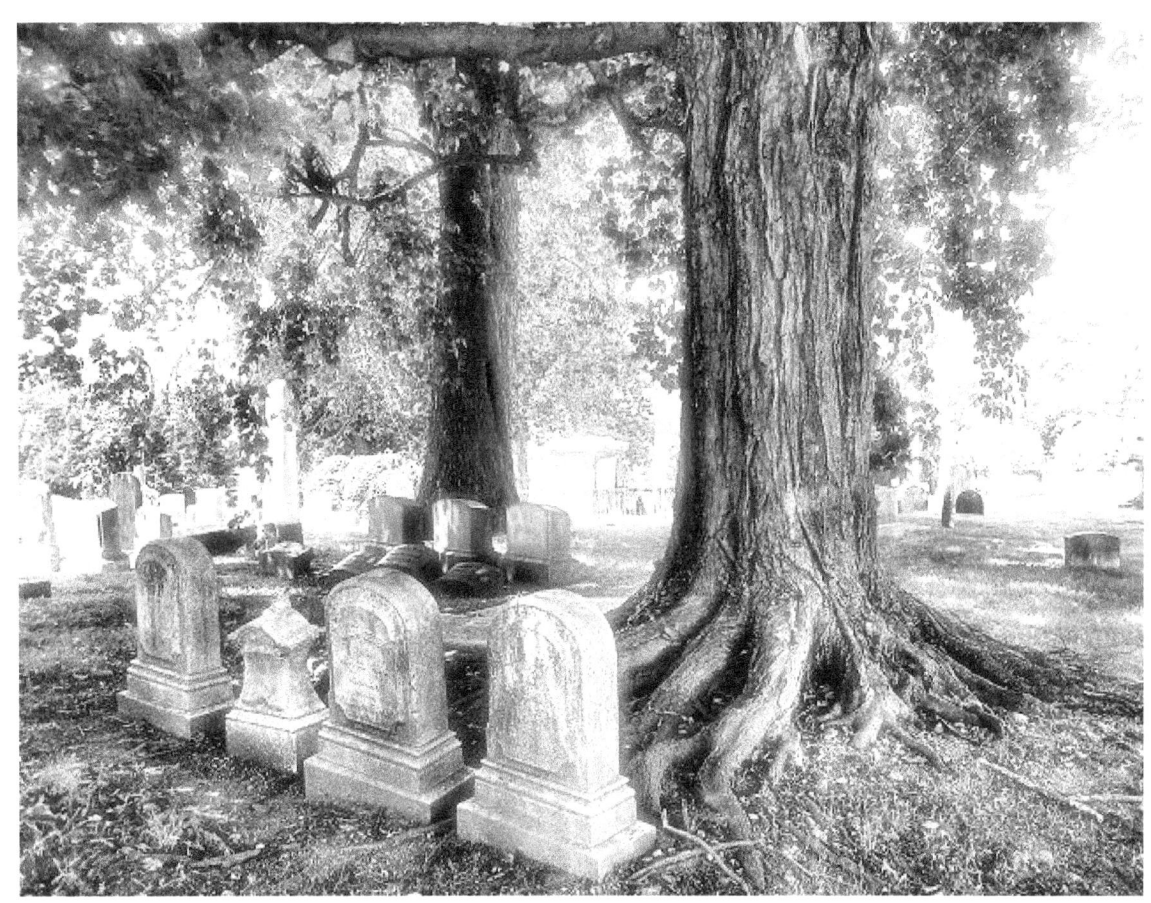

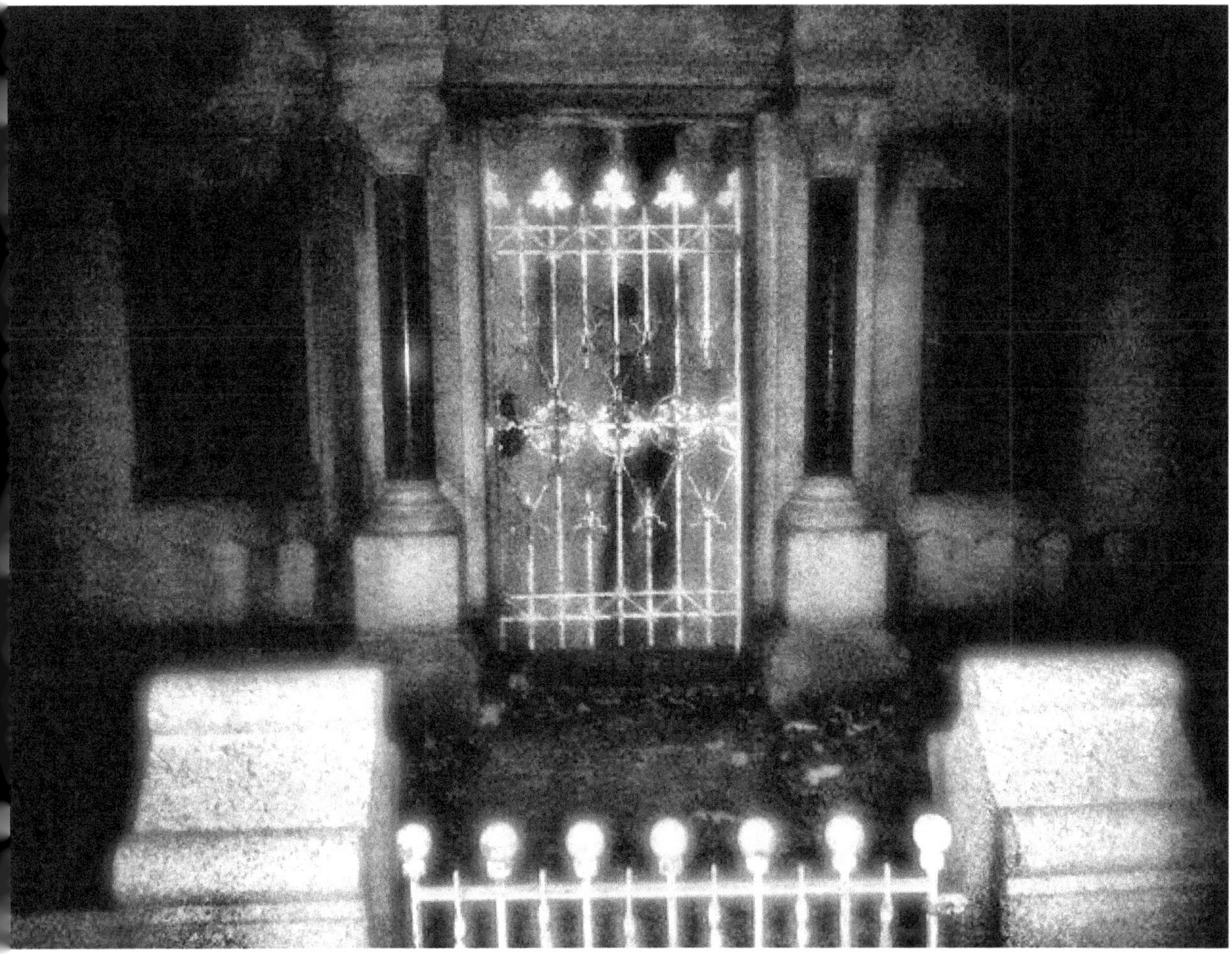

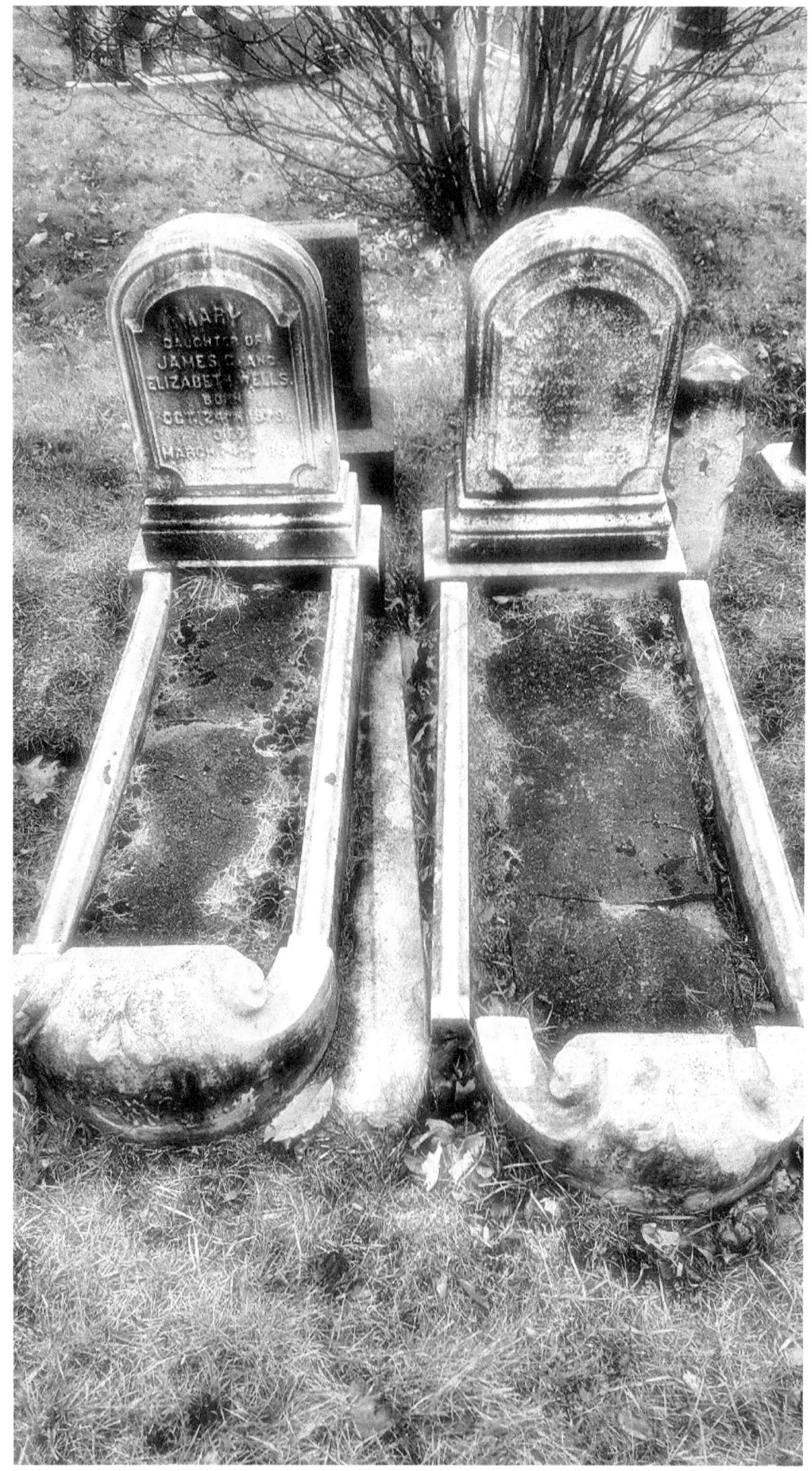

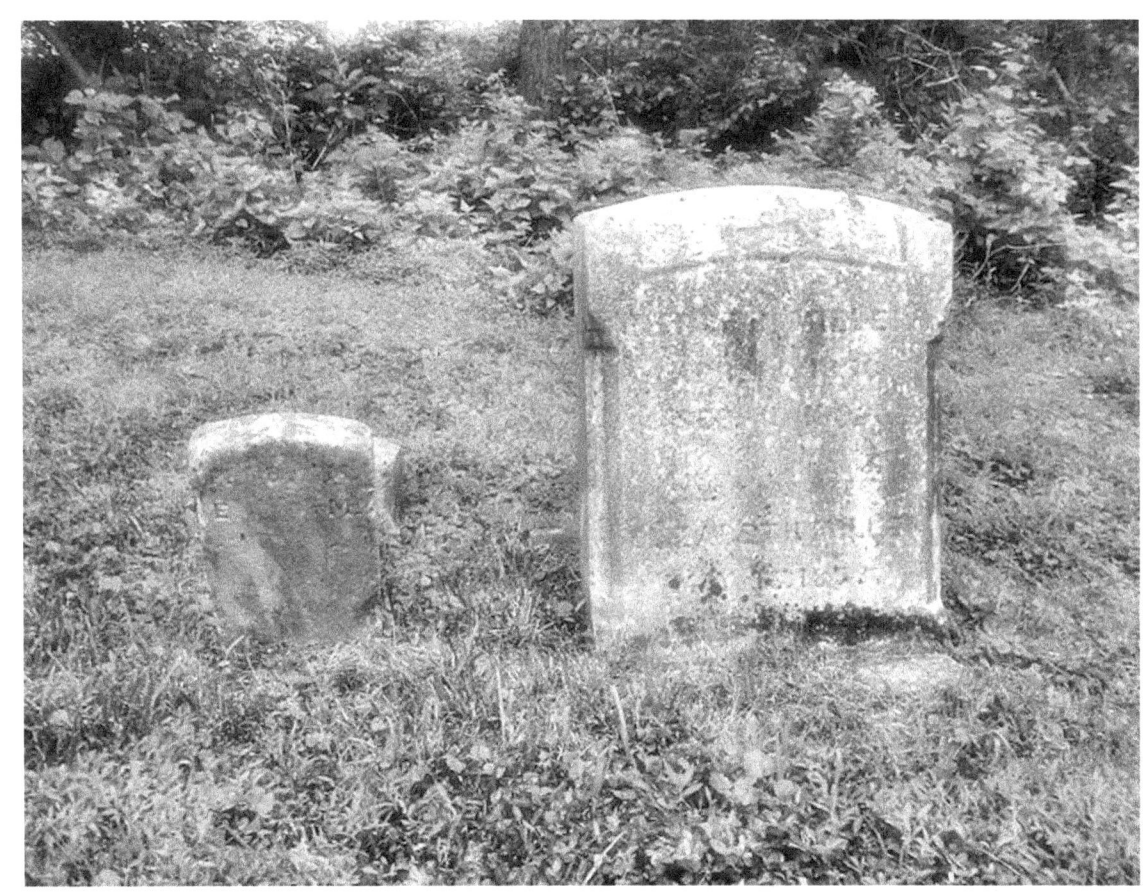

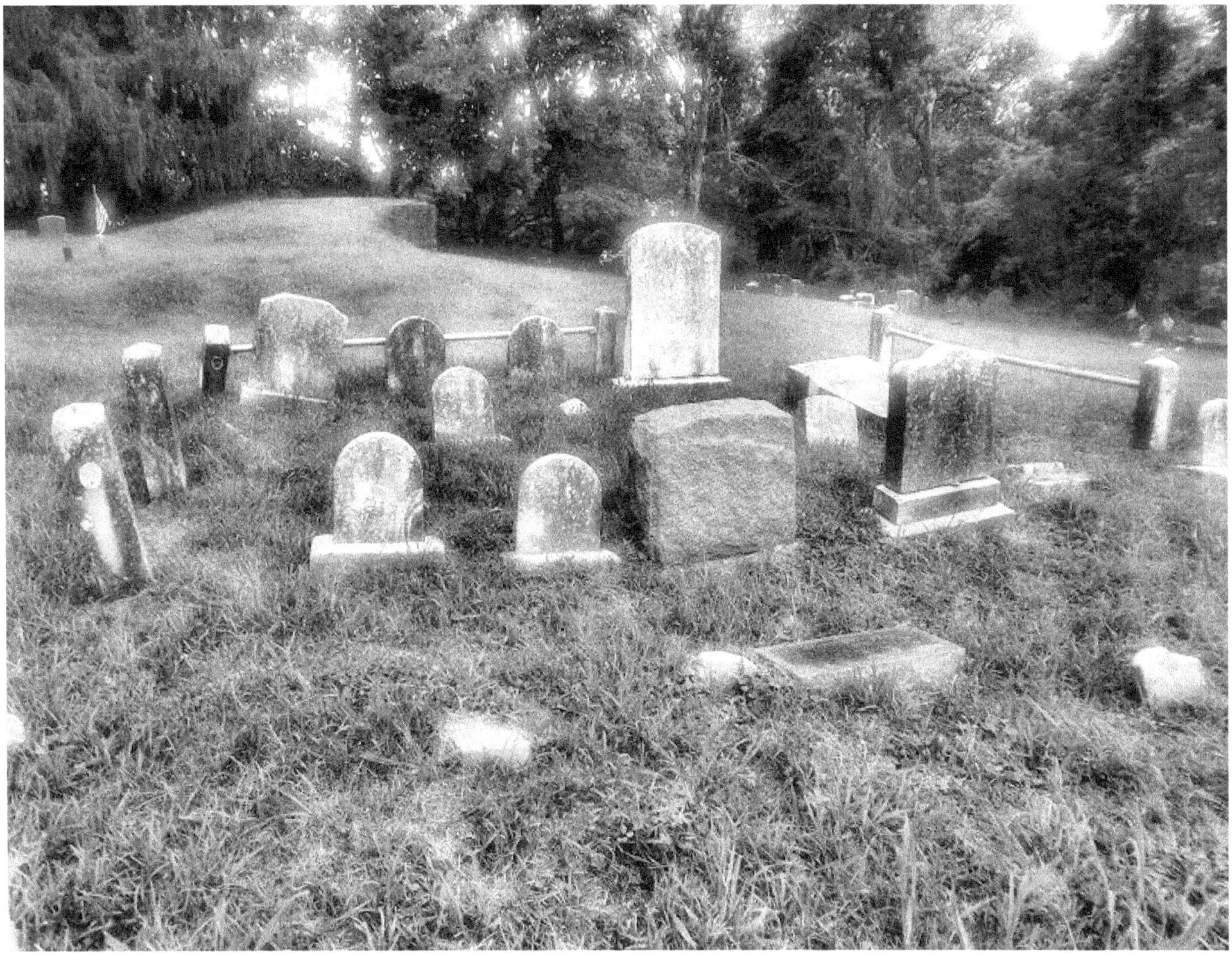

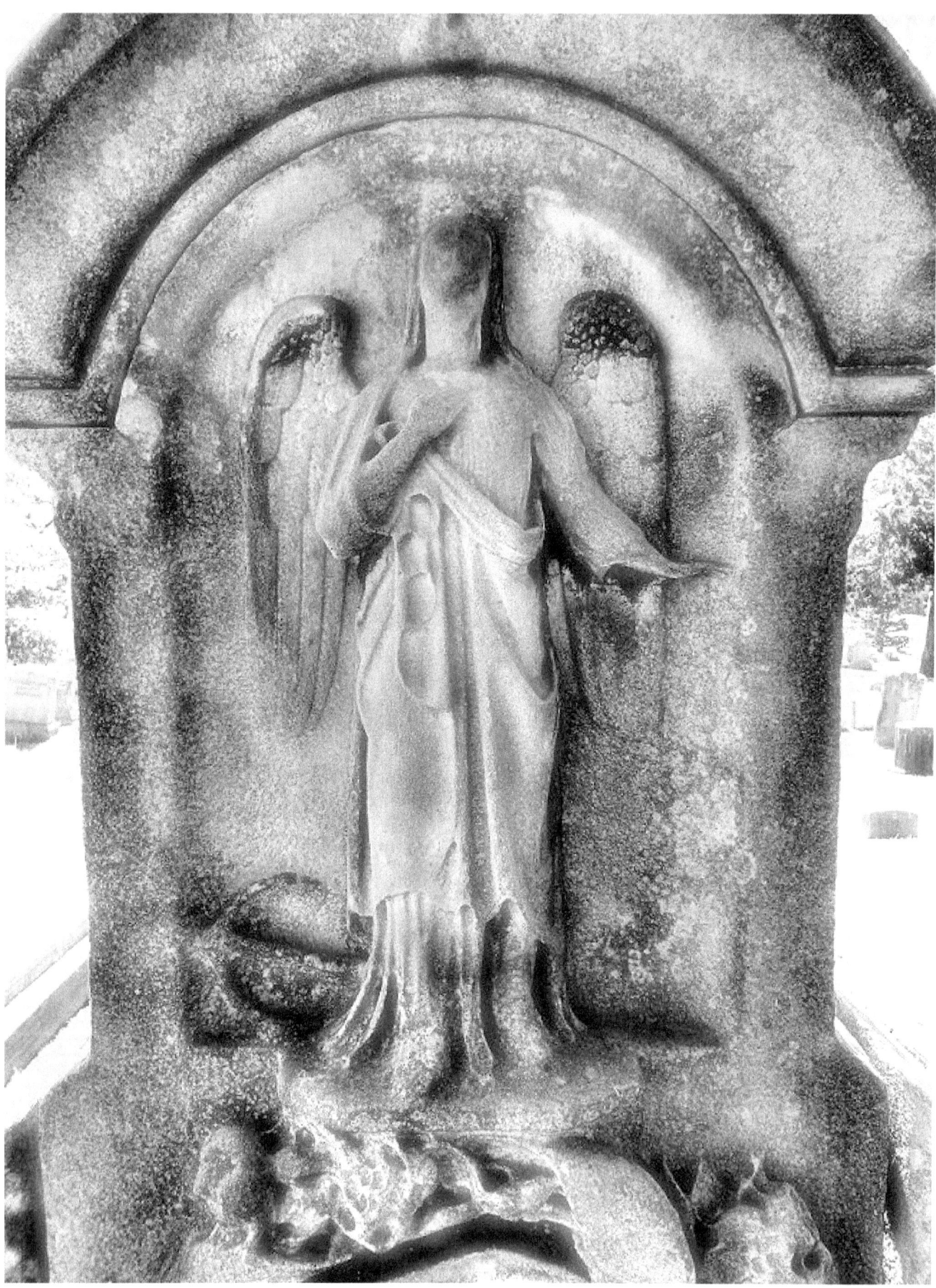

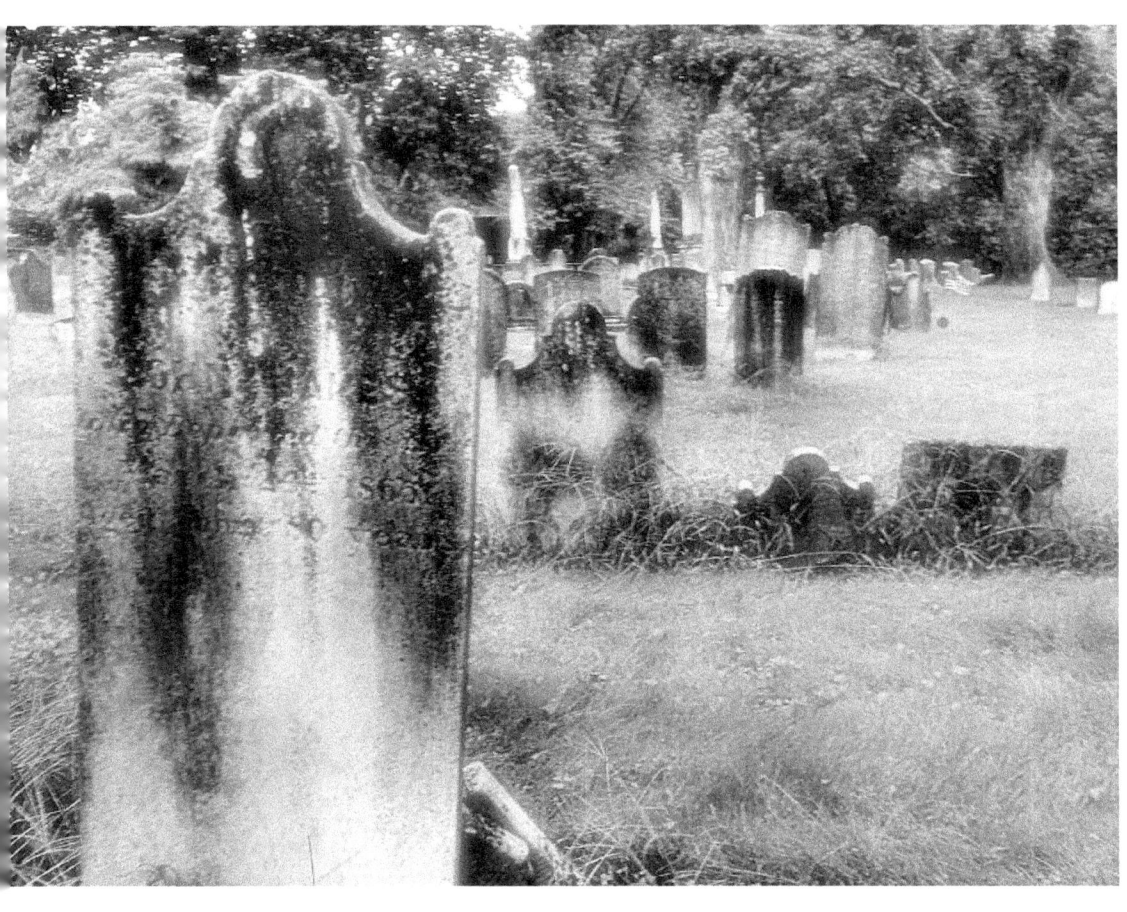

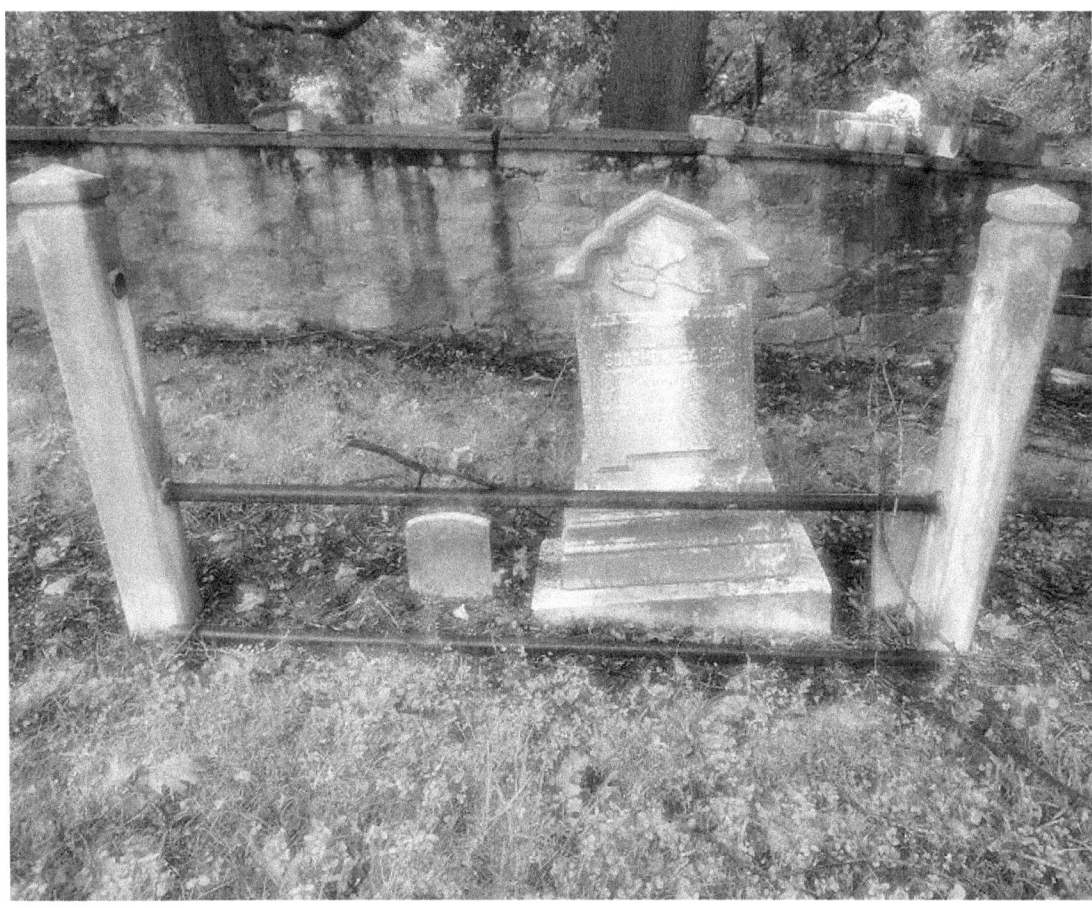

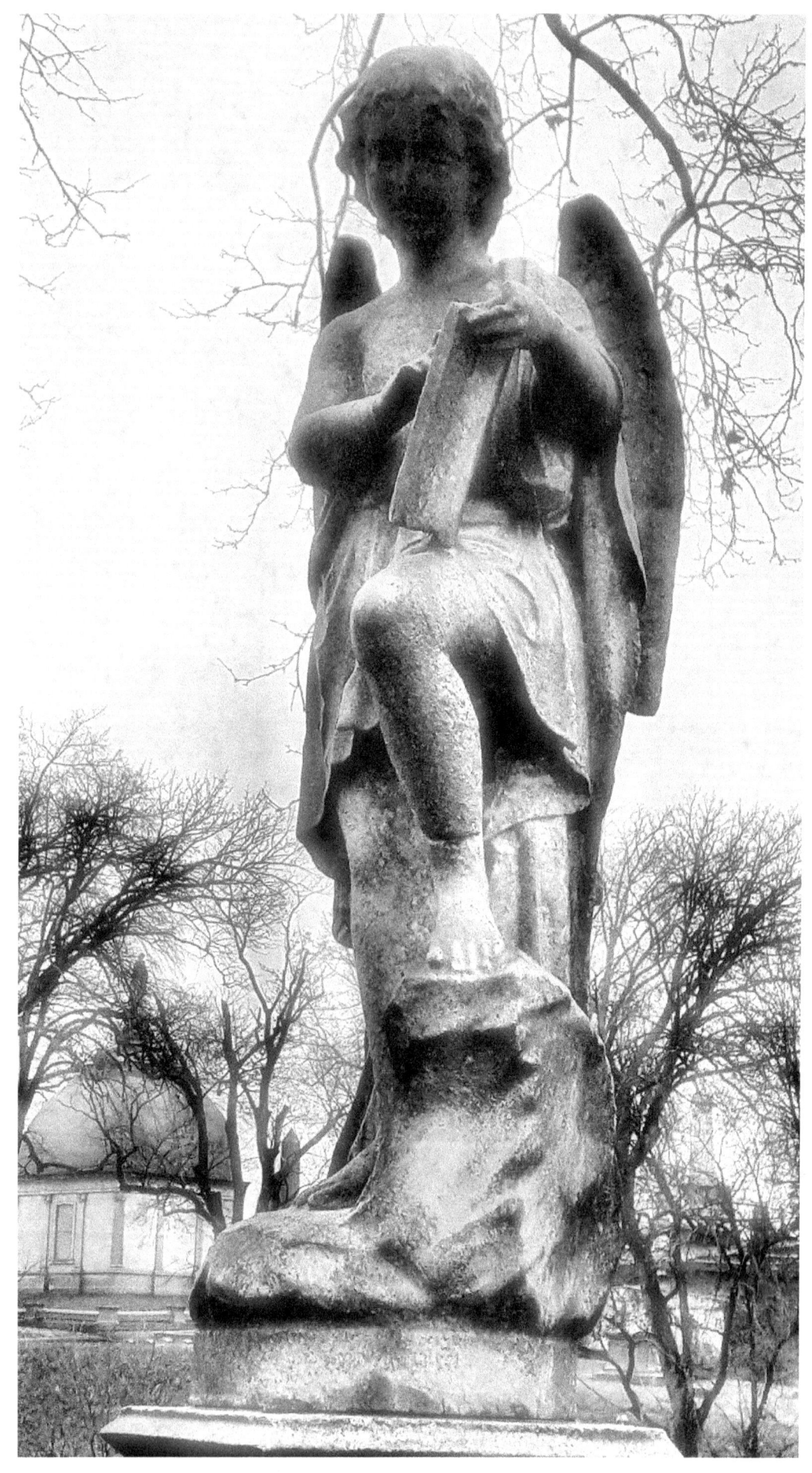

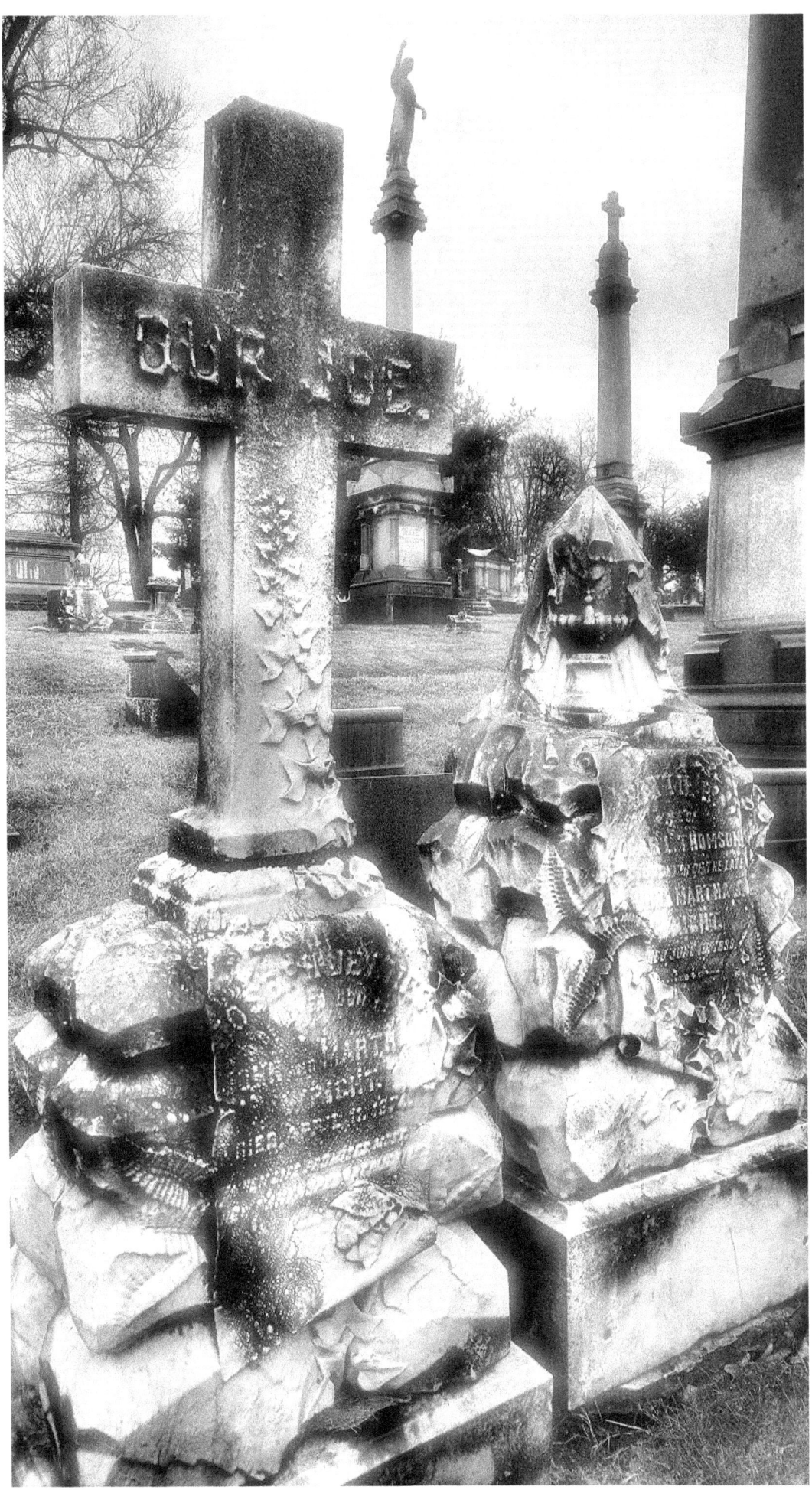

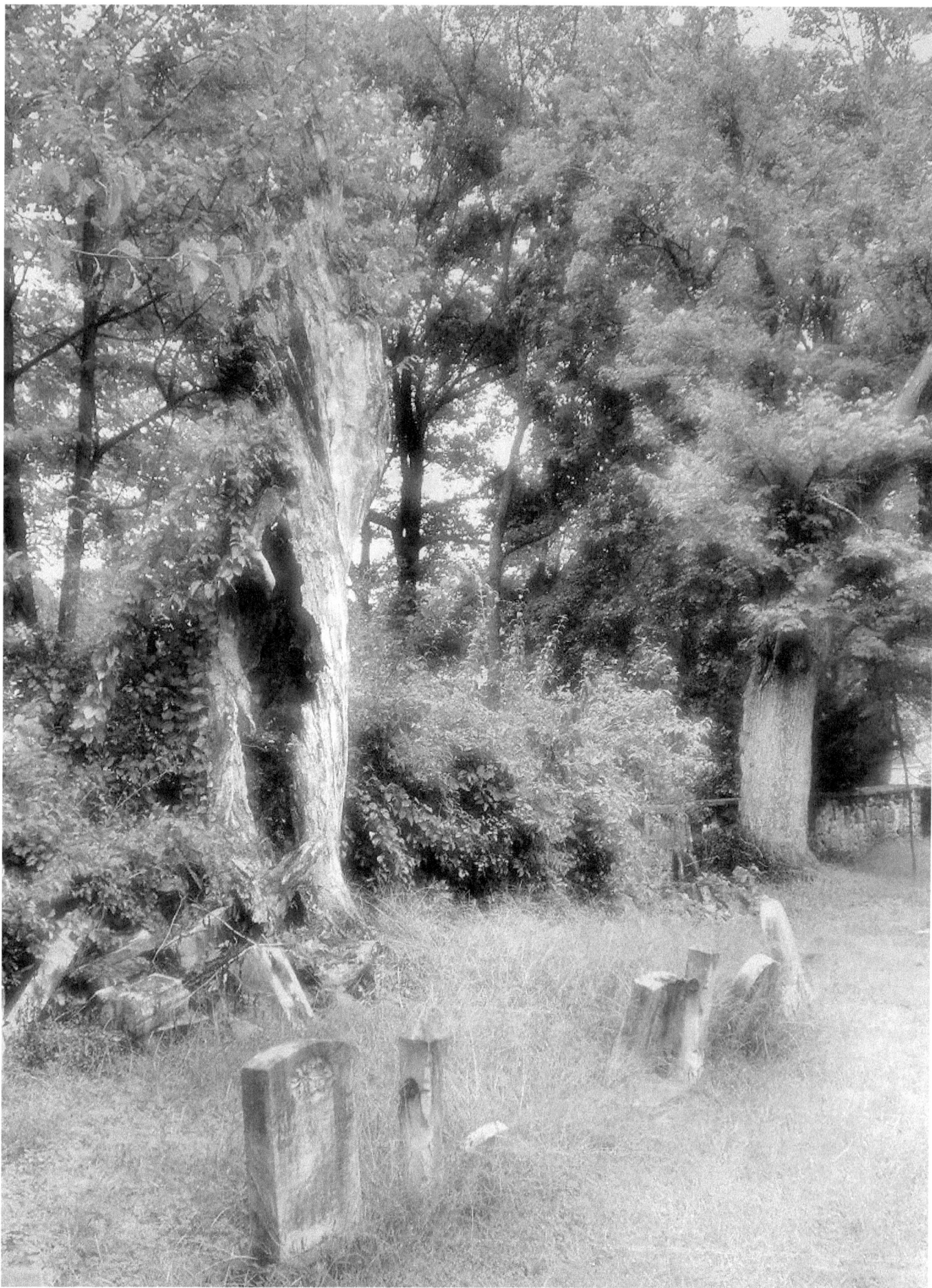

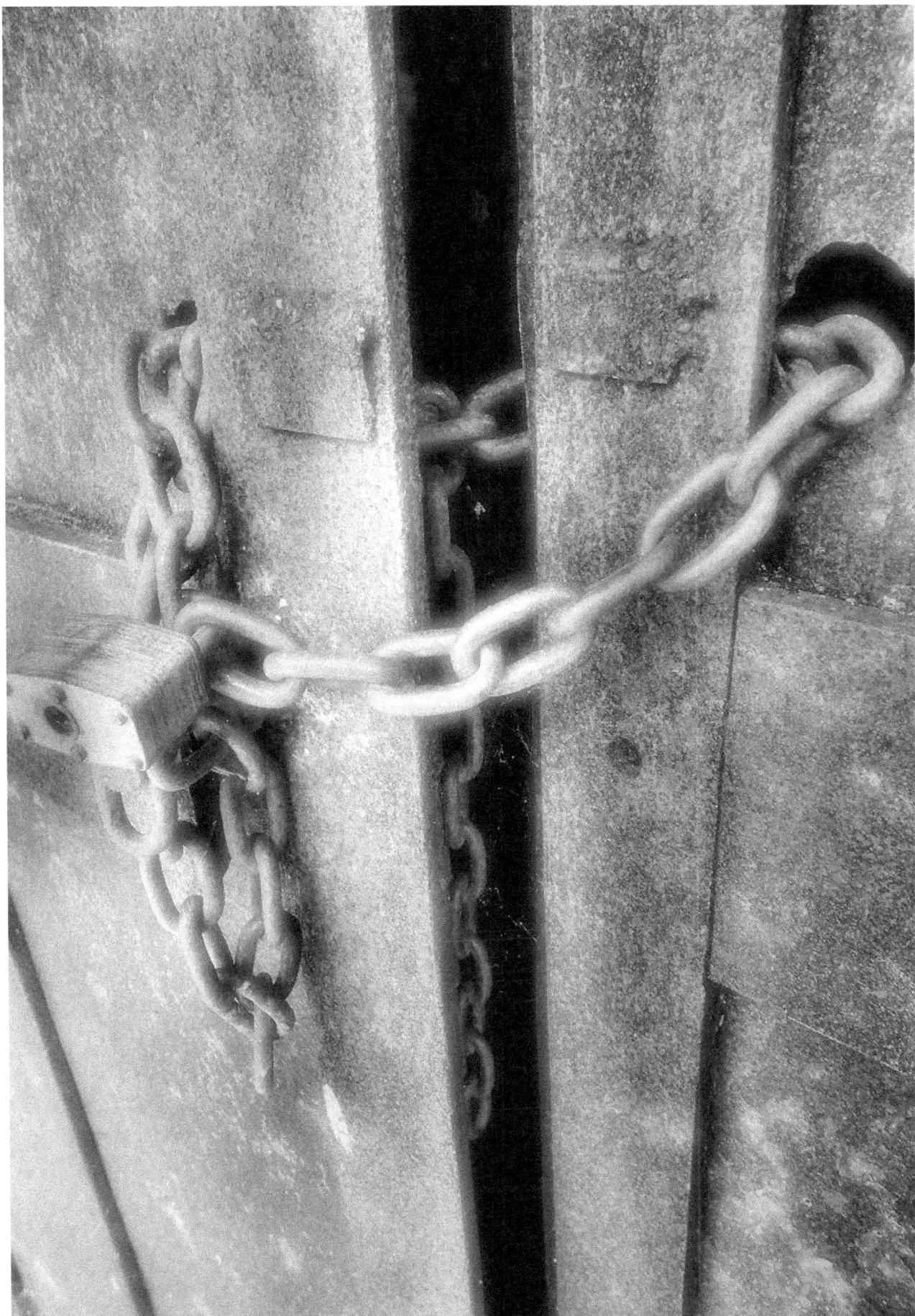

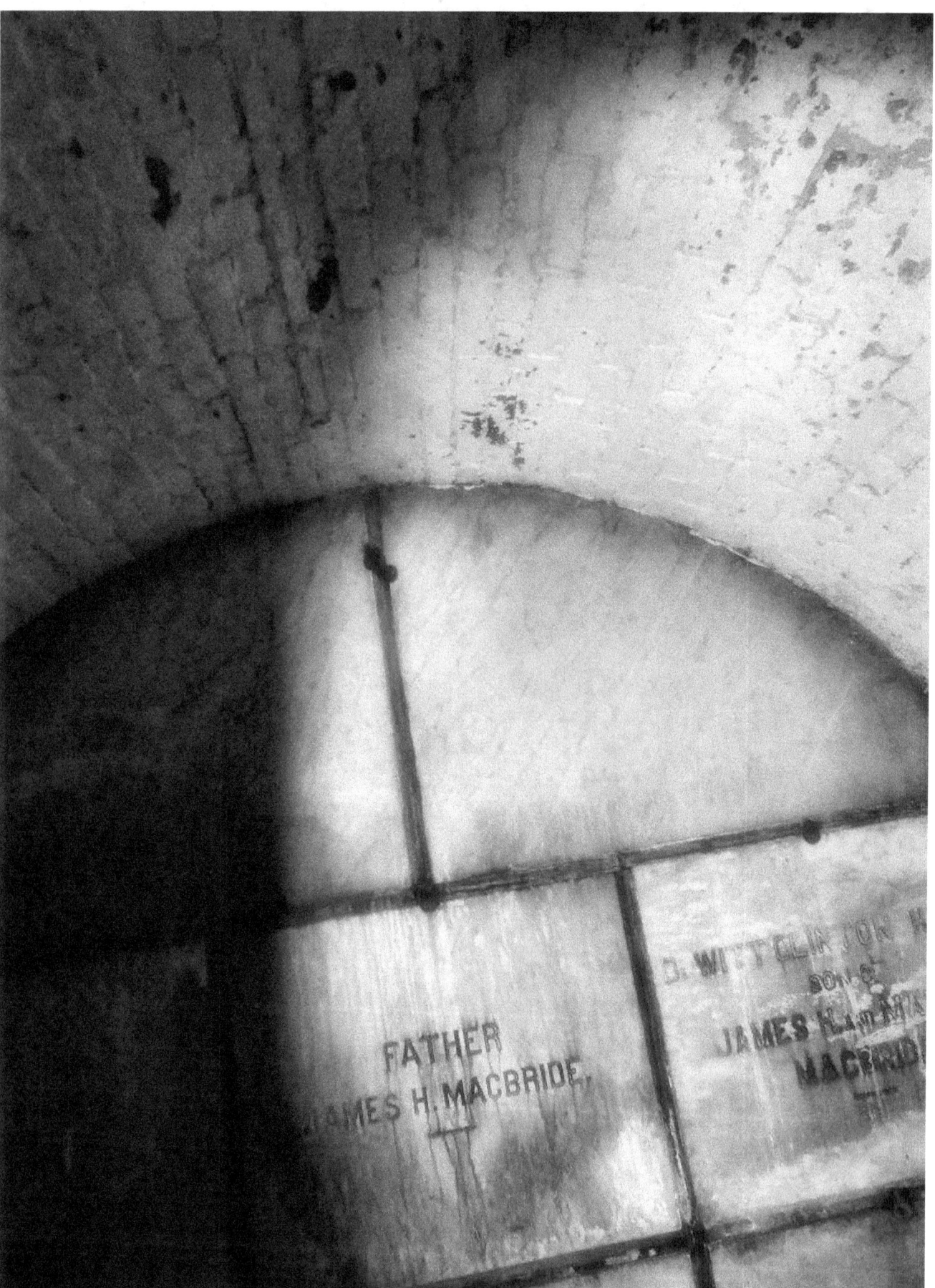

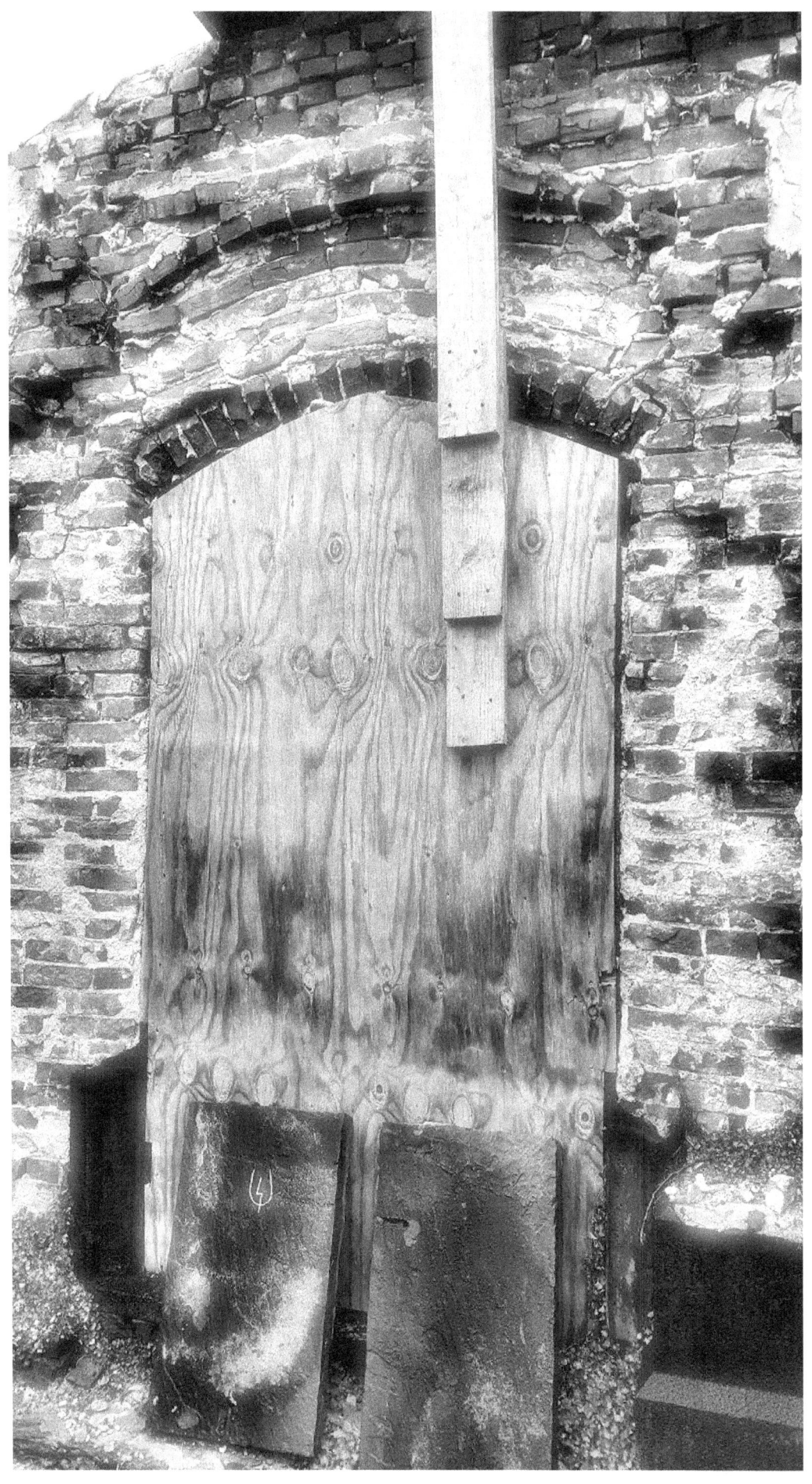

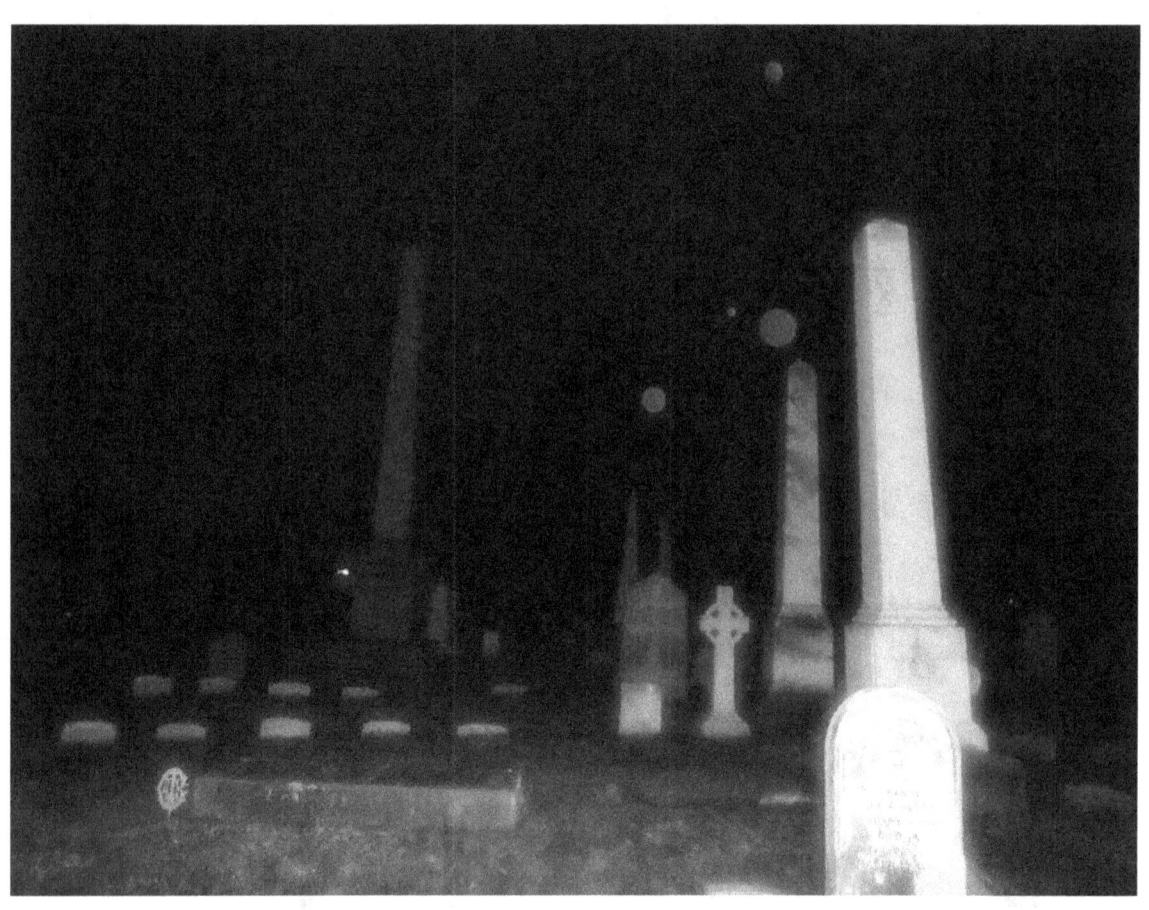

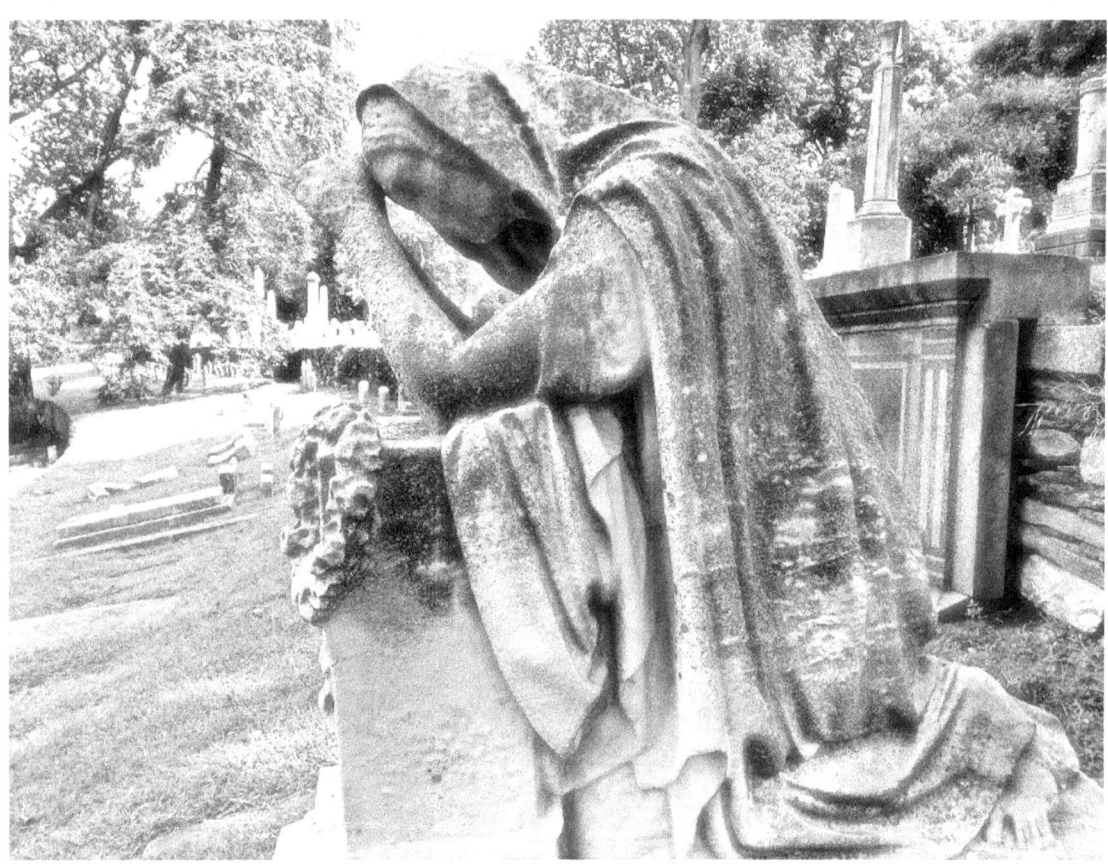

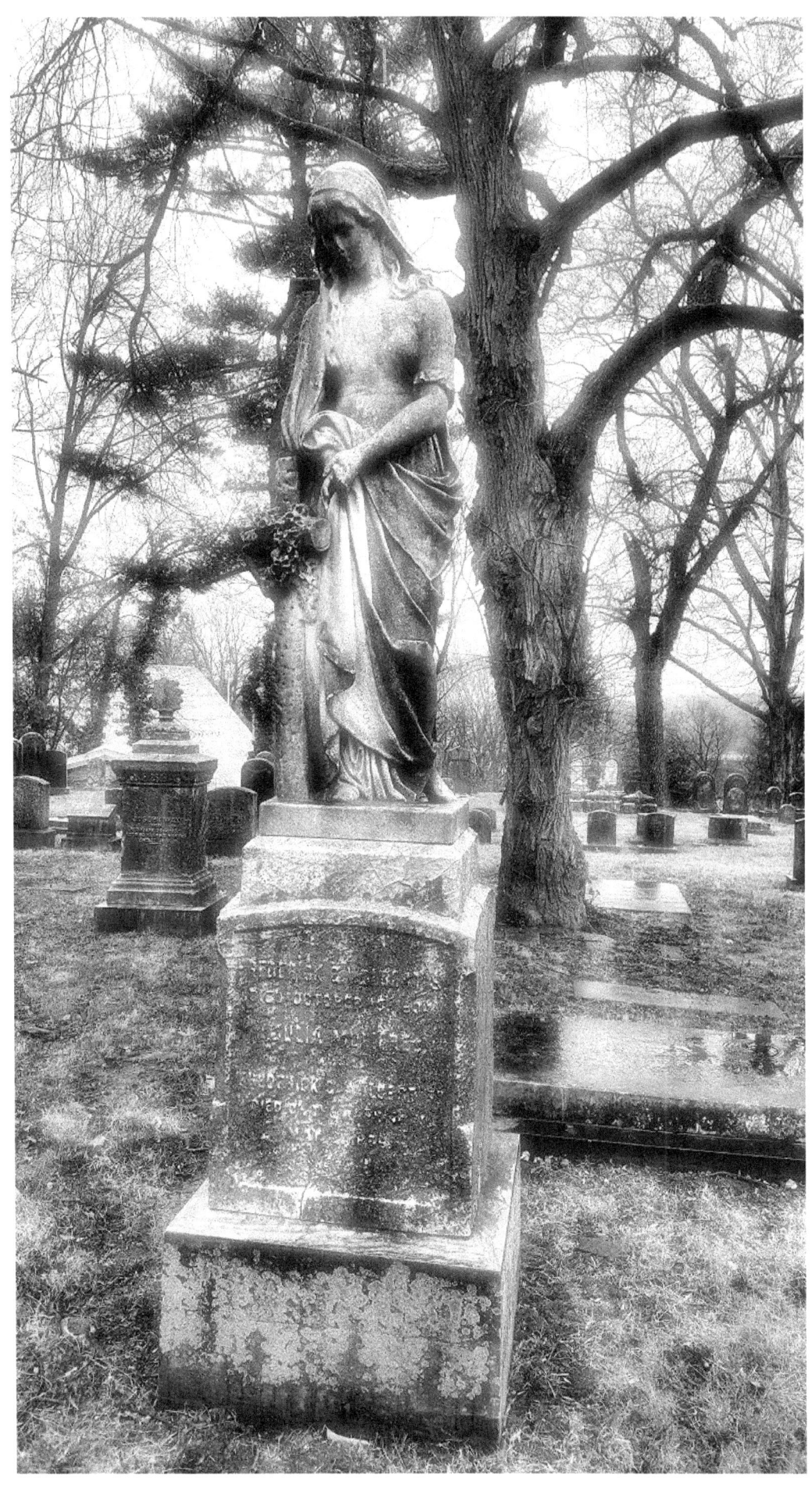

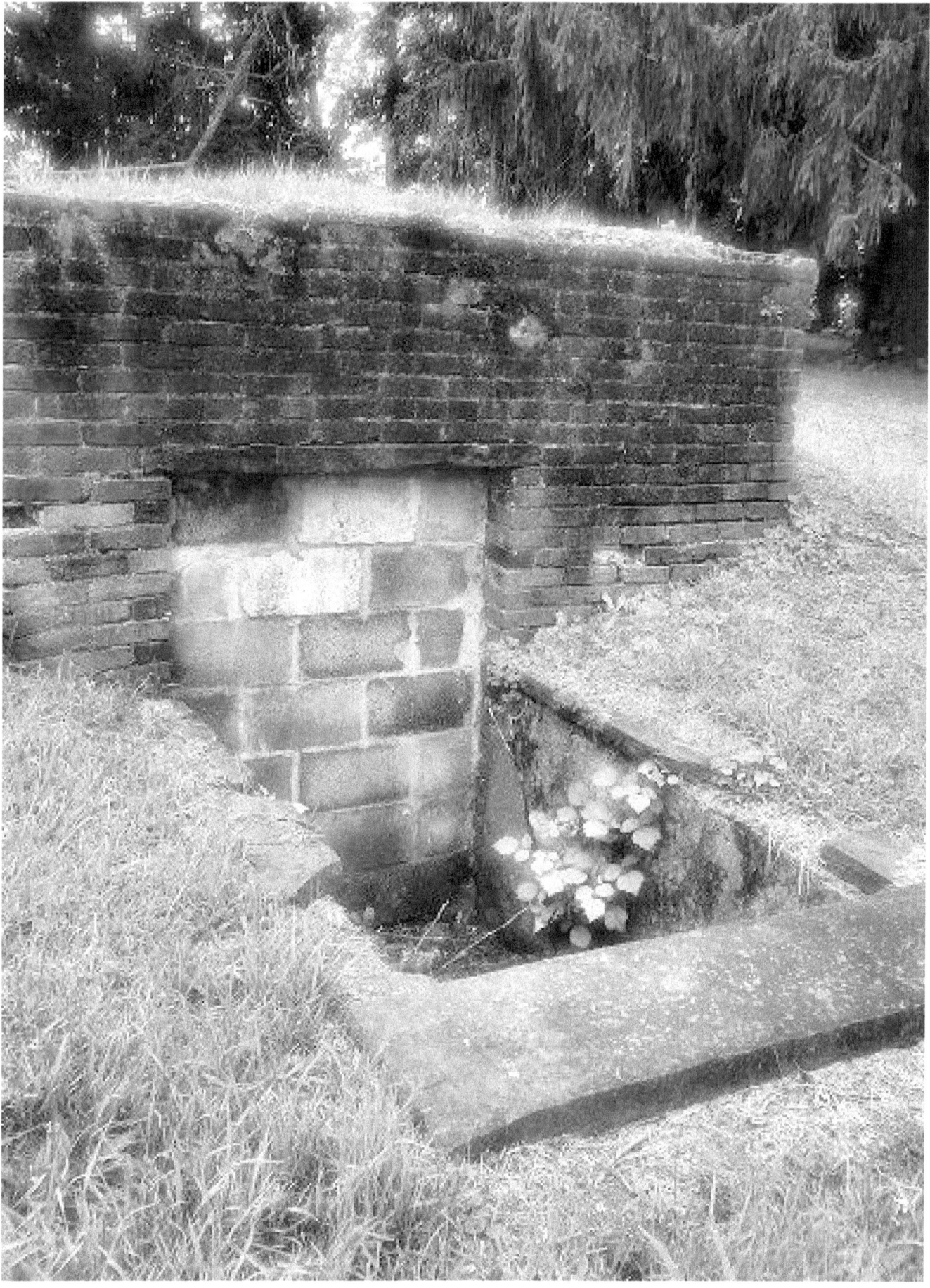

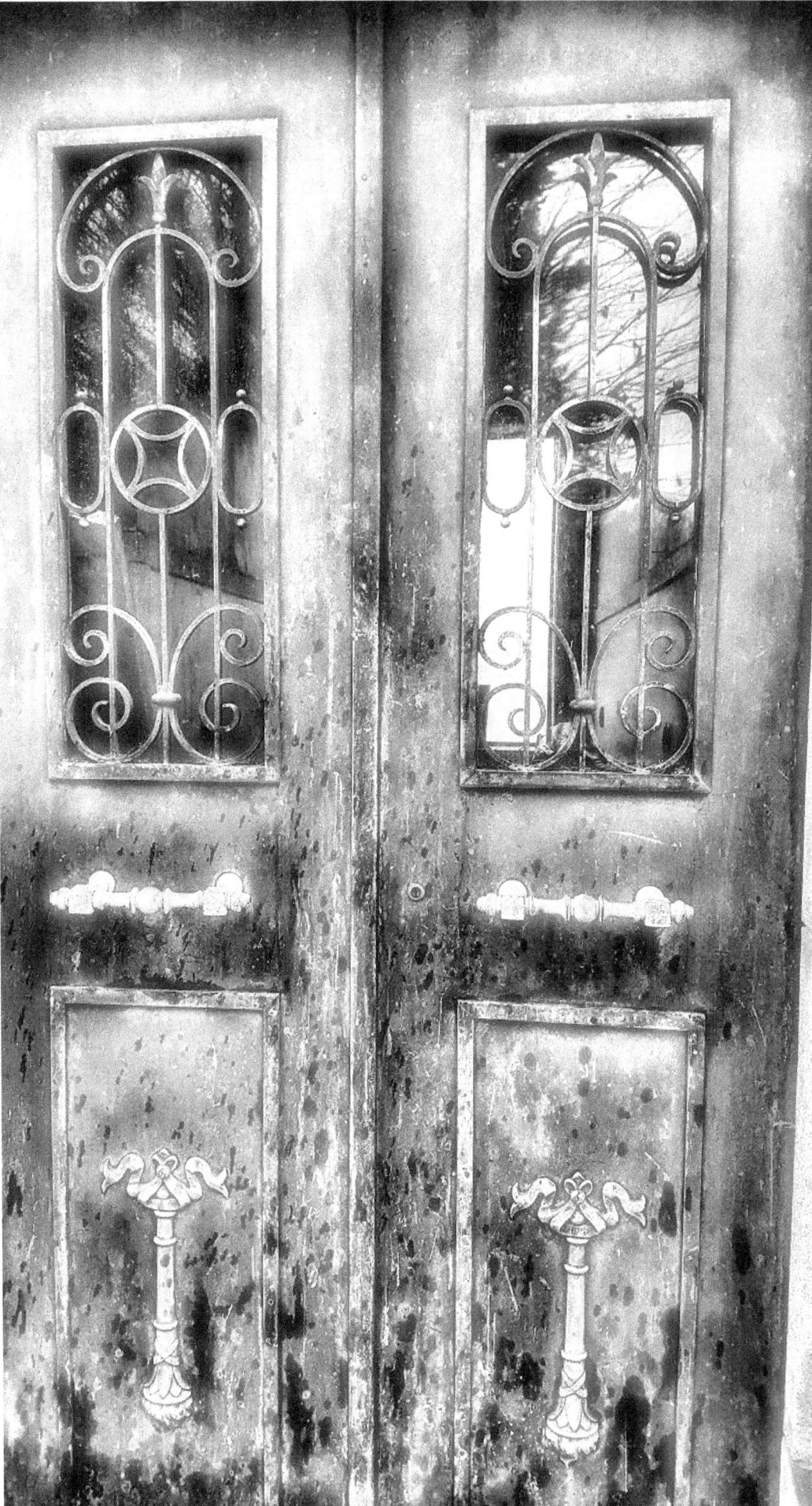

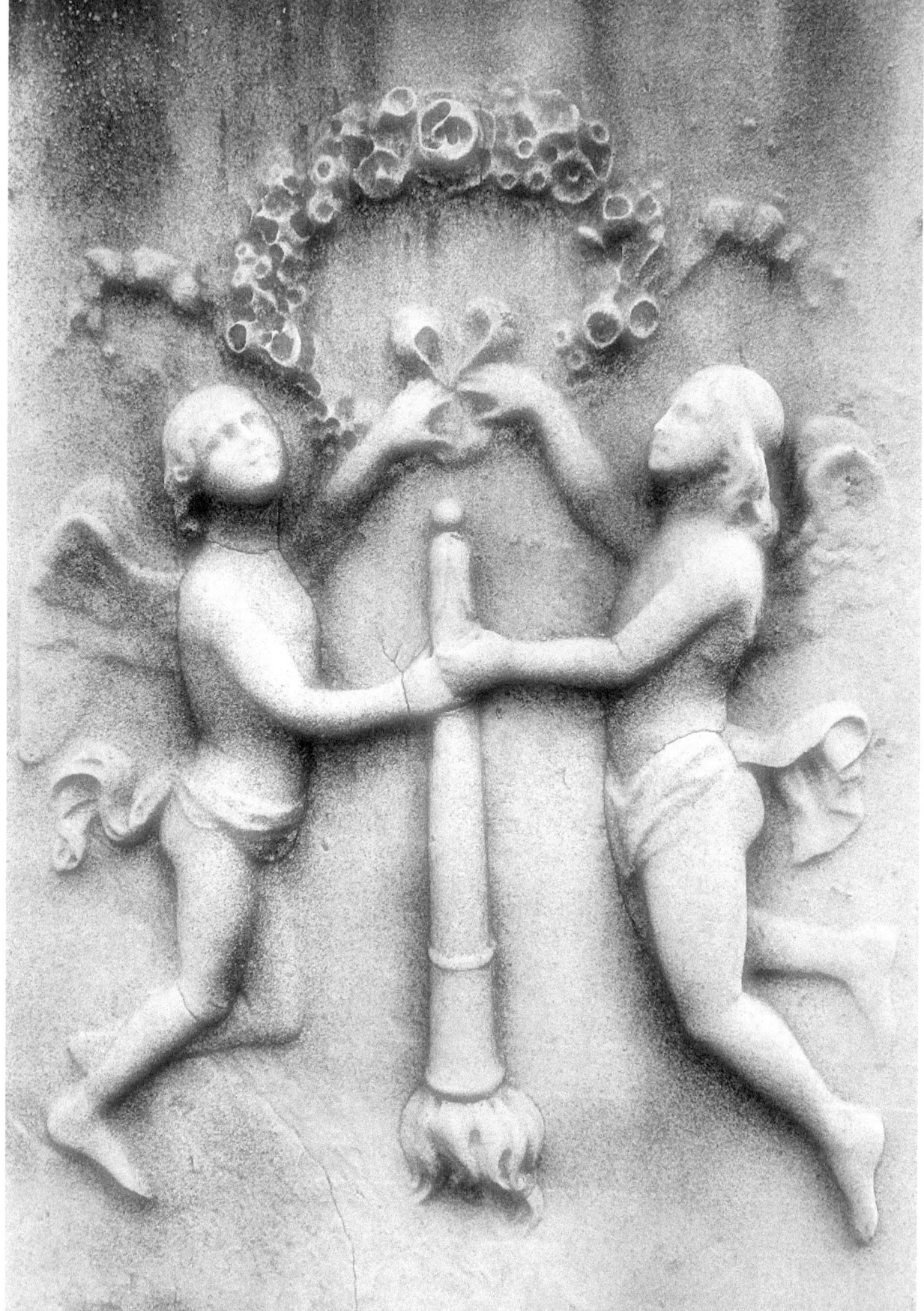

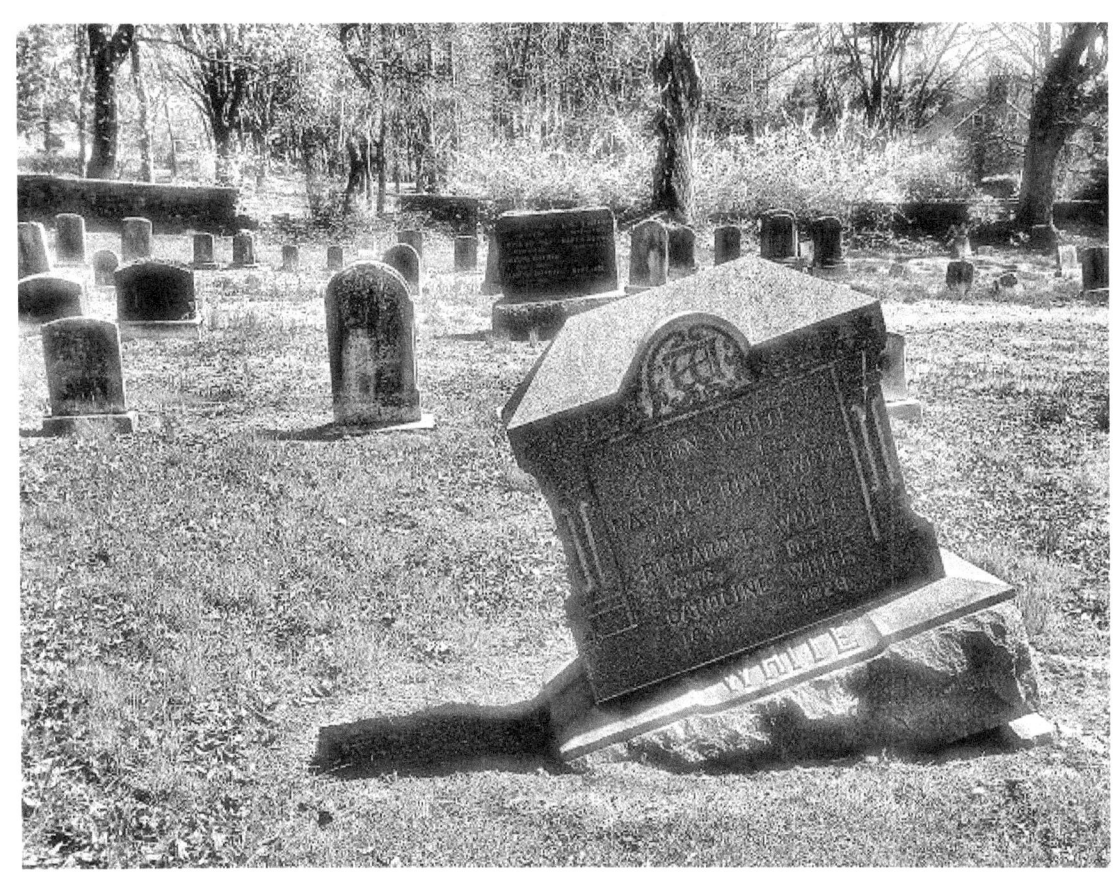

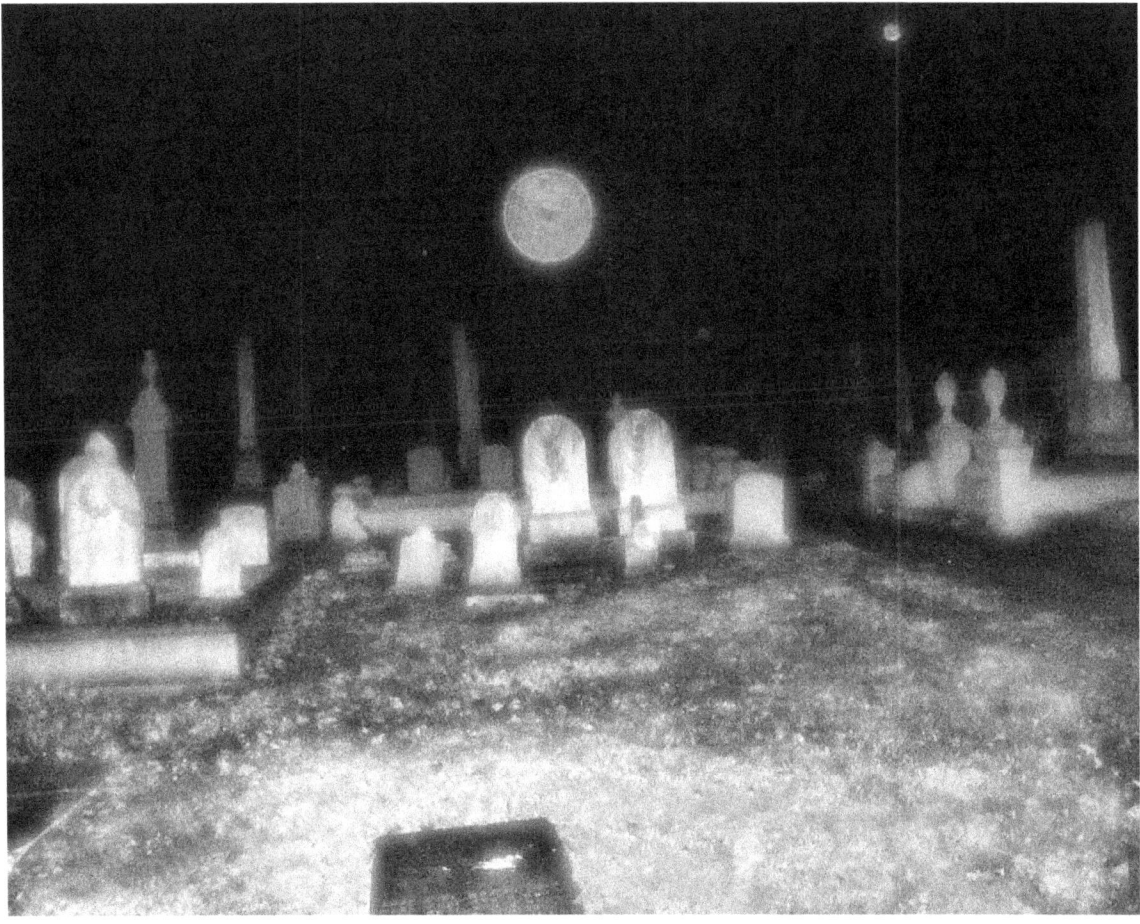

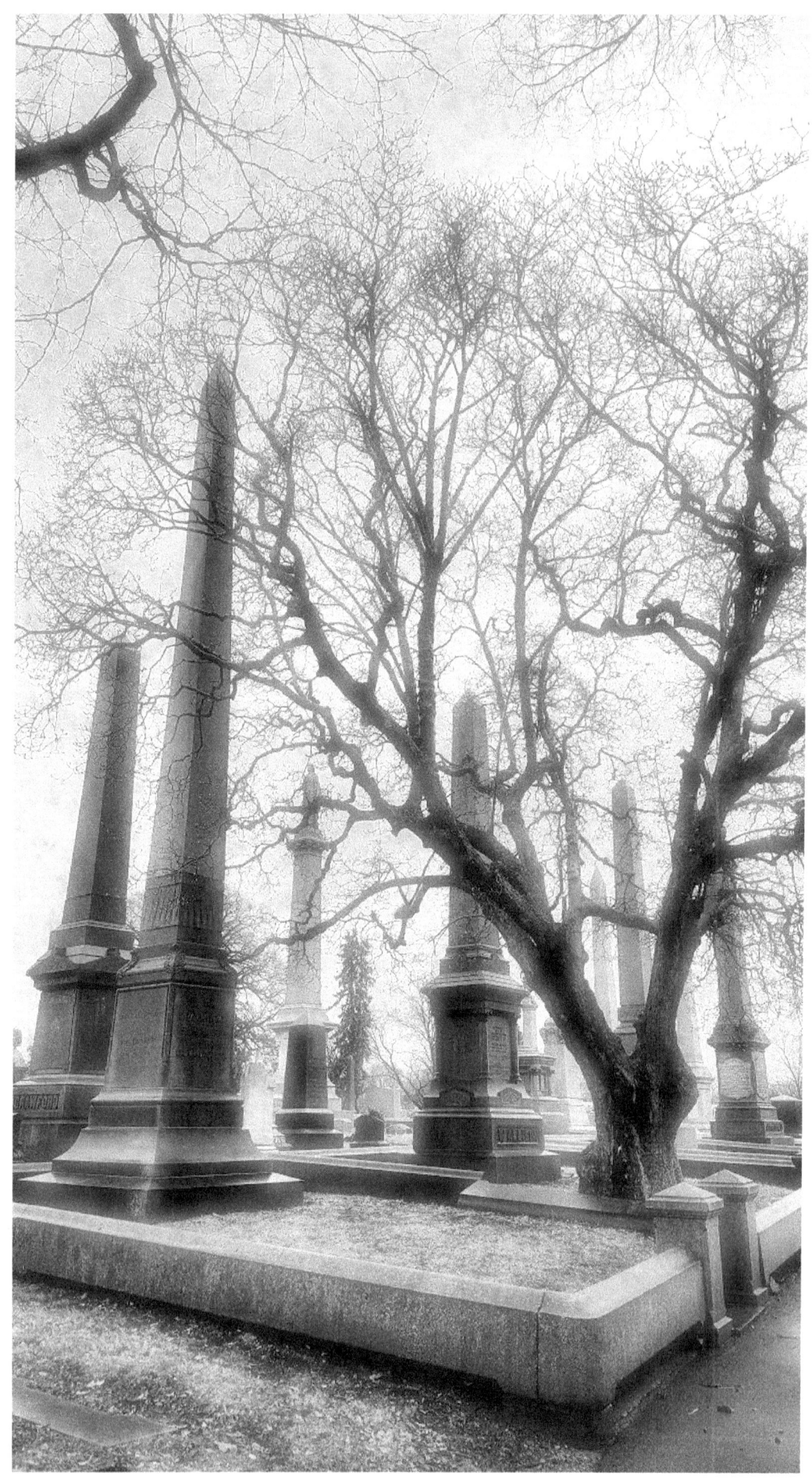

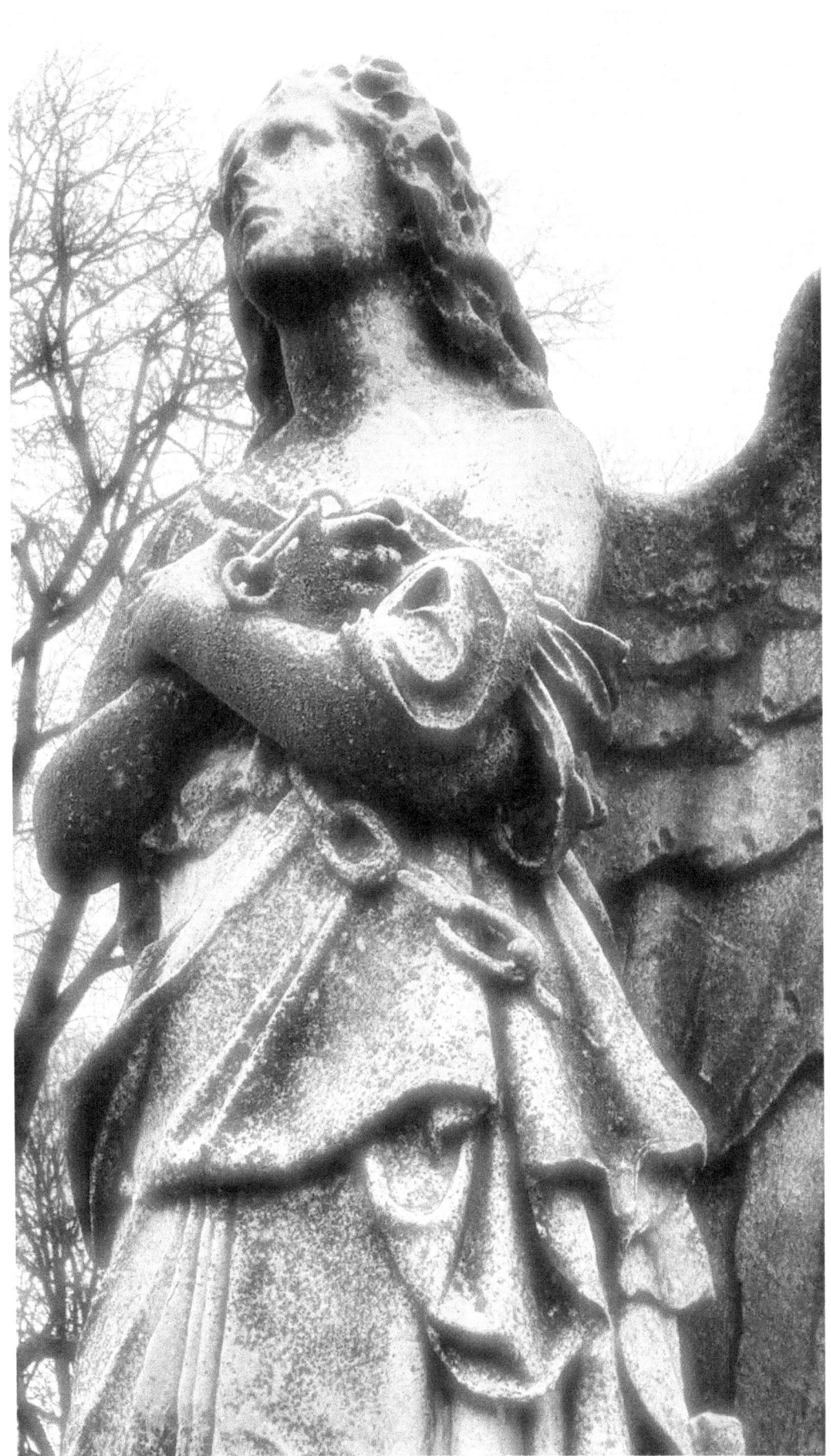

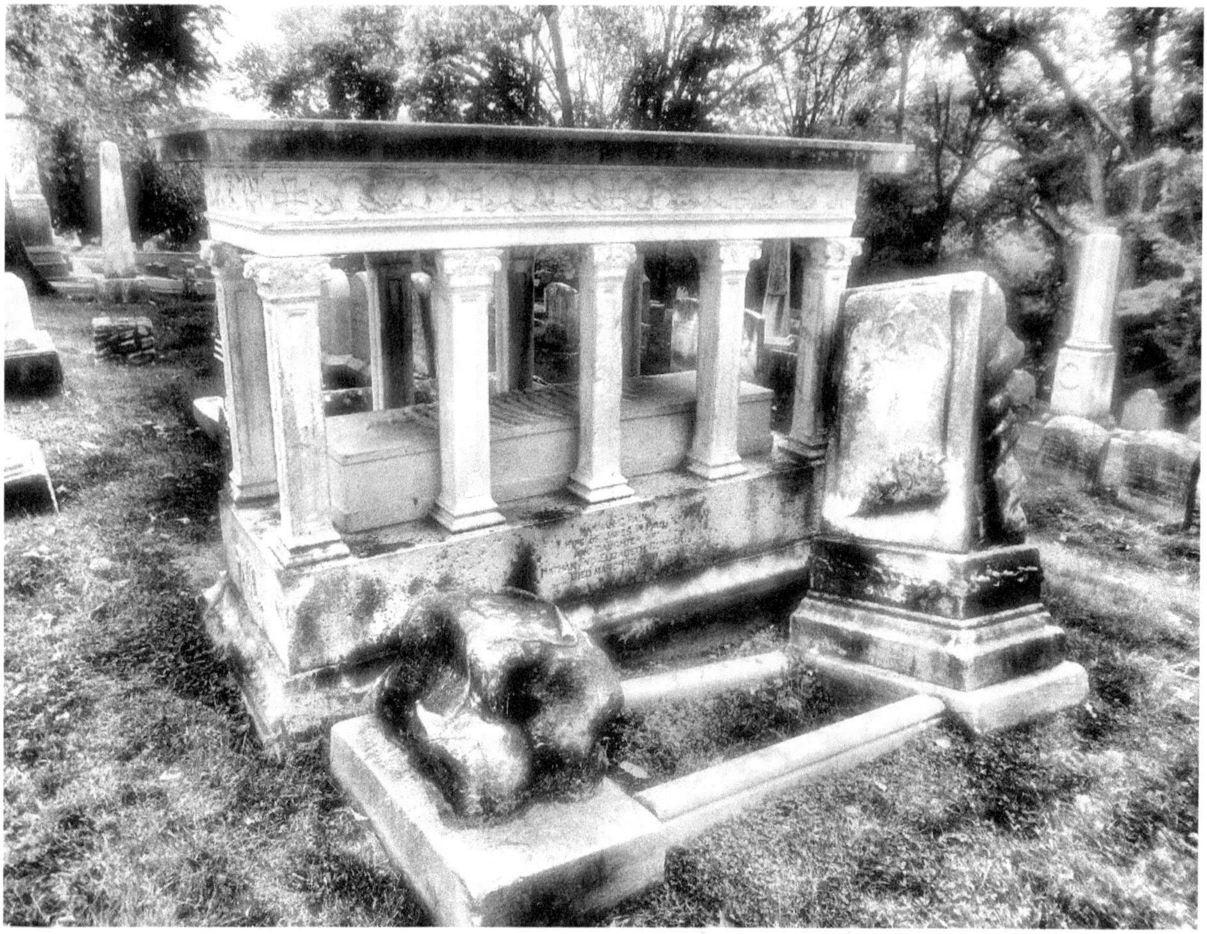

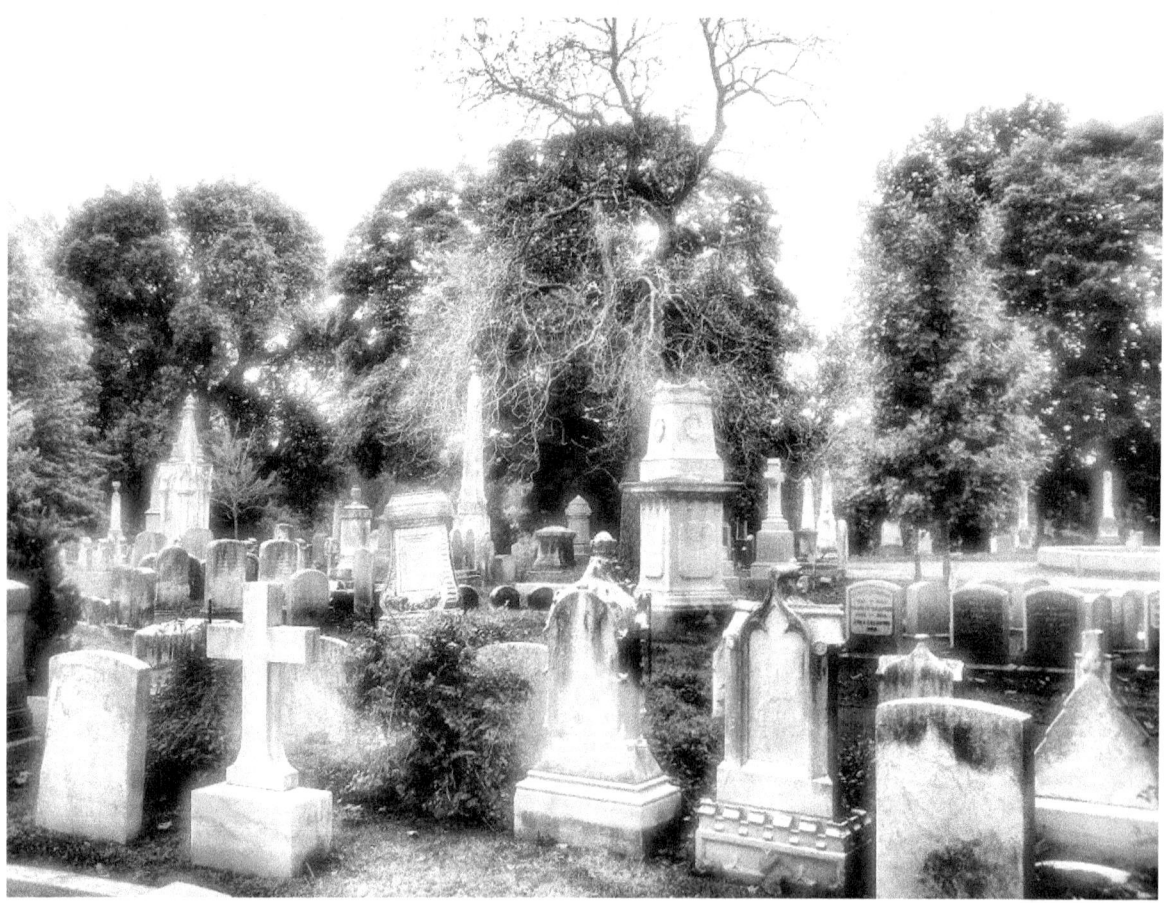

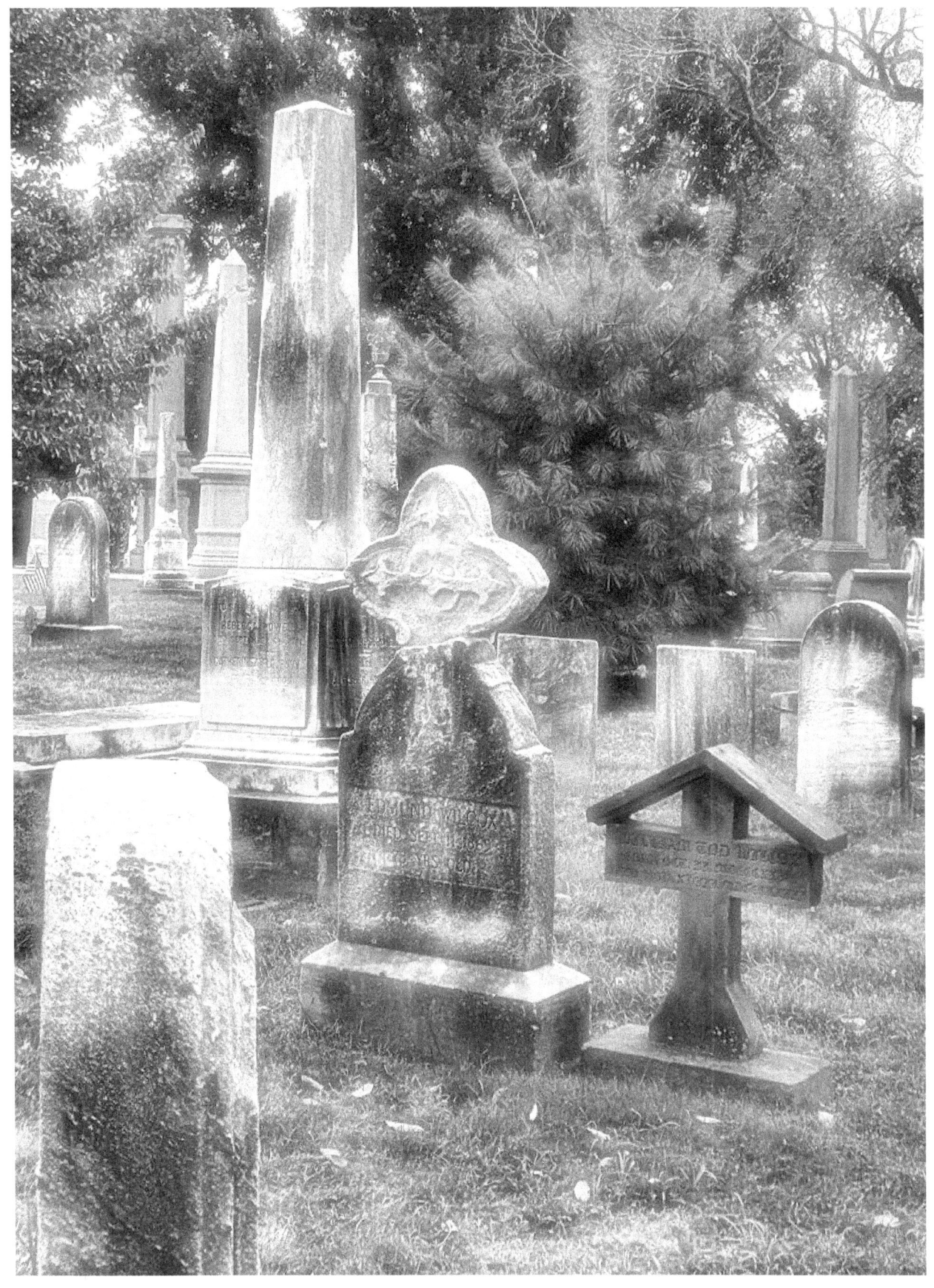

"Every man has his secret sorrows which the world knows not, and often times we call a man cold when he is only sad. " ---Henry Wadsworth Longfellow

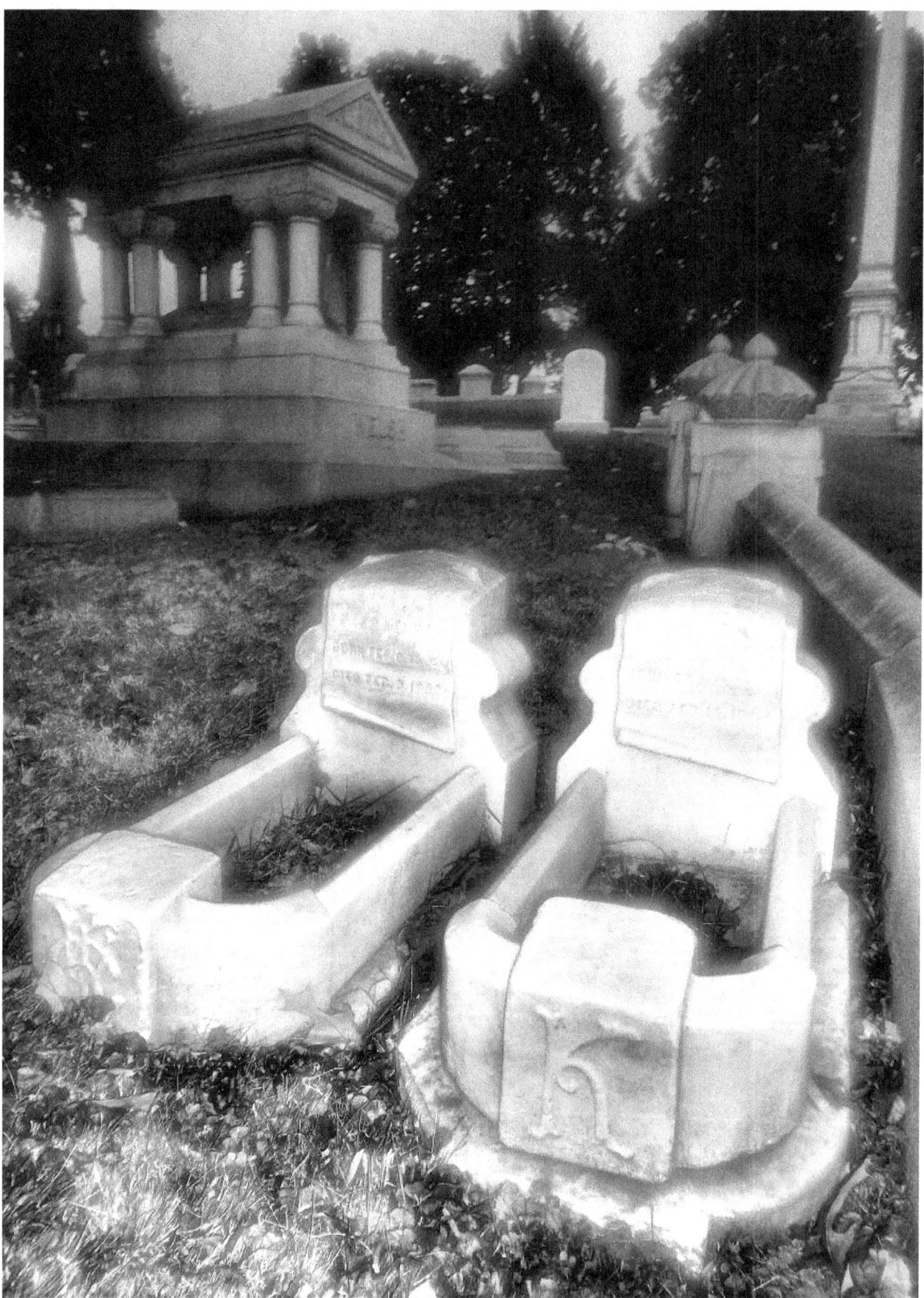

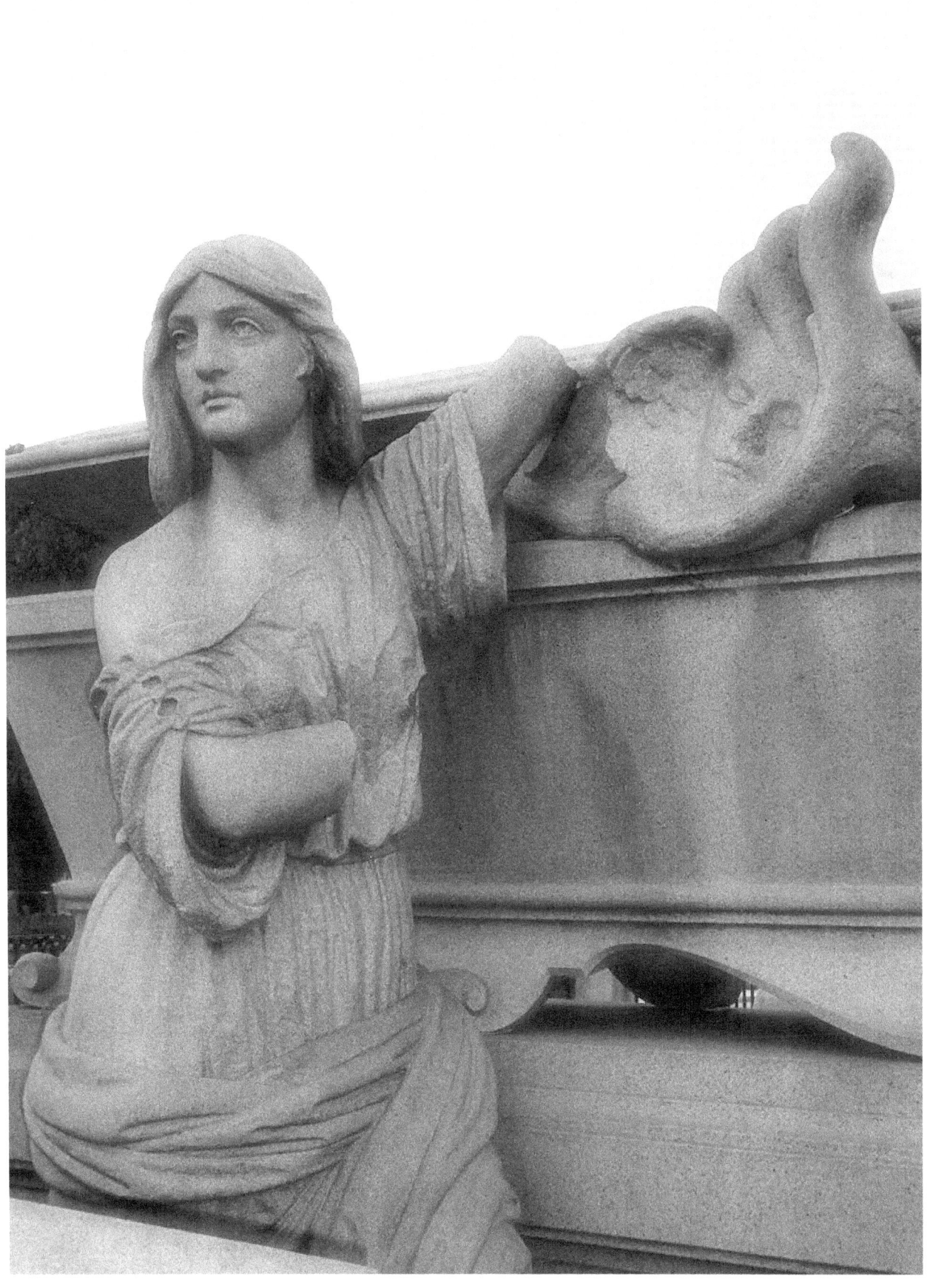

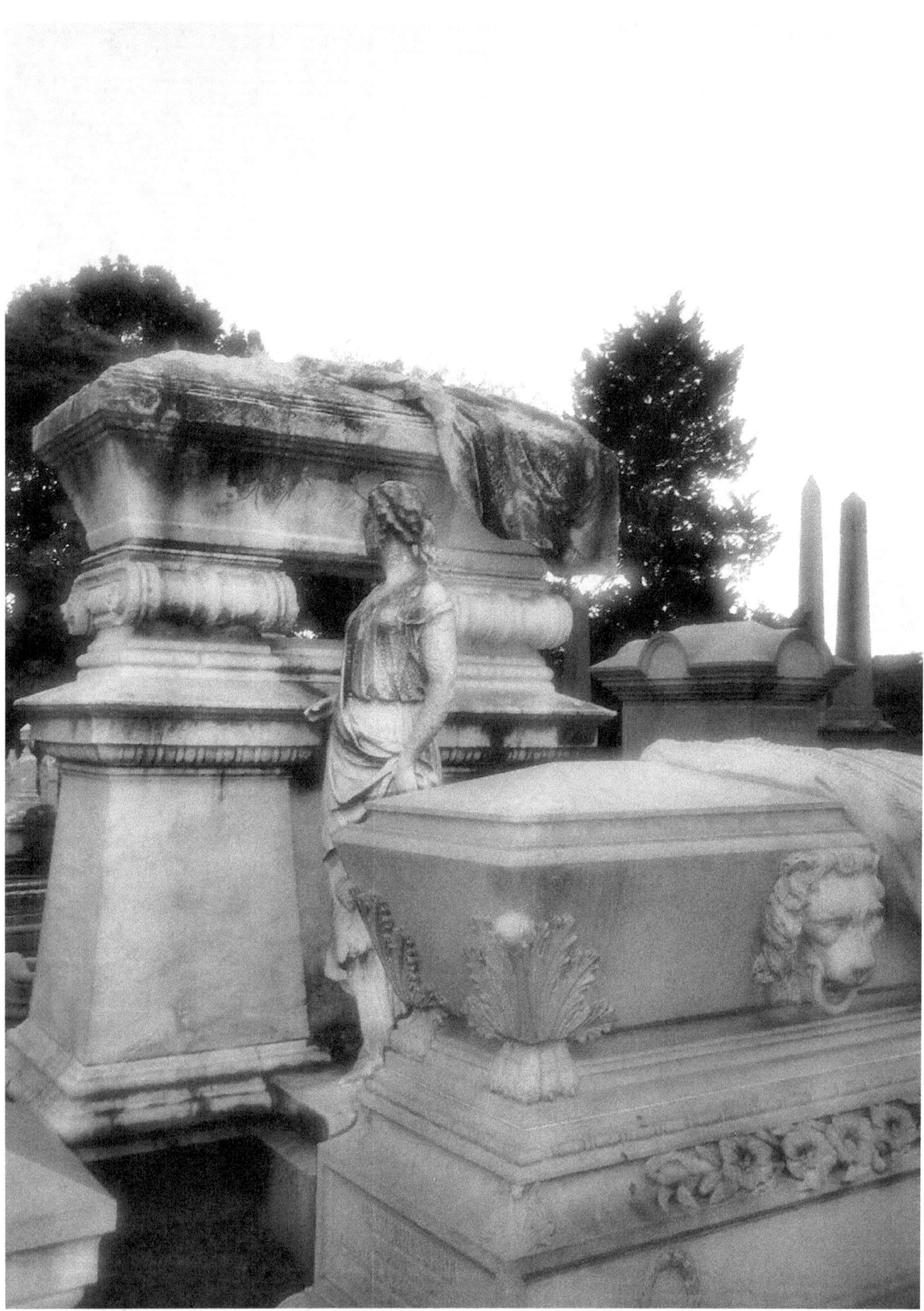

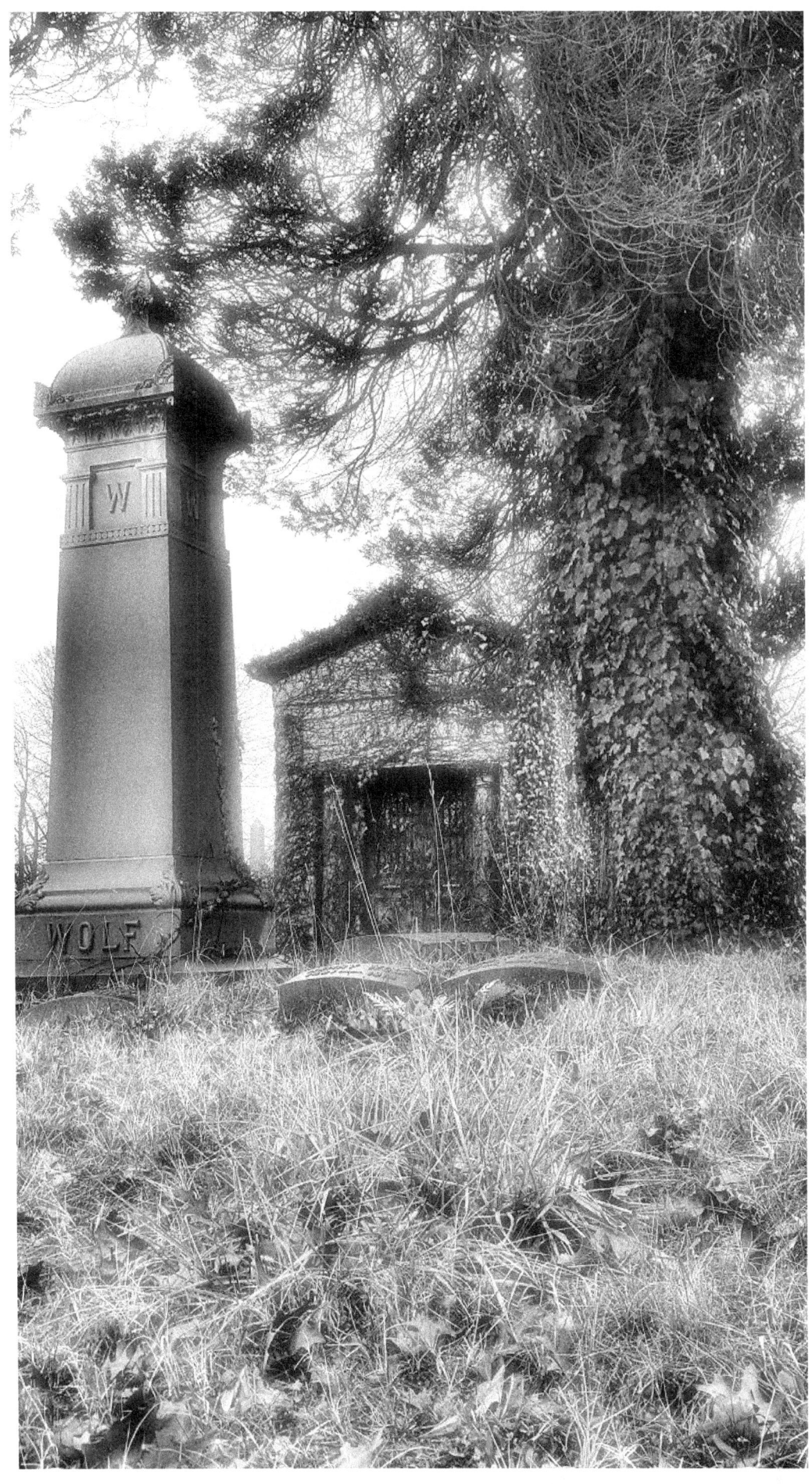

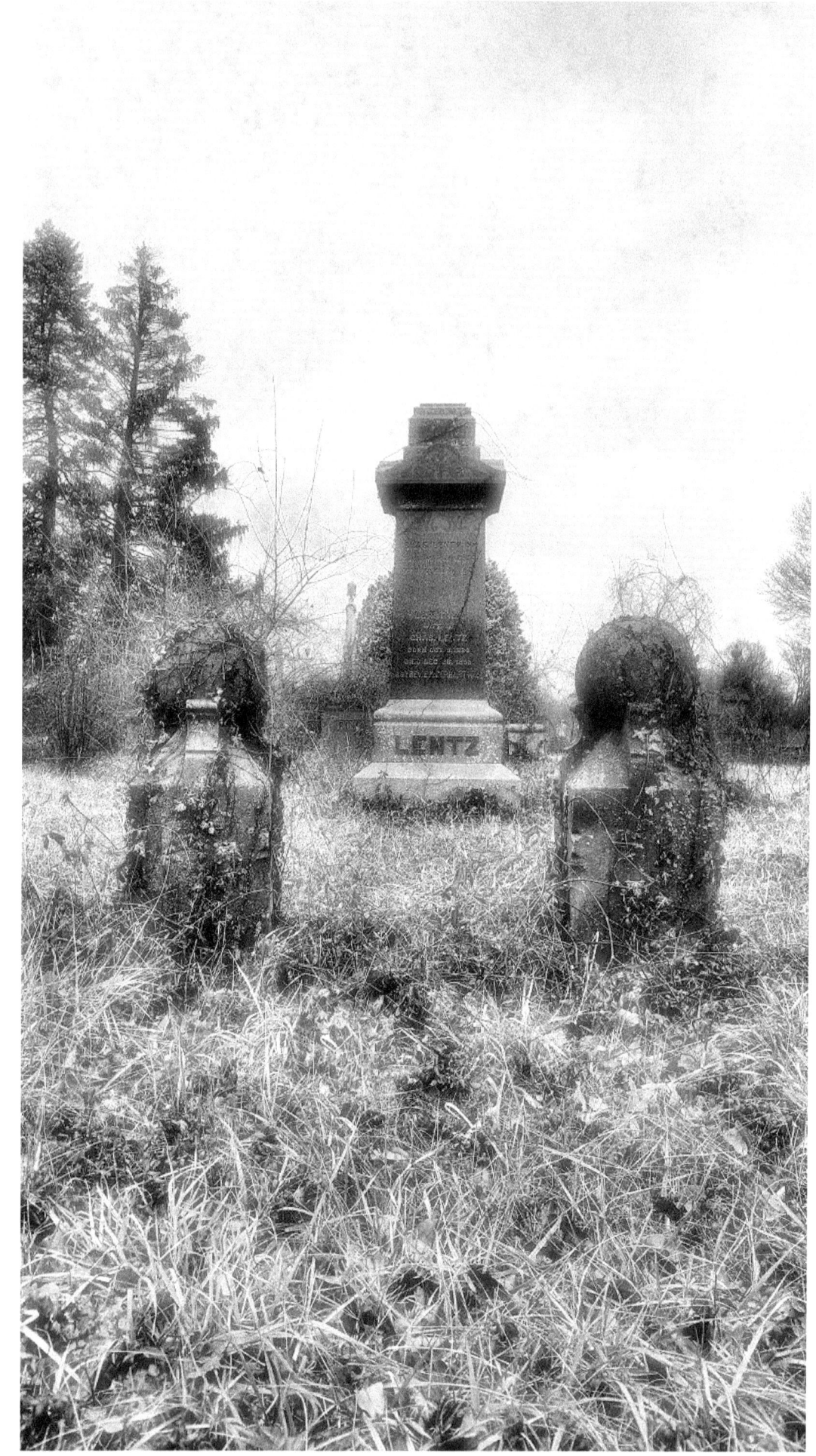

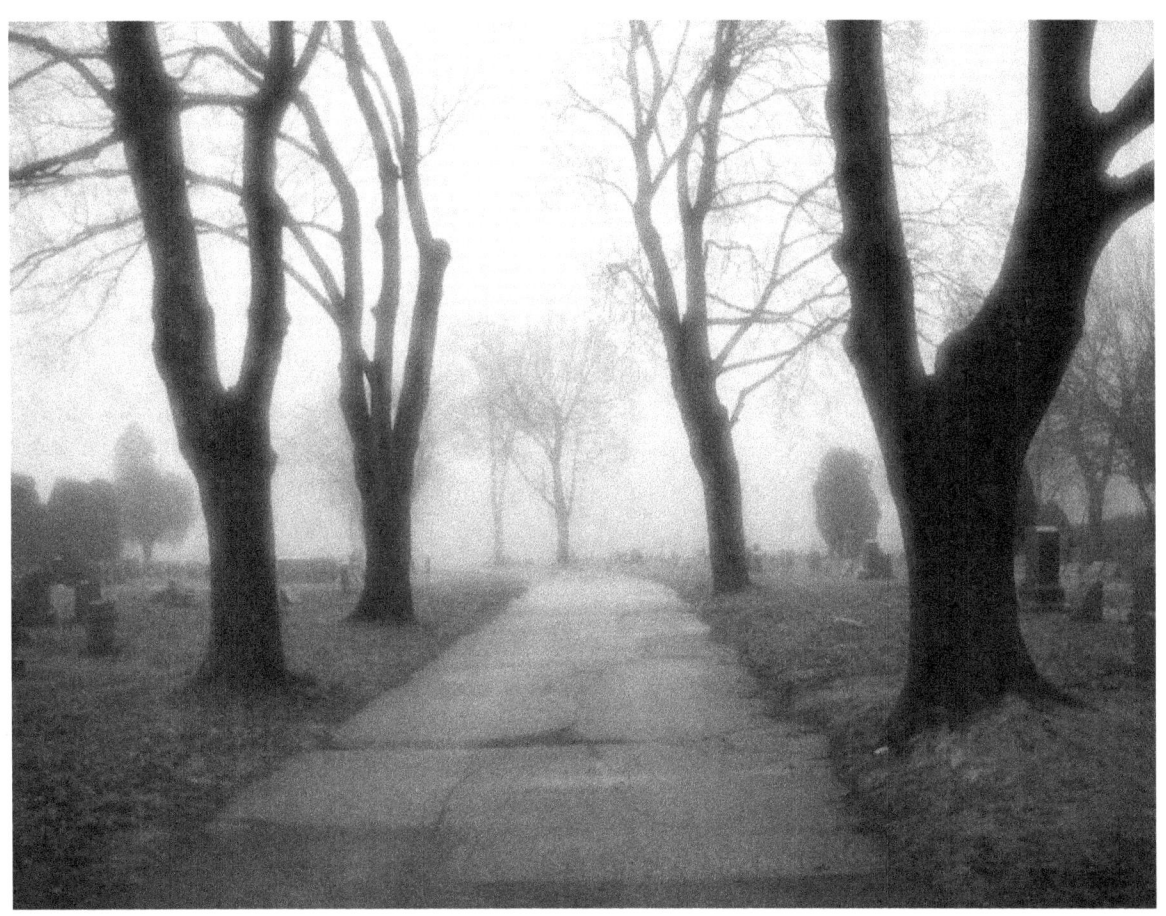

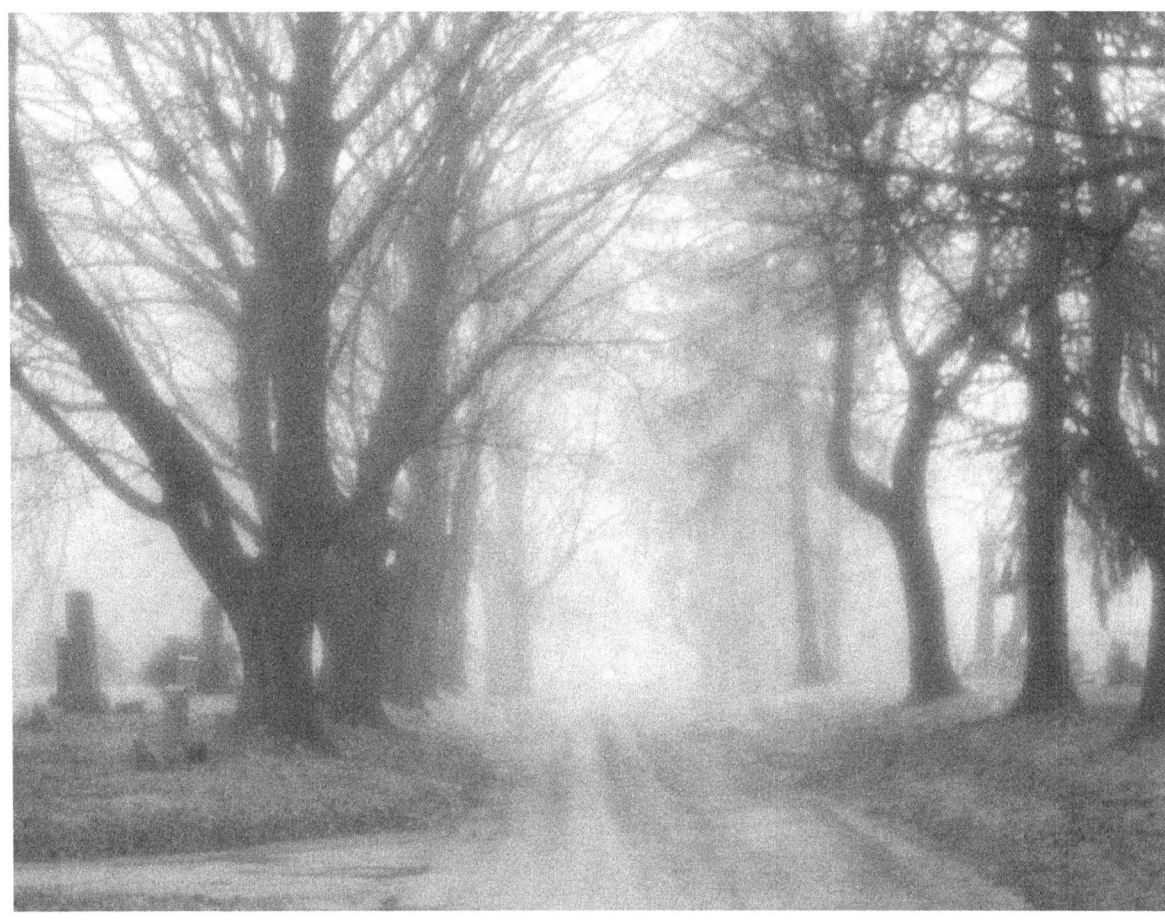

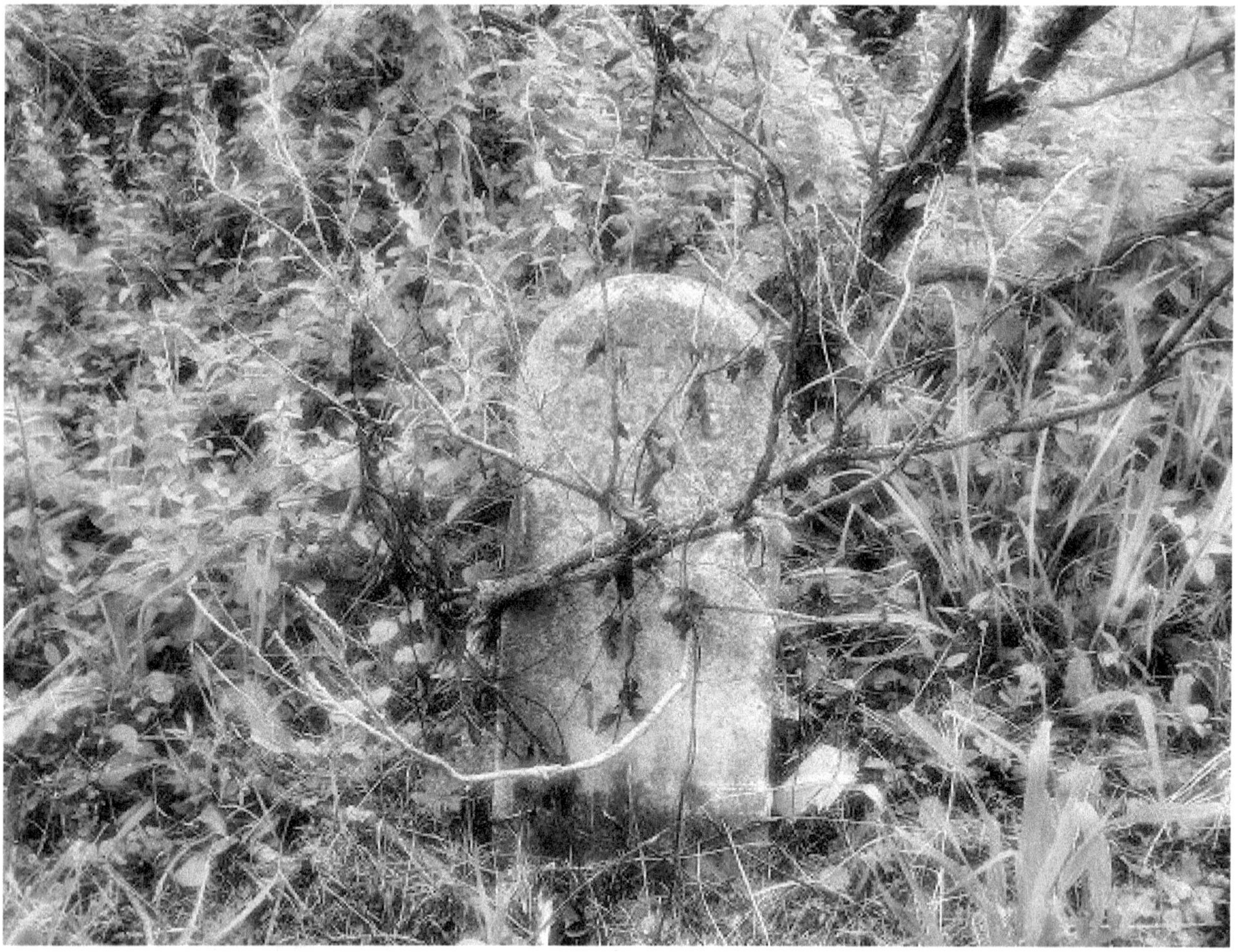

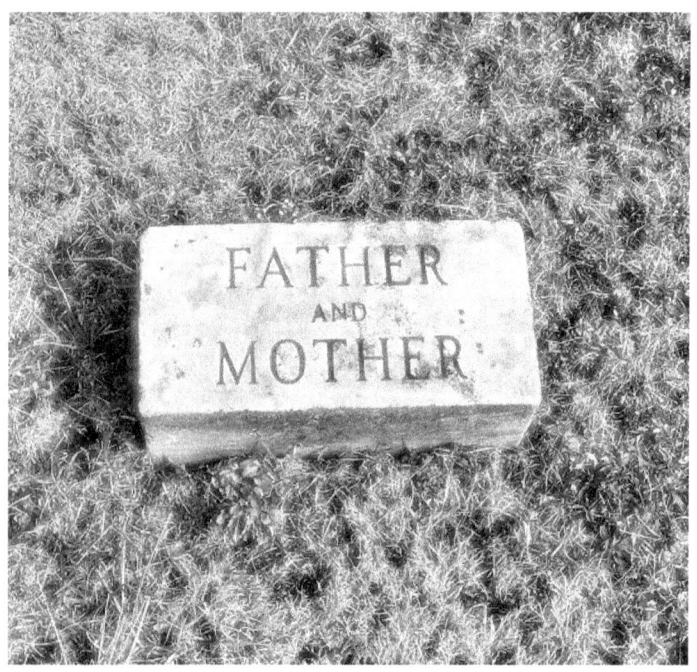

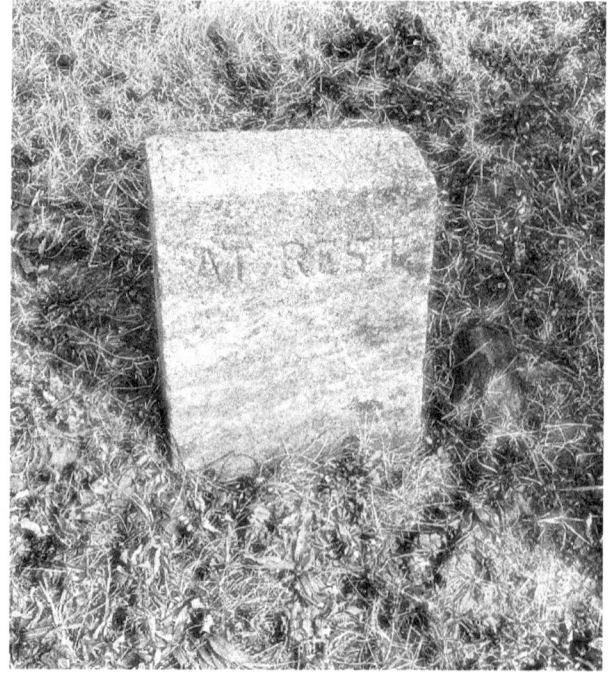

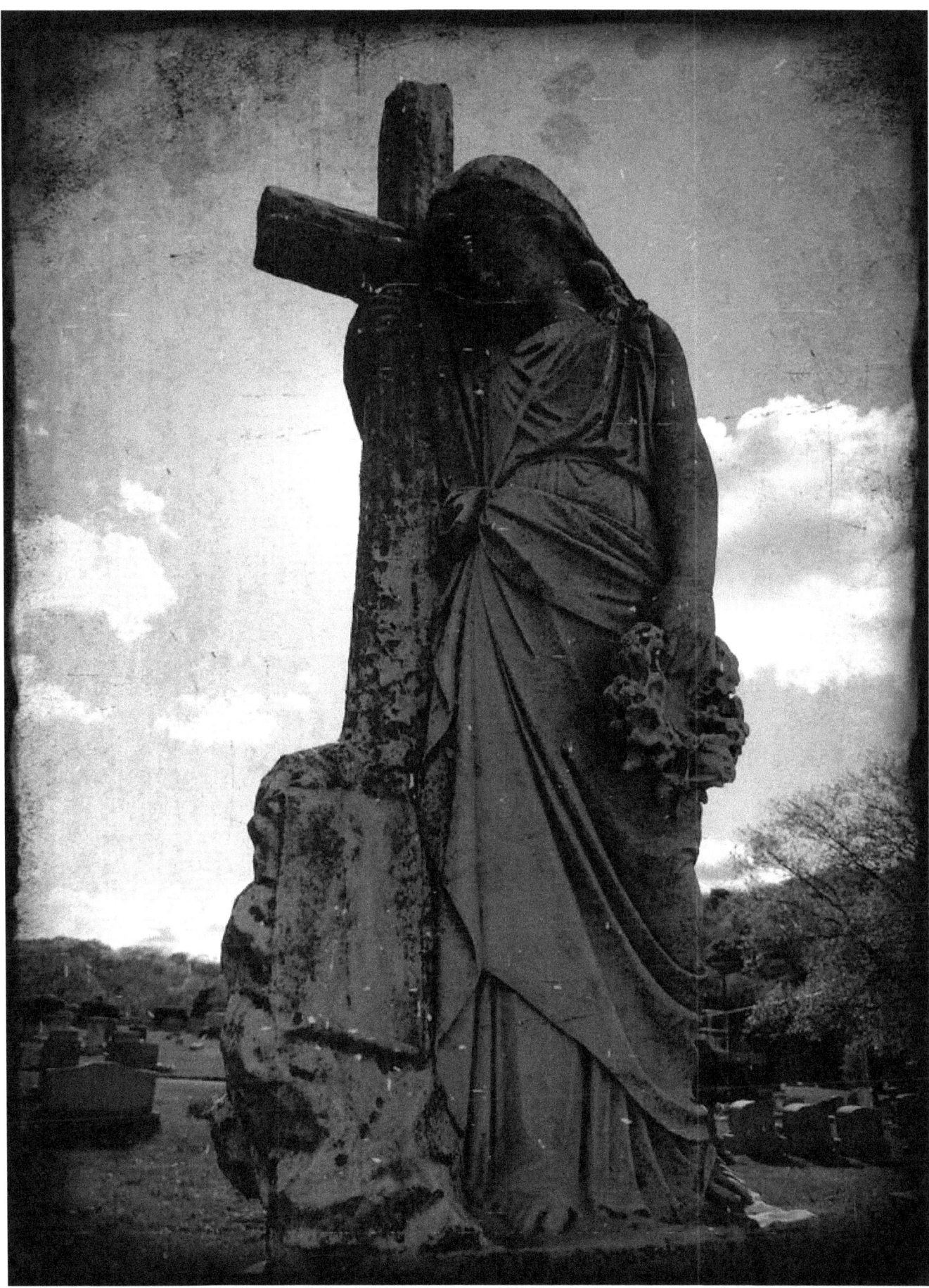

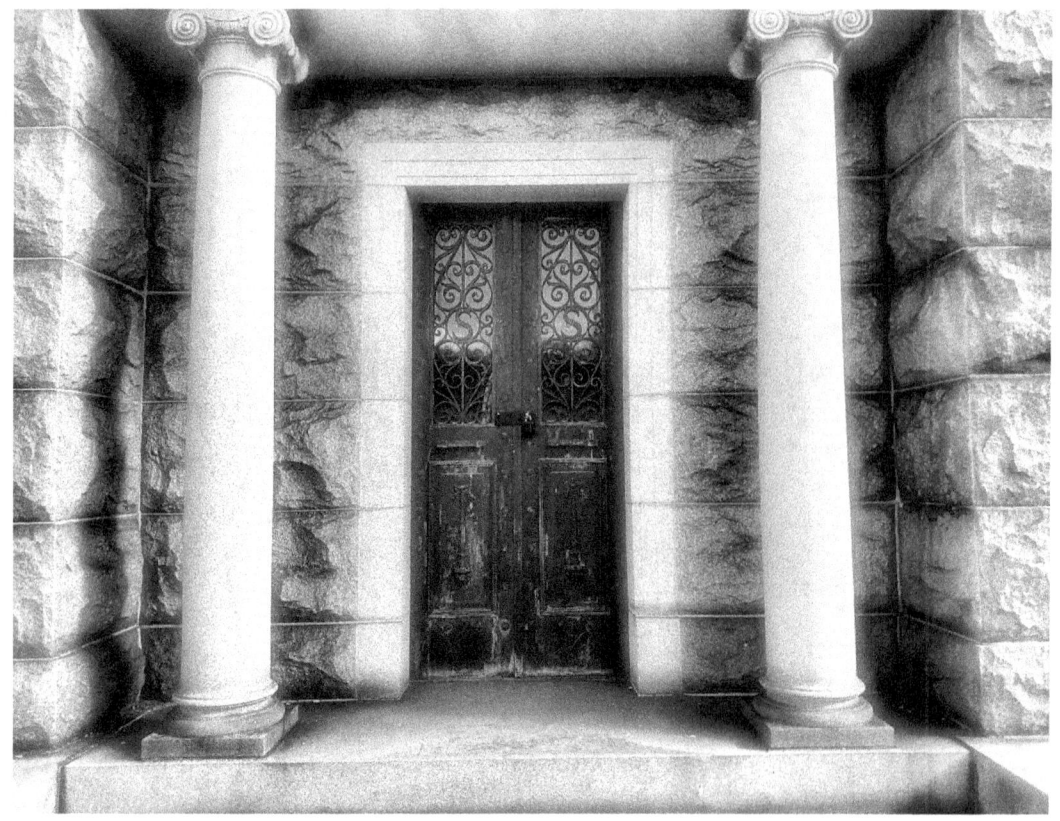

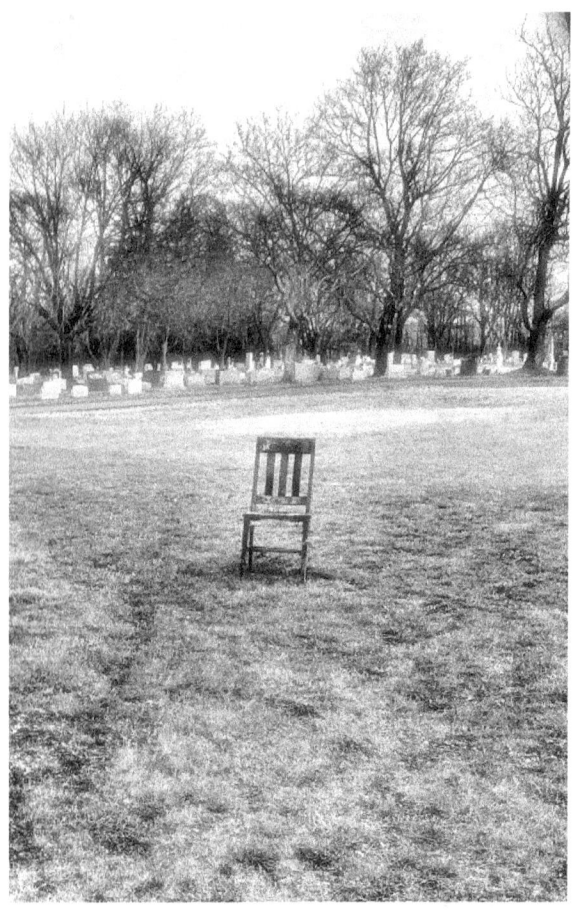

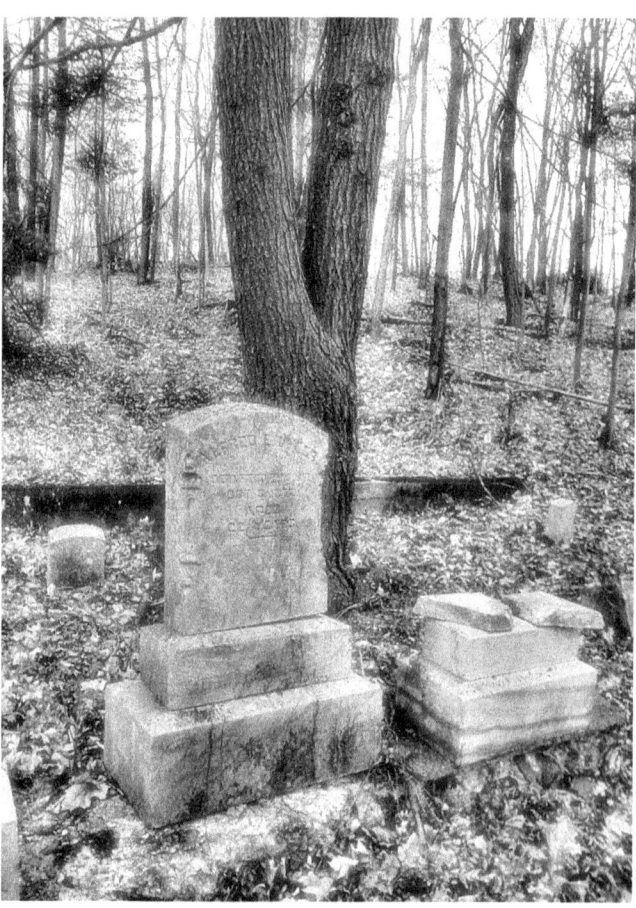

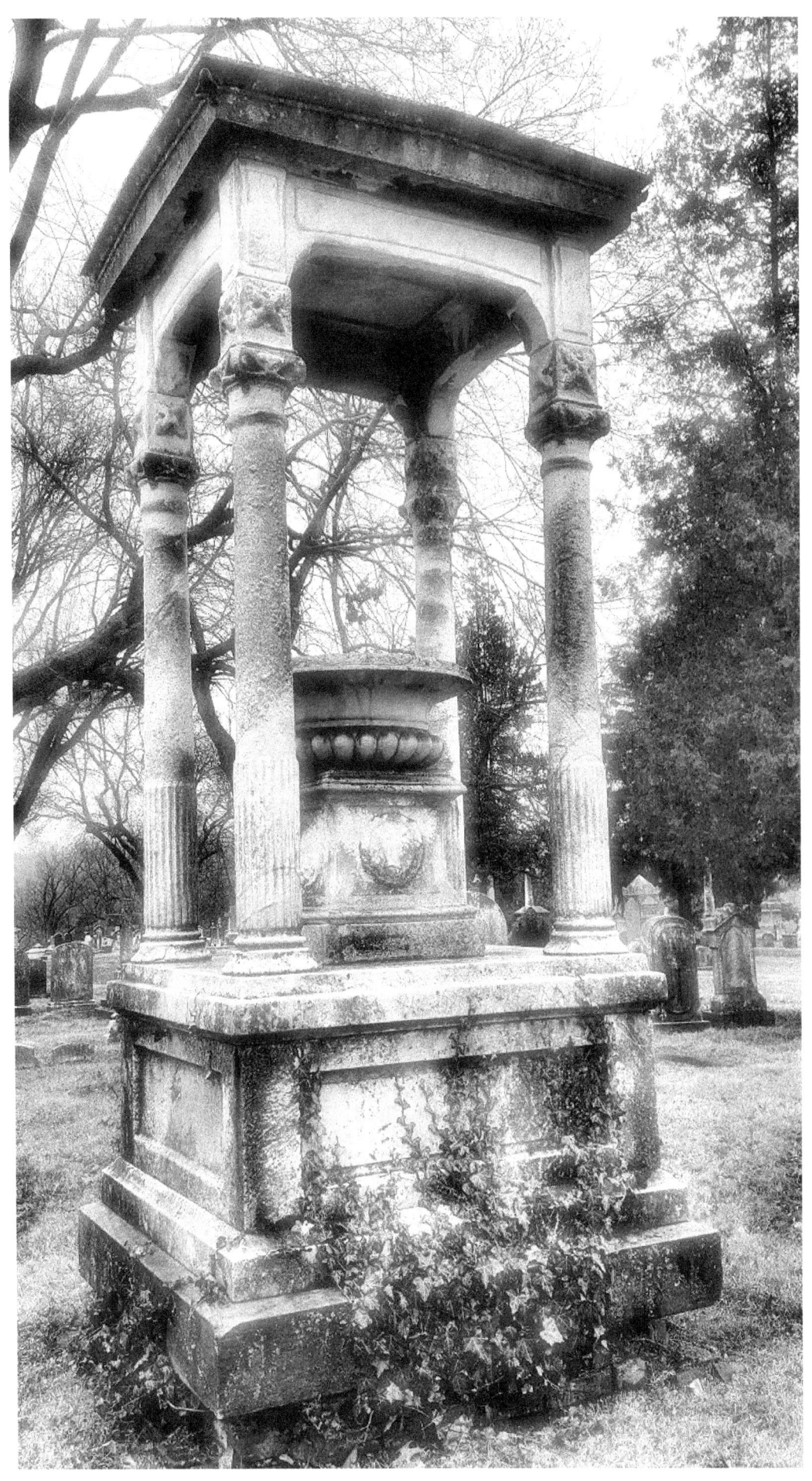

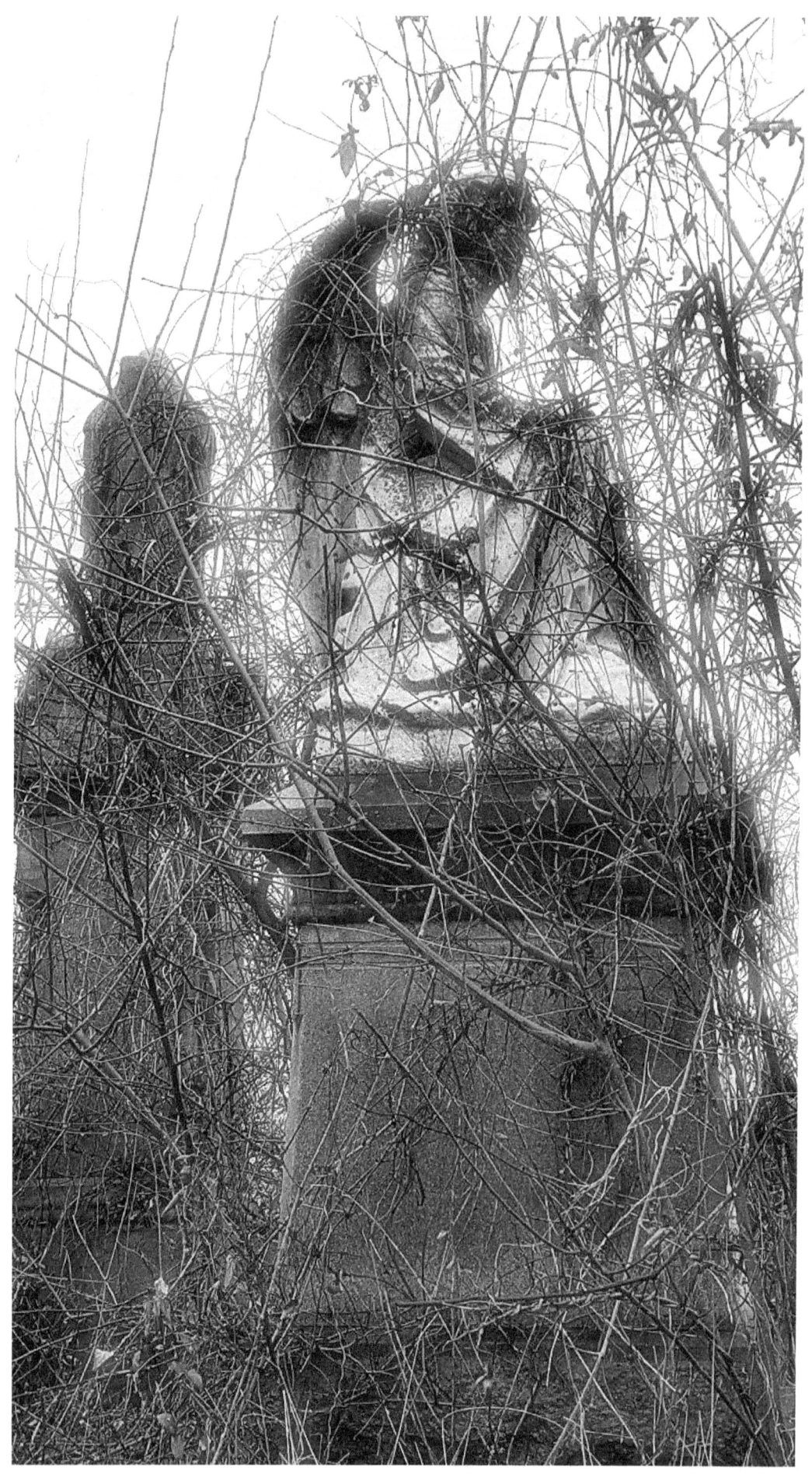

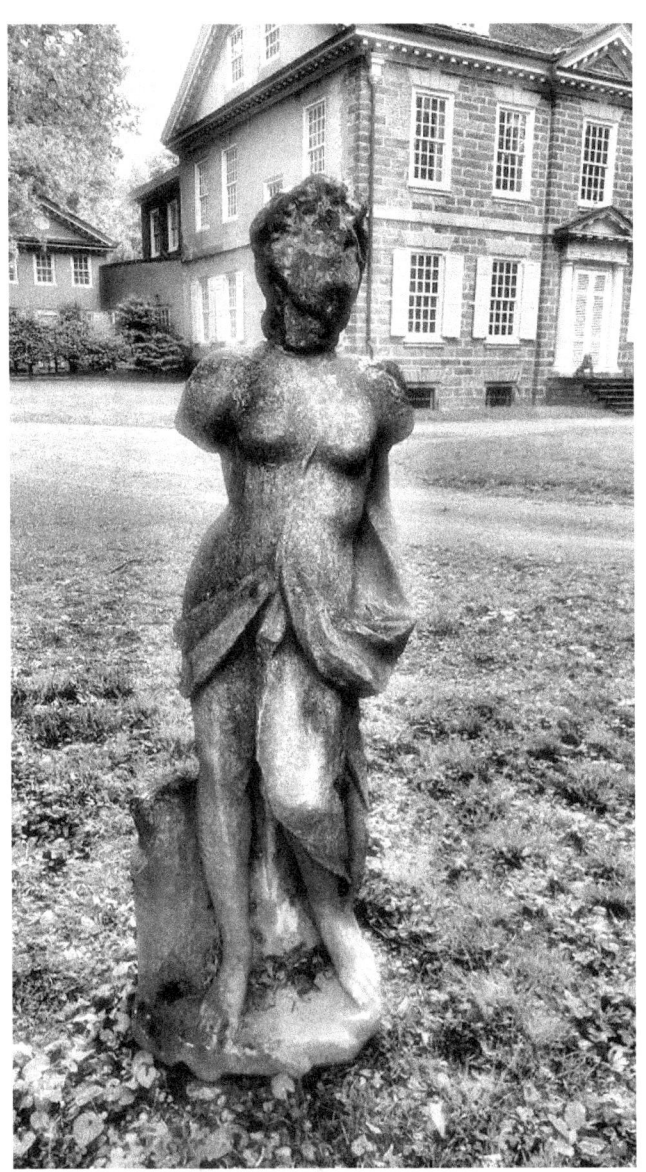

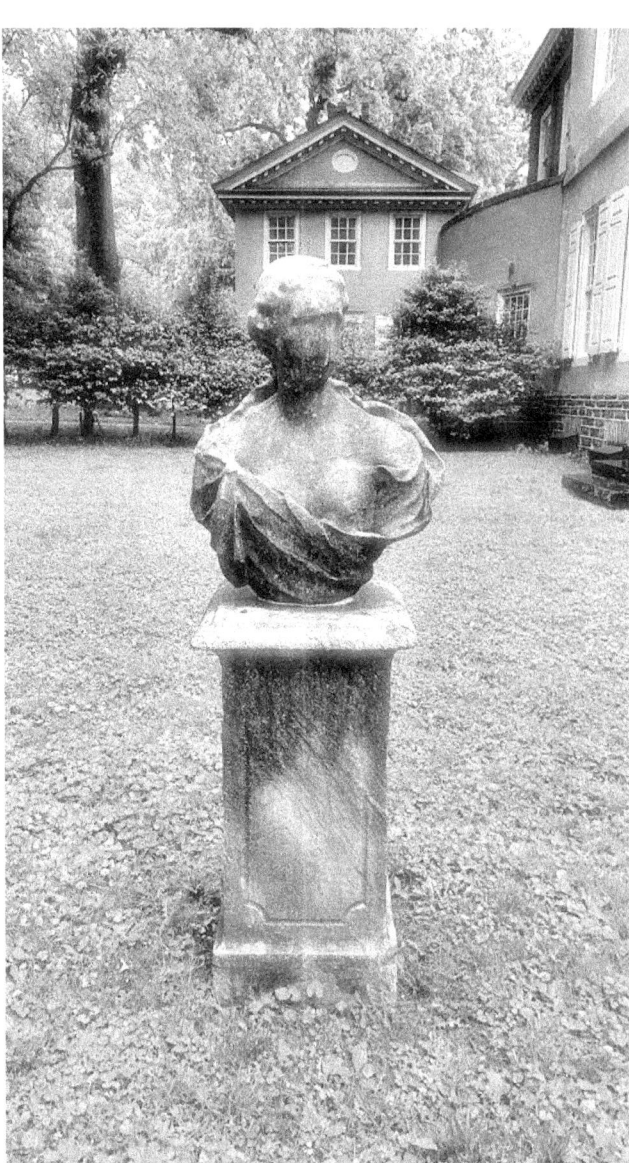

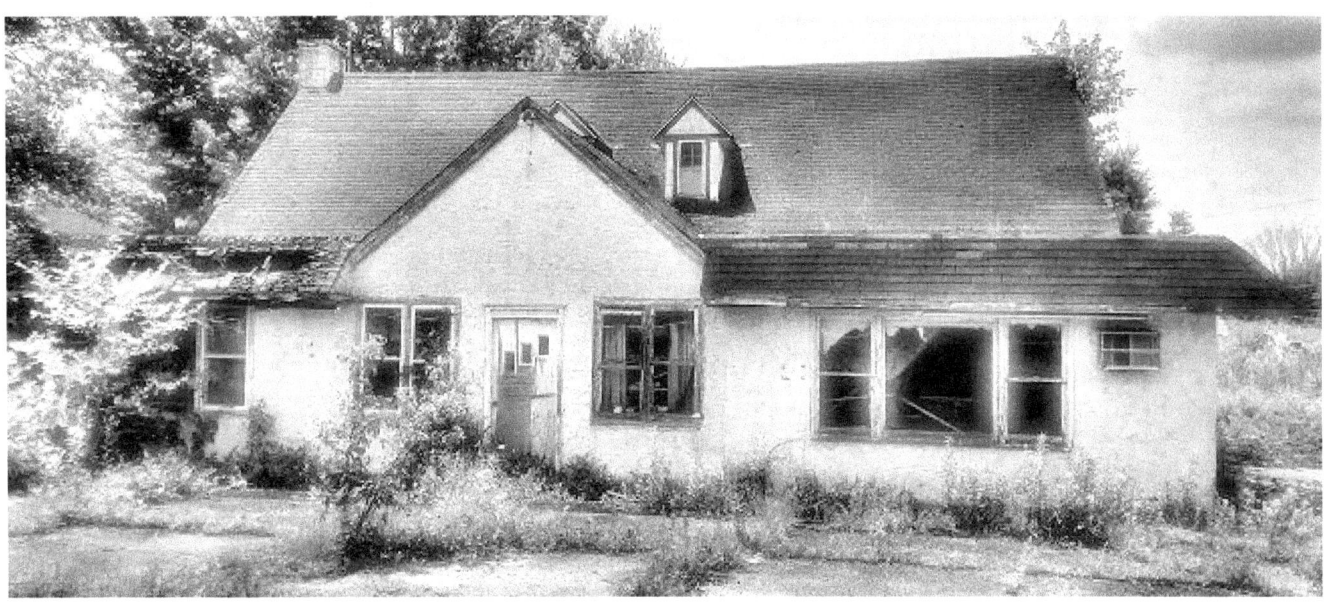

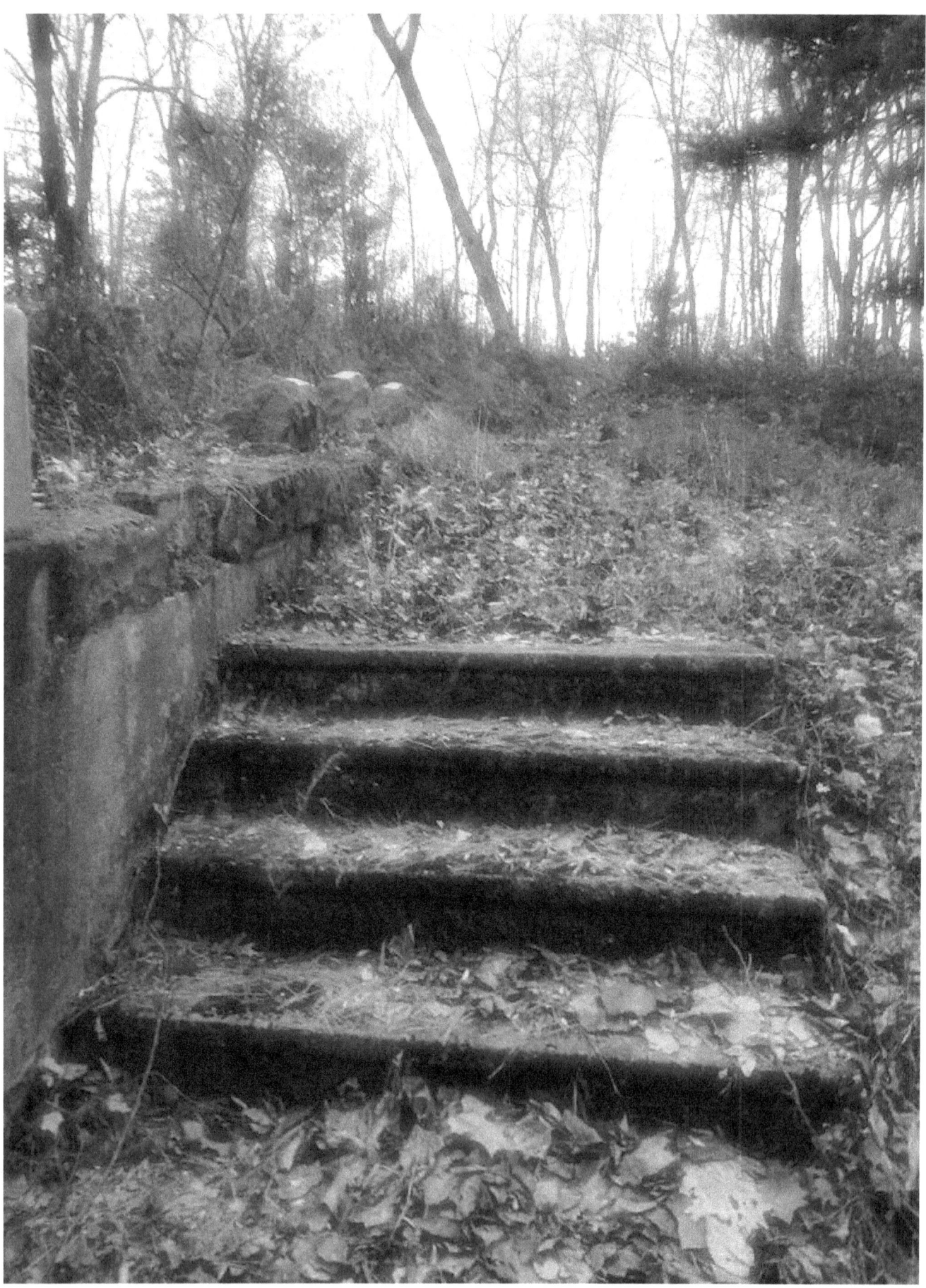

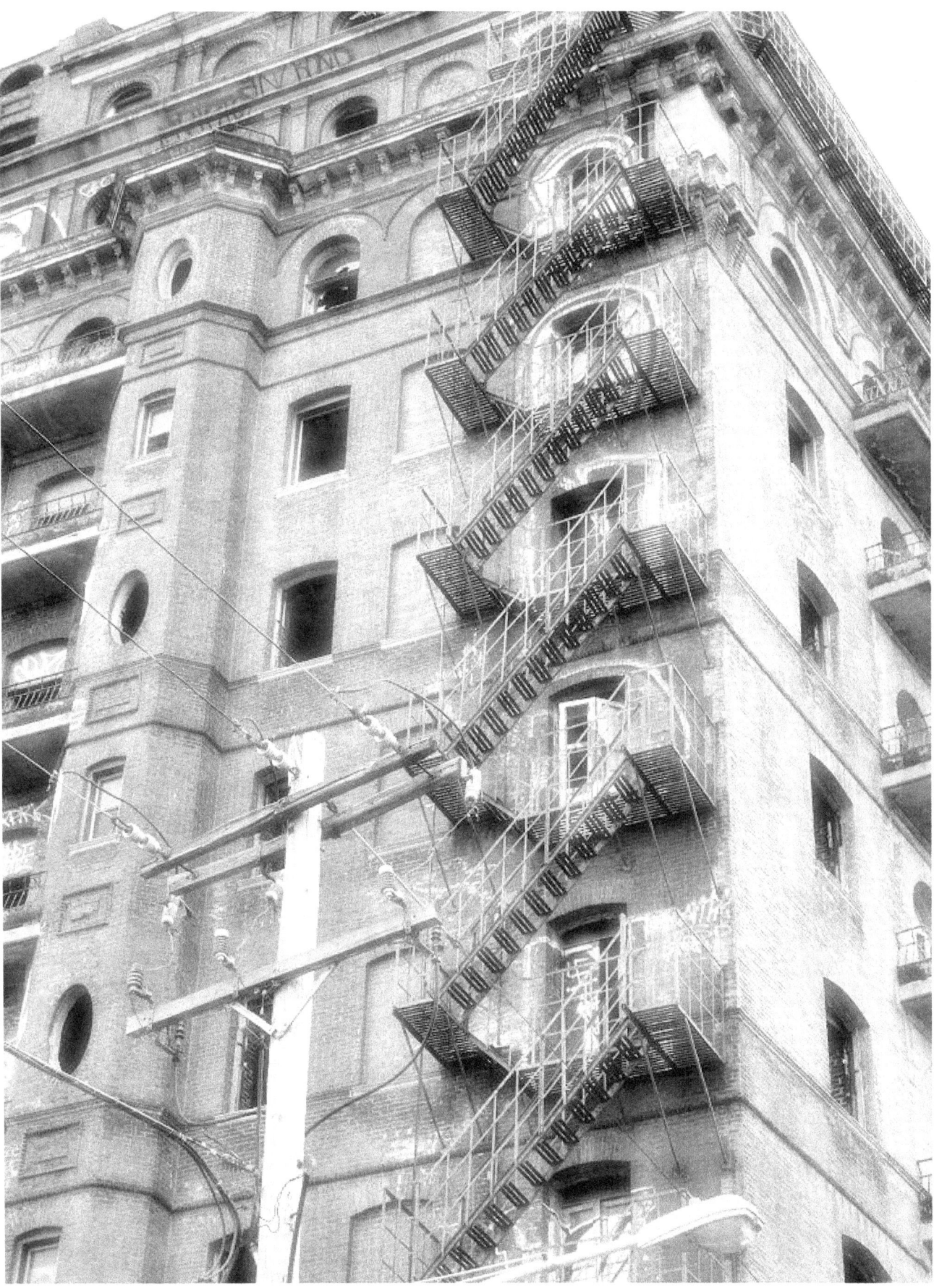

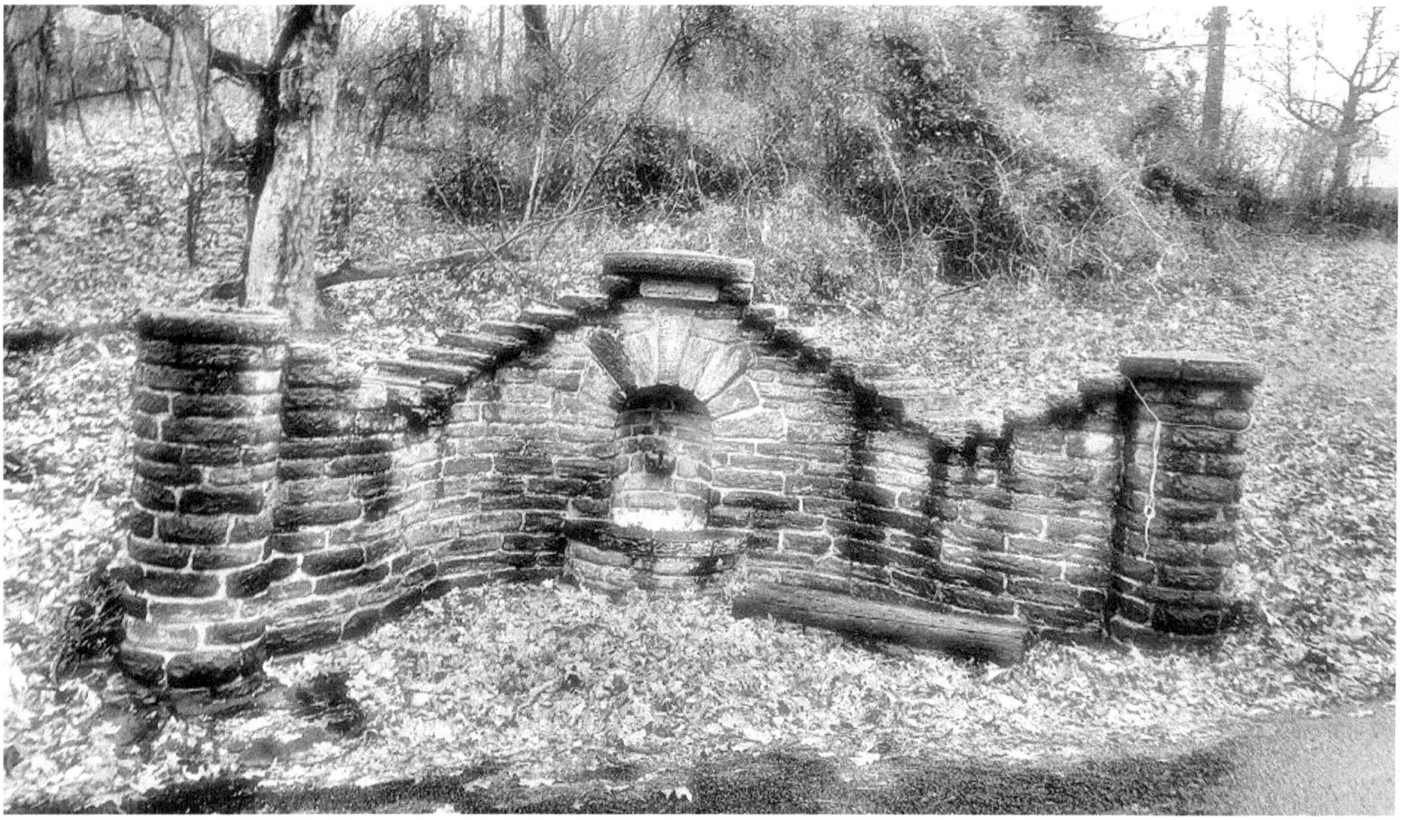

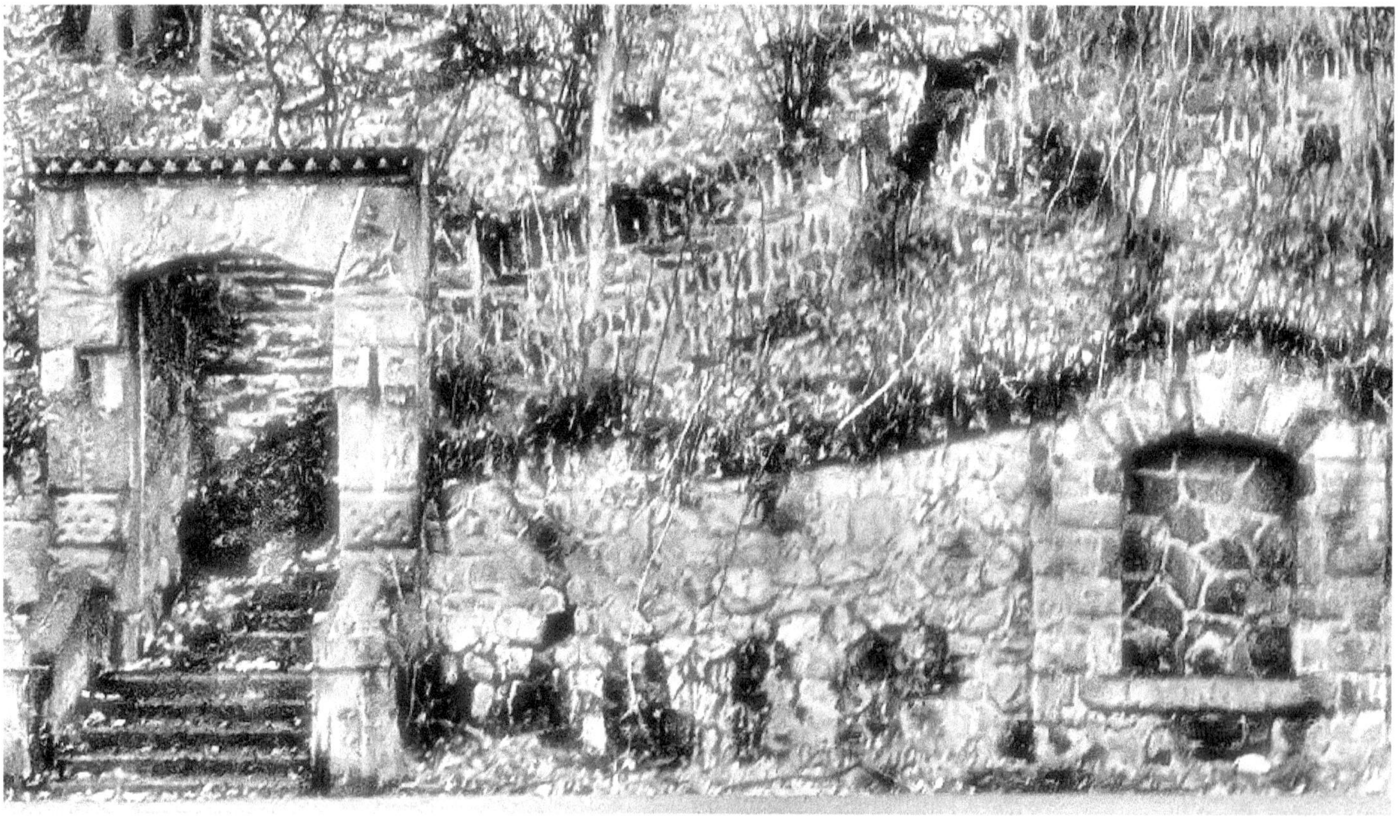

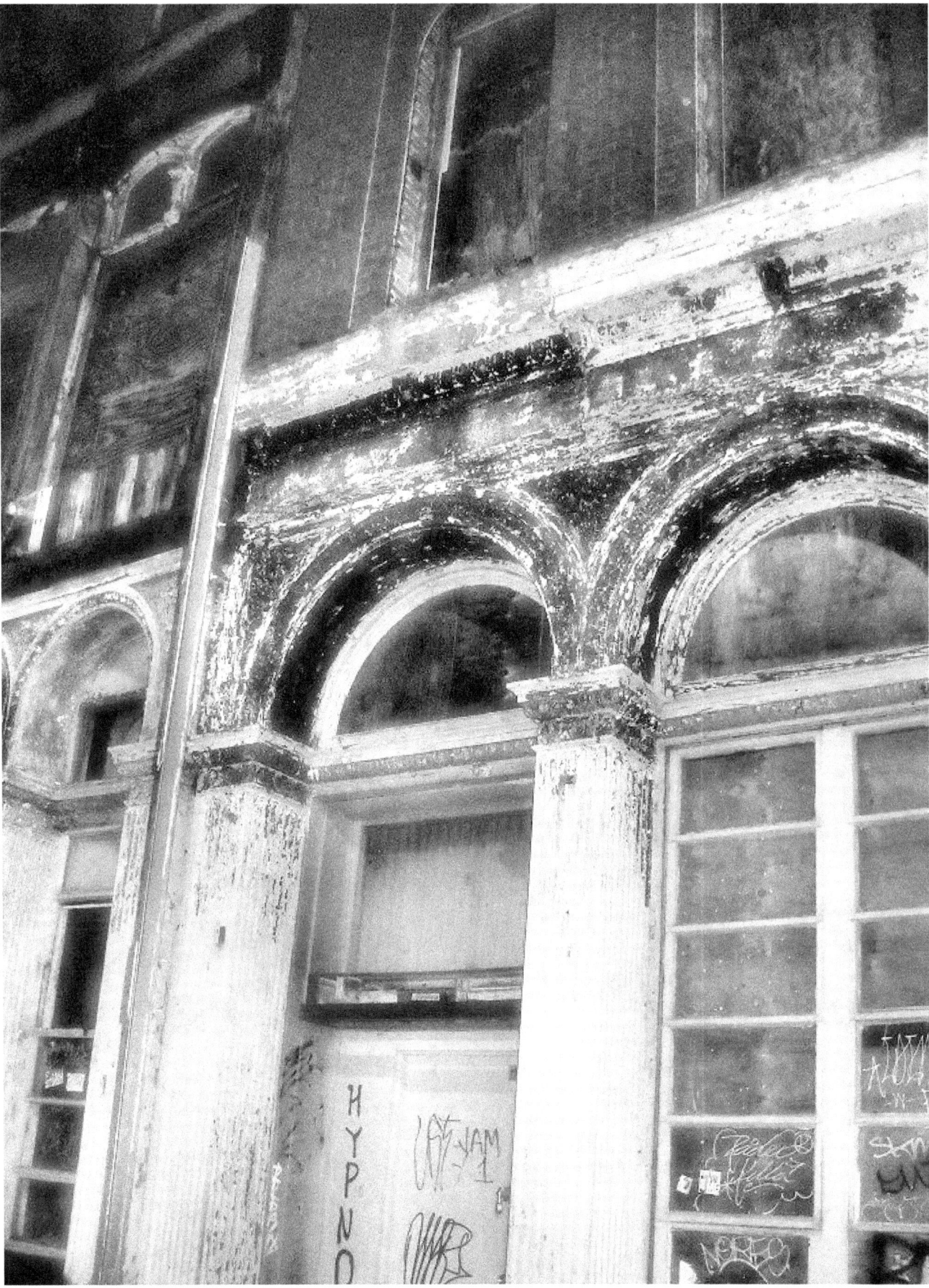

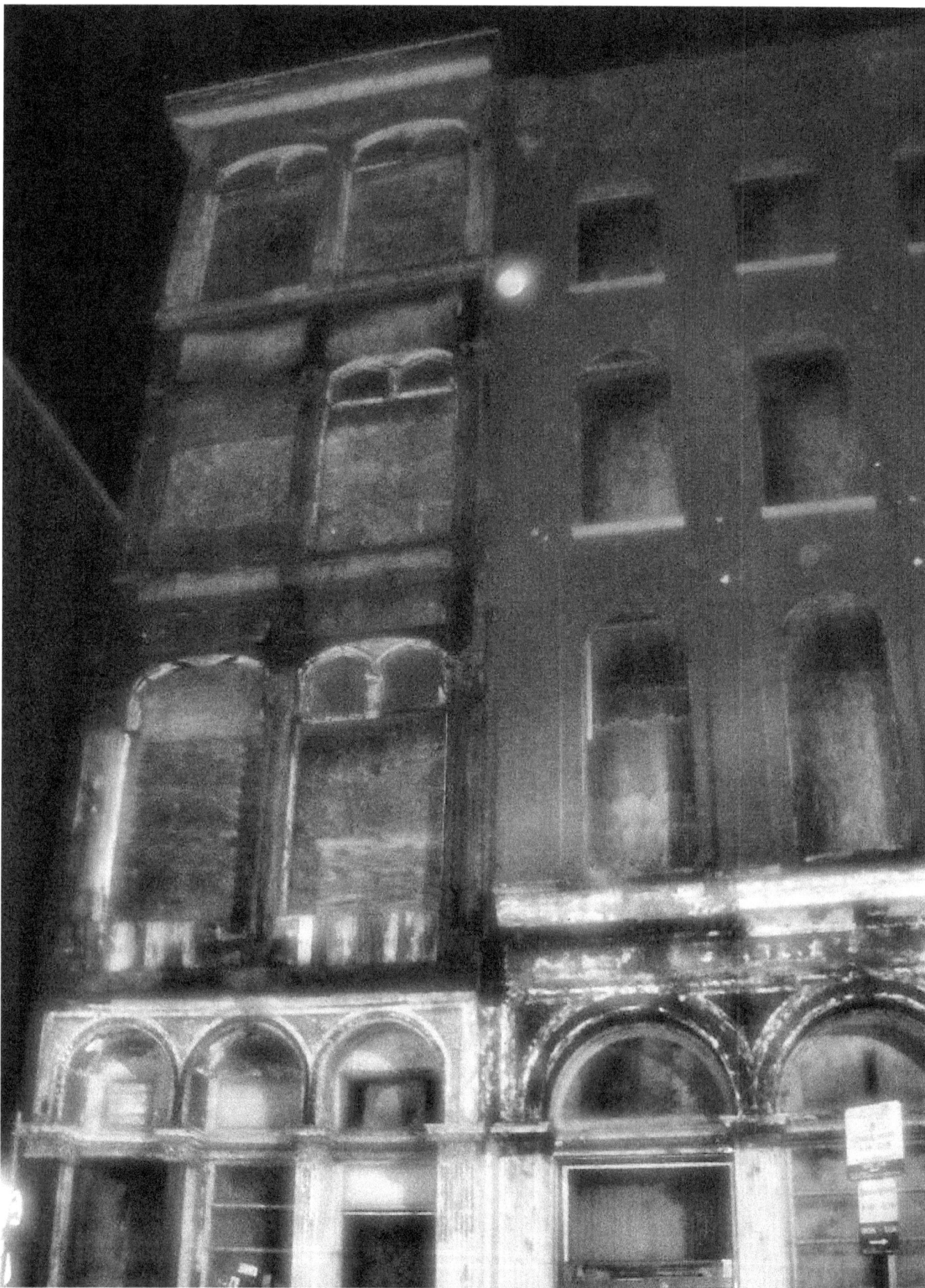

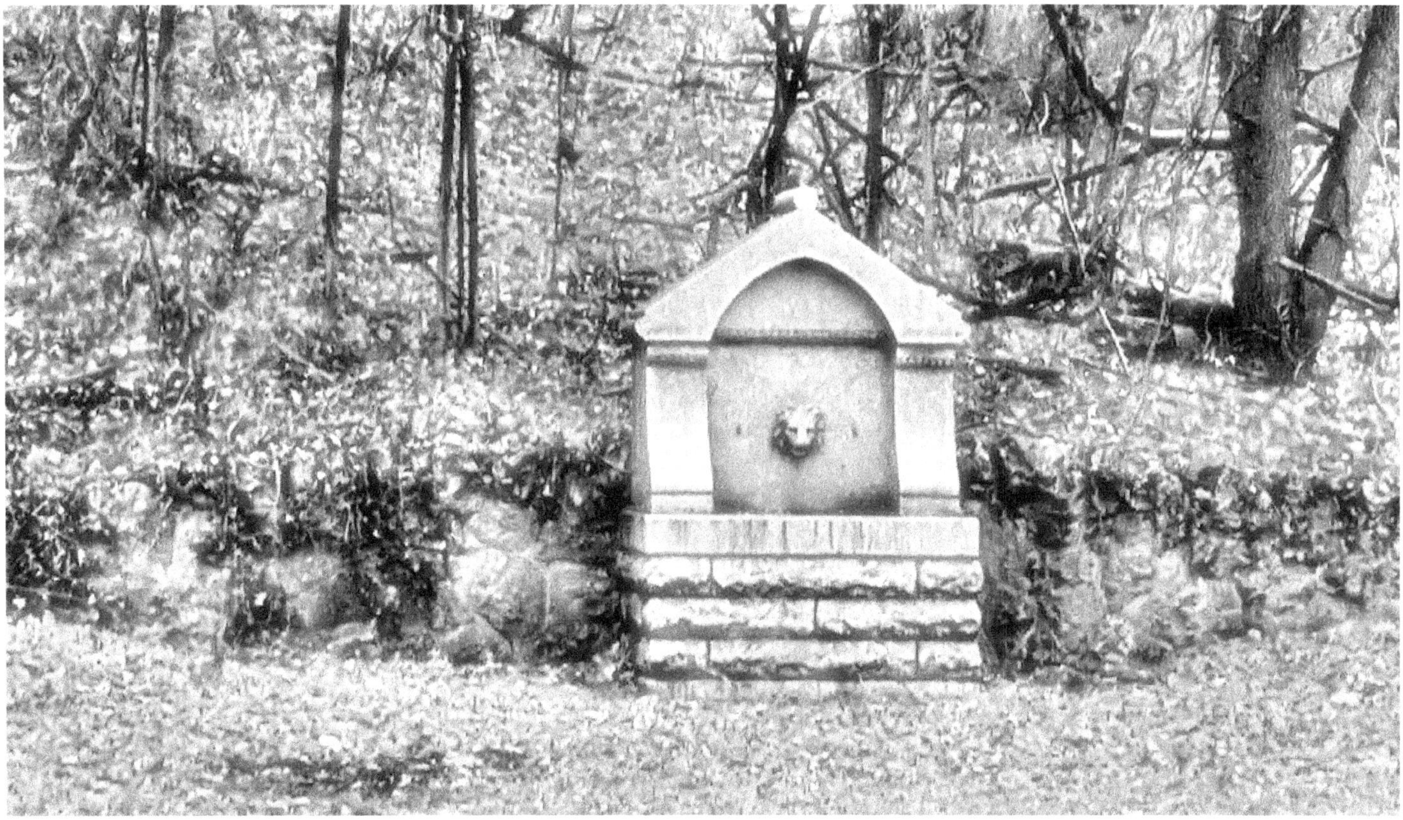

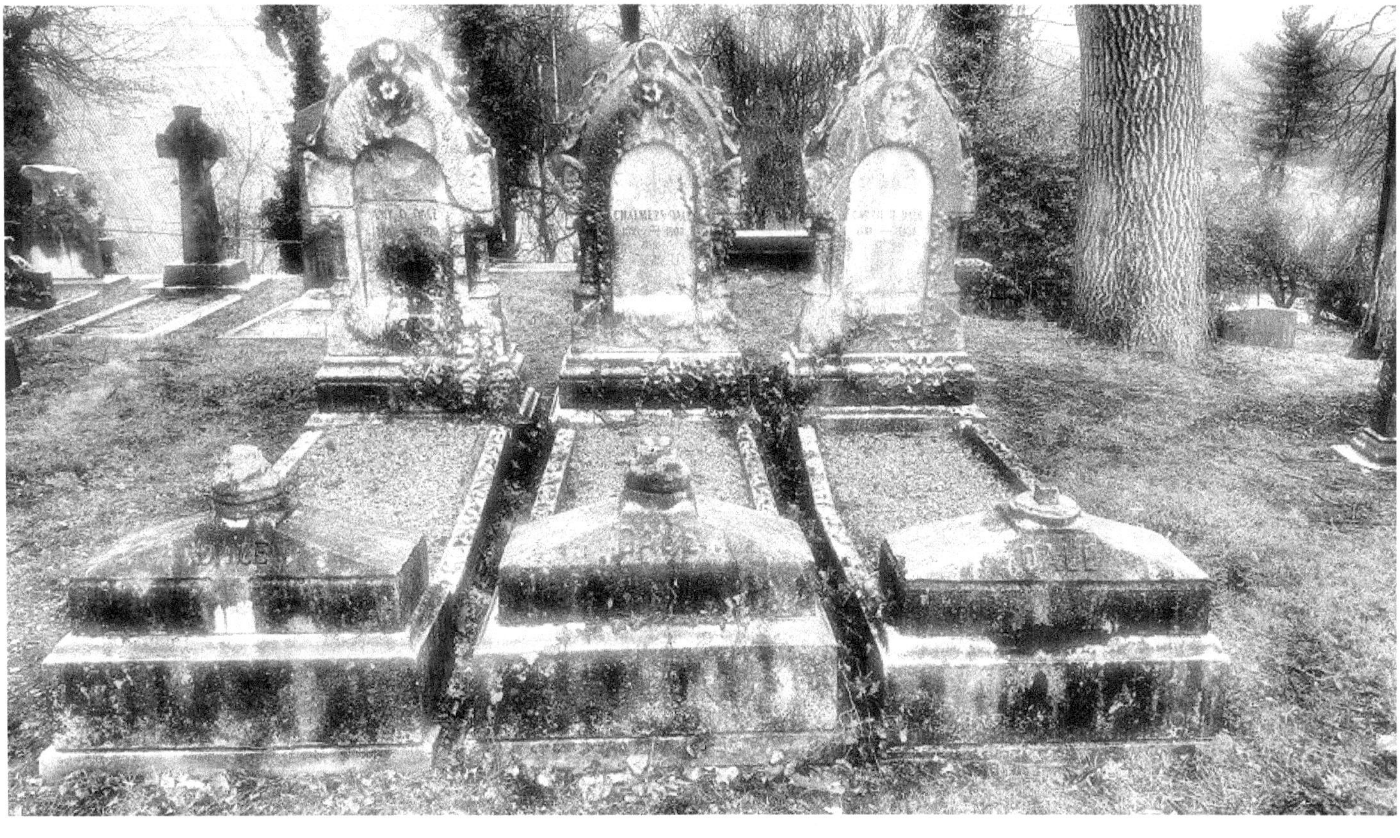
CHALMERS

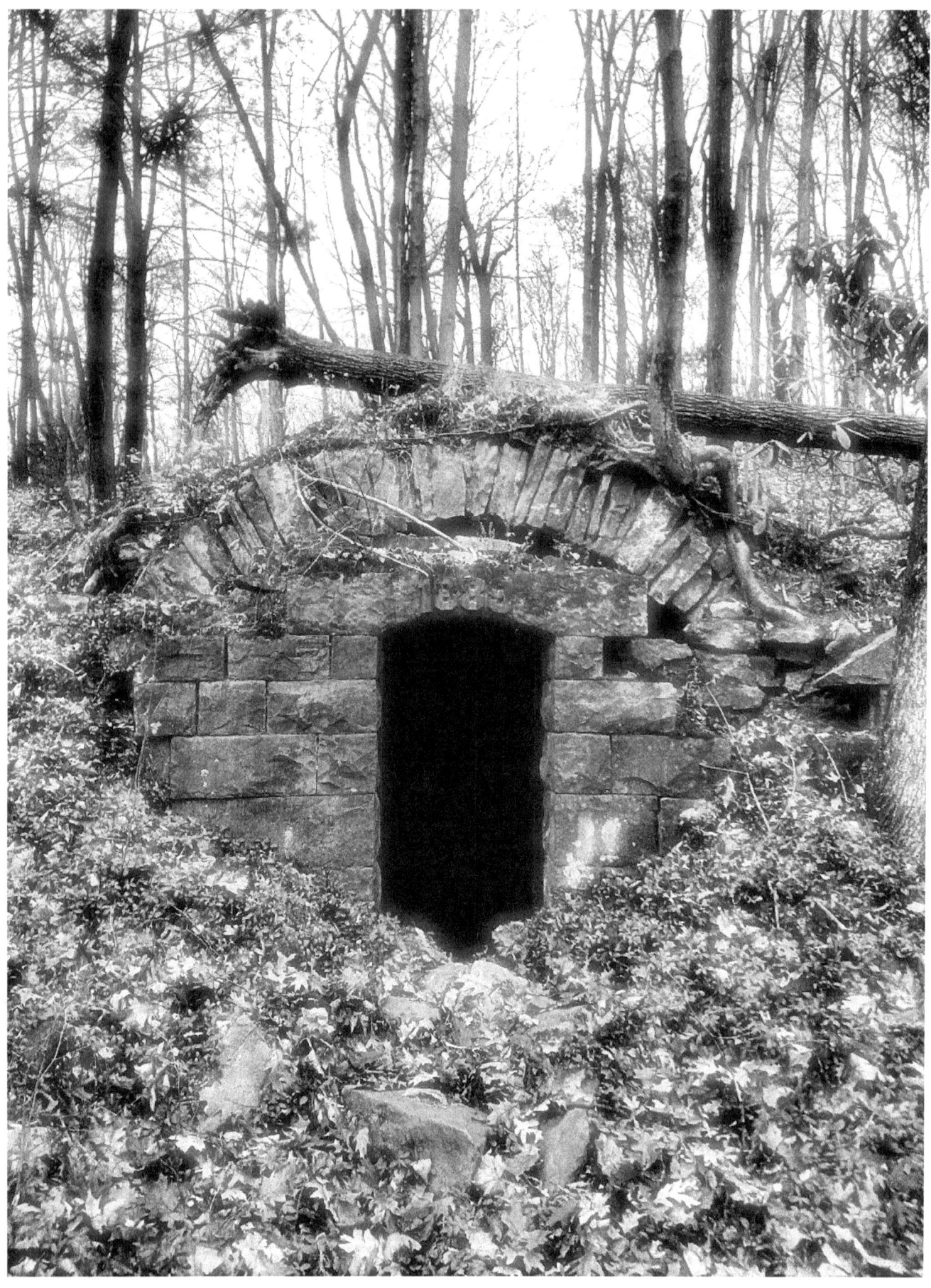

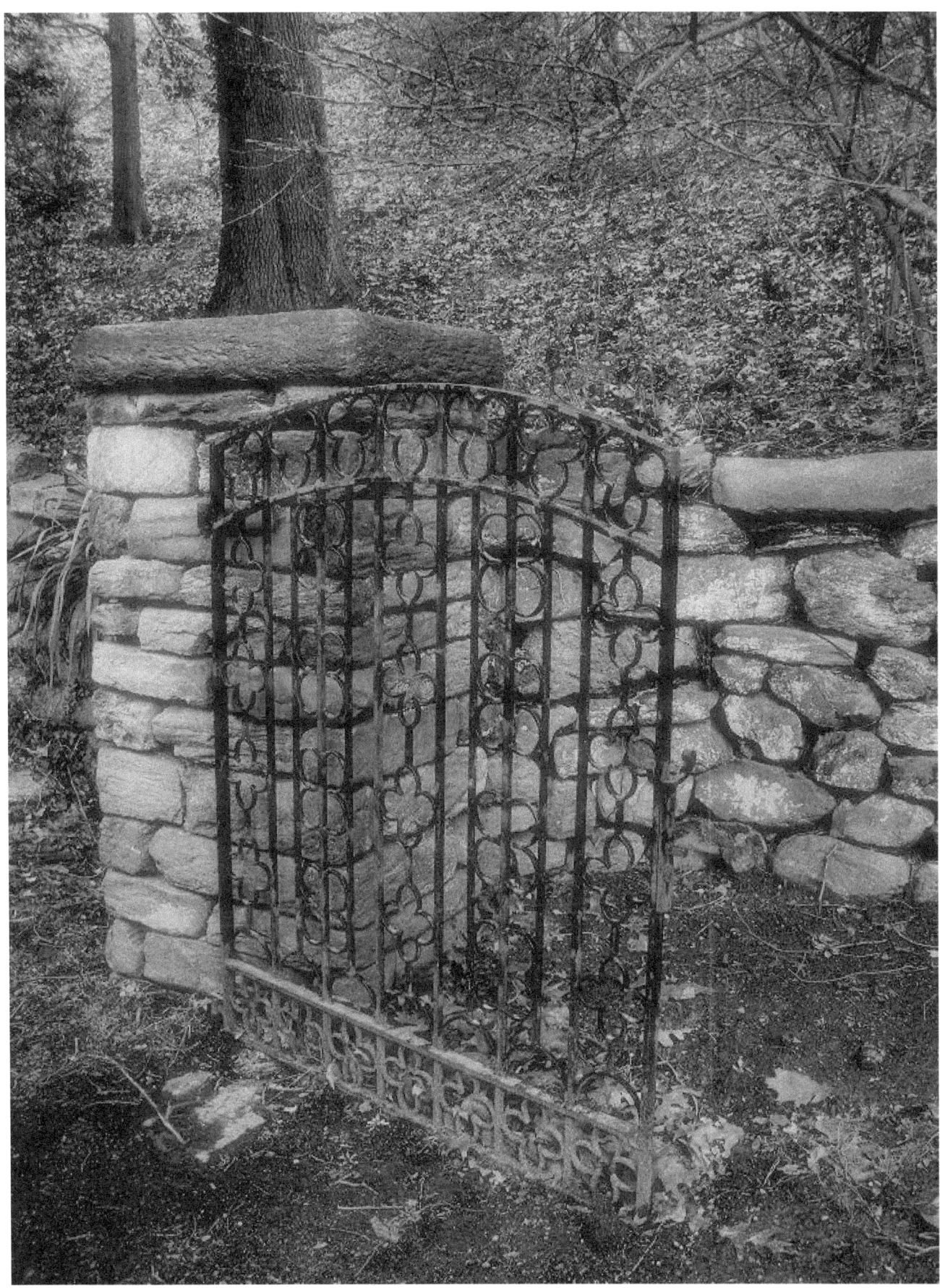

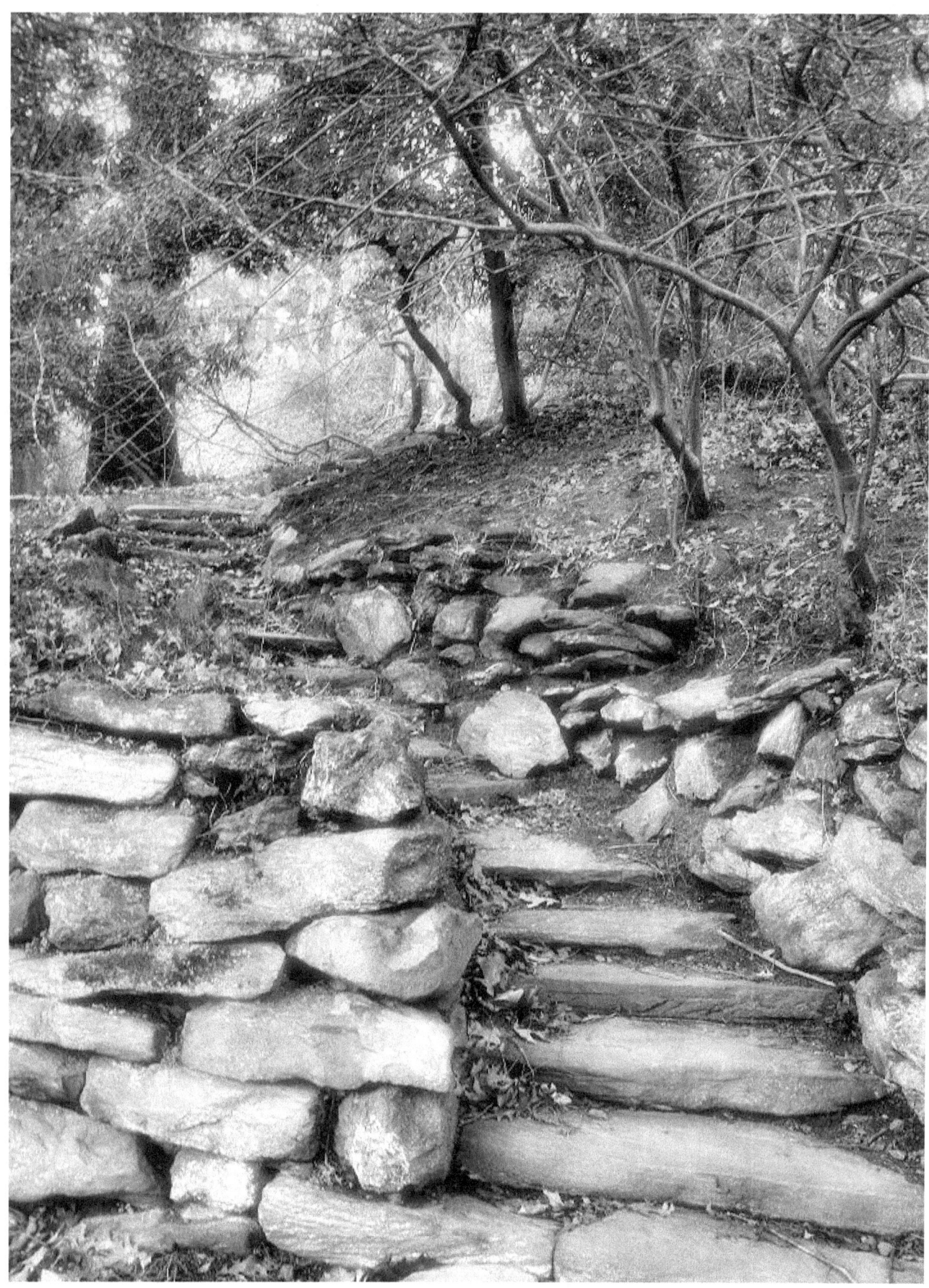

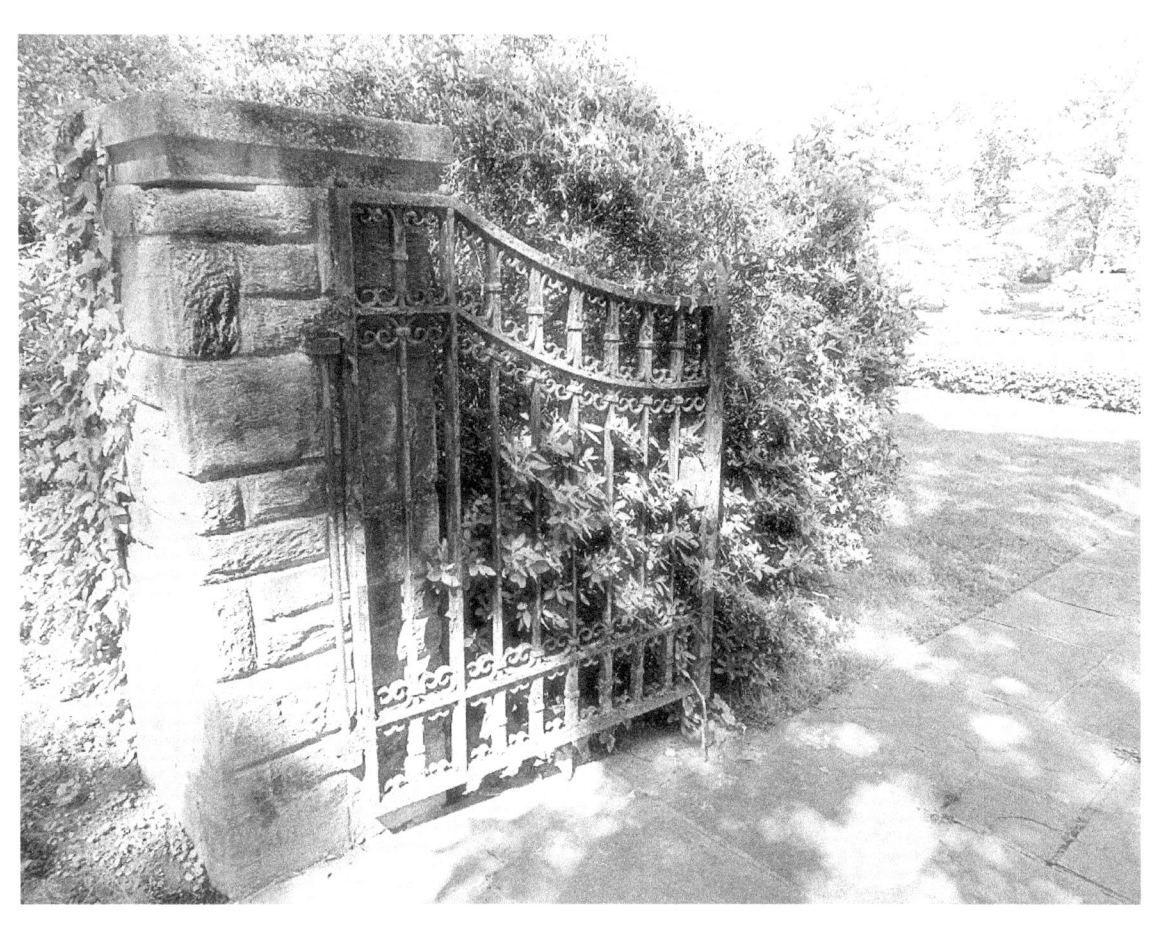

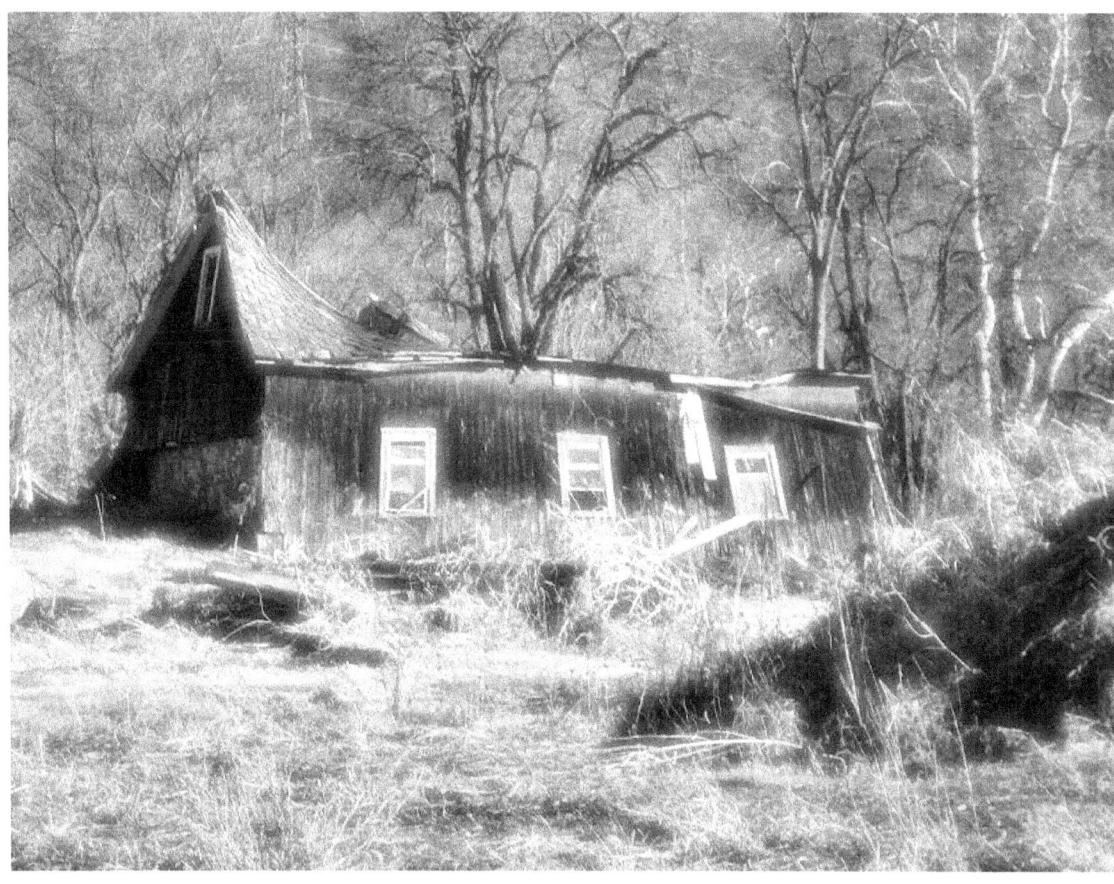

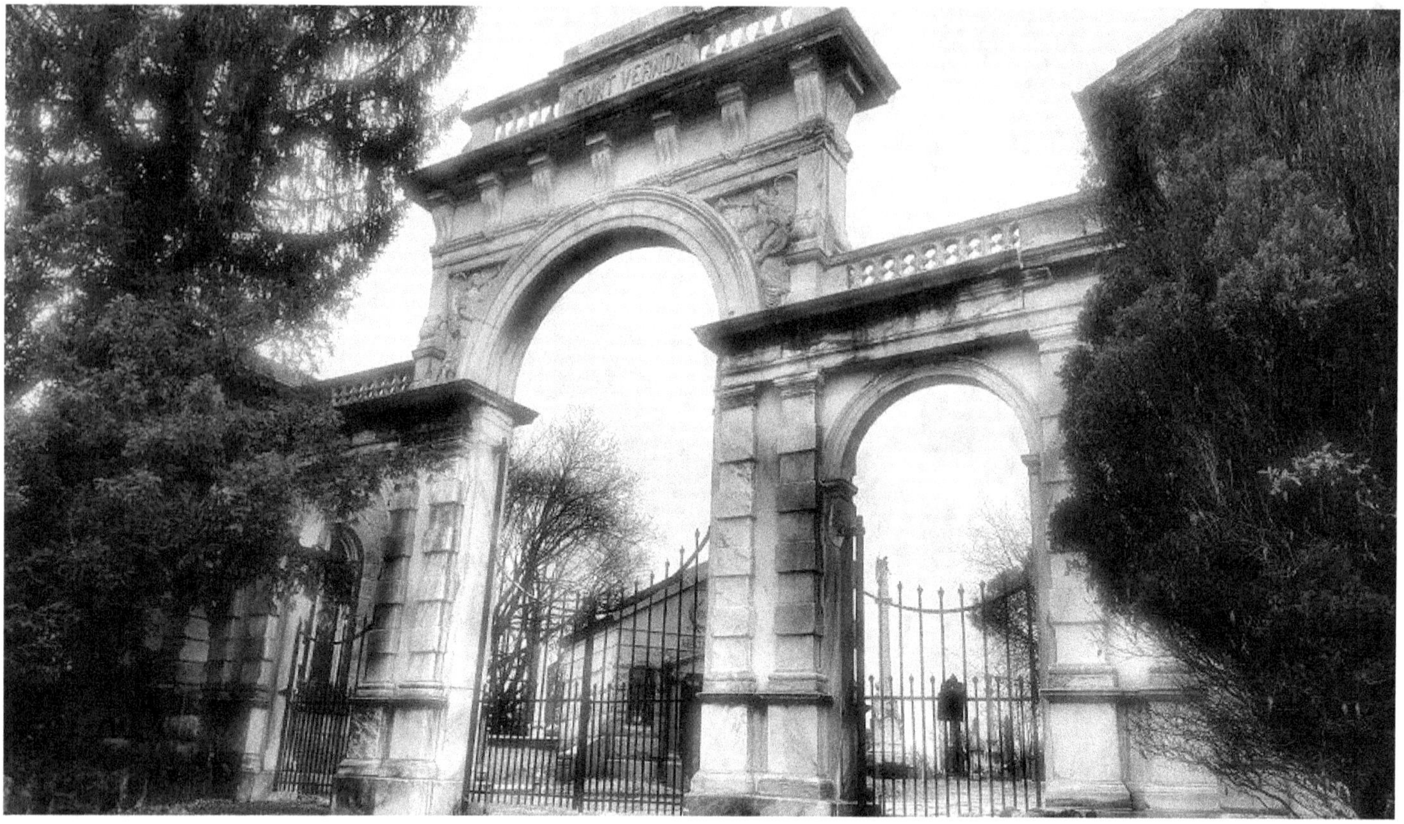

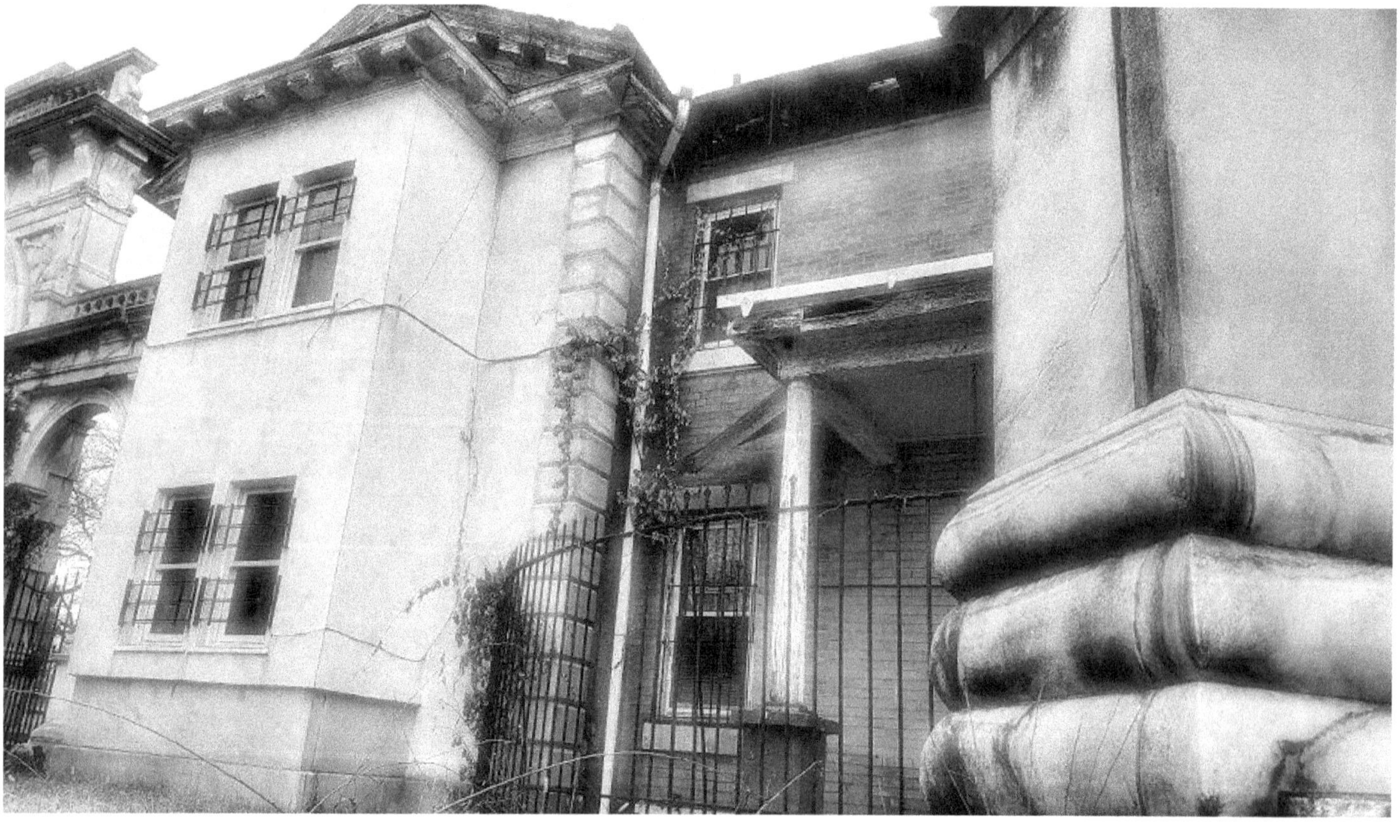

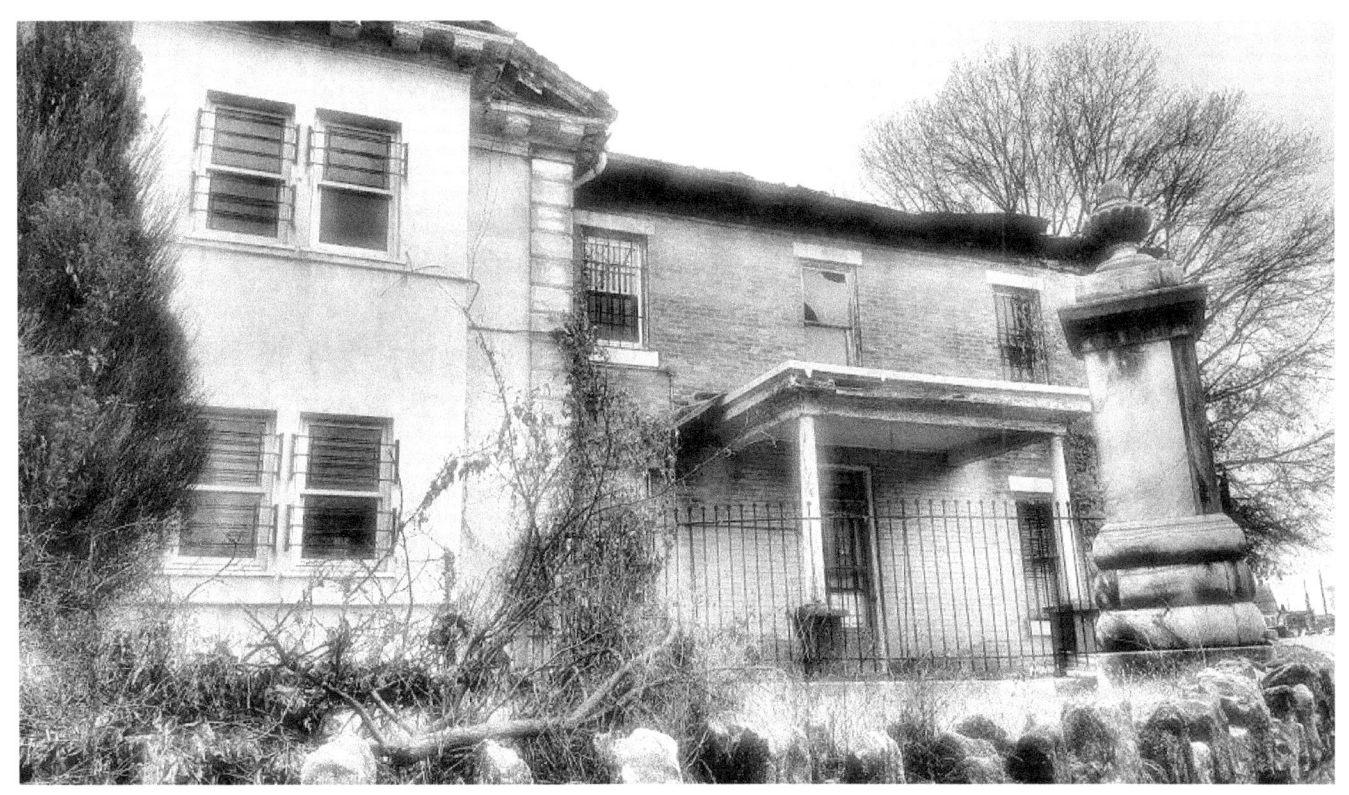

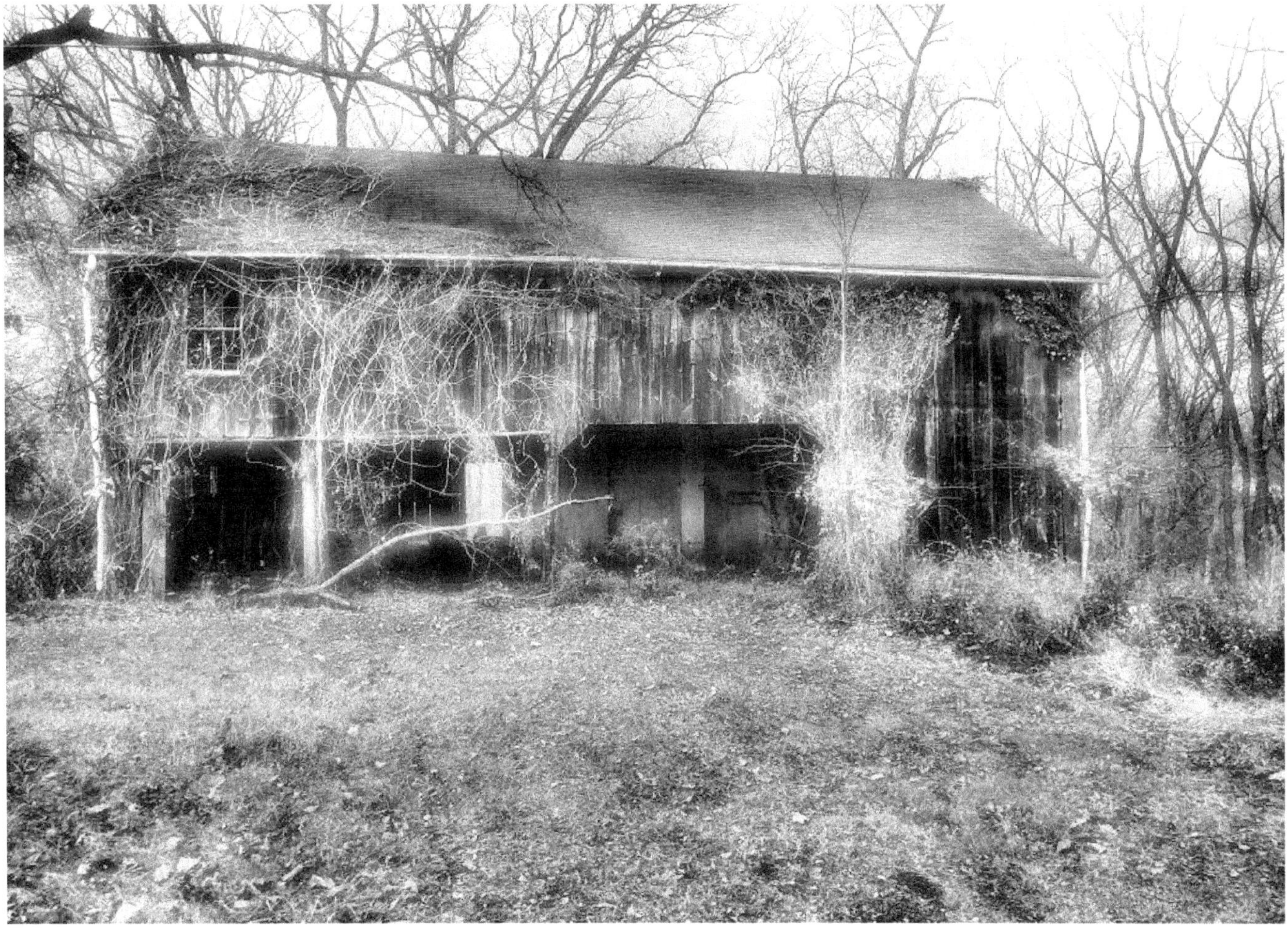

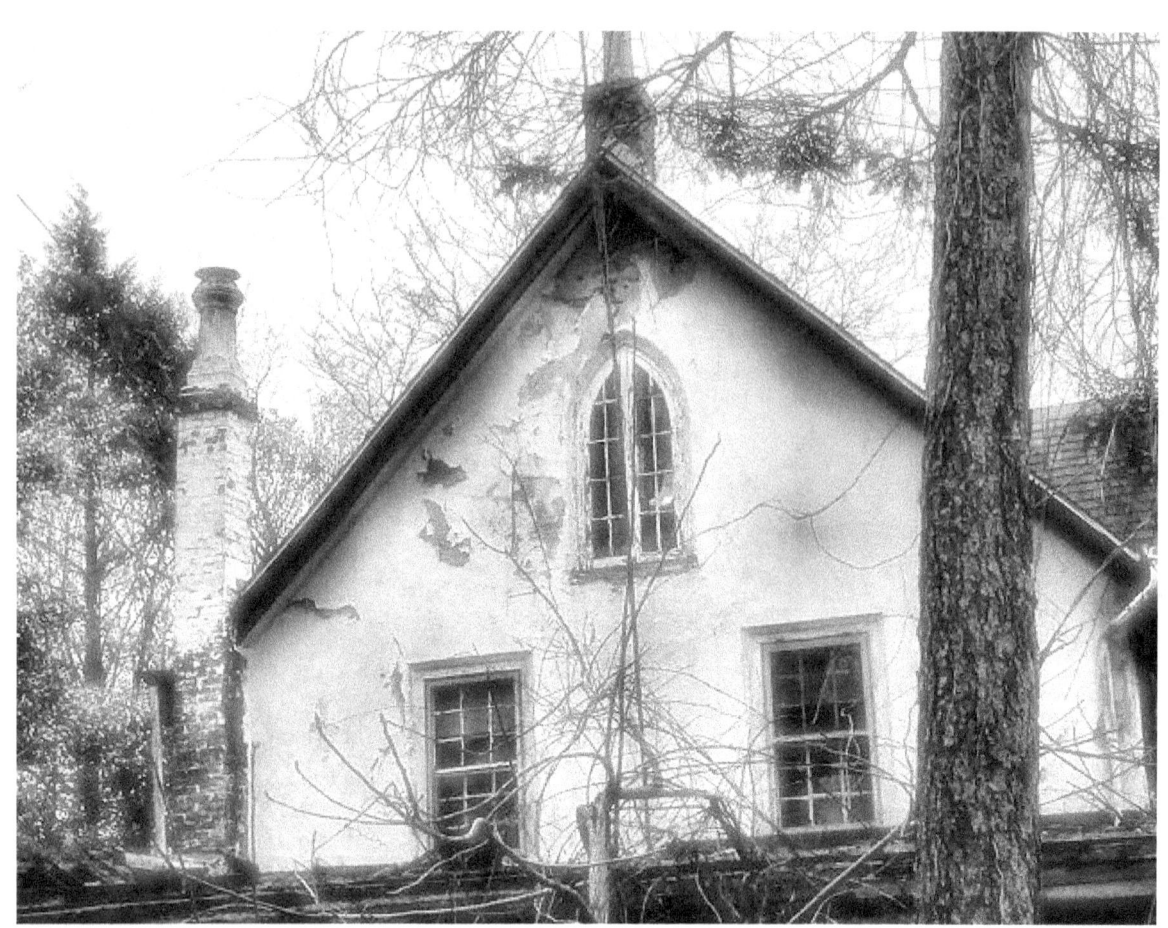

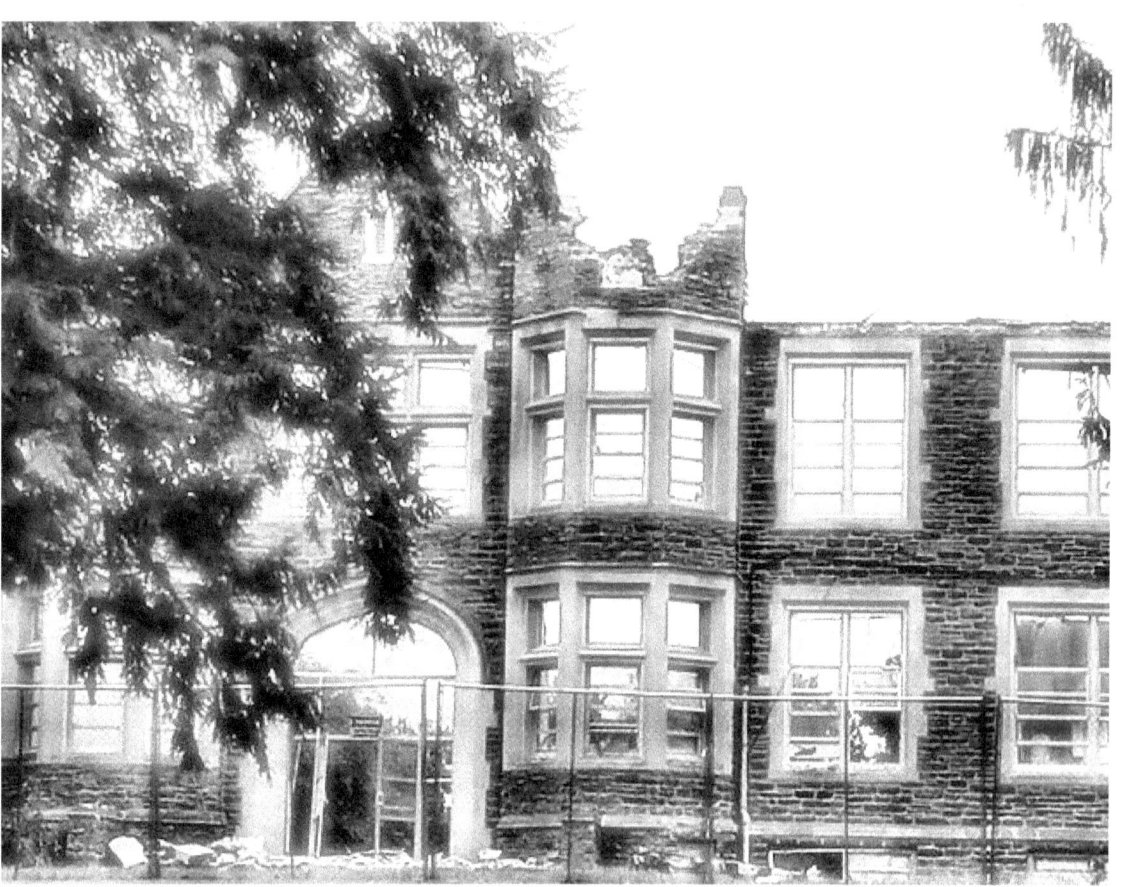

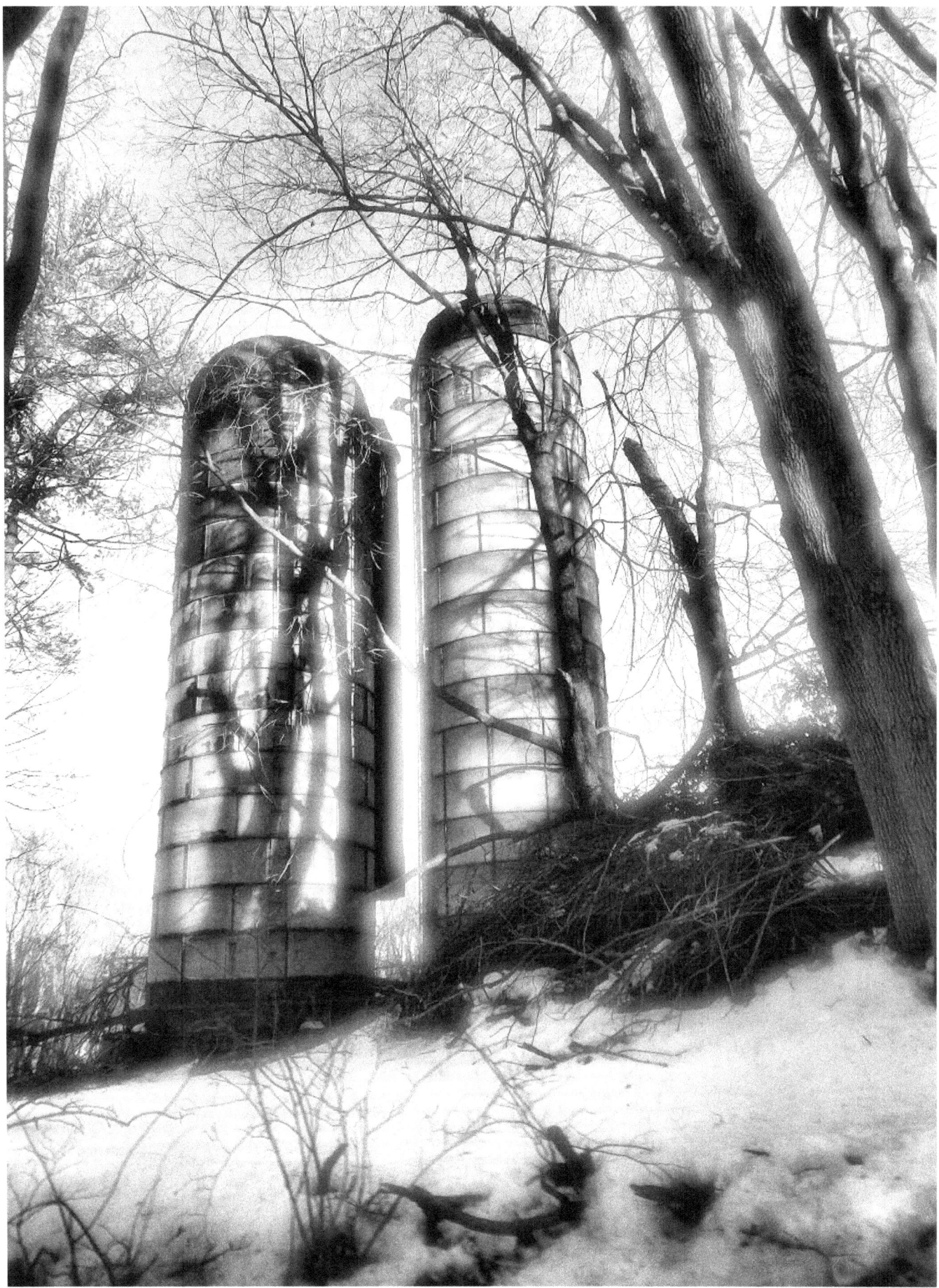

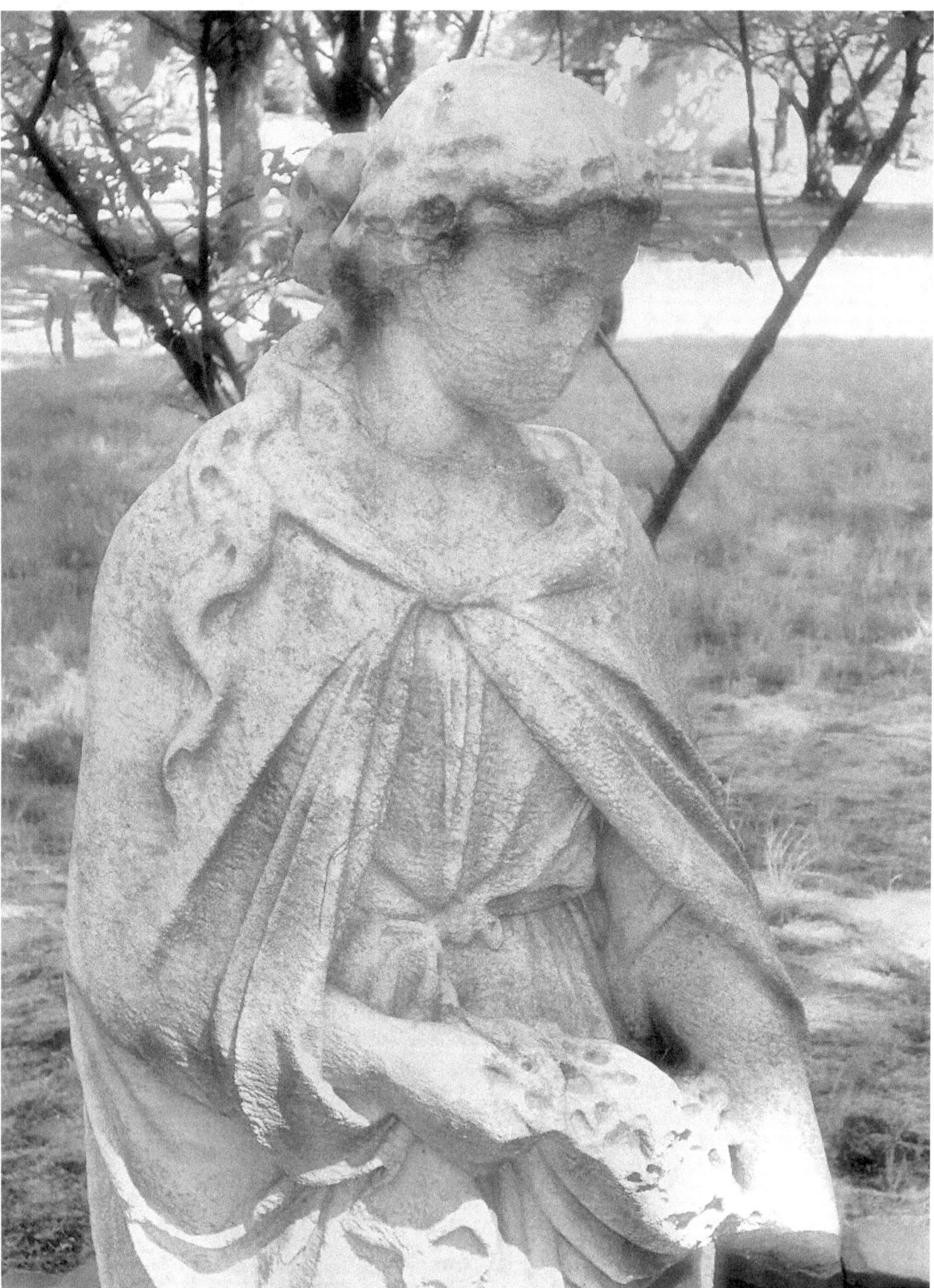

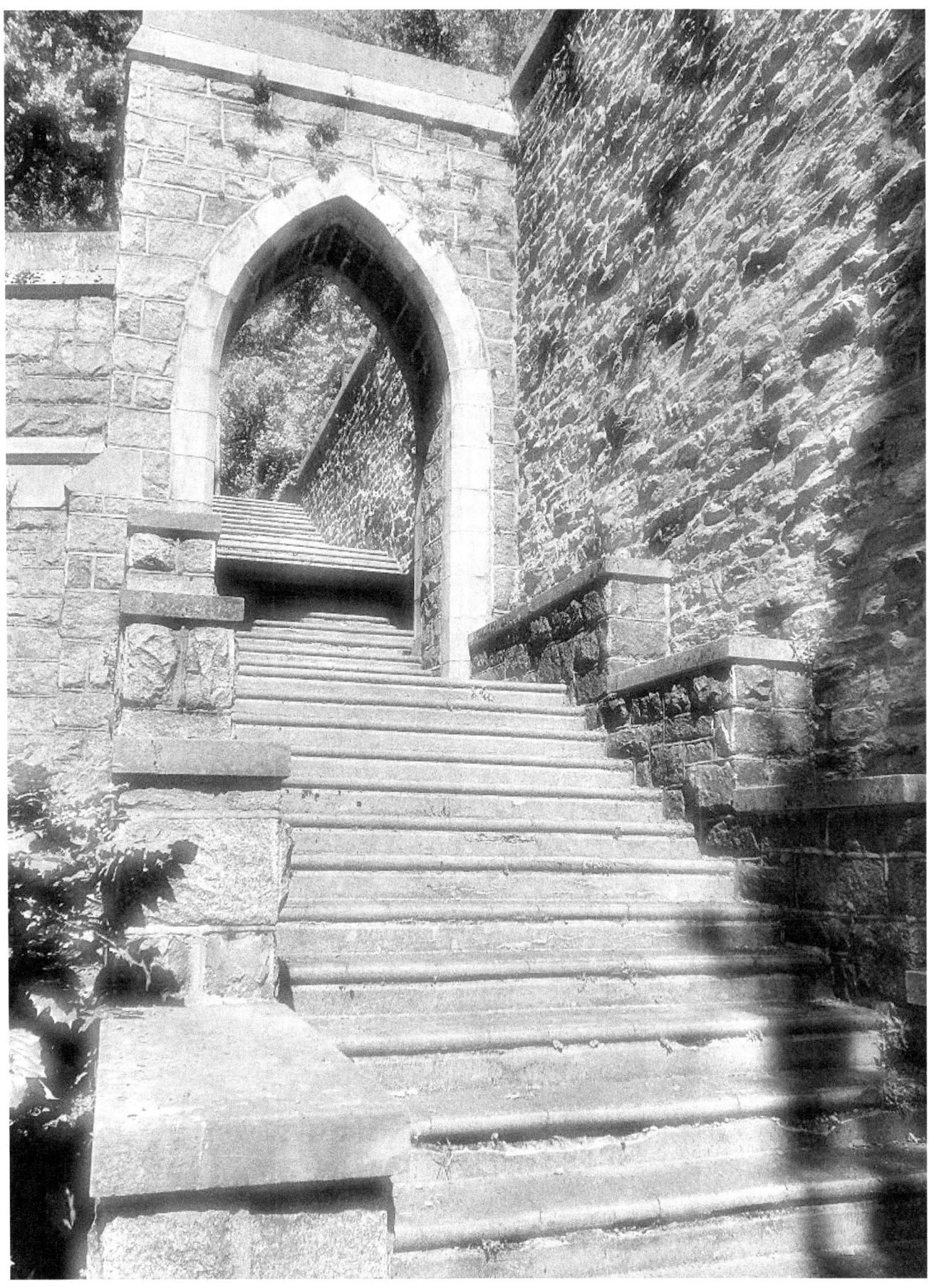

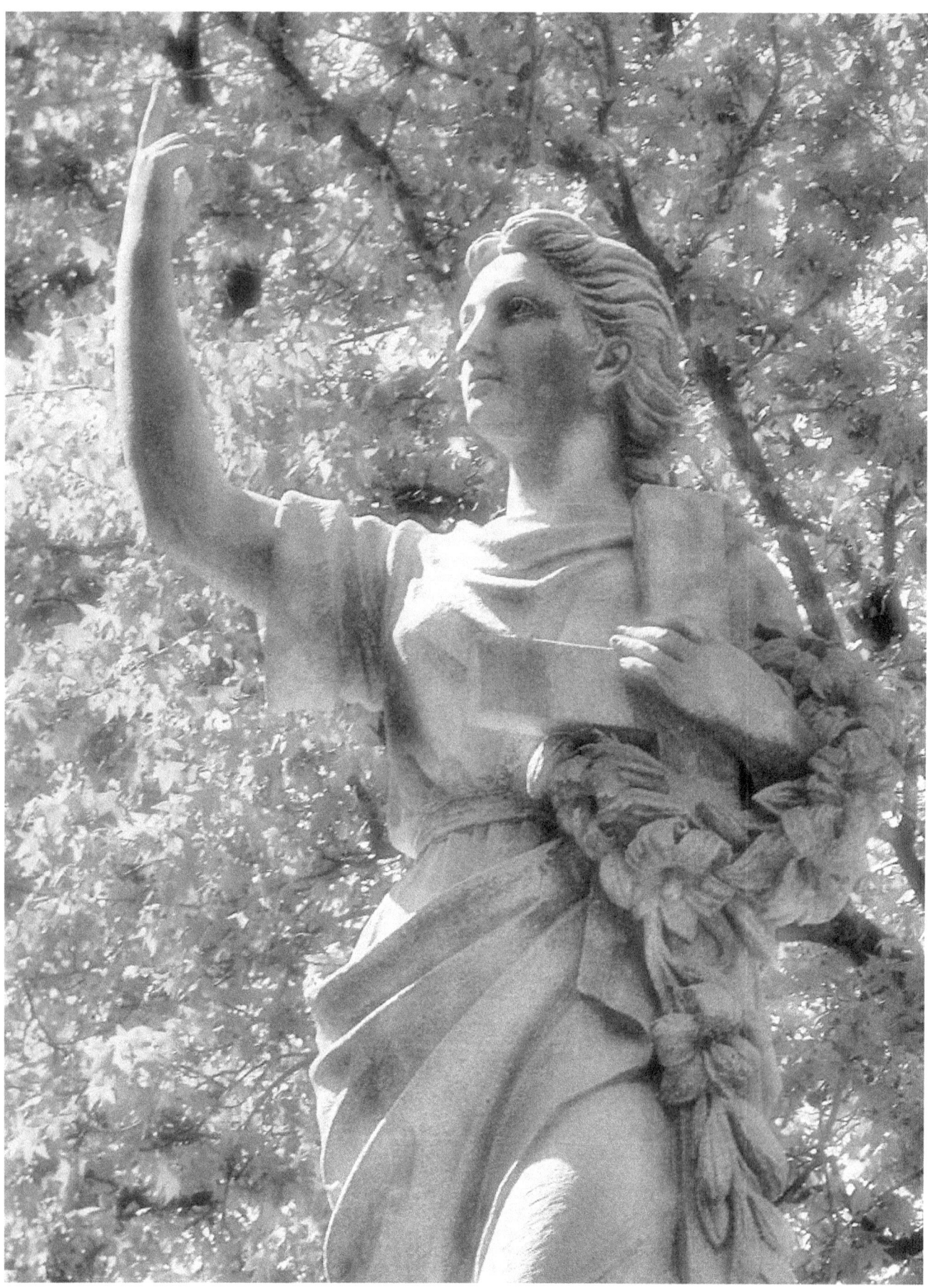

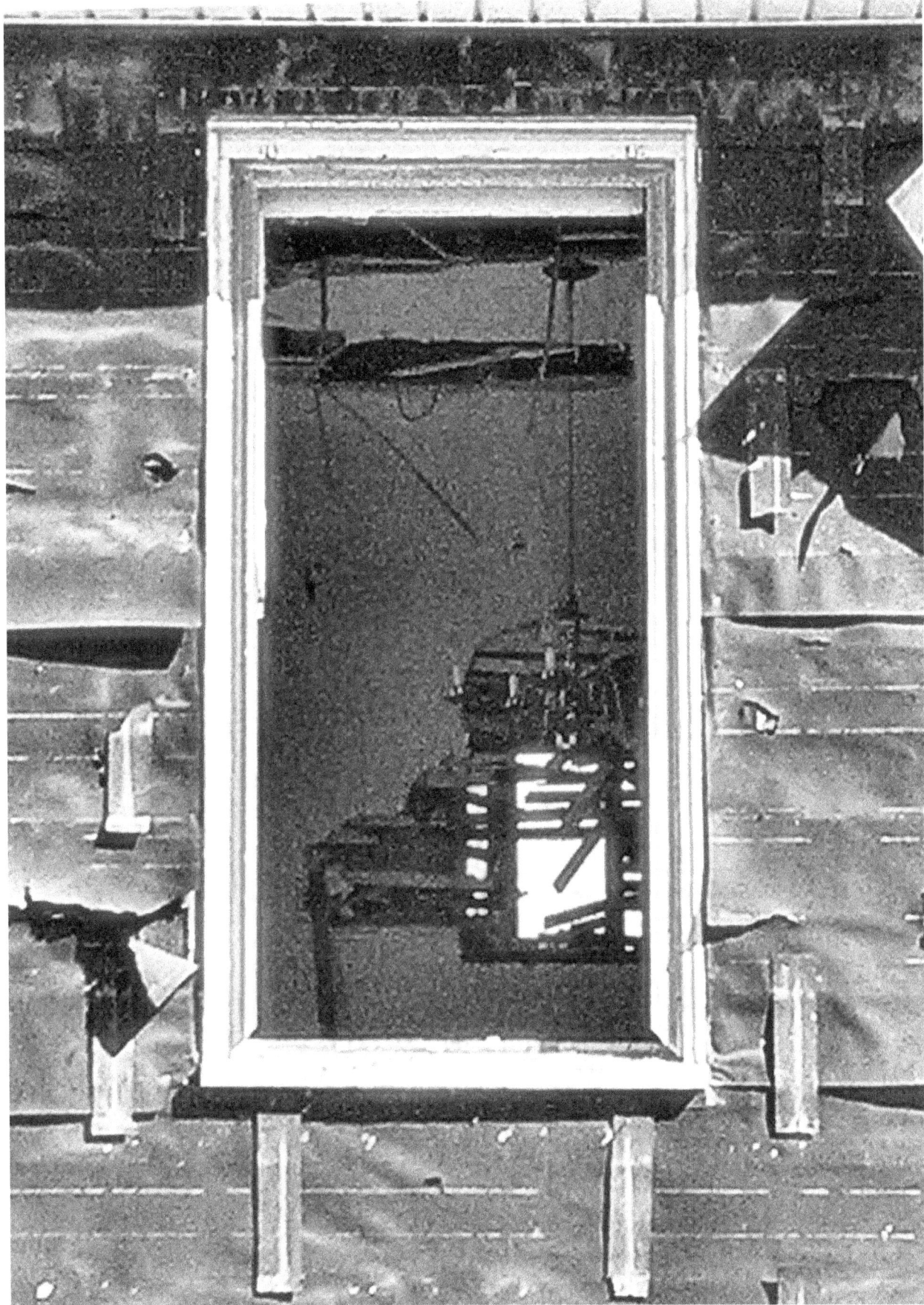

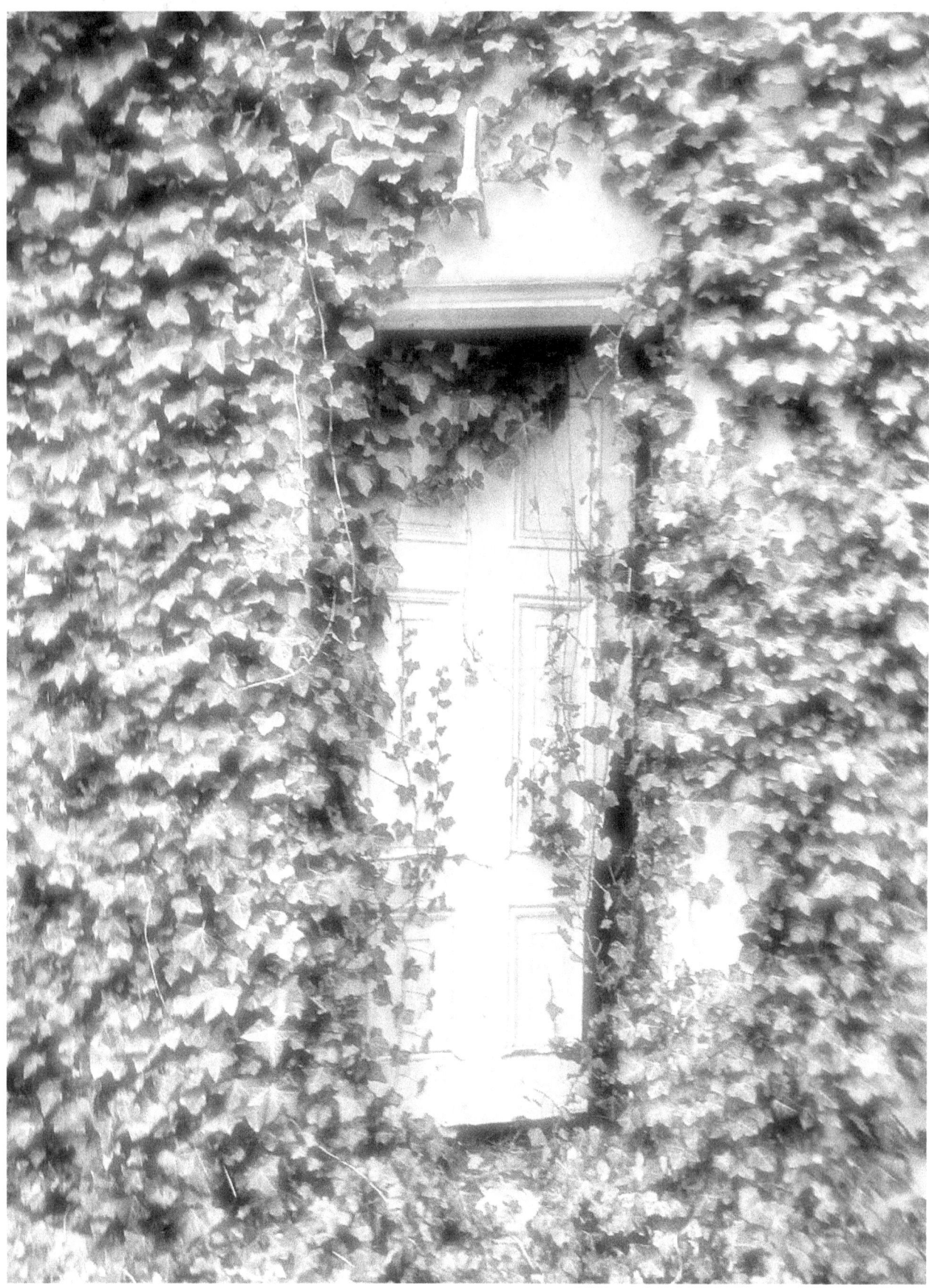

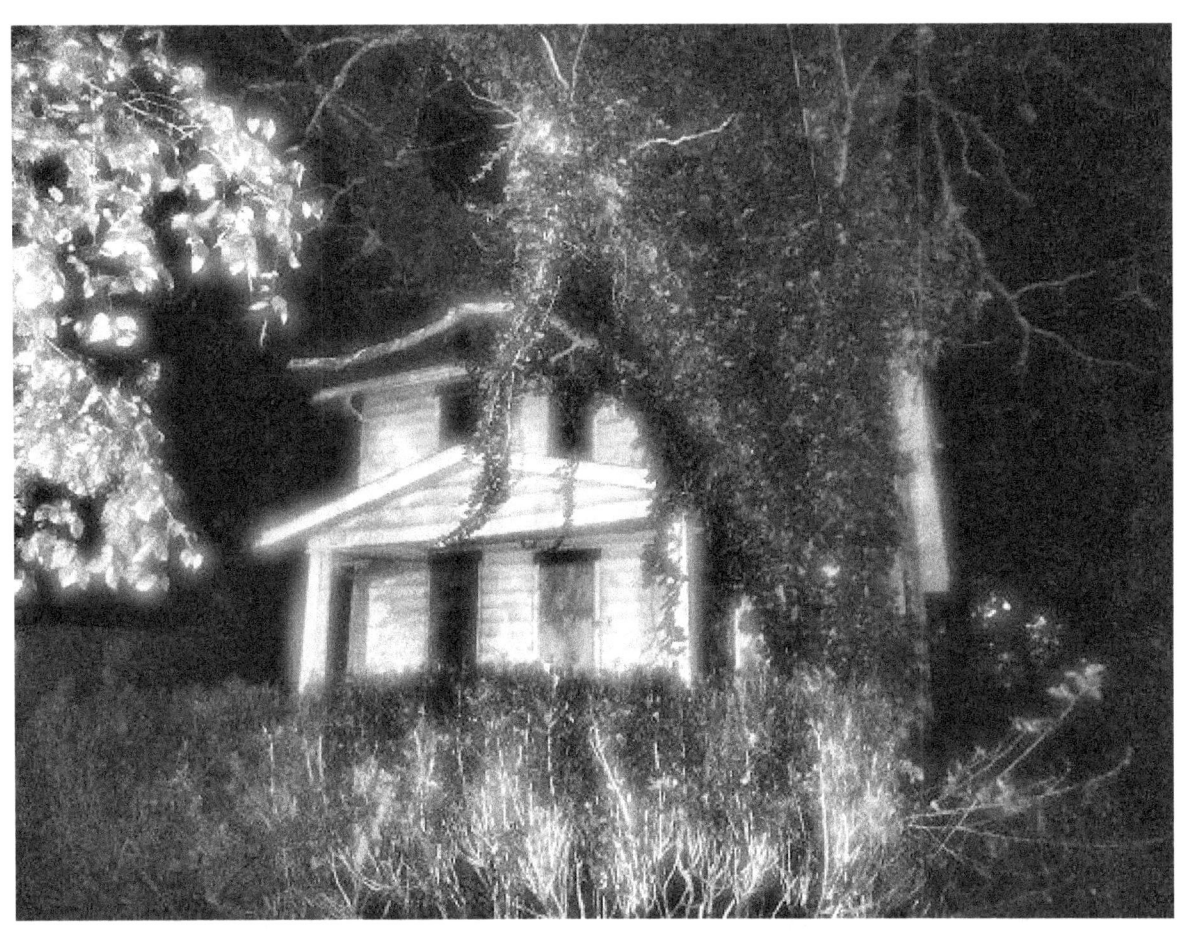

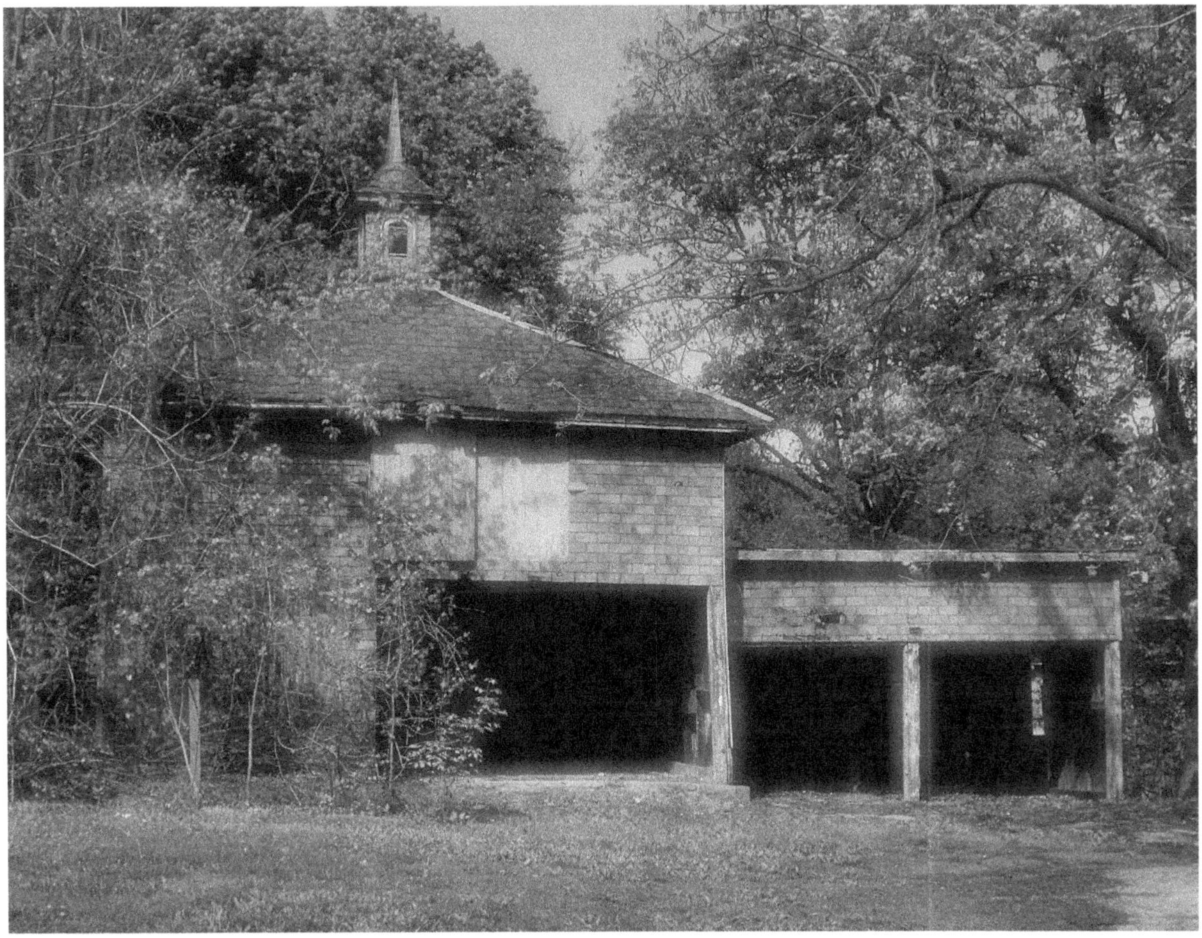

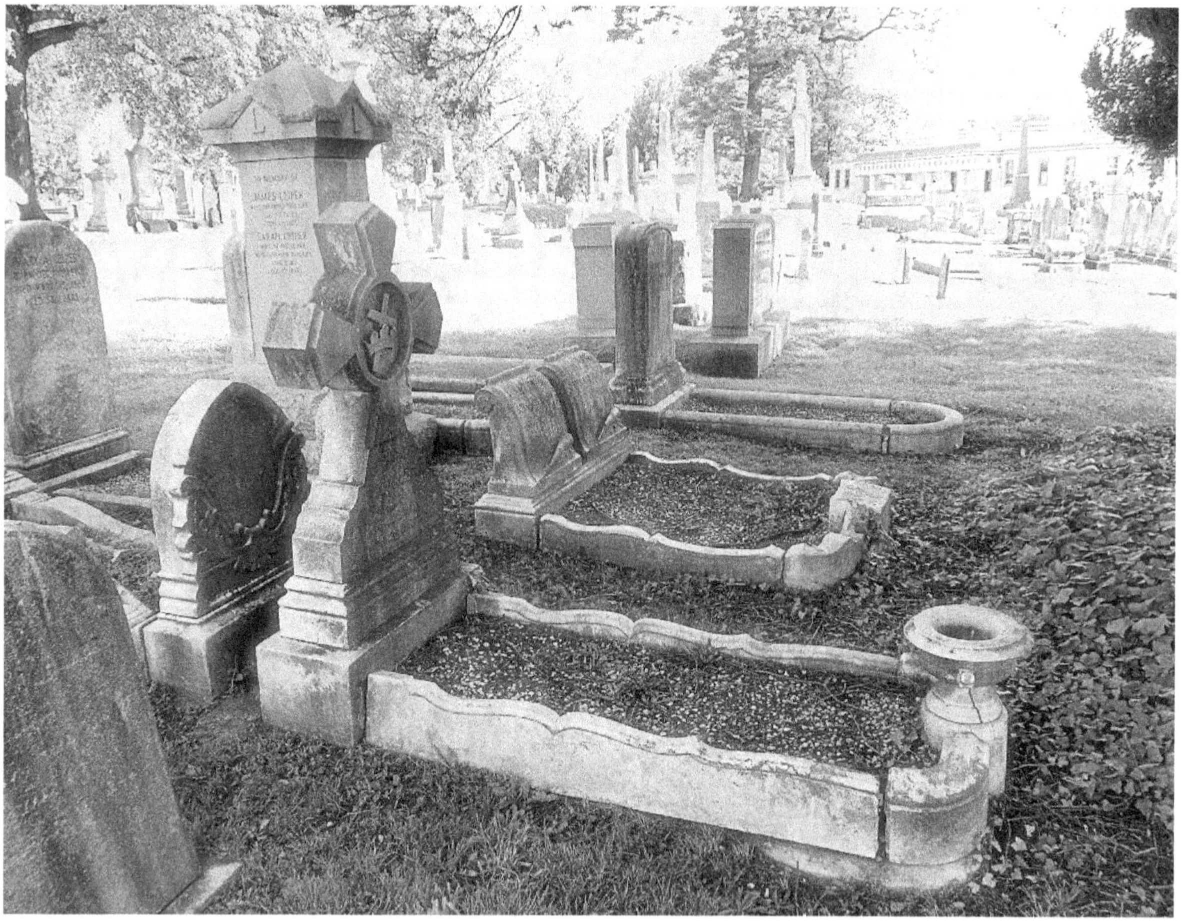

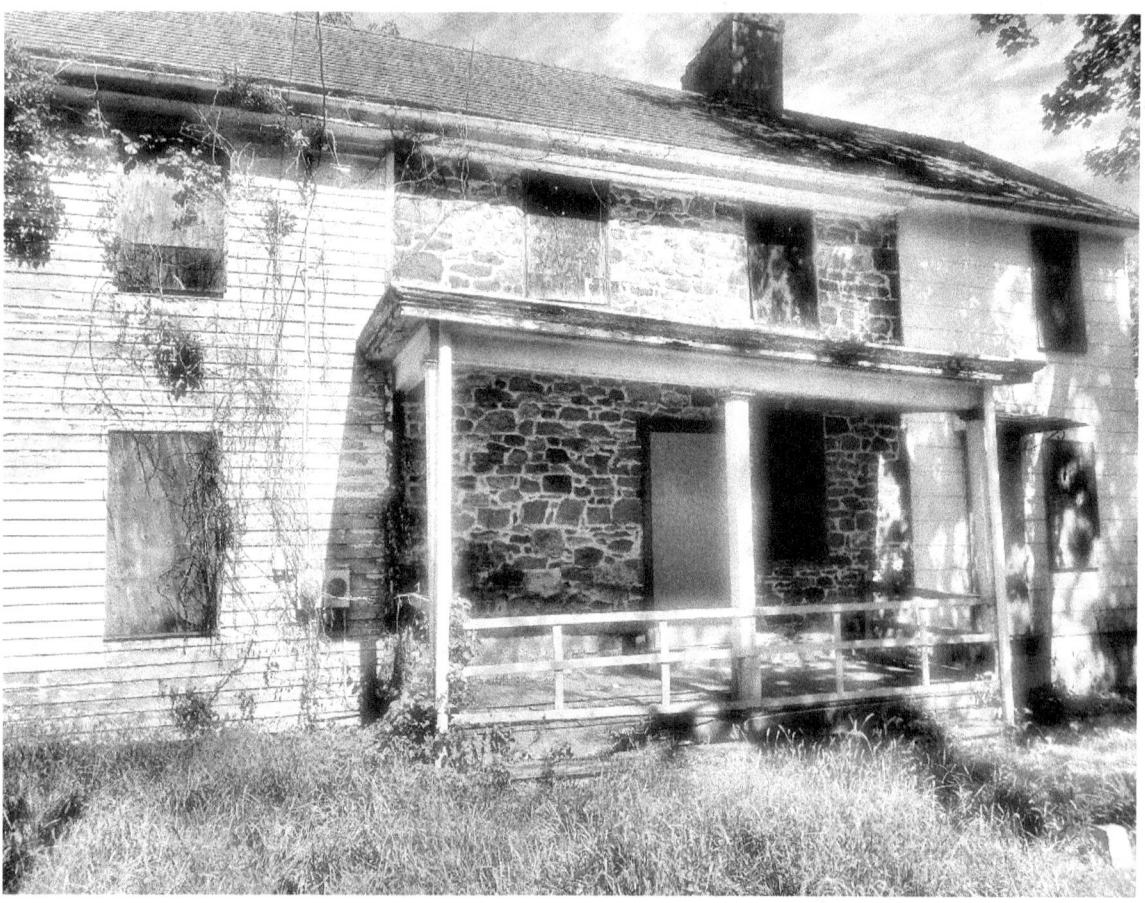

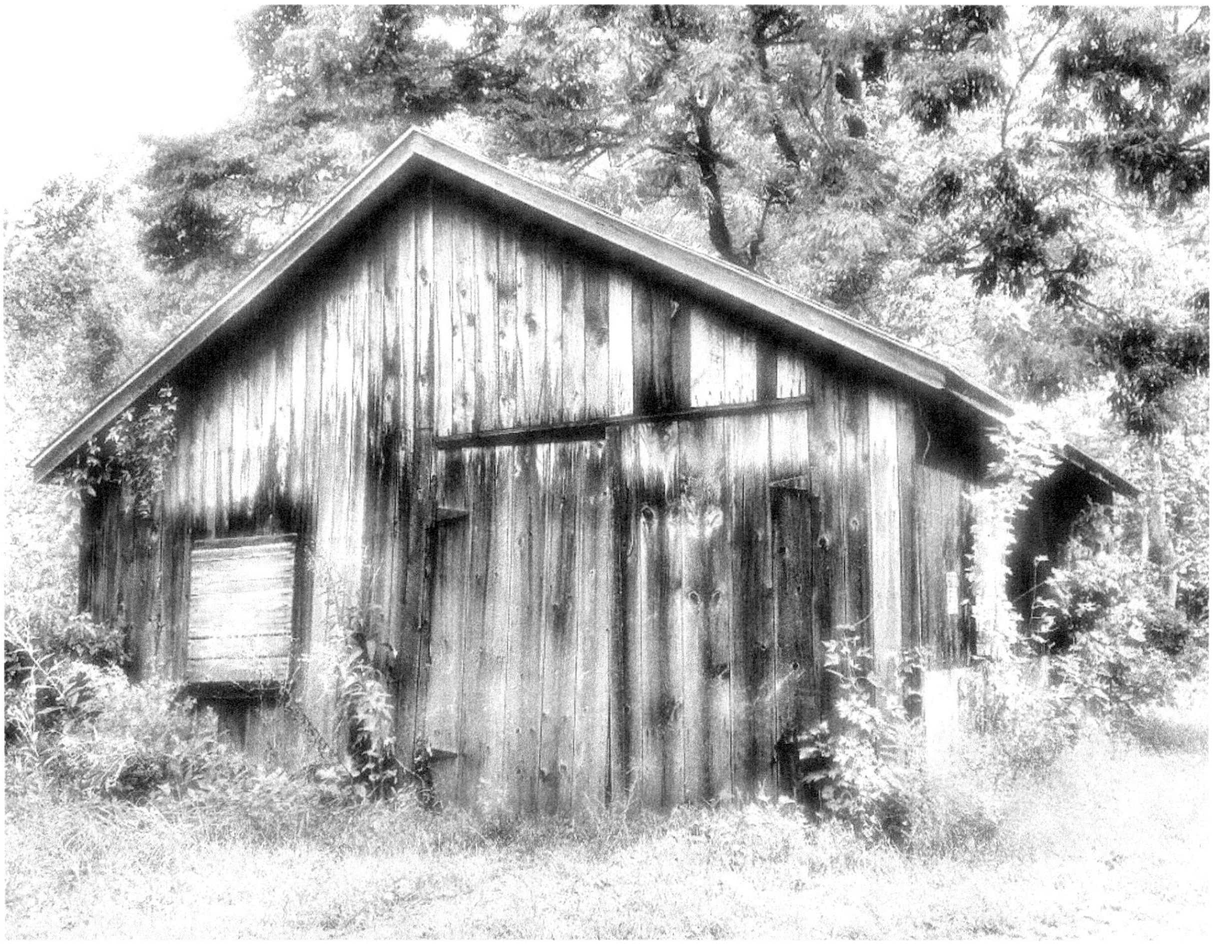

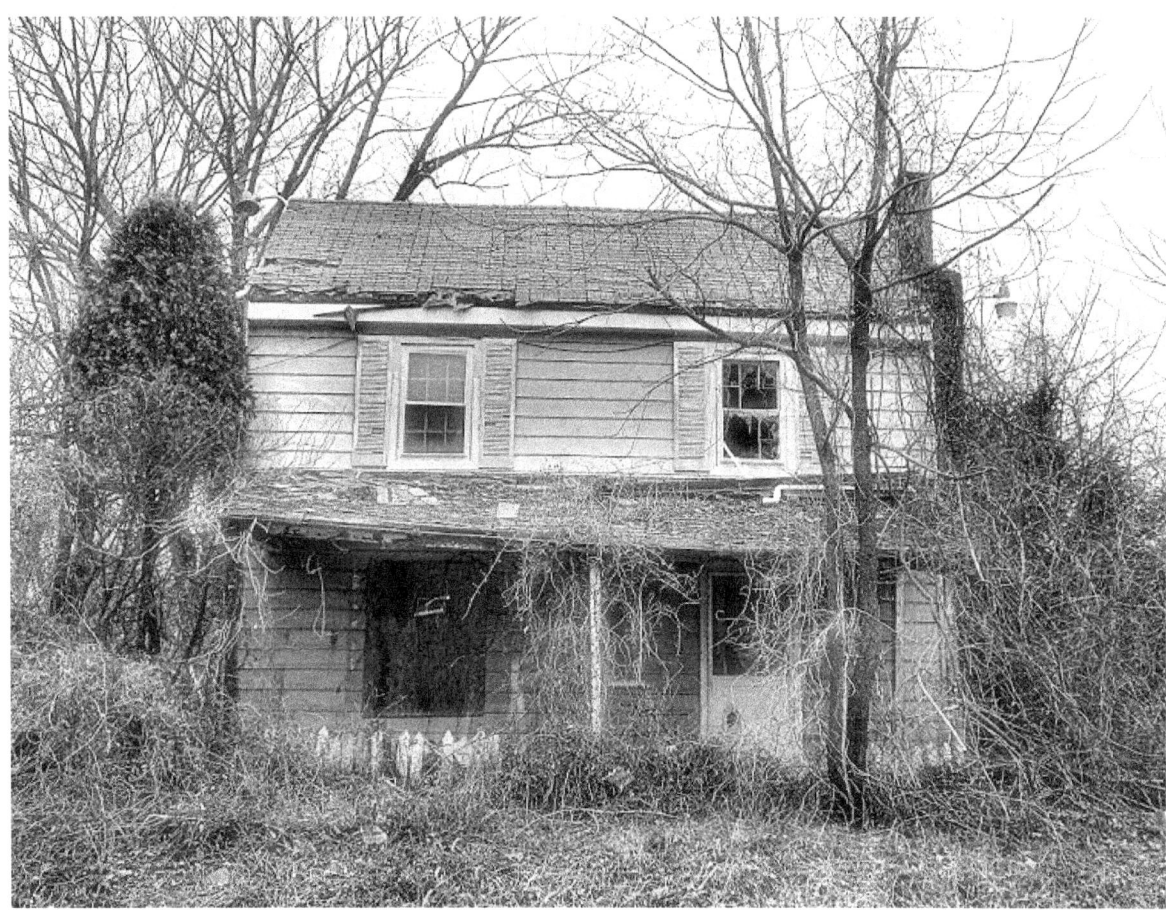

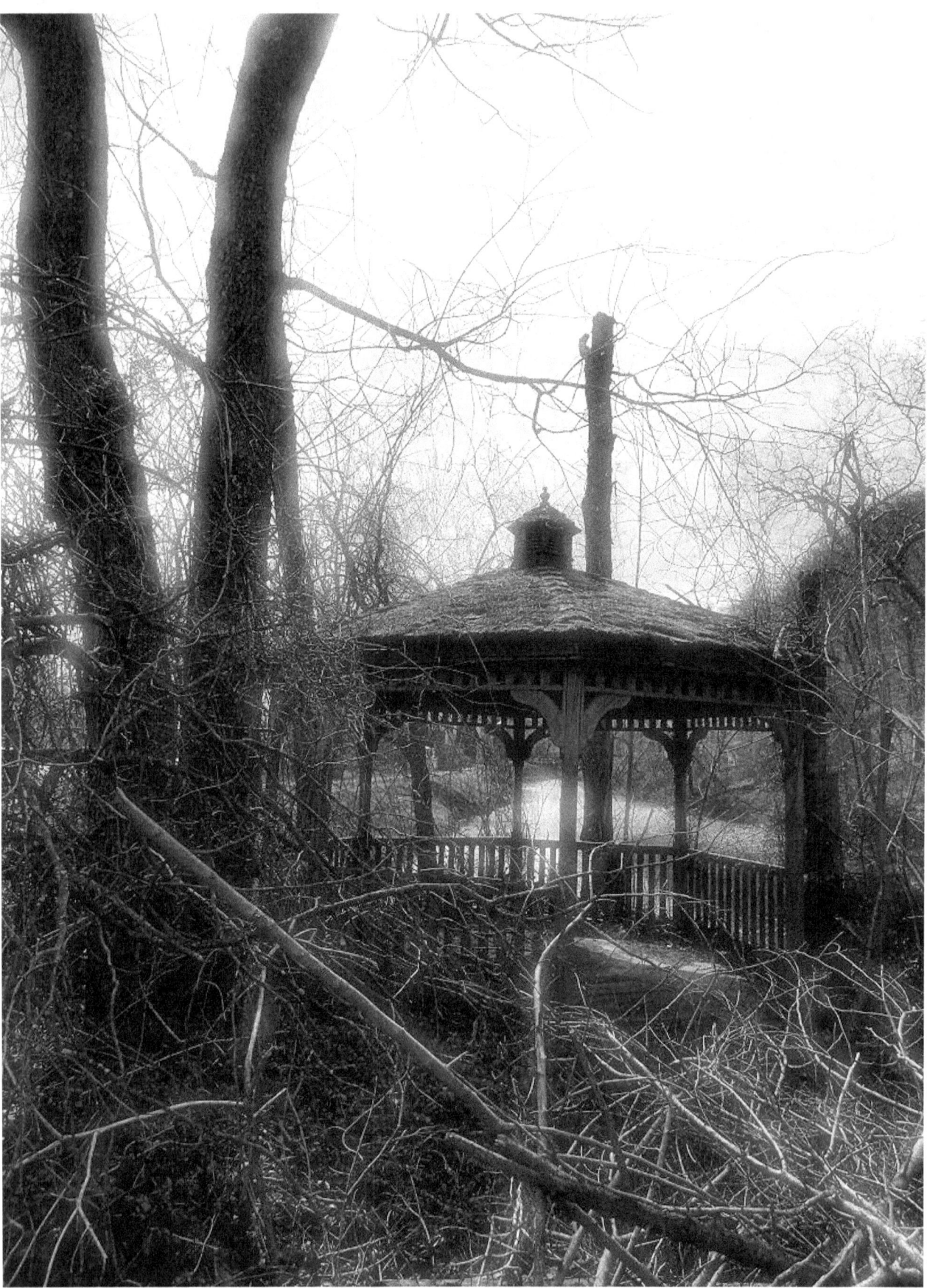

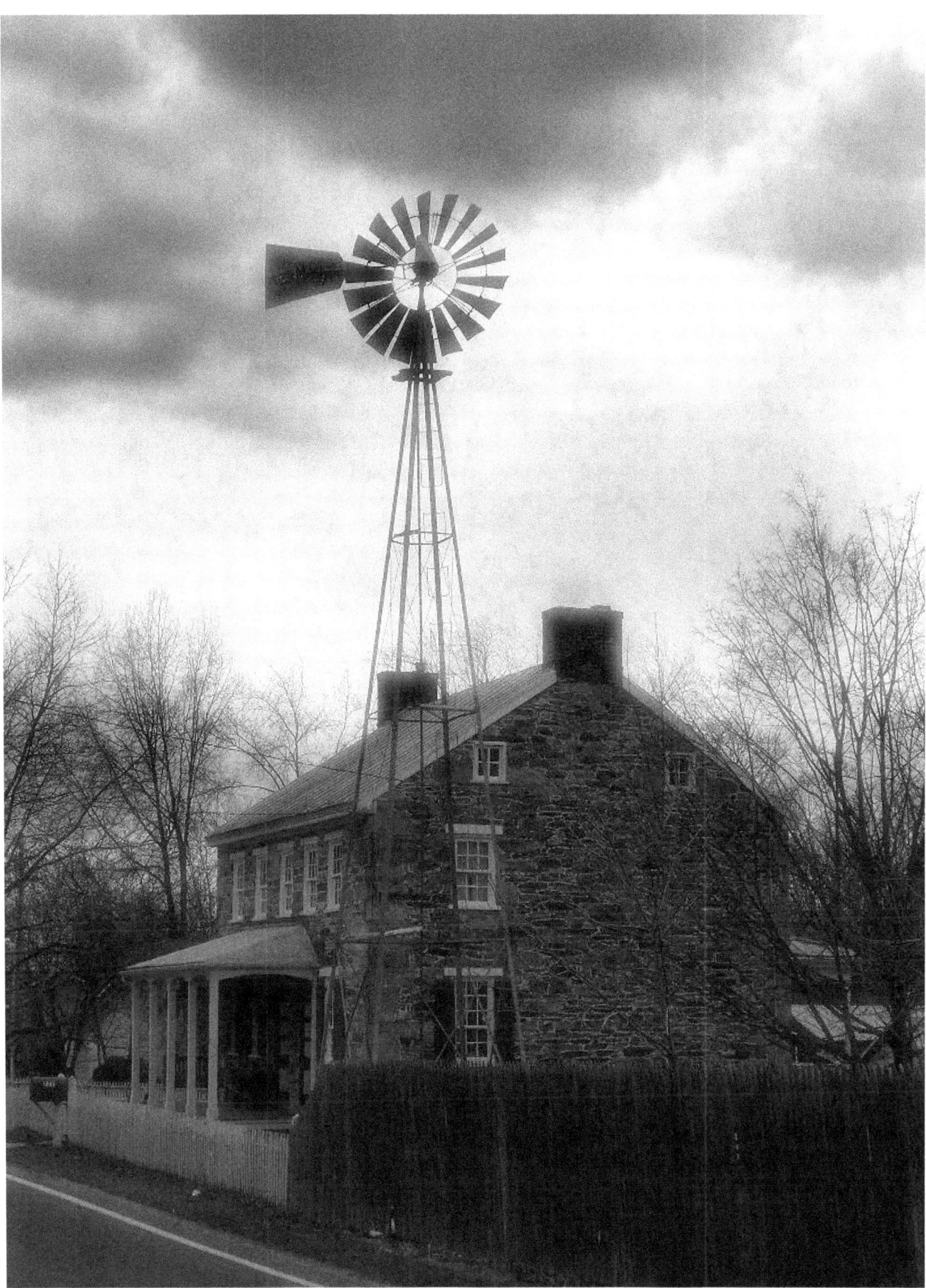

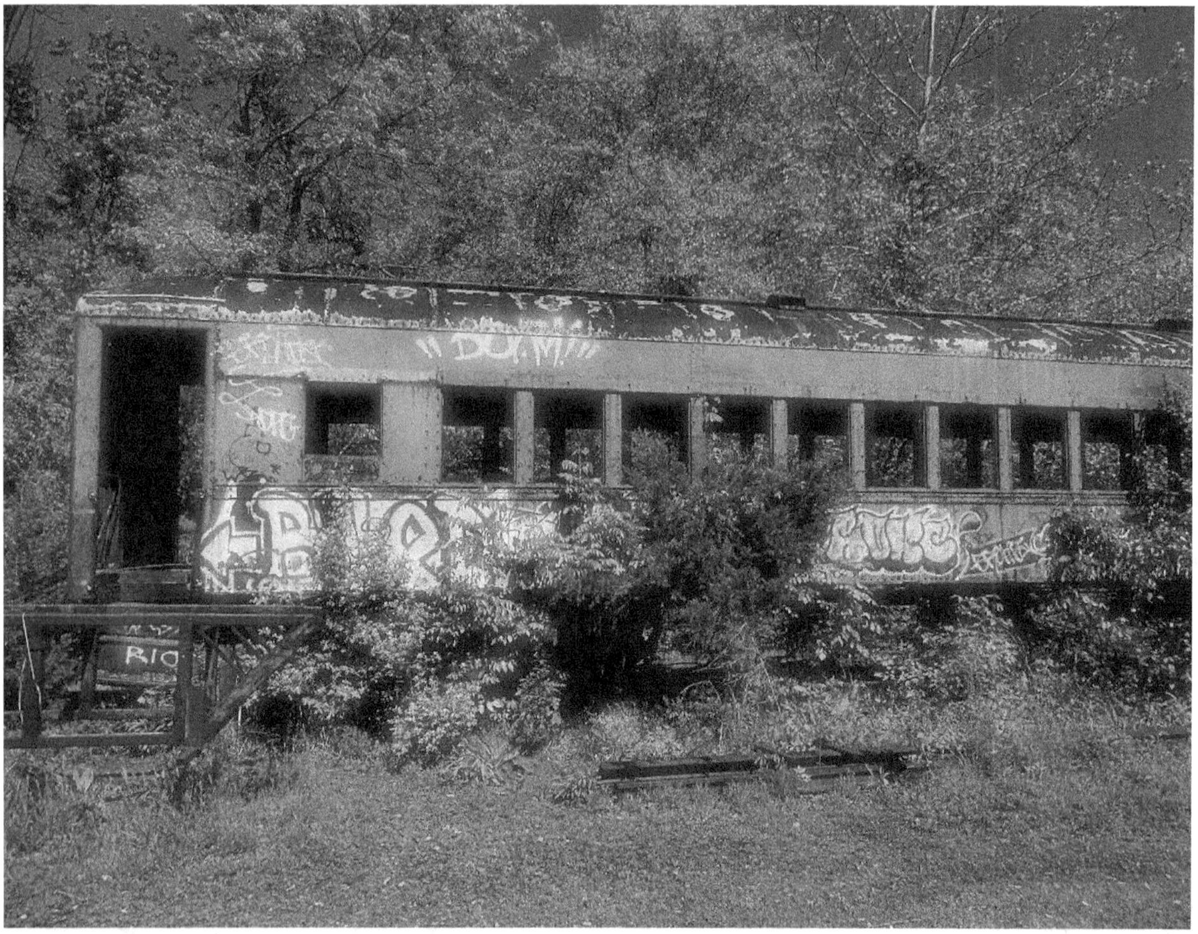

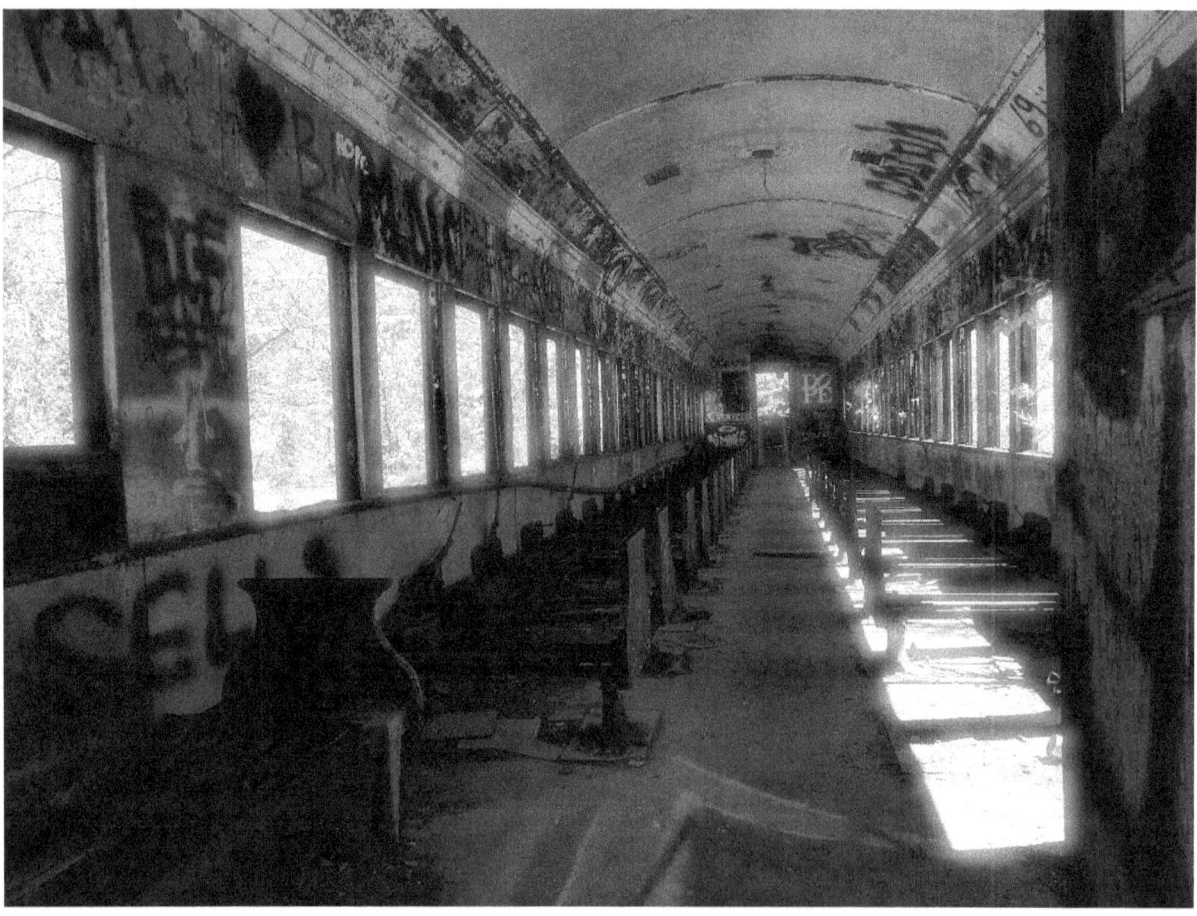

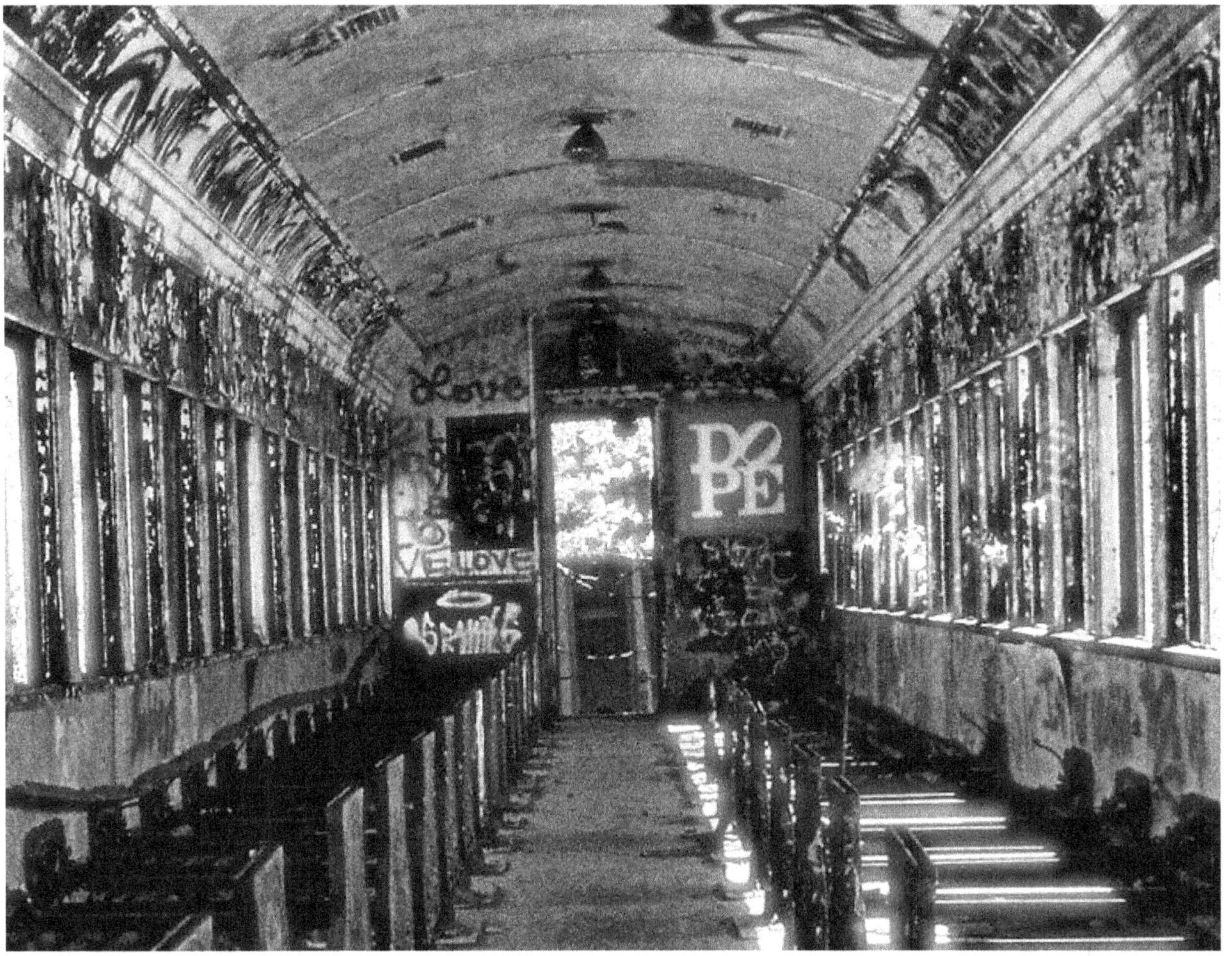

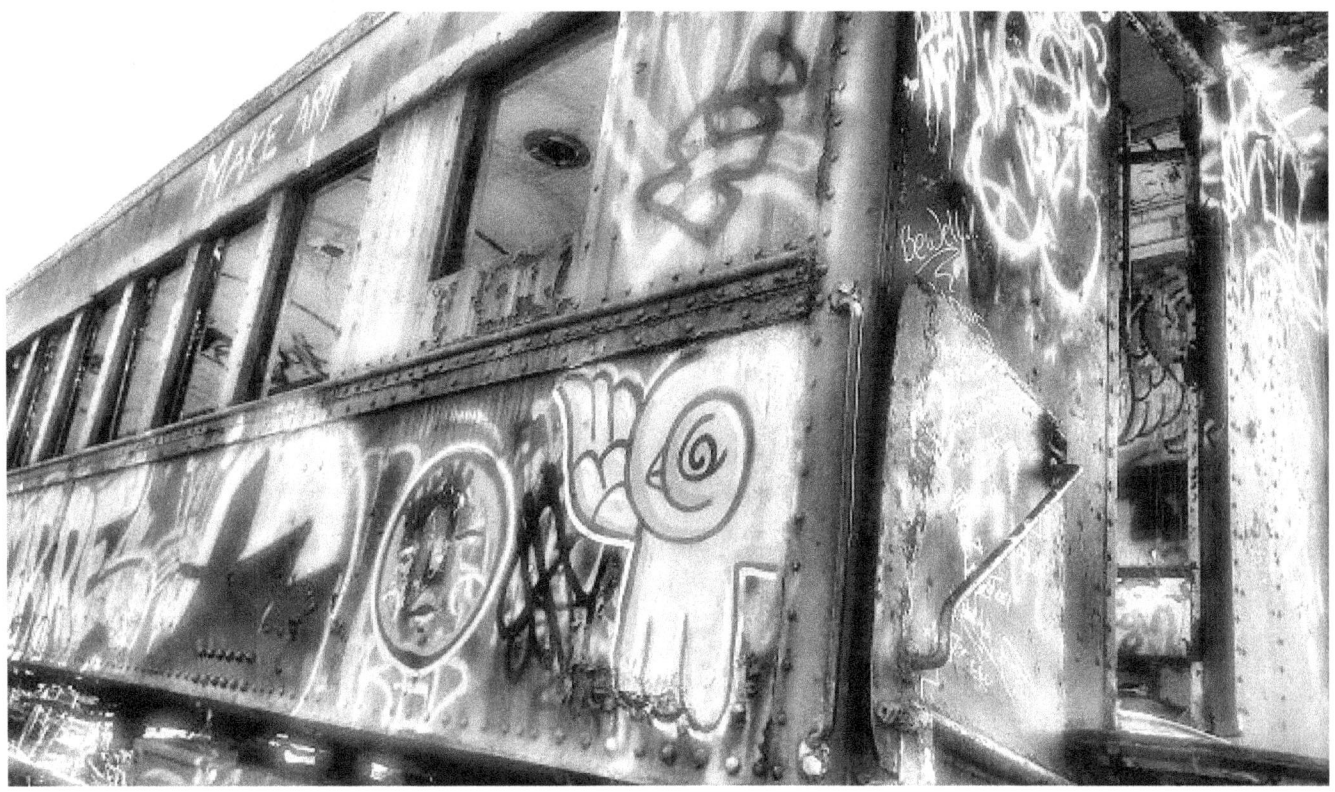

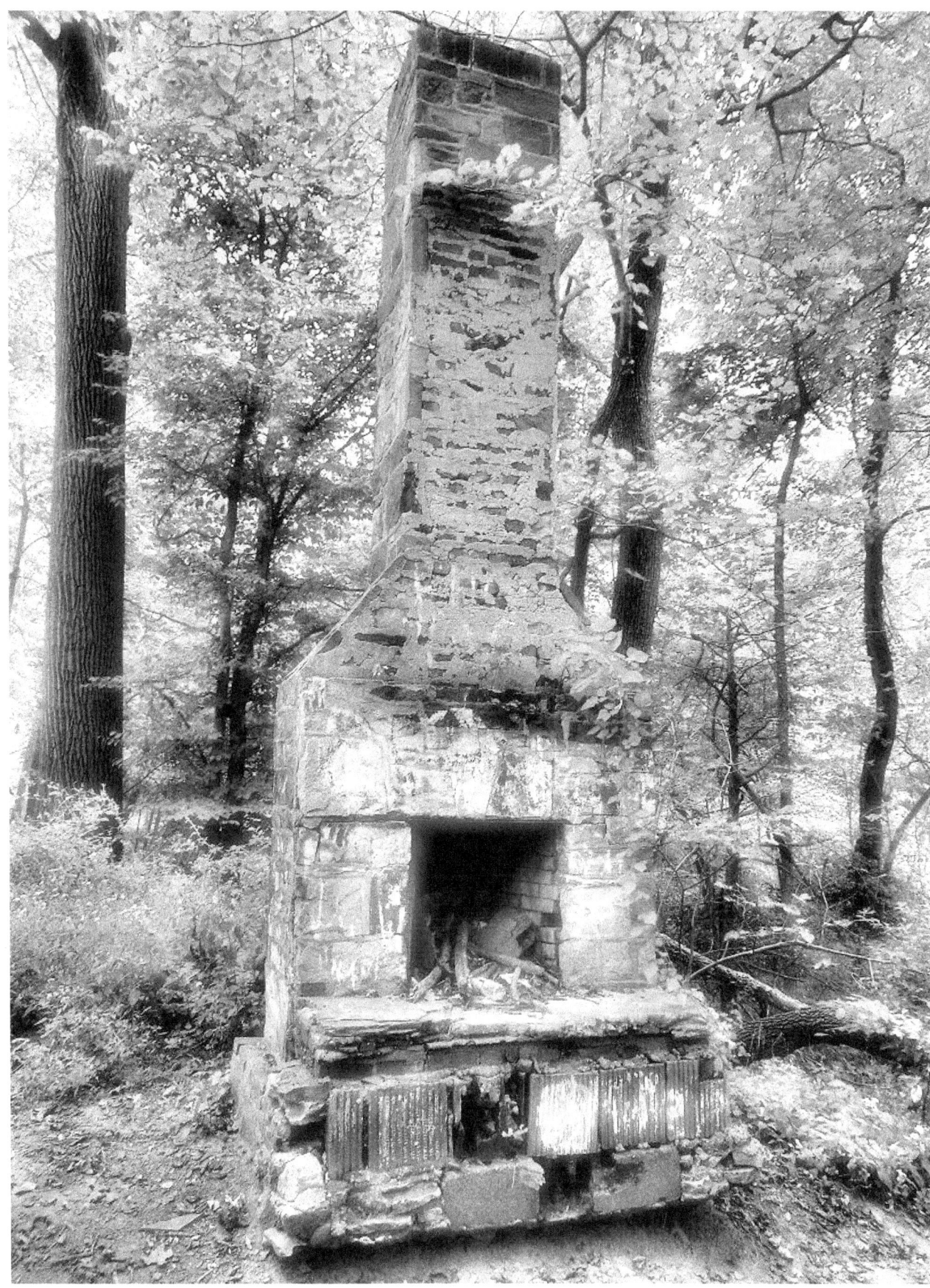

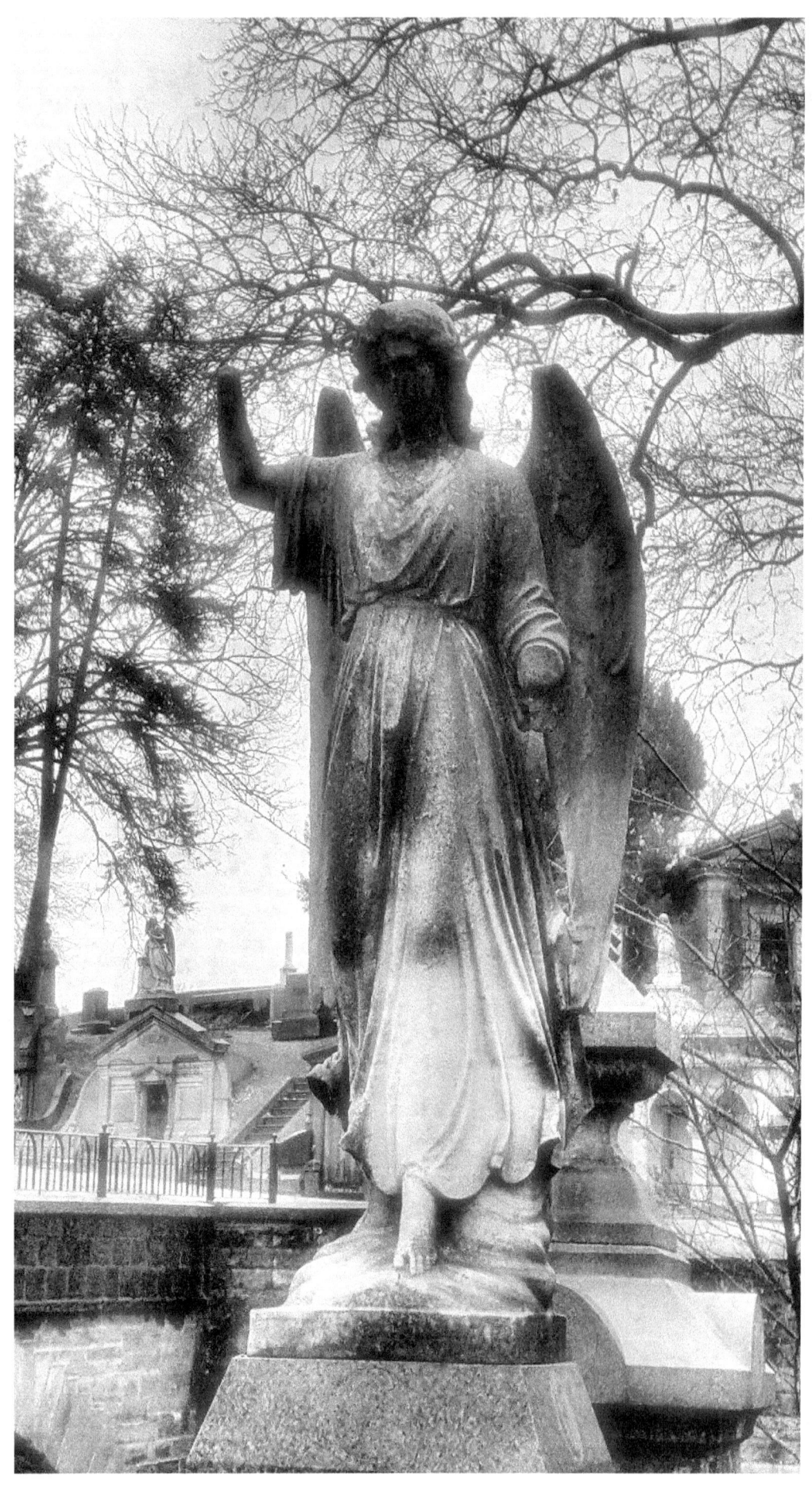

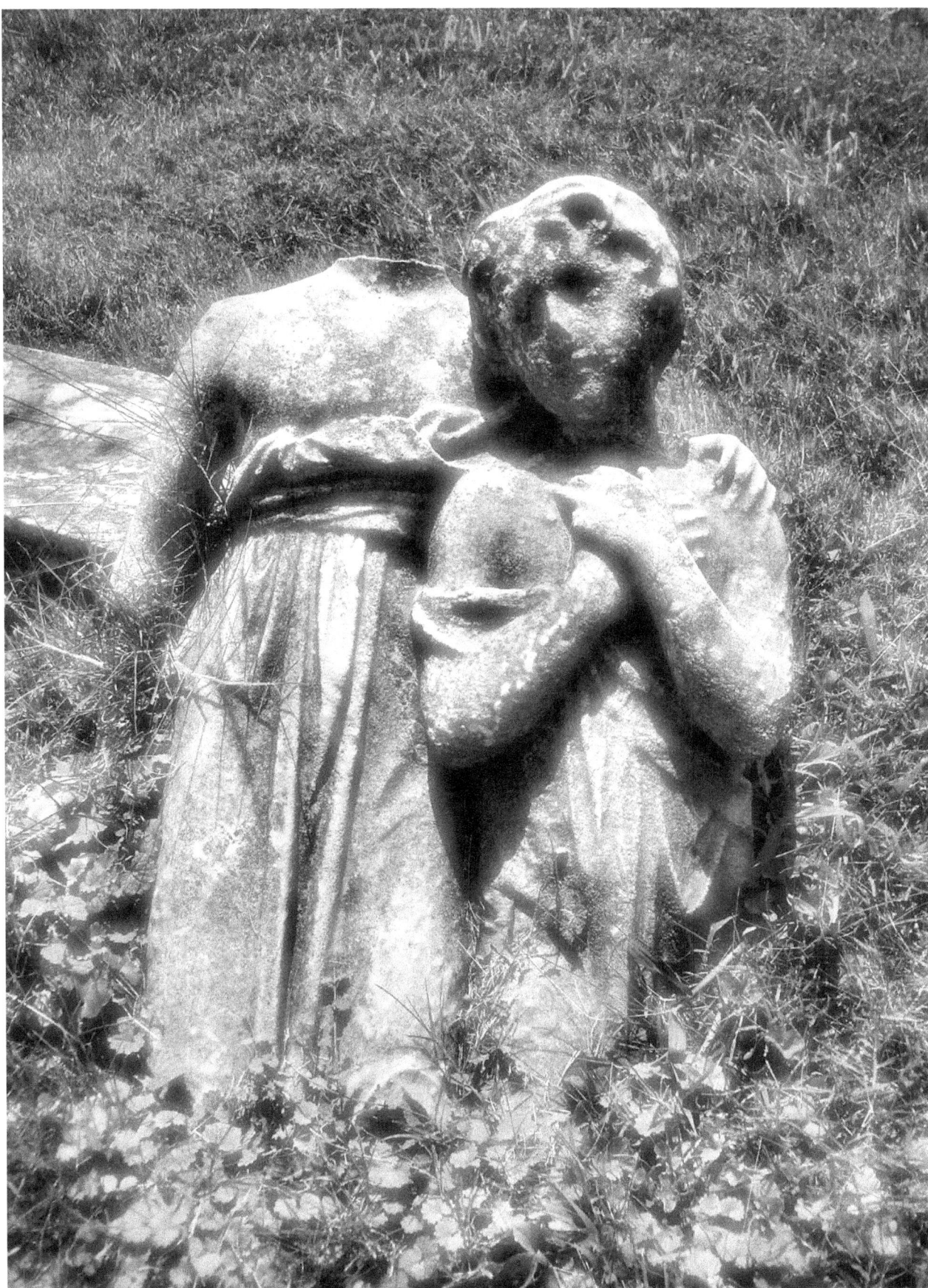

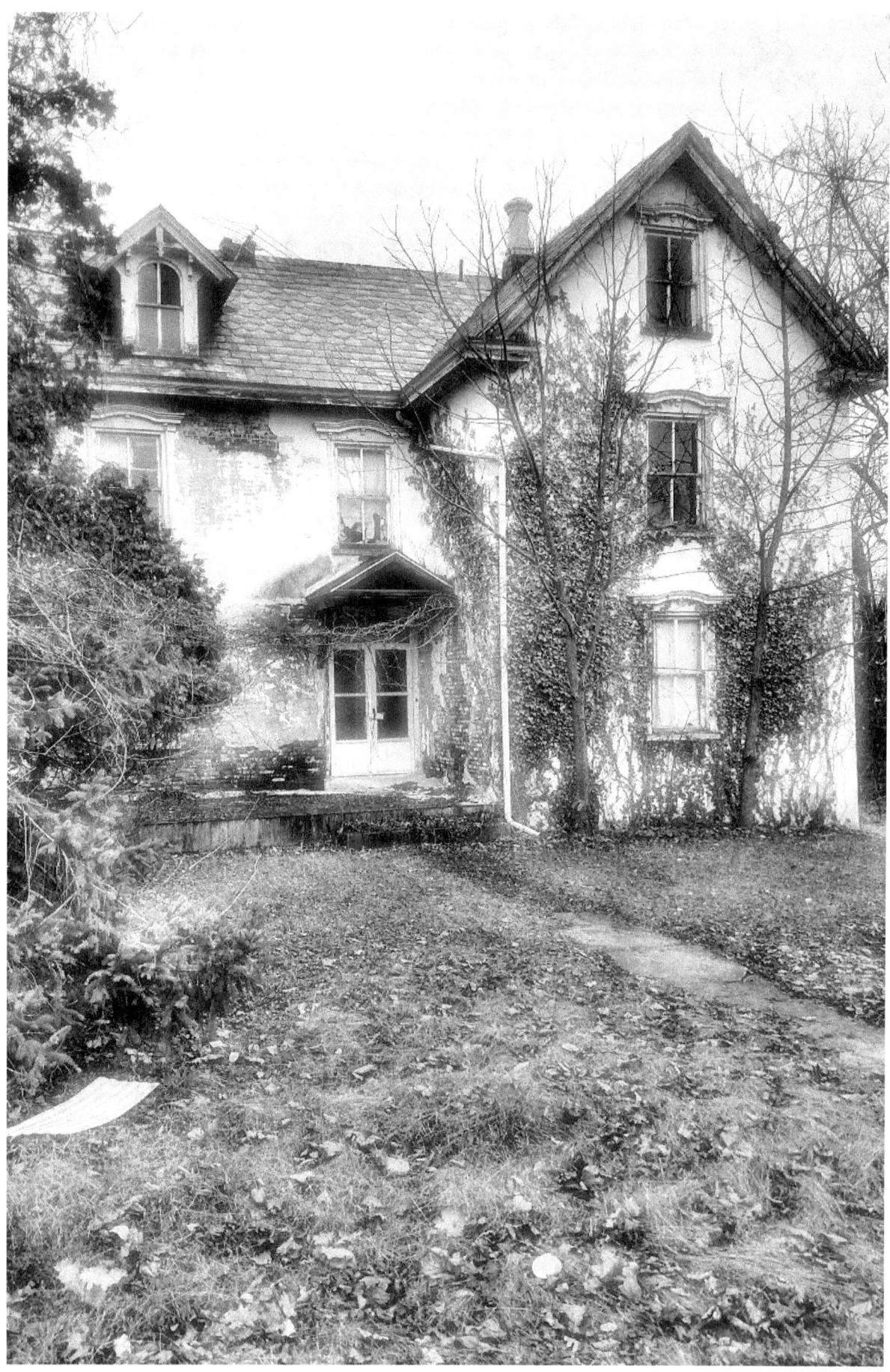

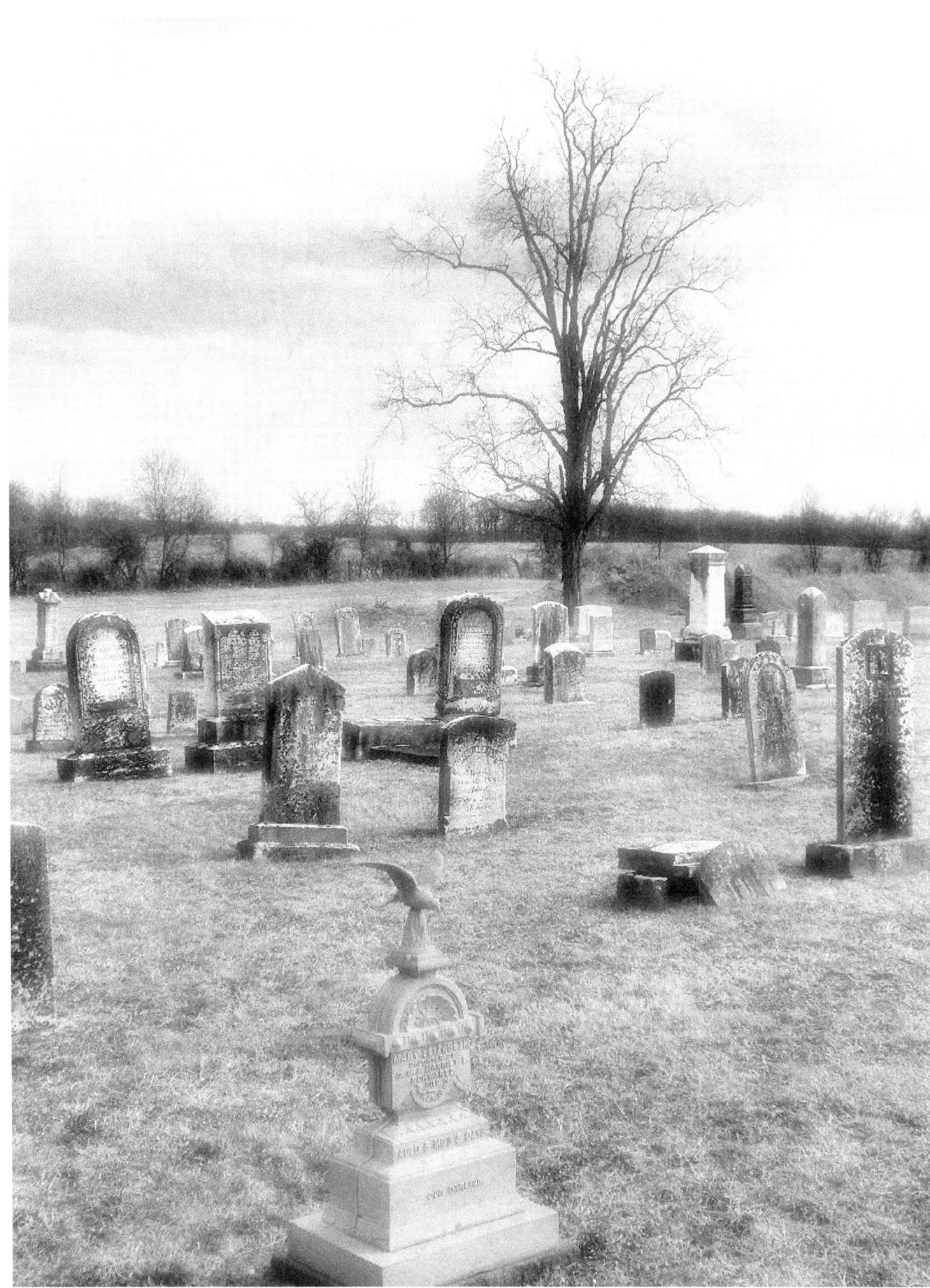

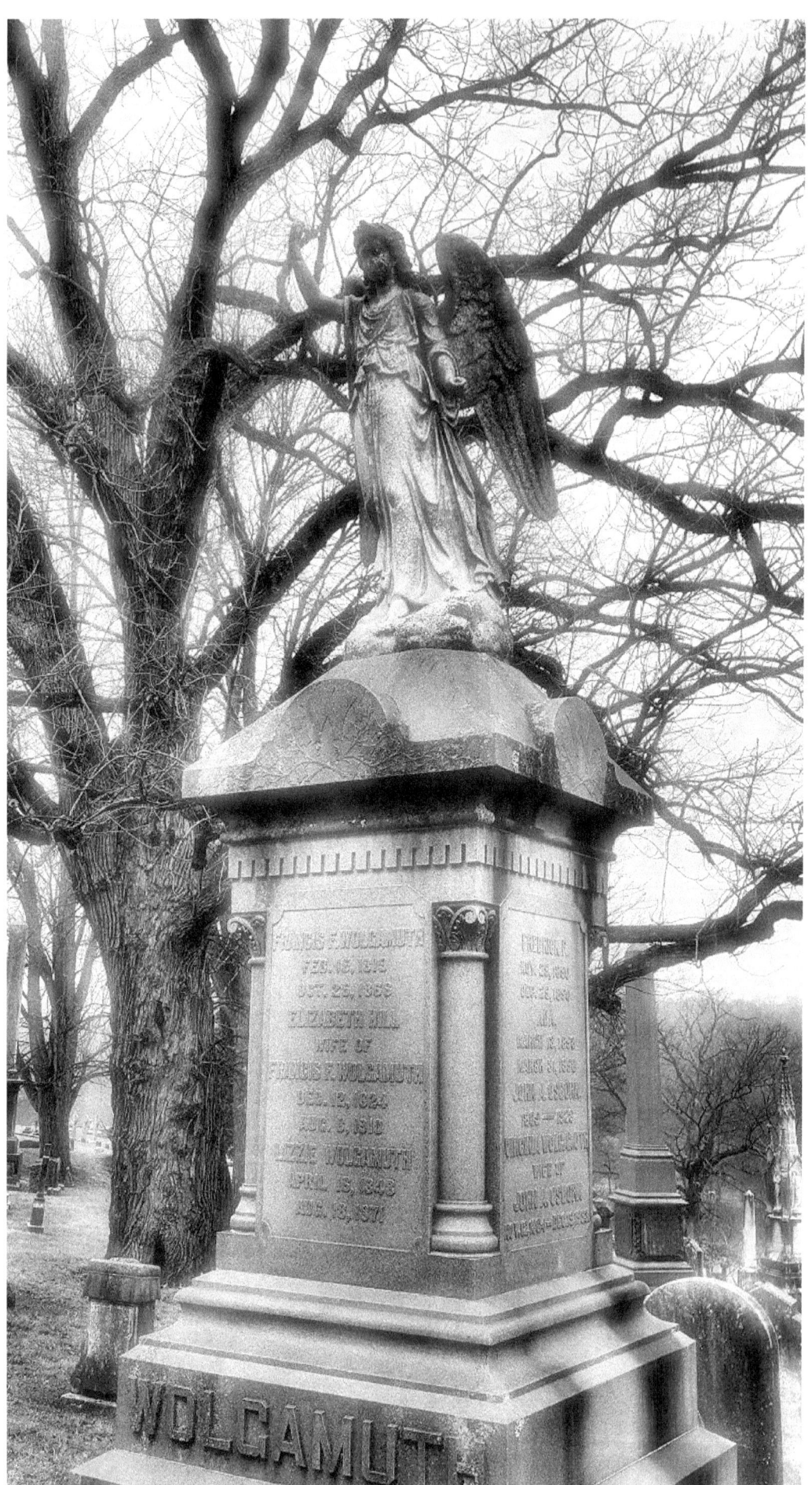

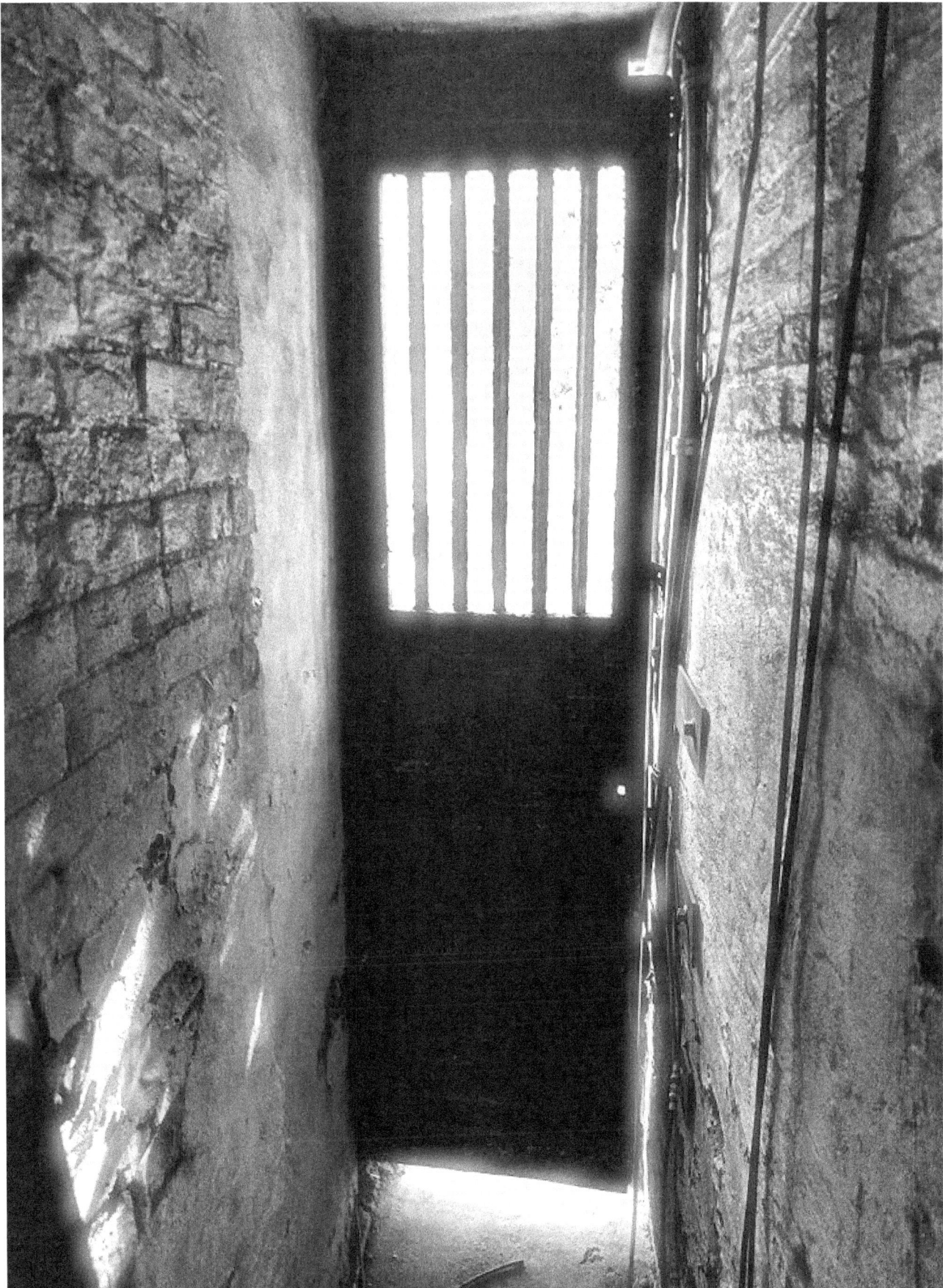

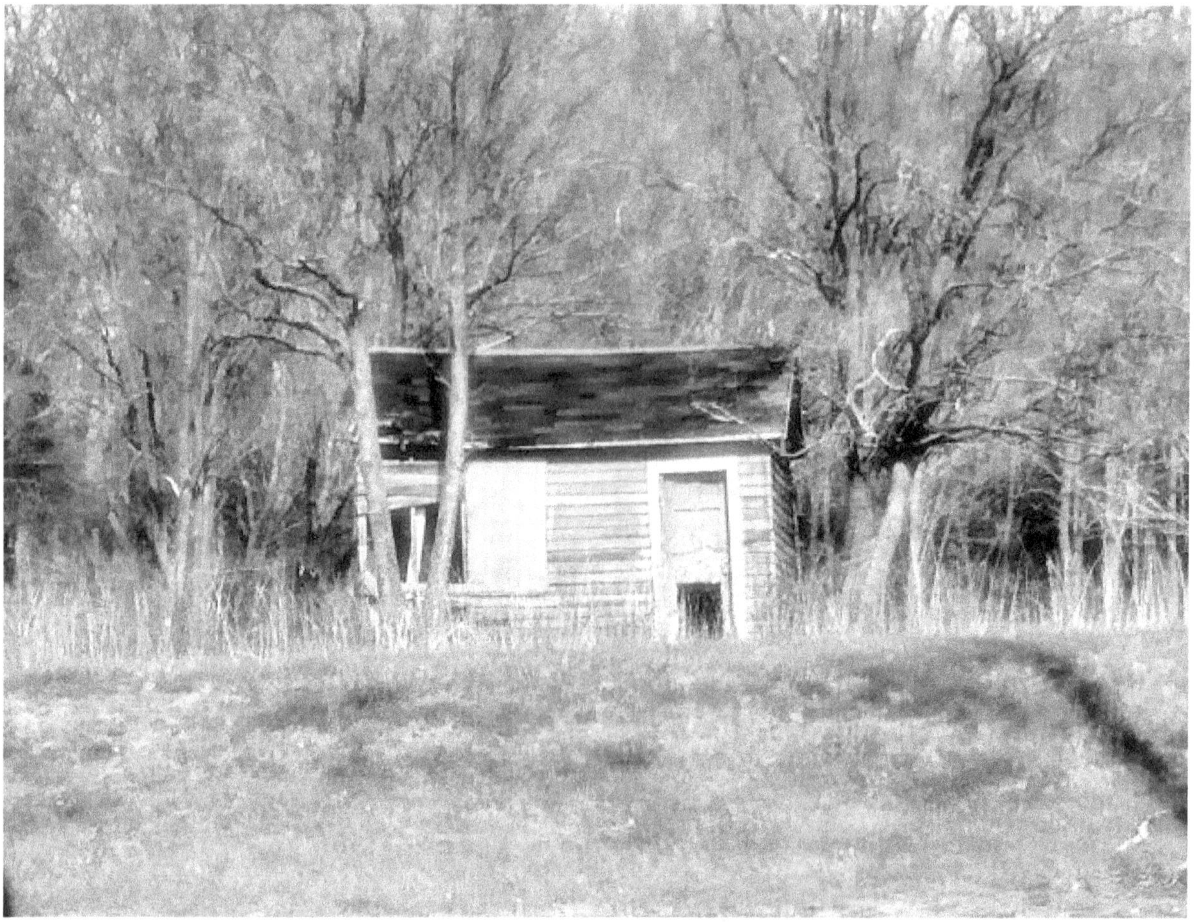

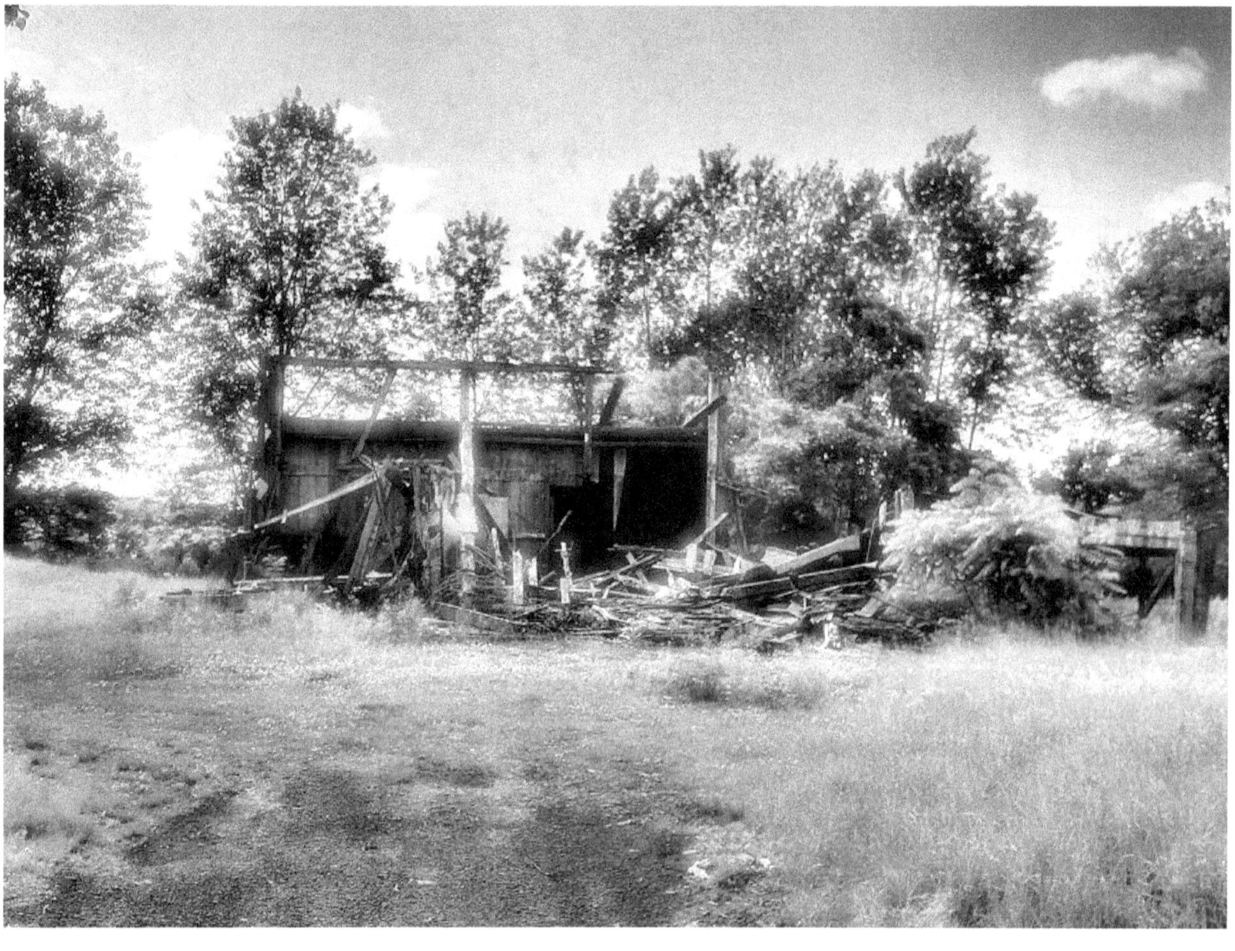

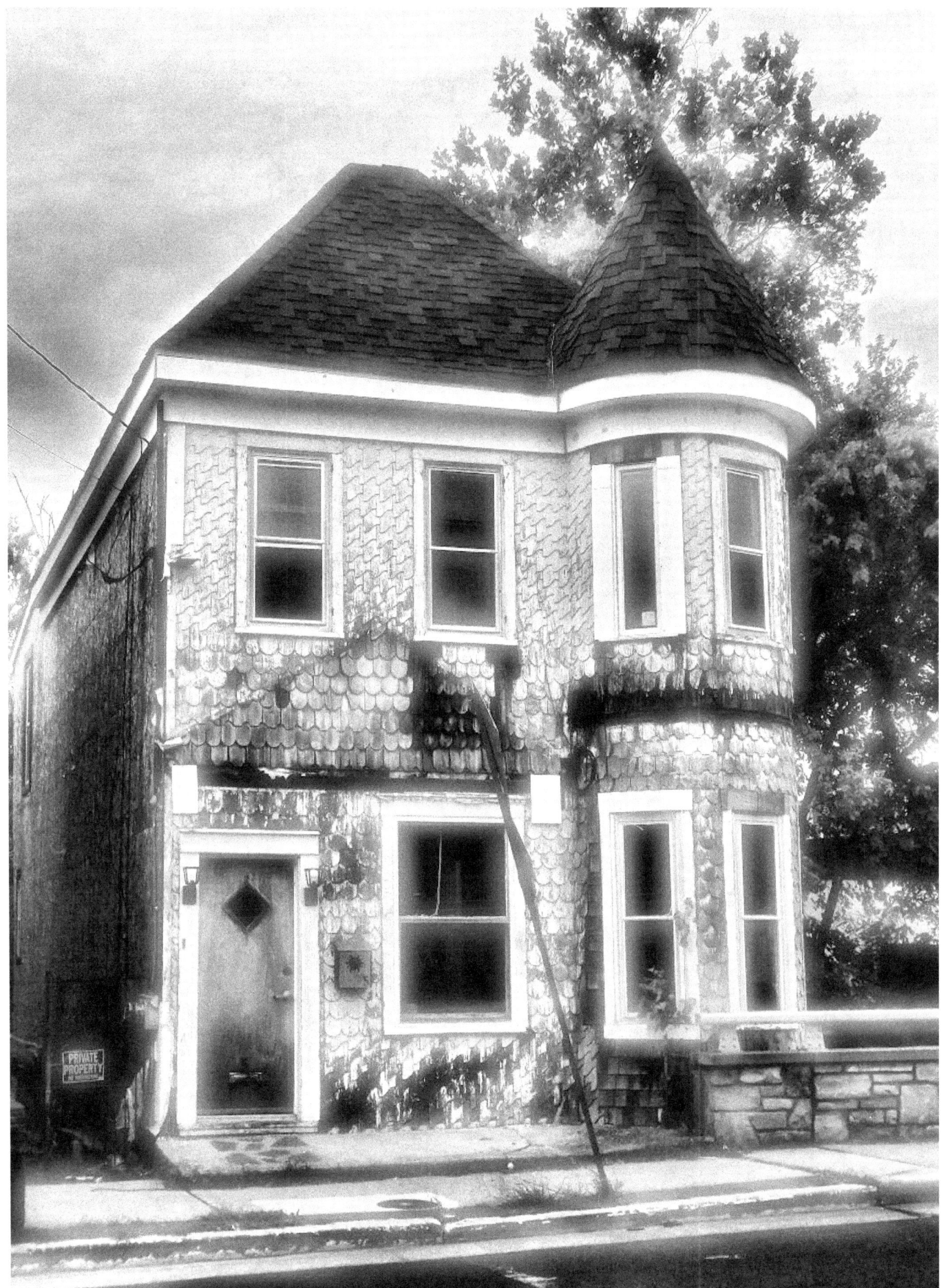

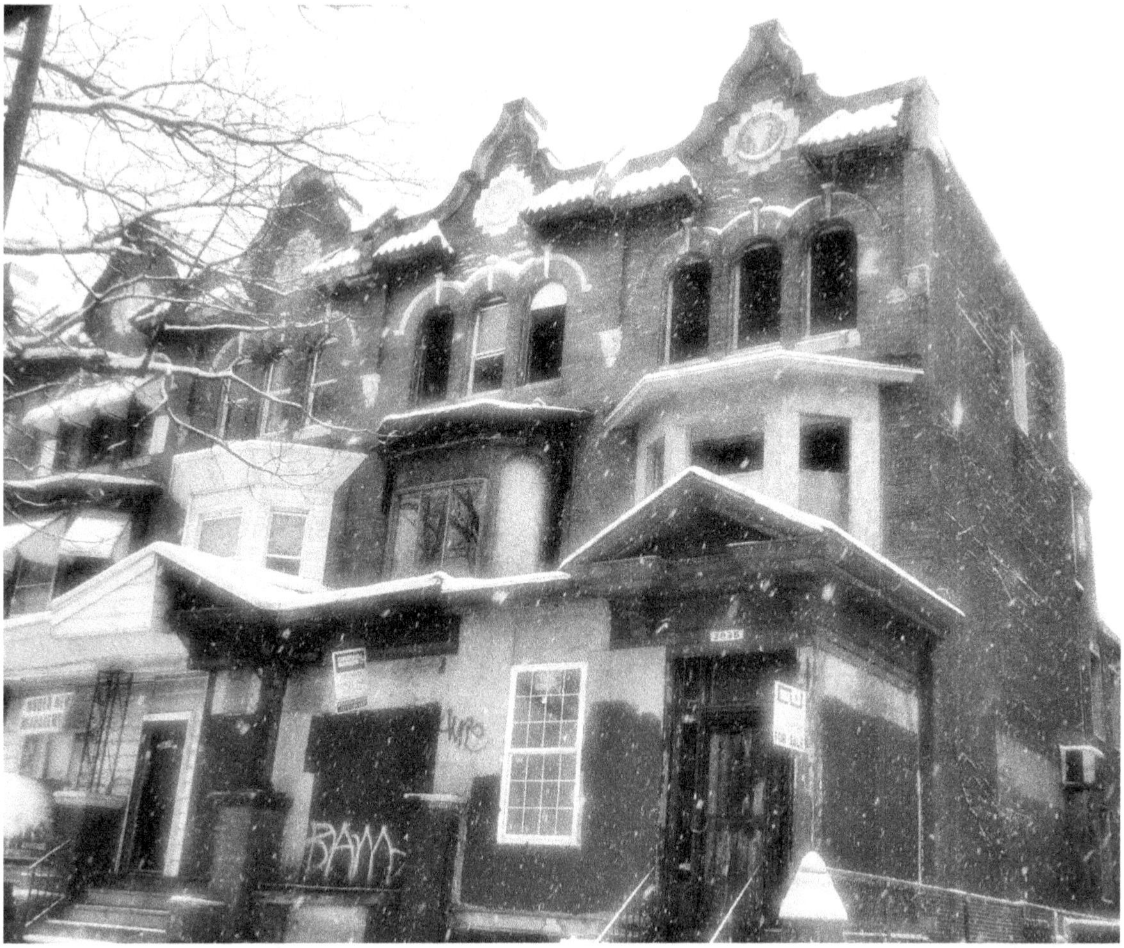

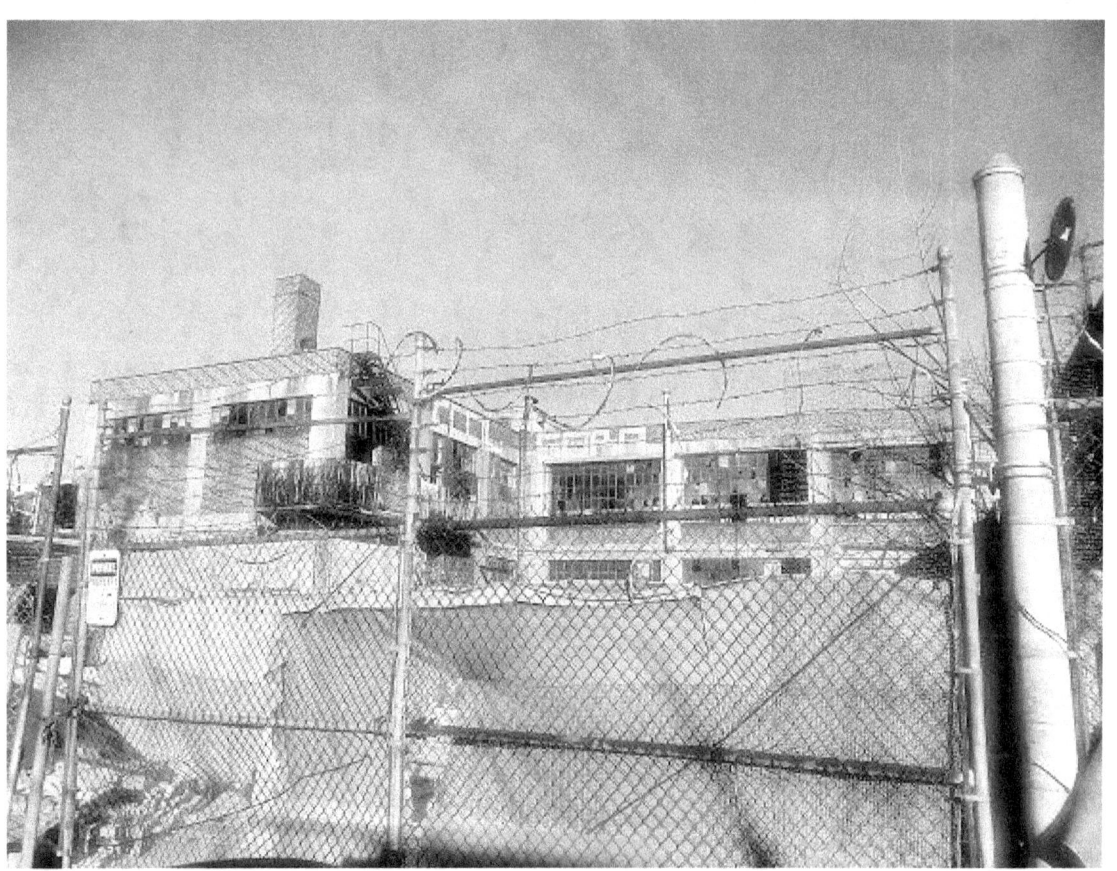

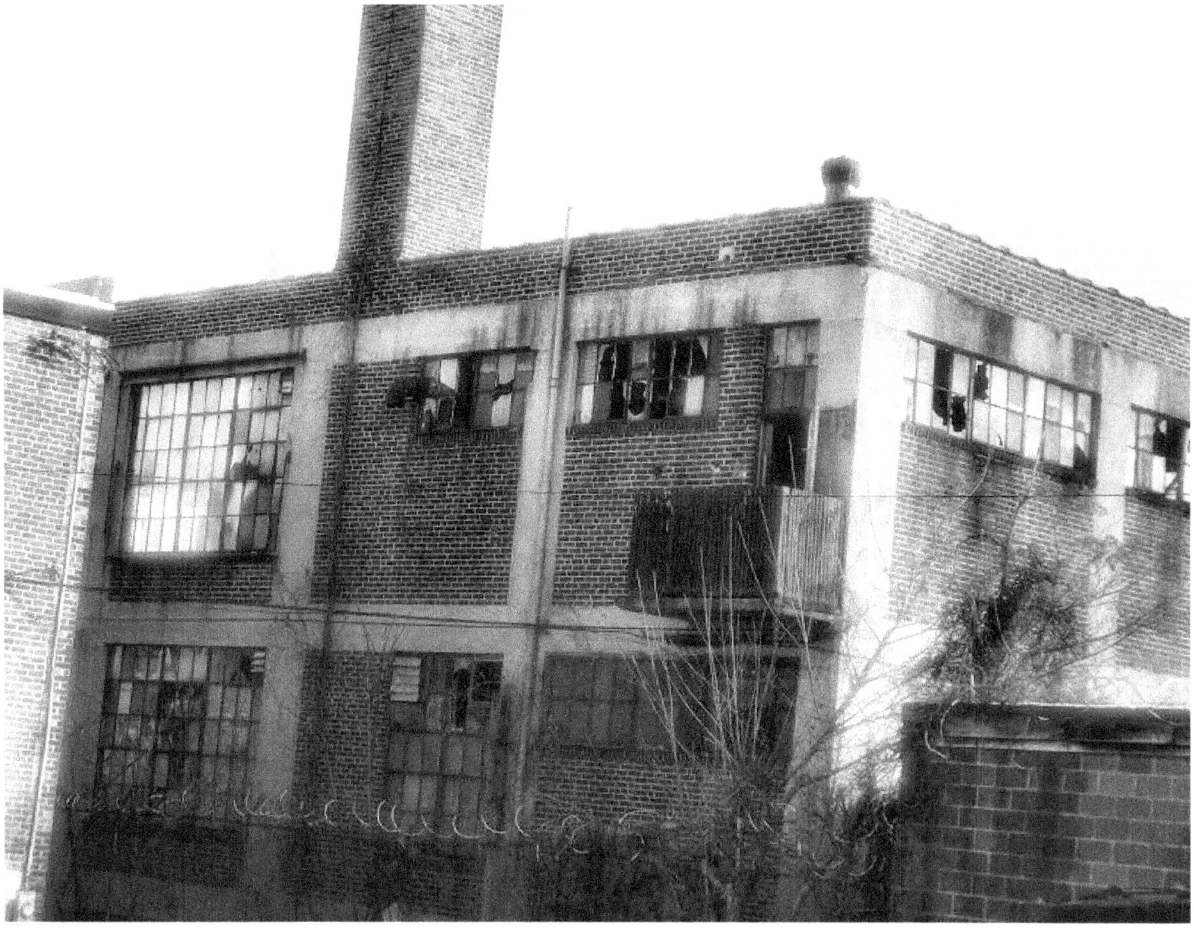

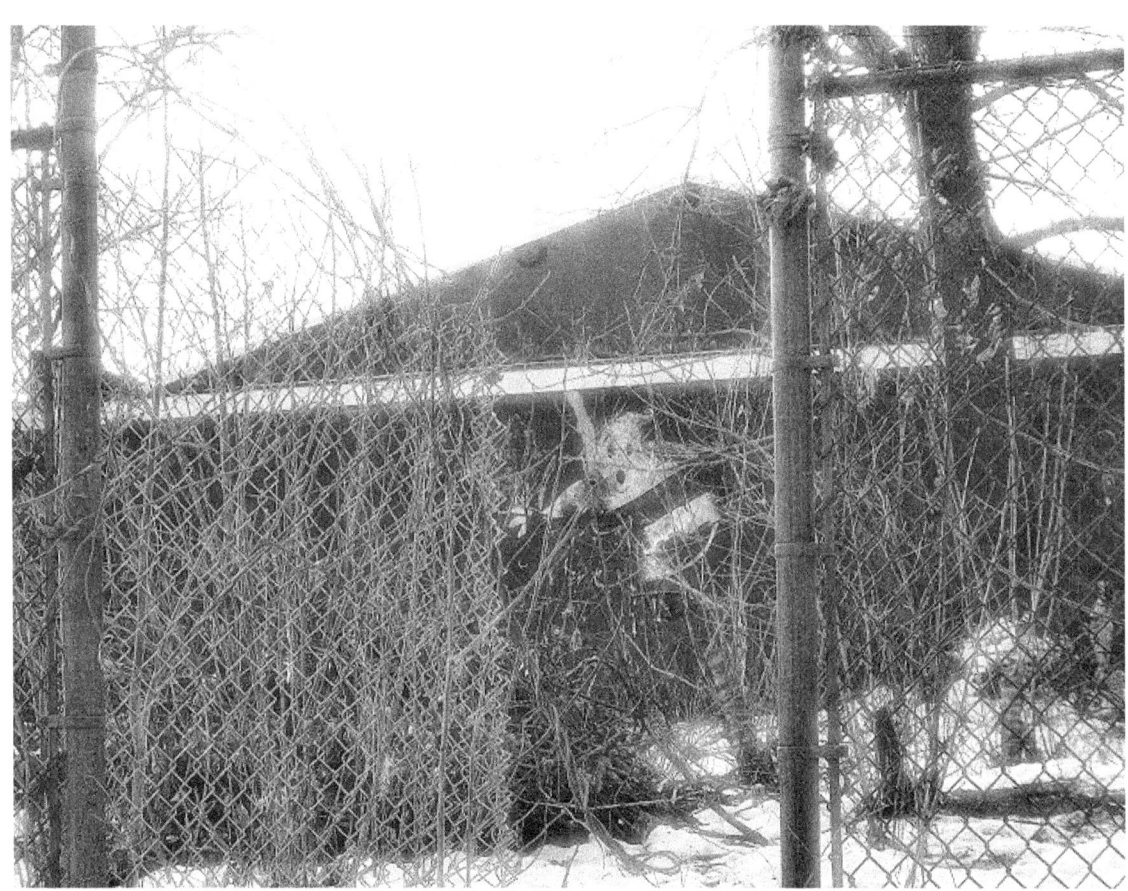

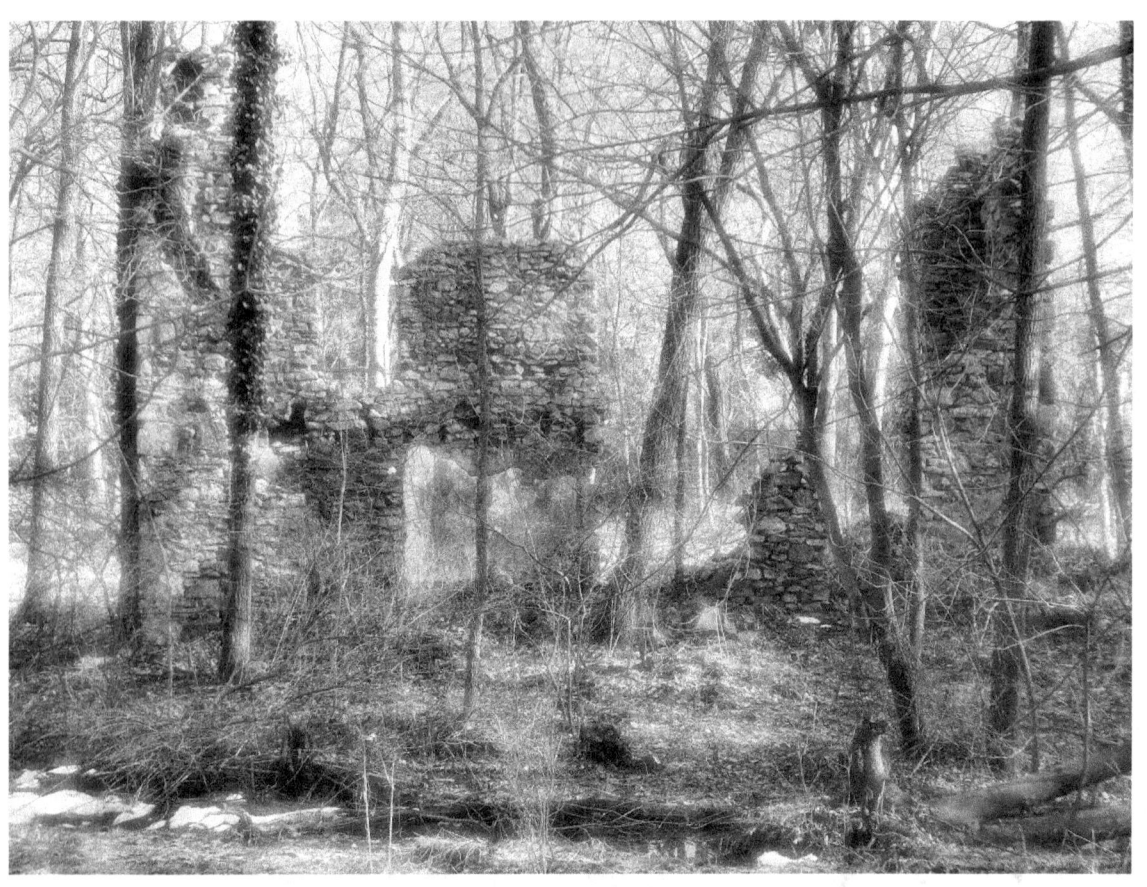

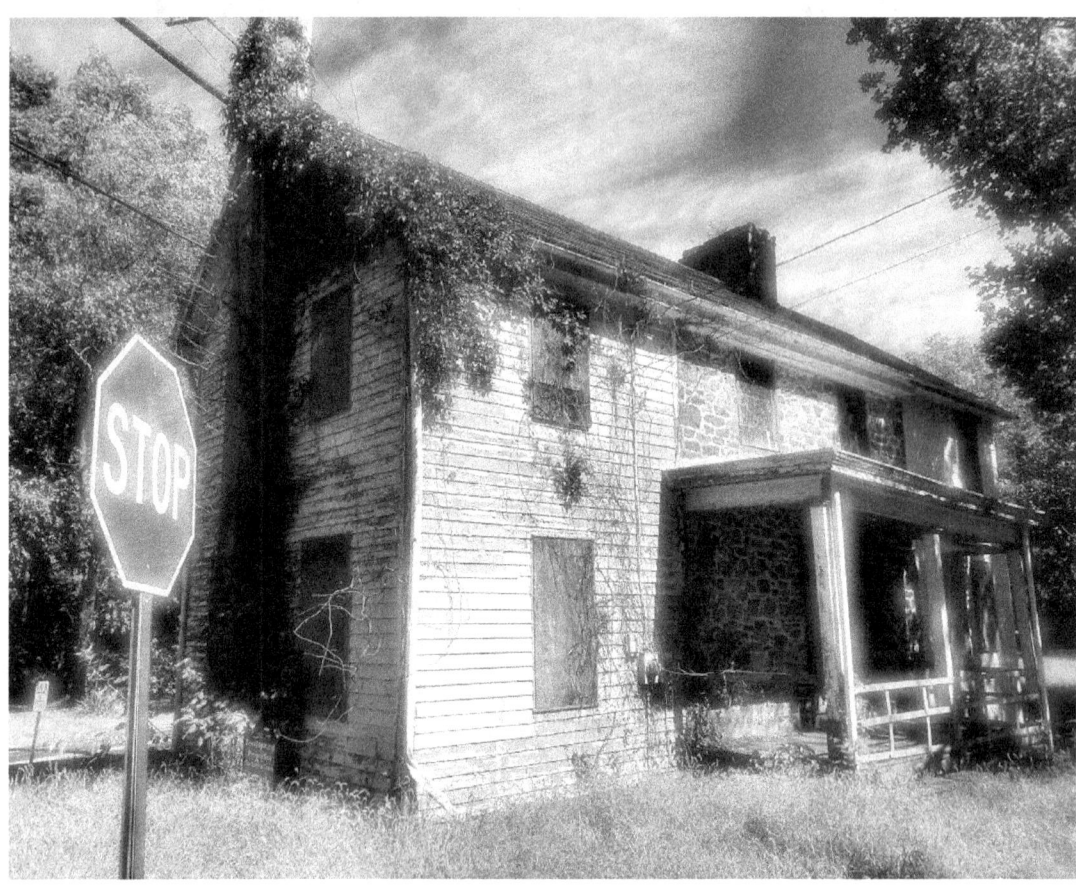

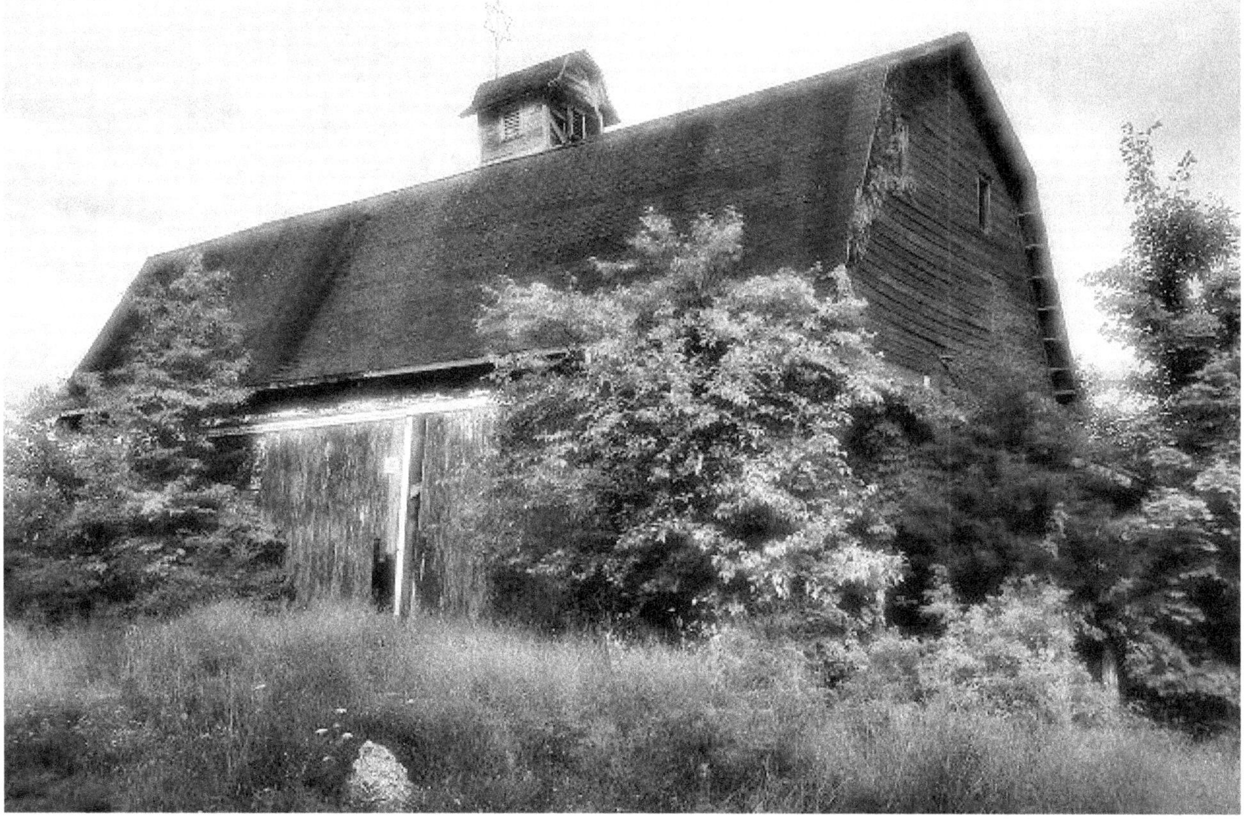

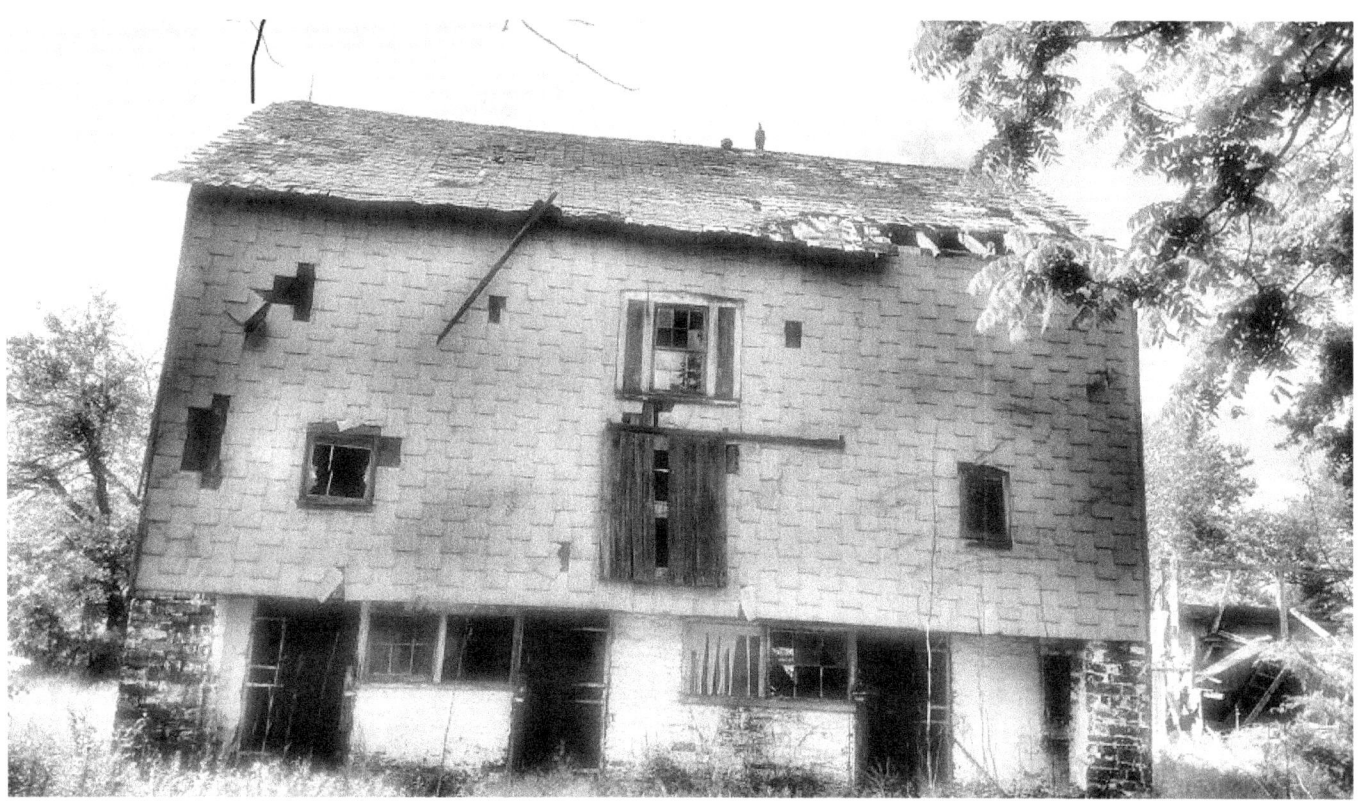

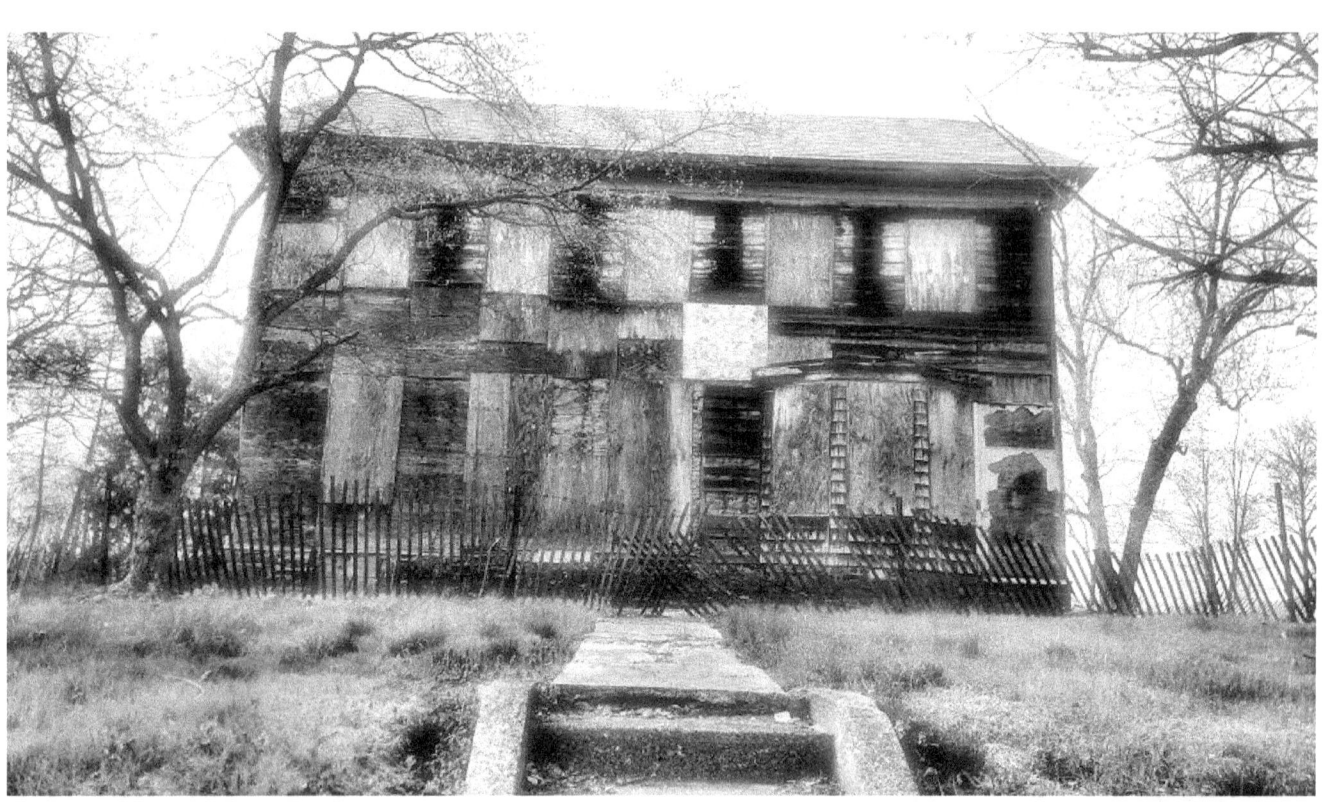

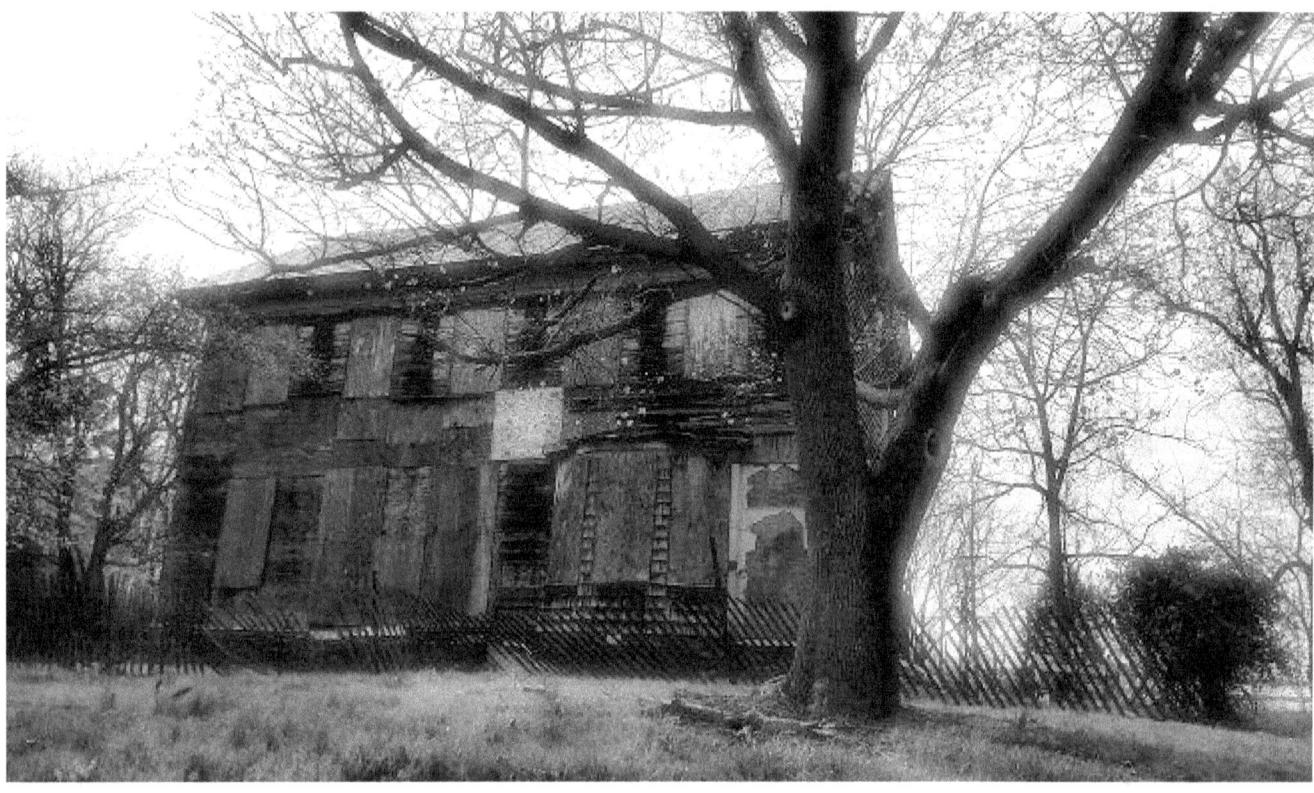

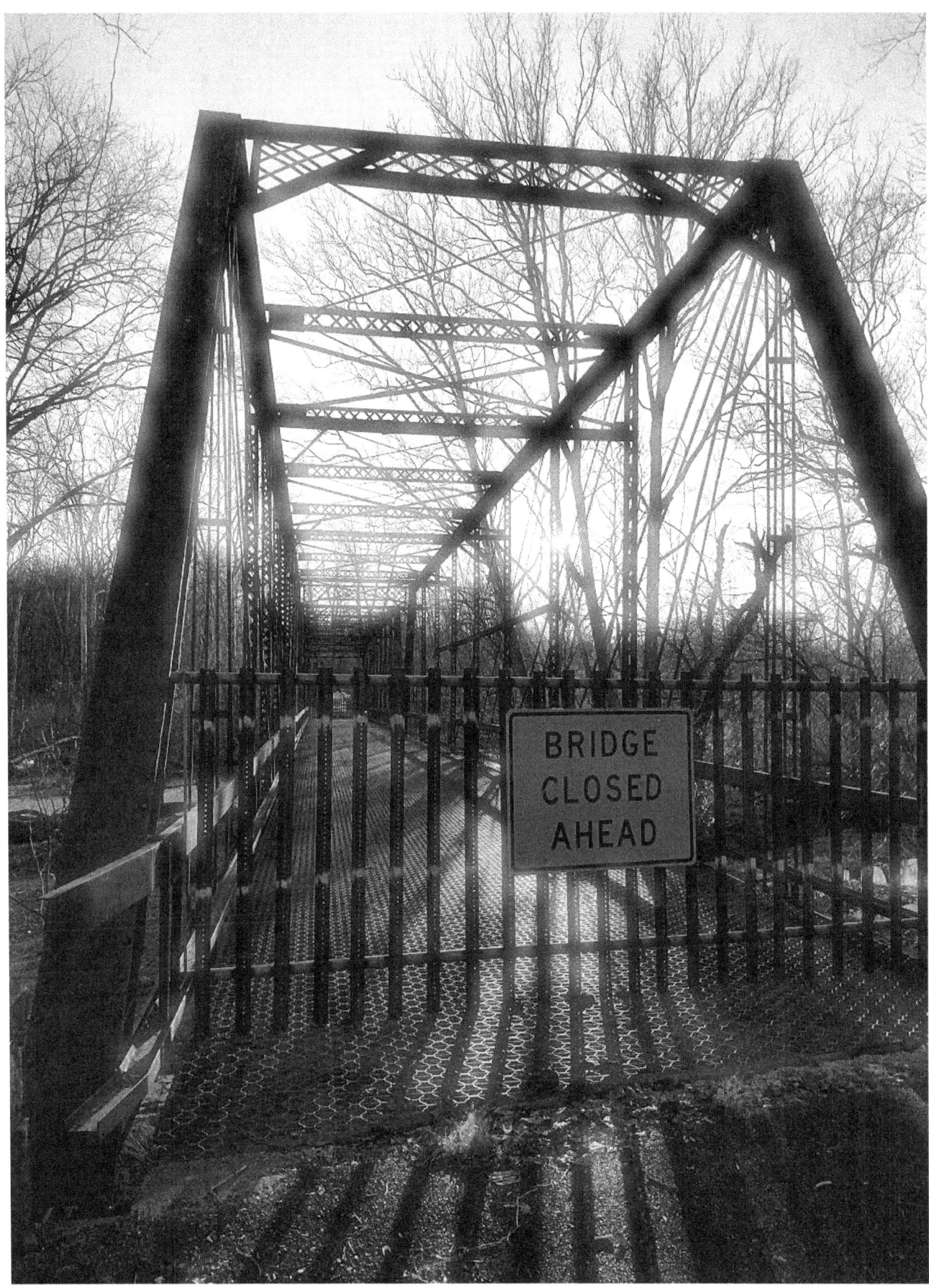

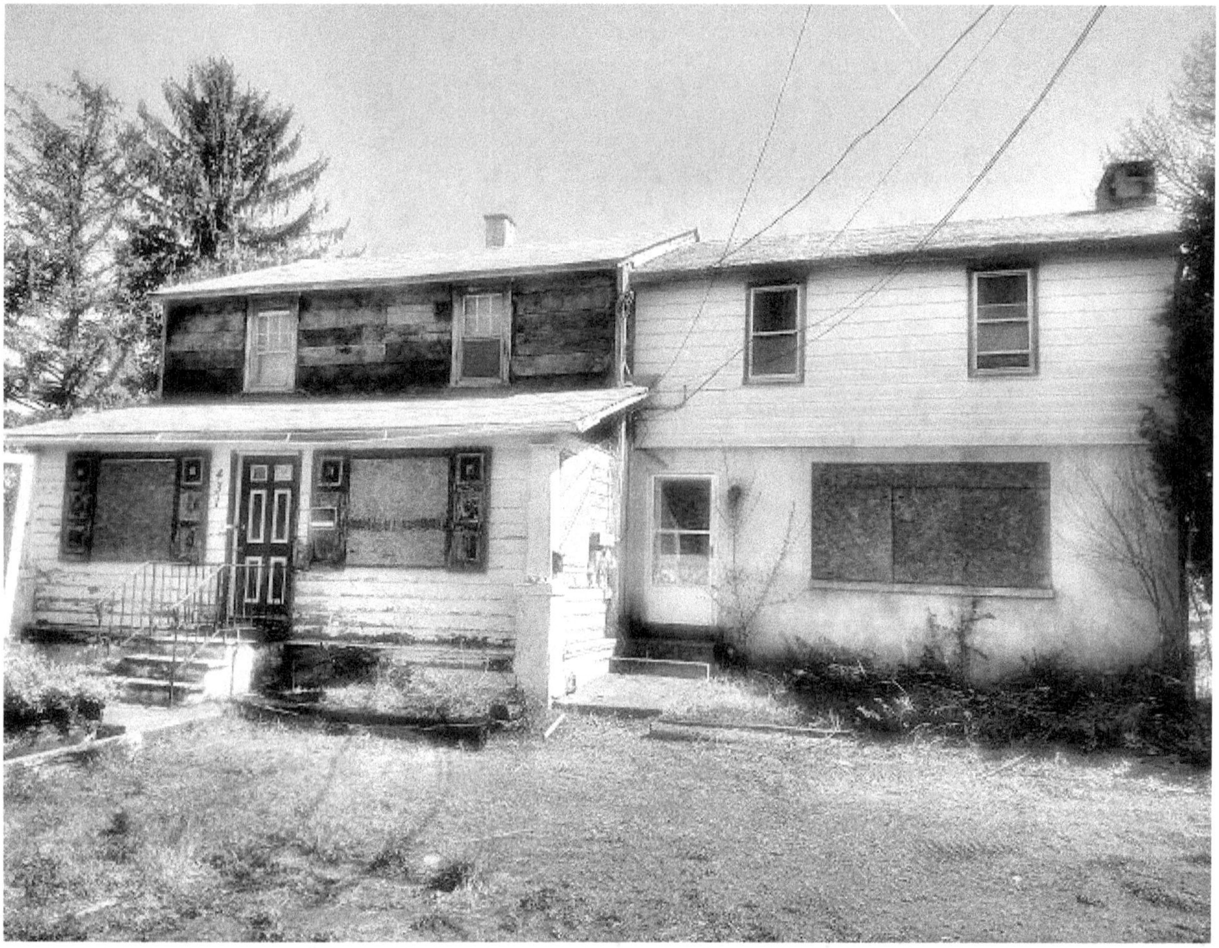

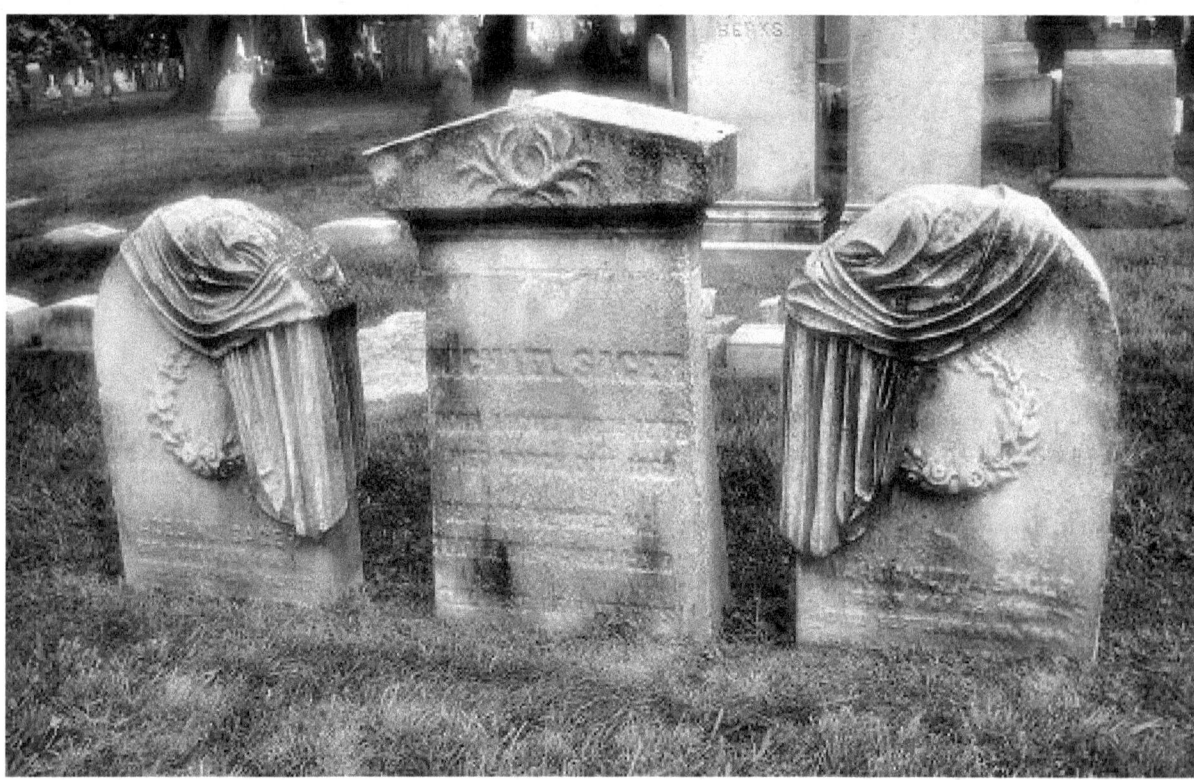

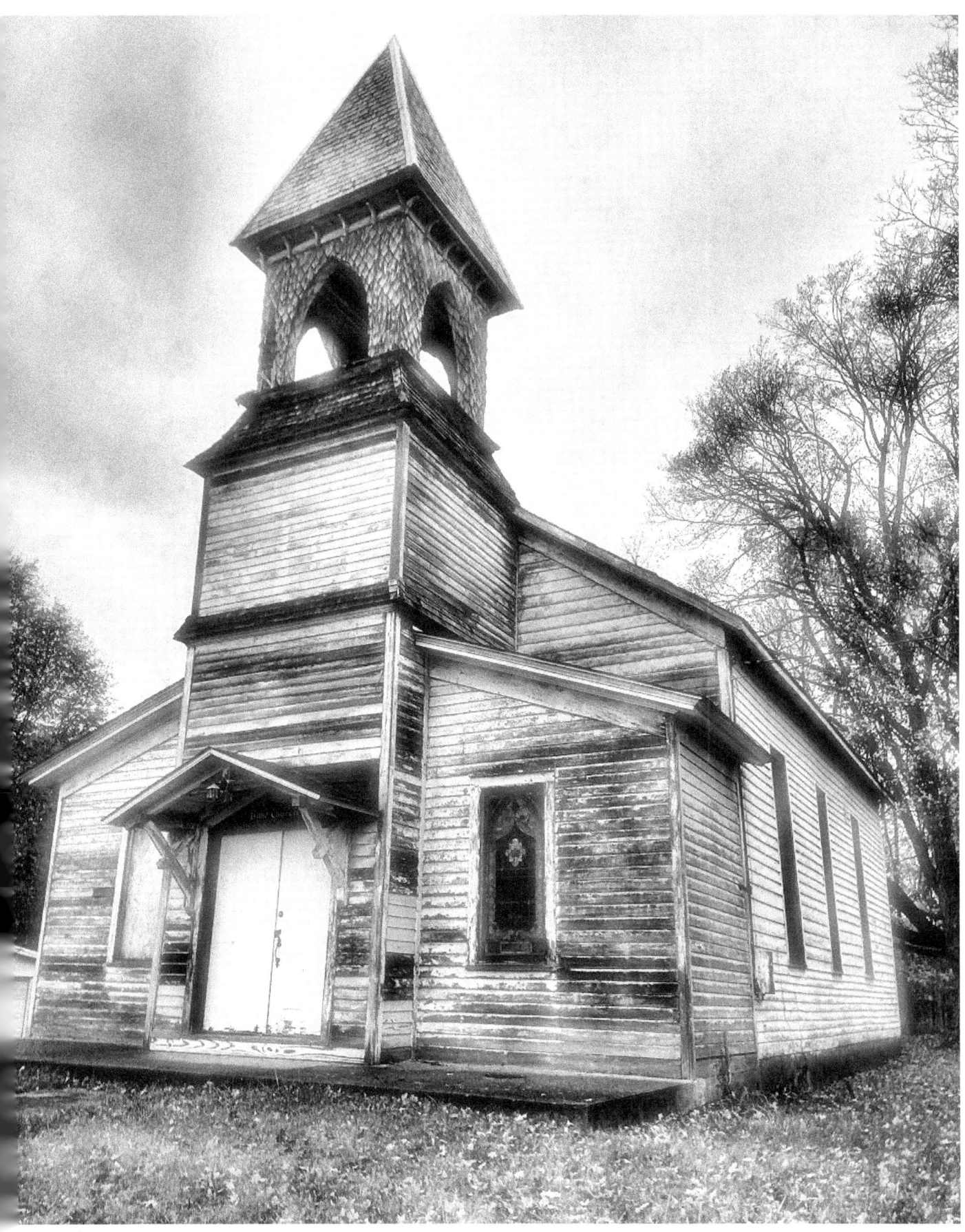

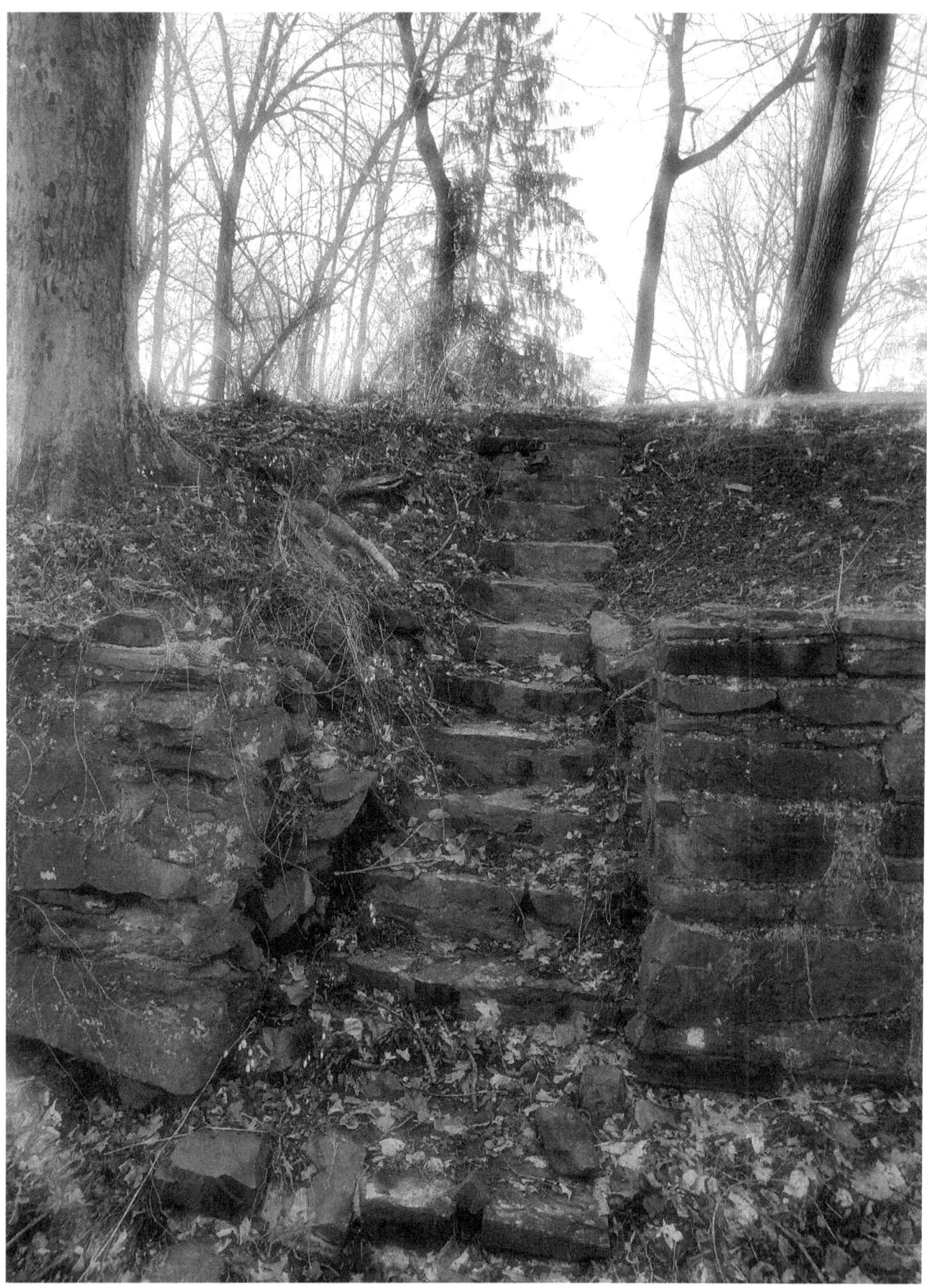

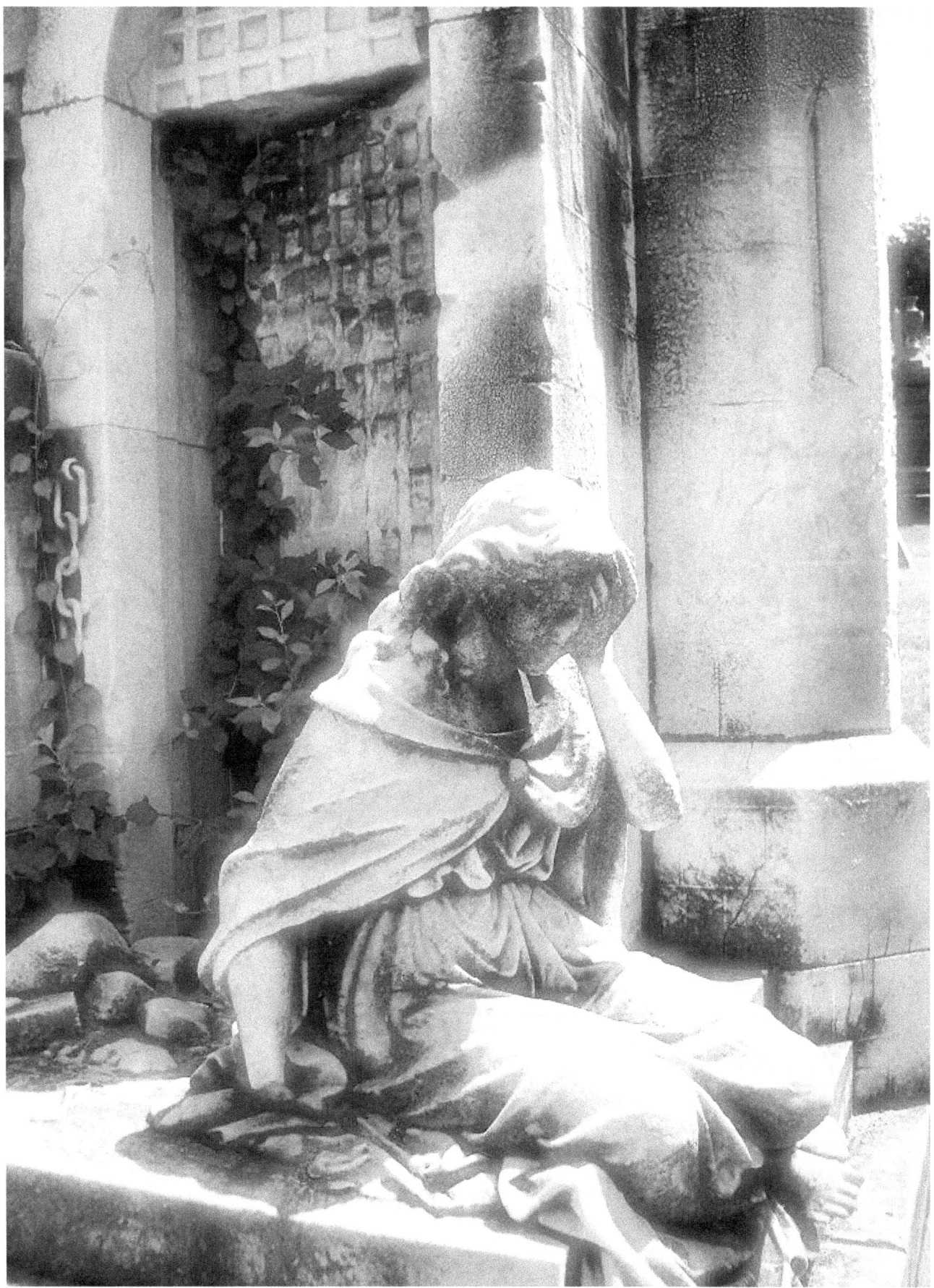

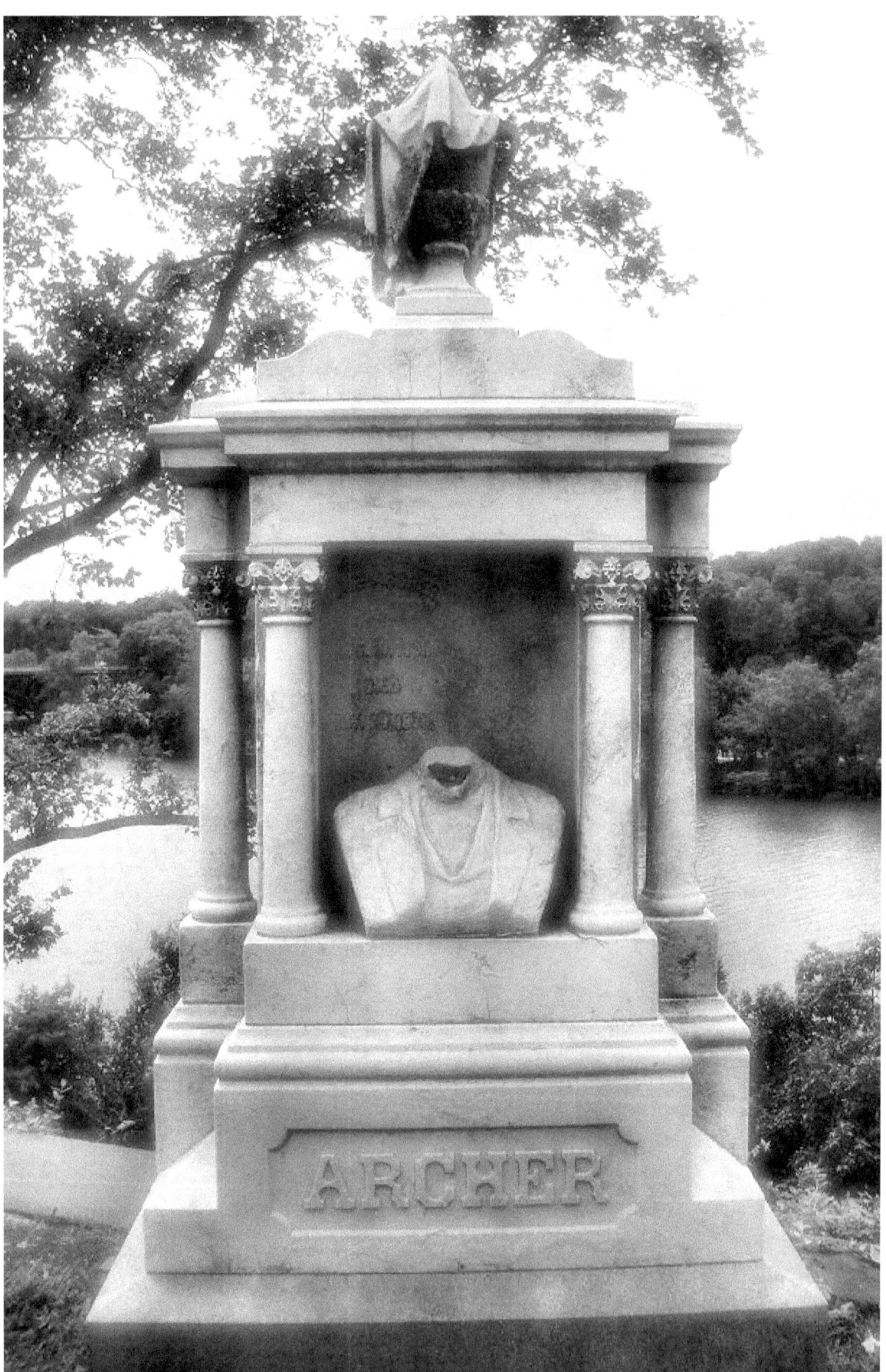

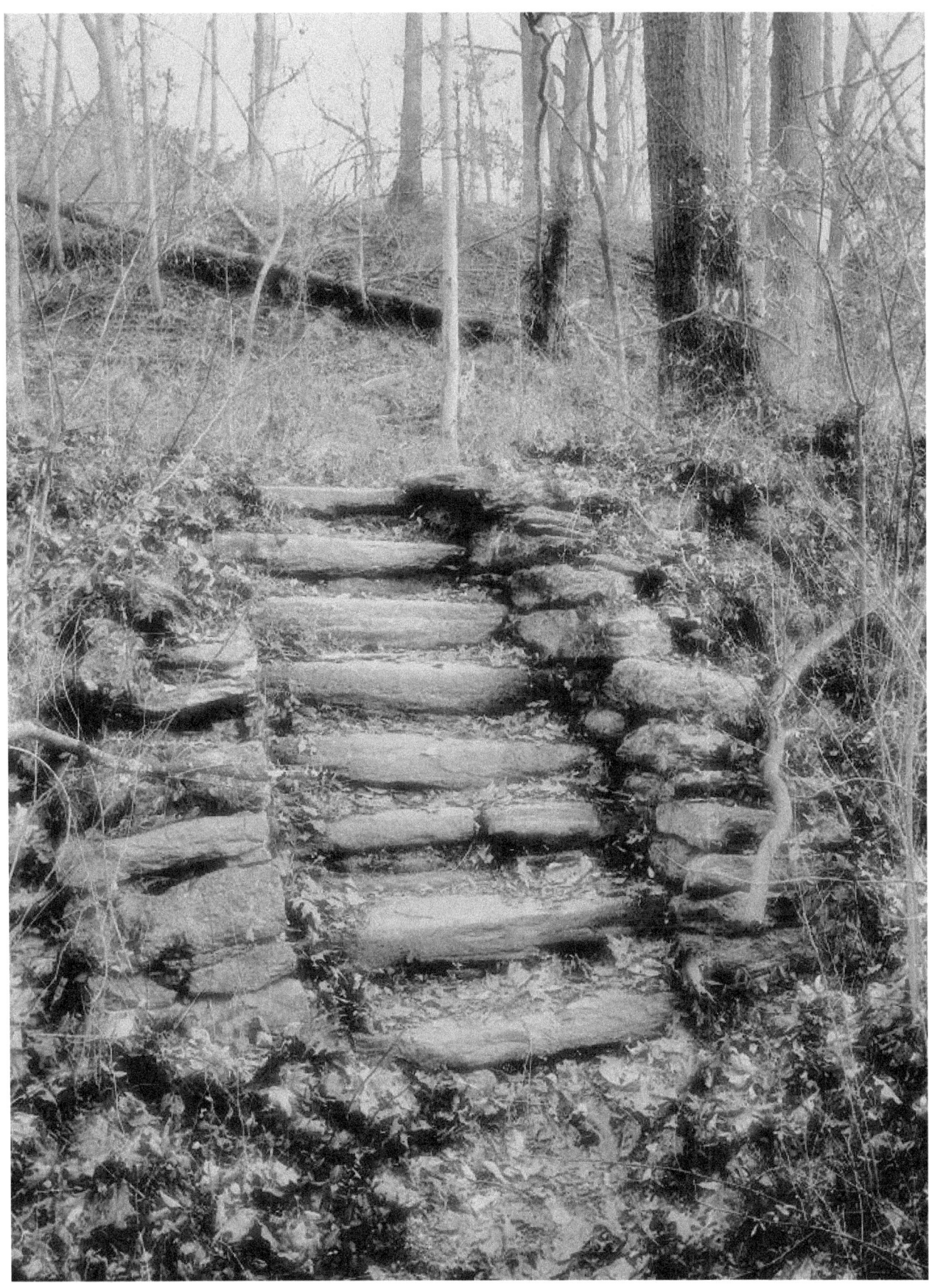

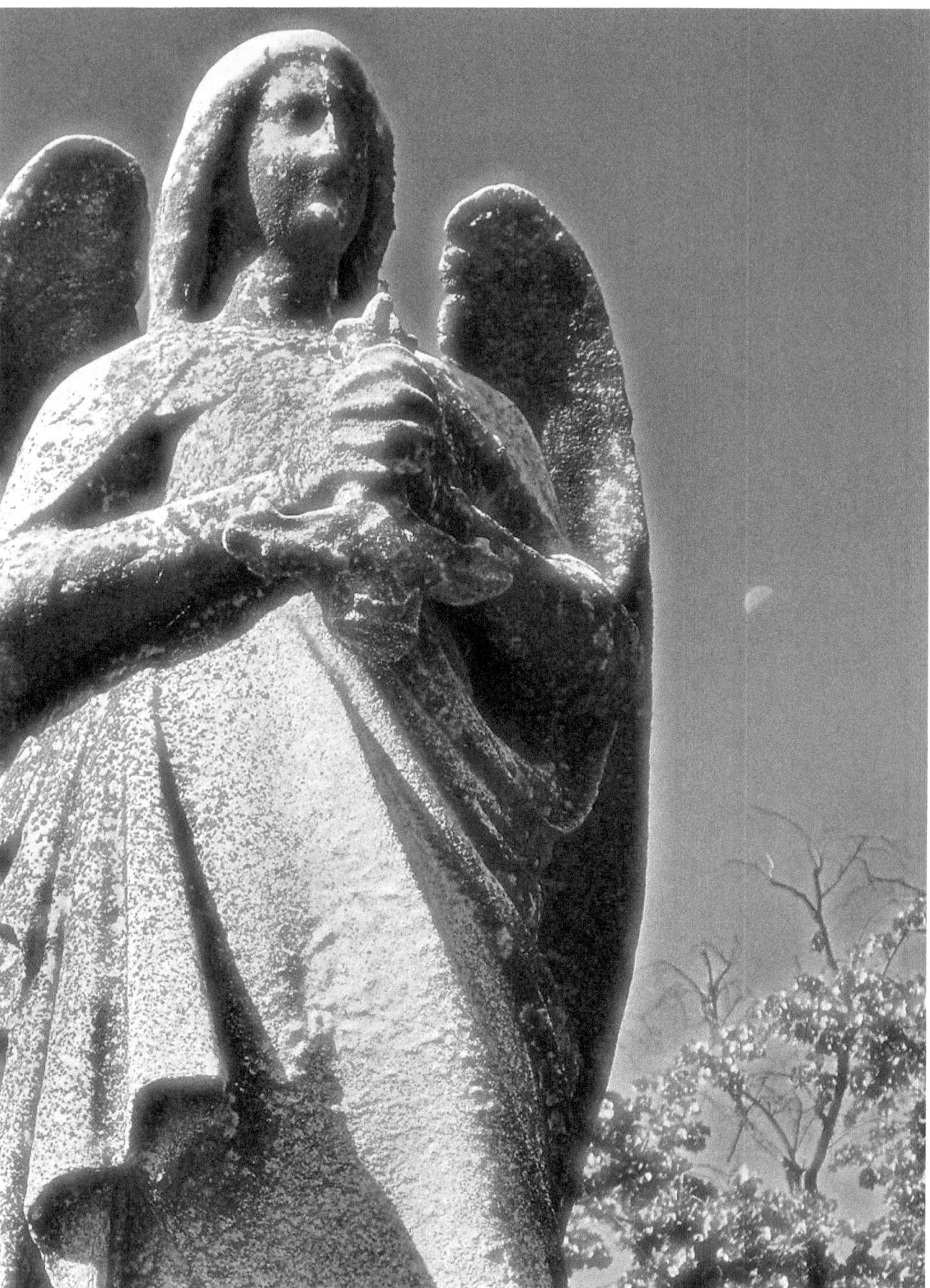

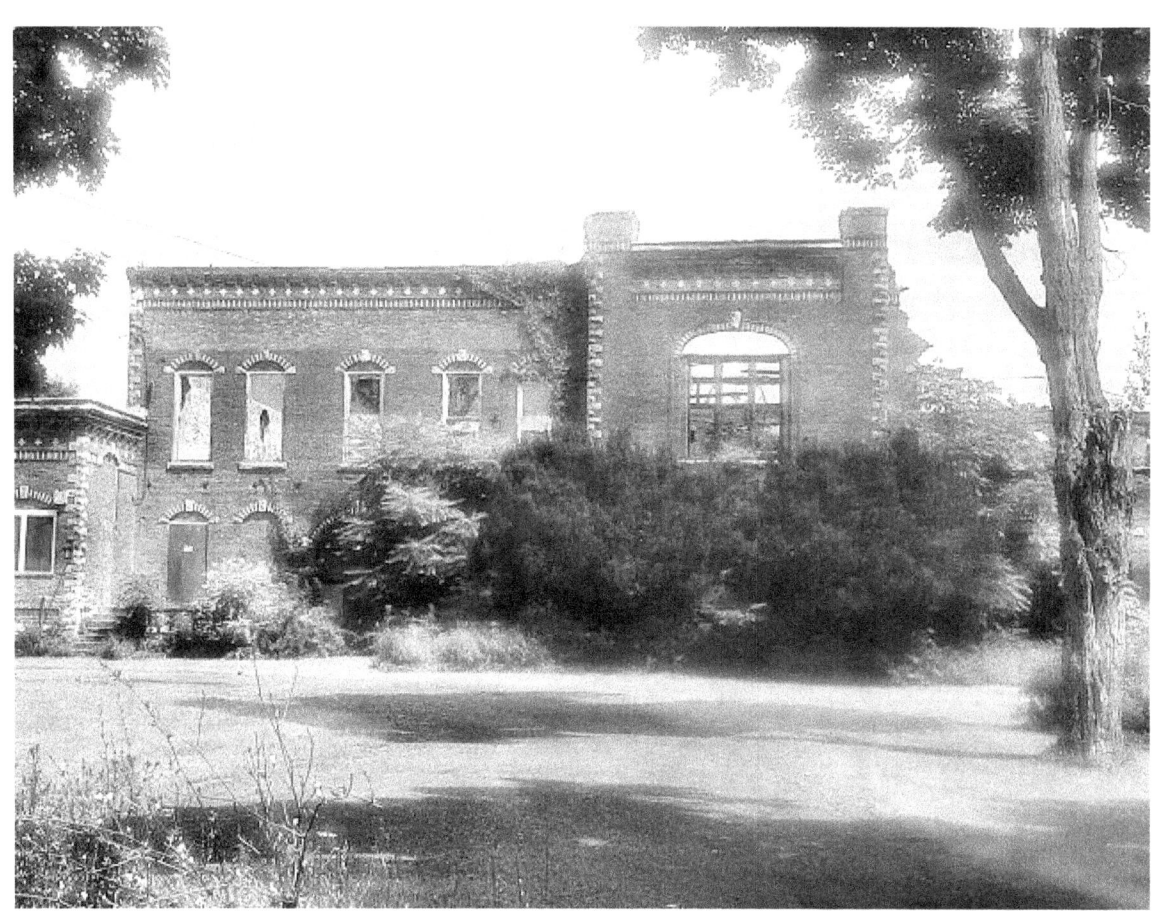

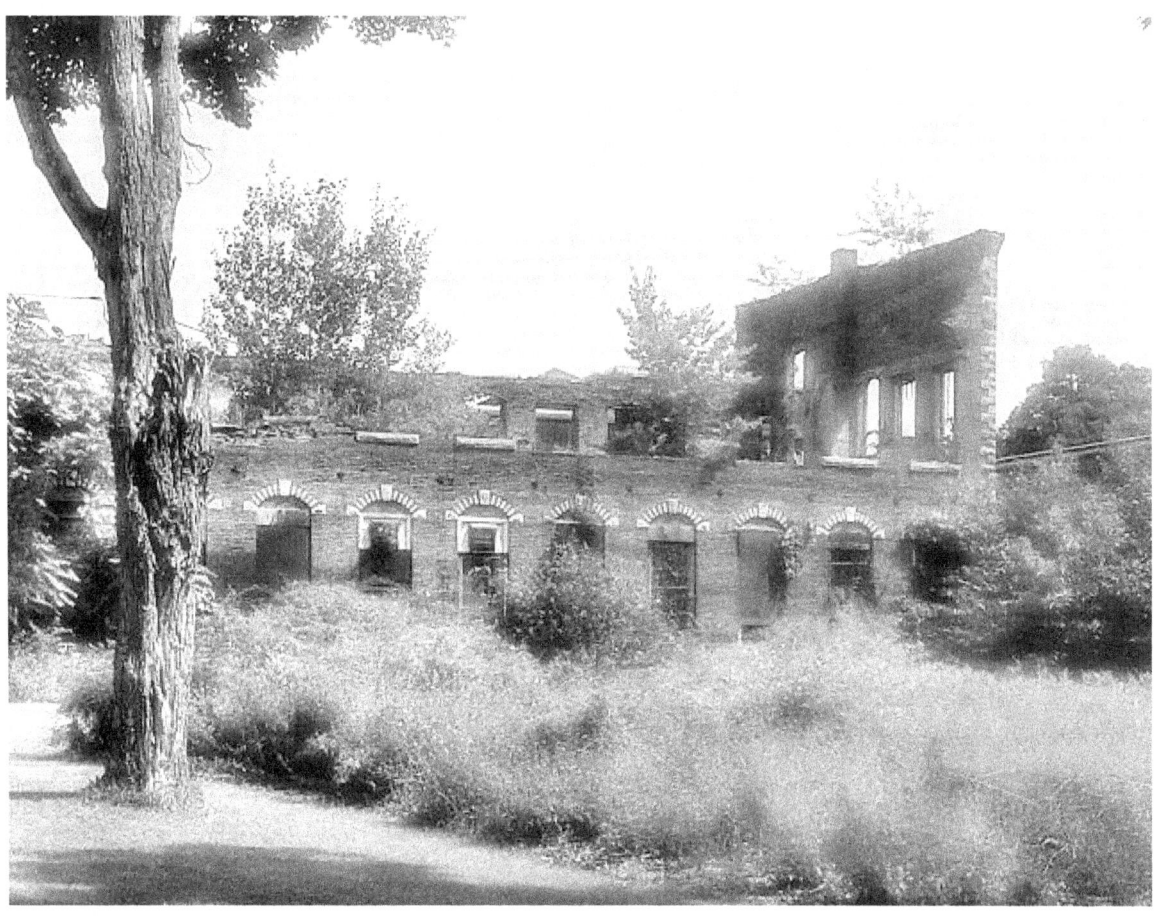

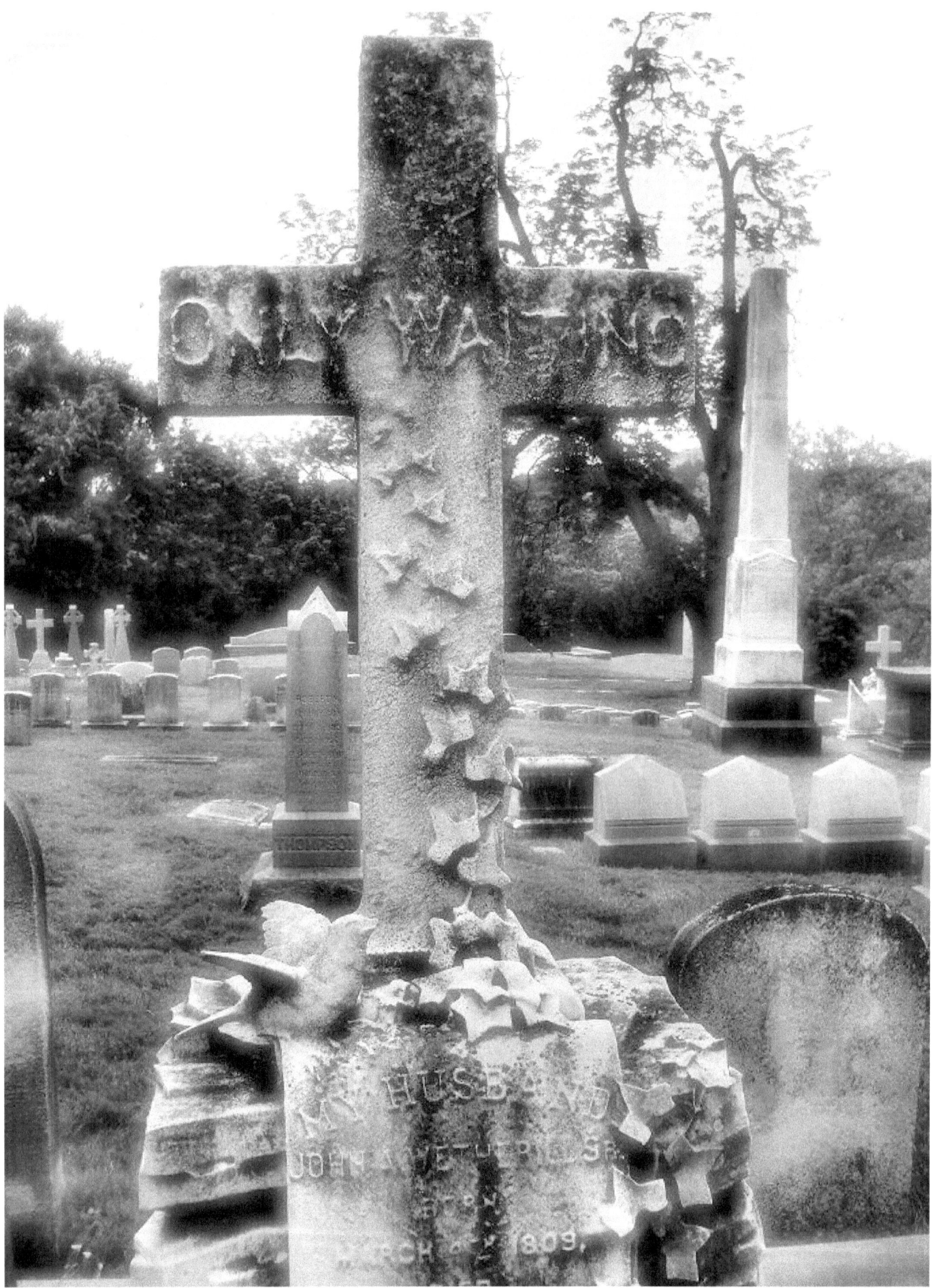

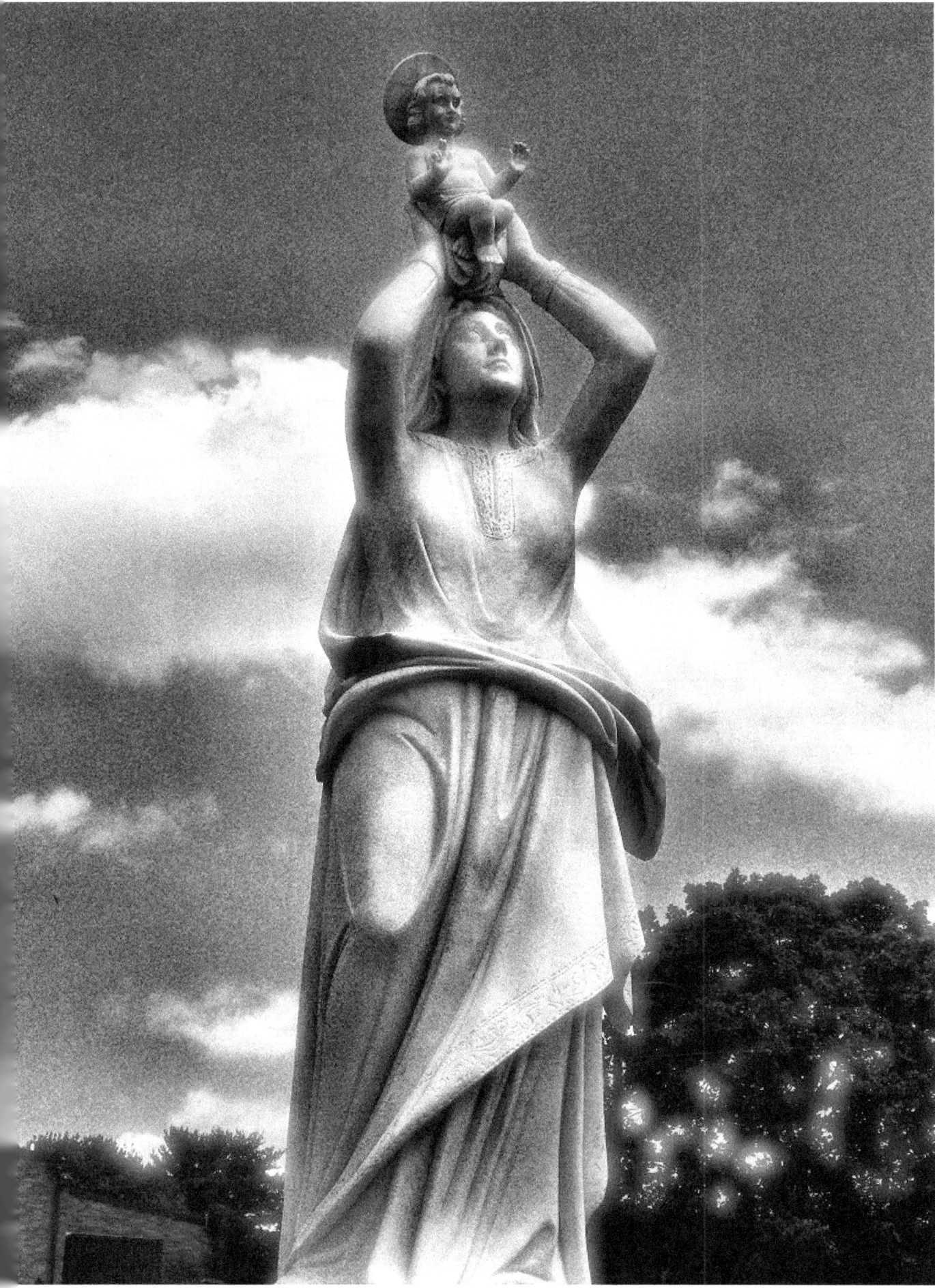

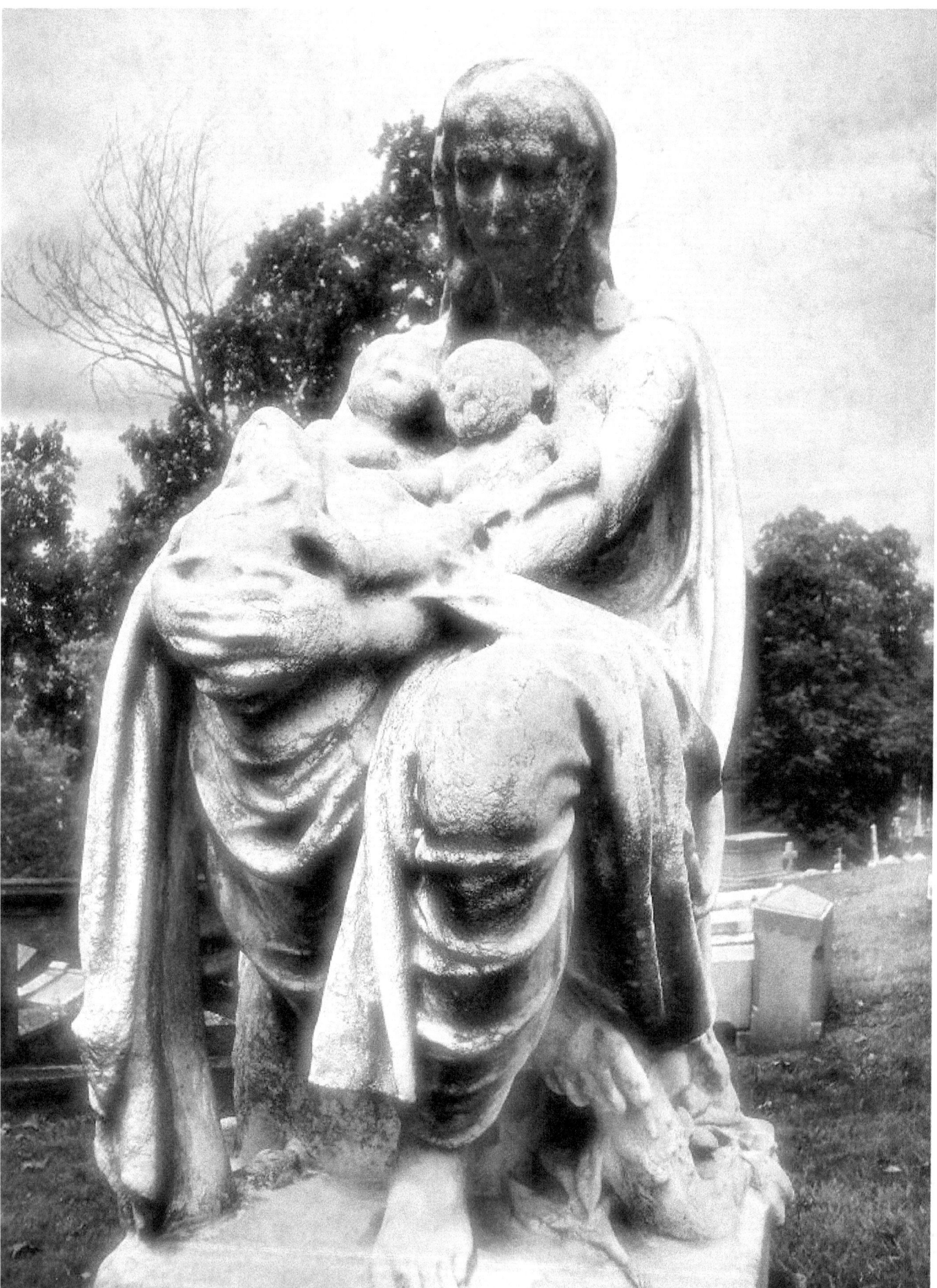

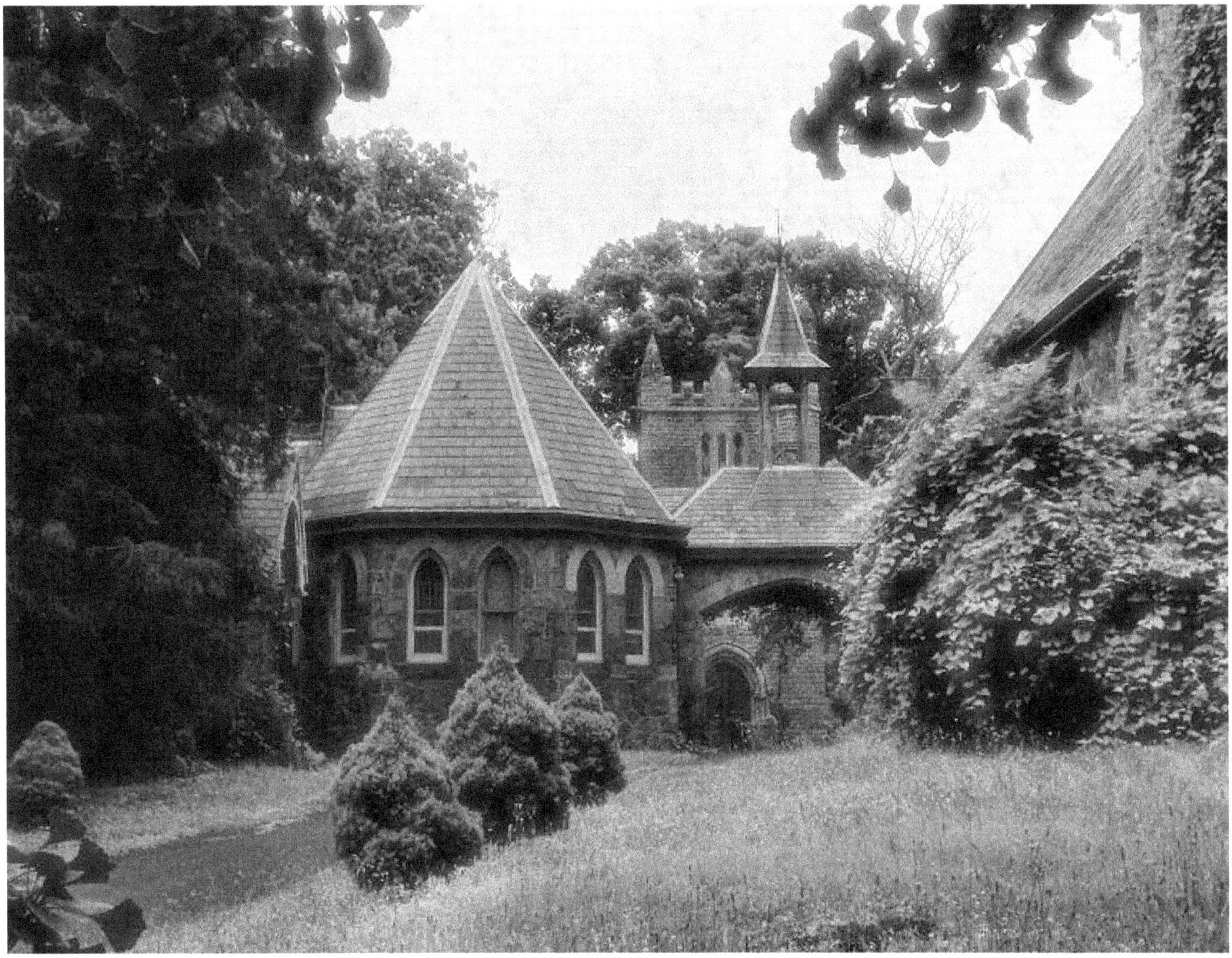

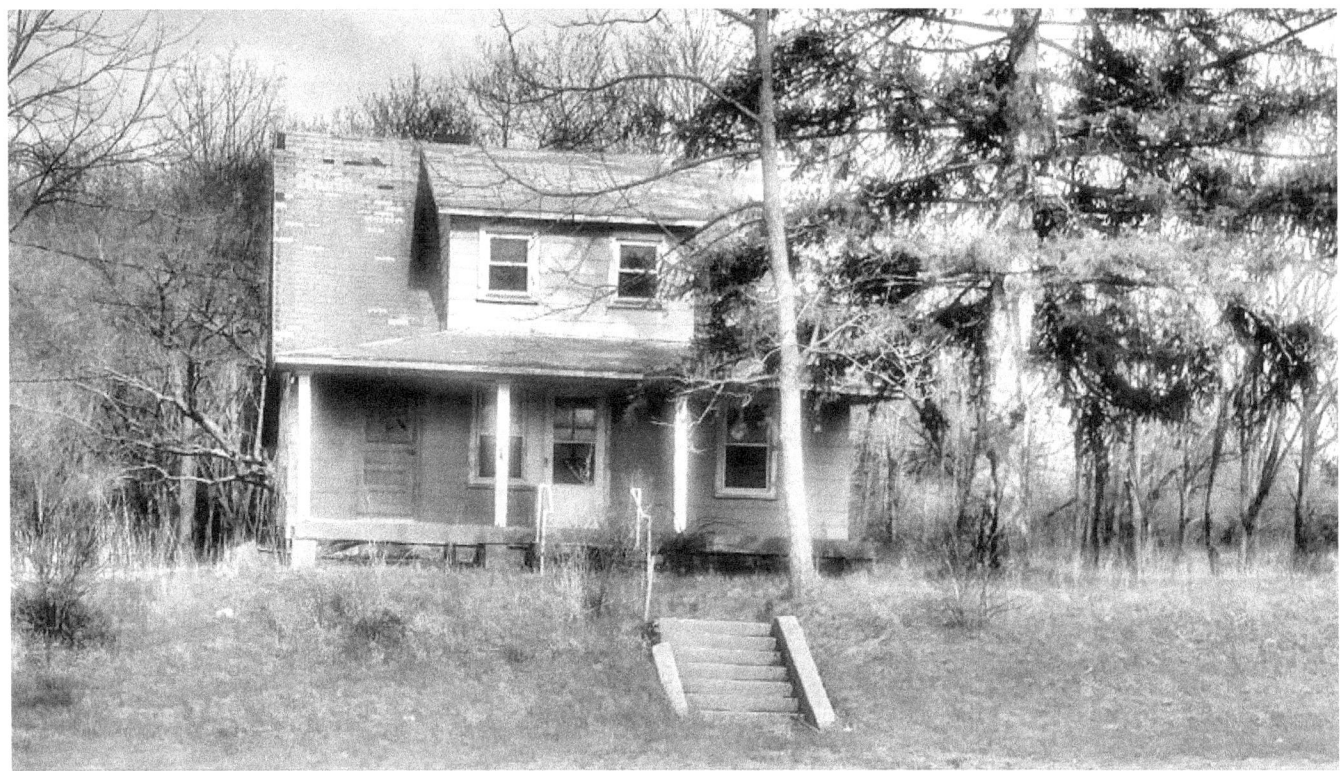

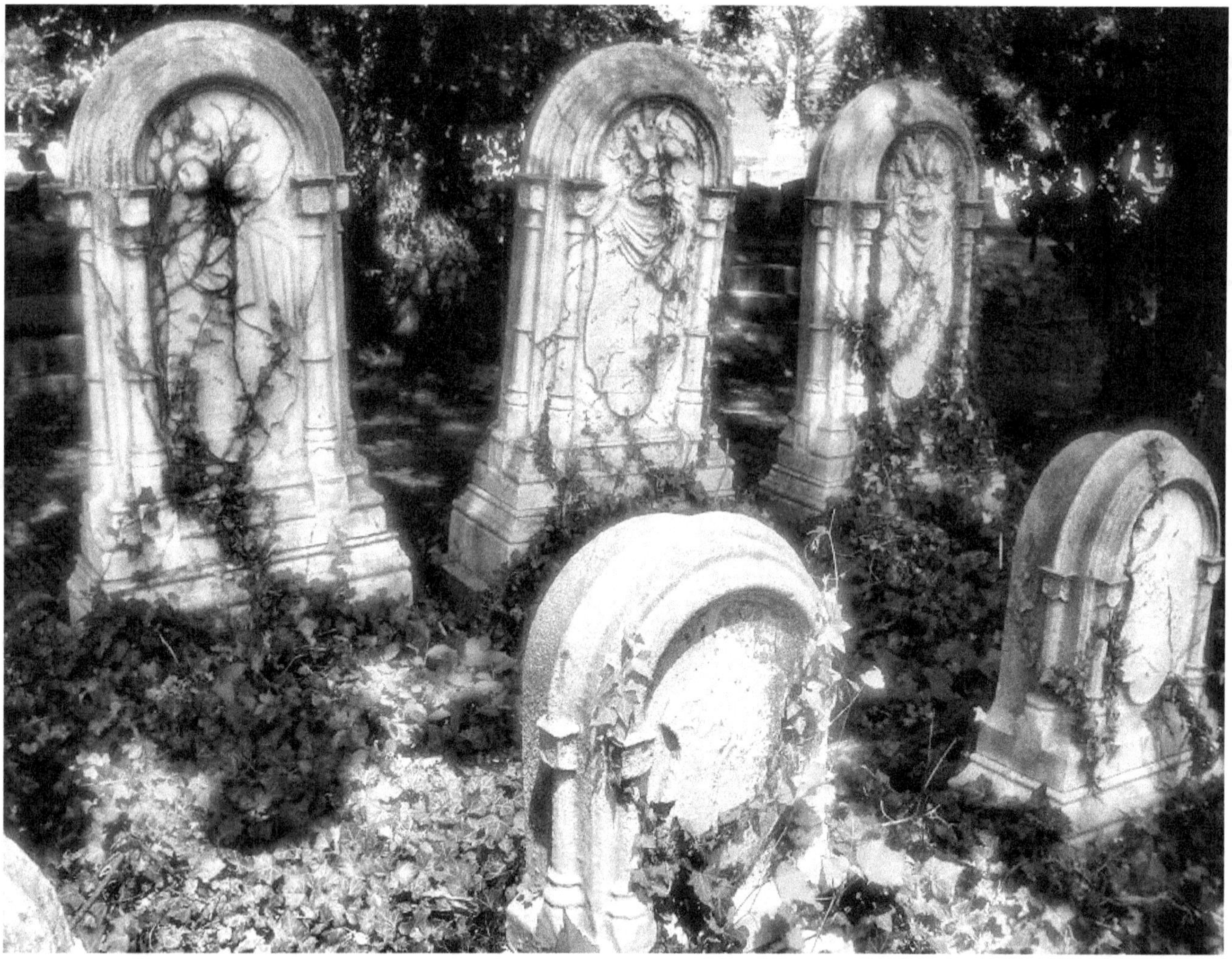

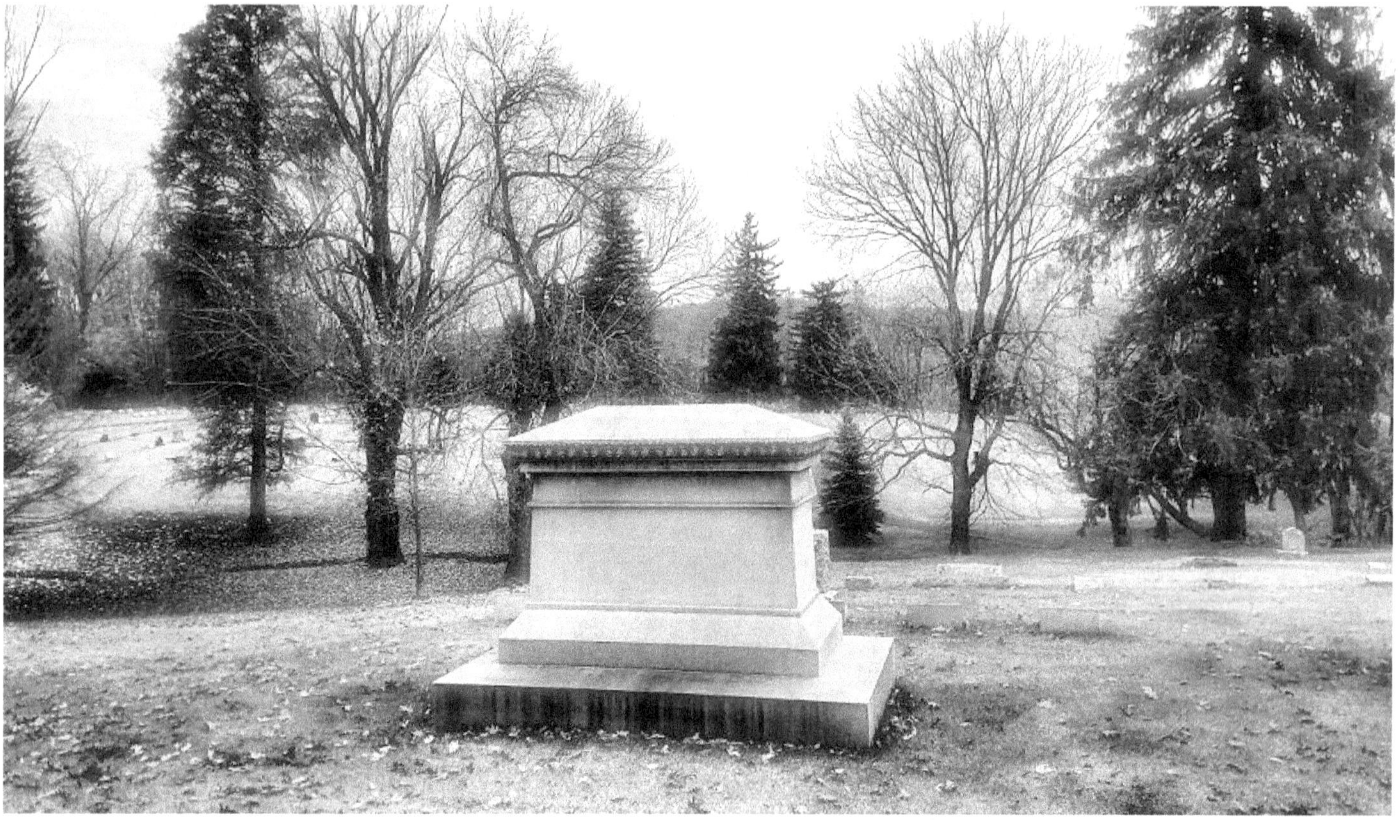

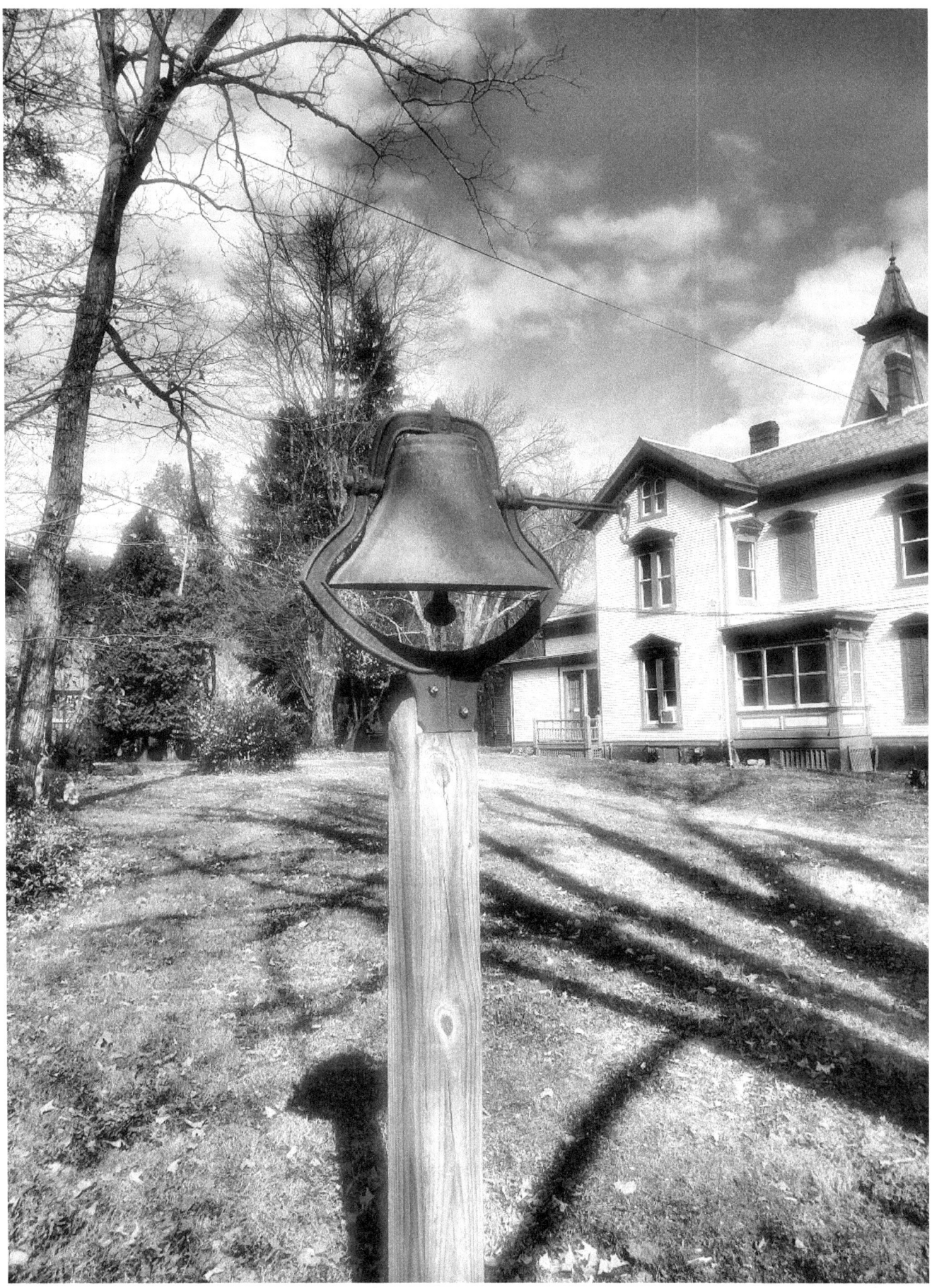

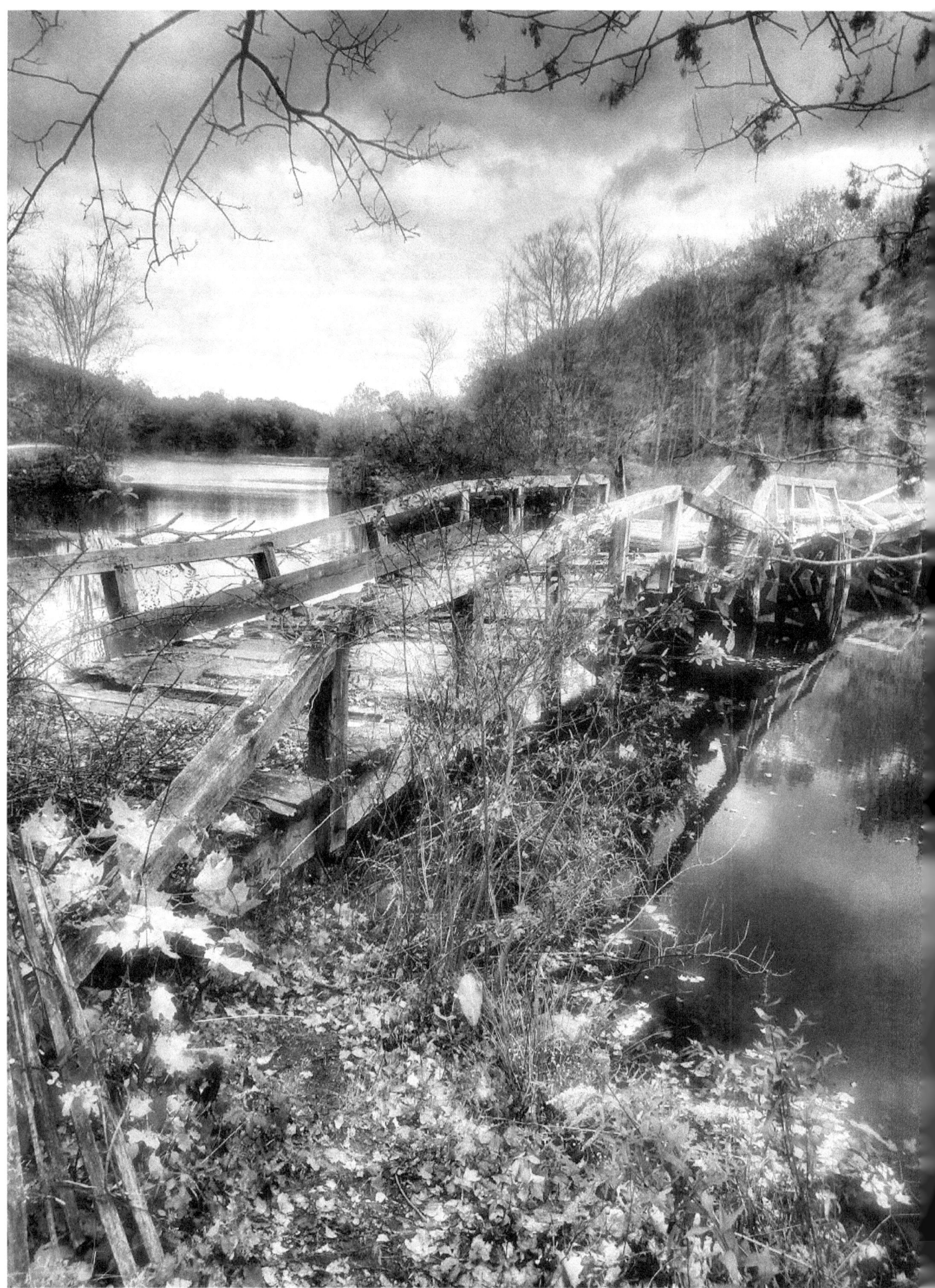

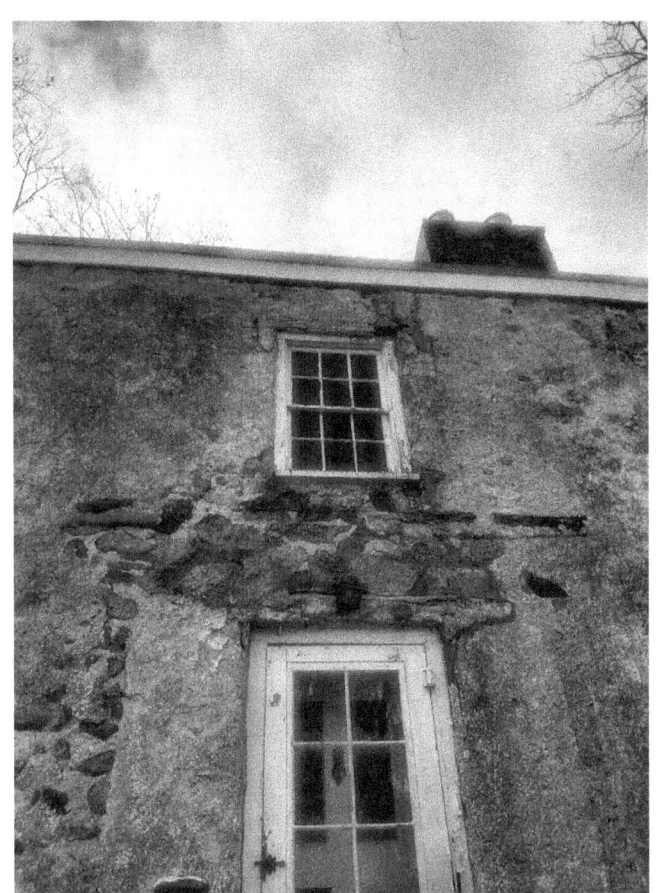
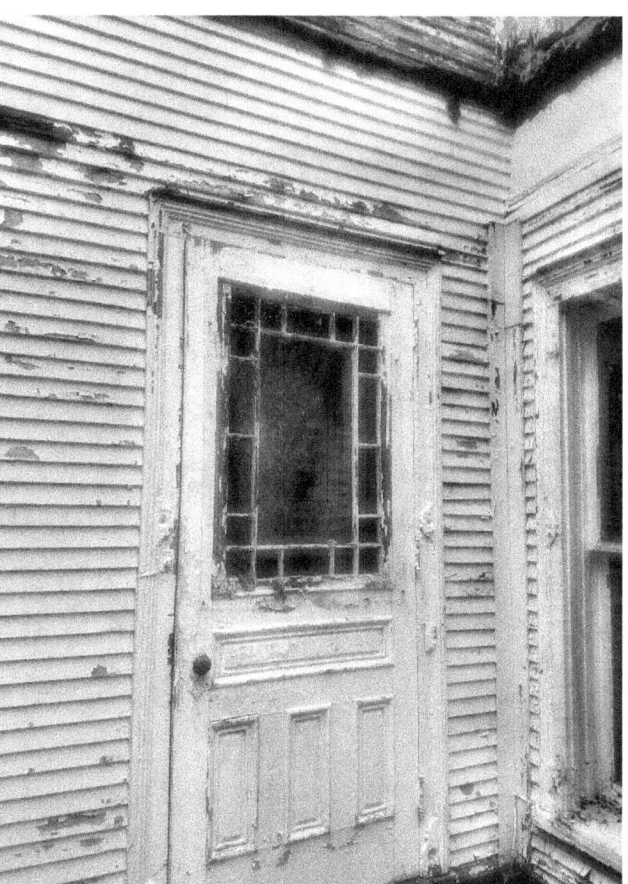

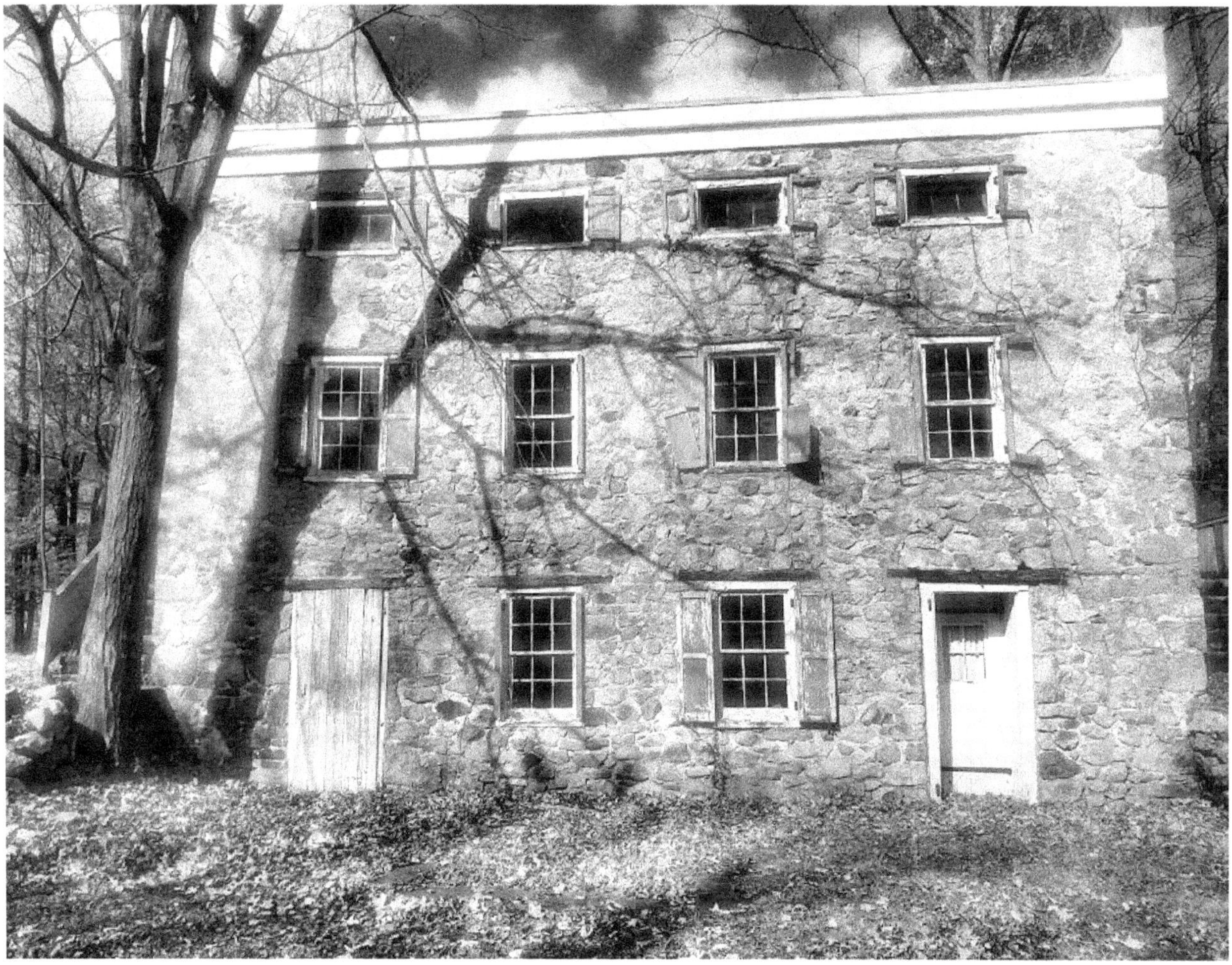

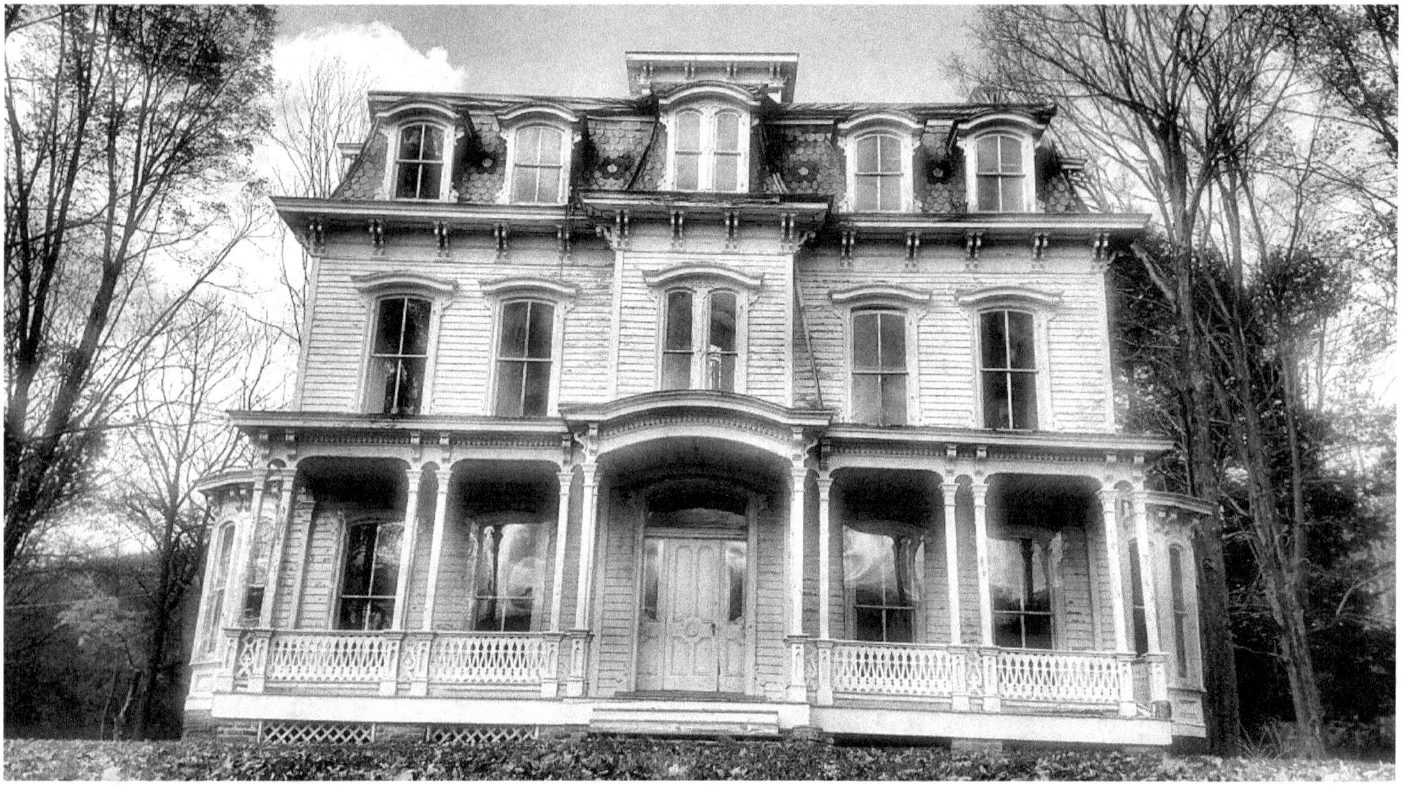

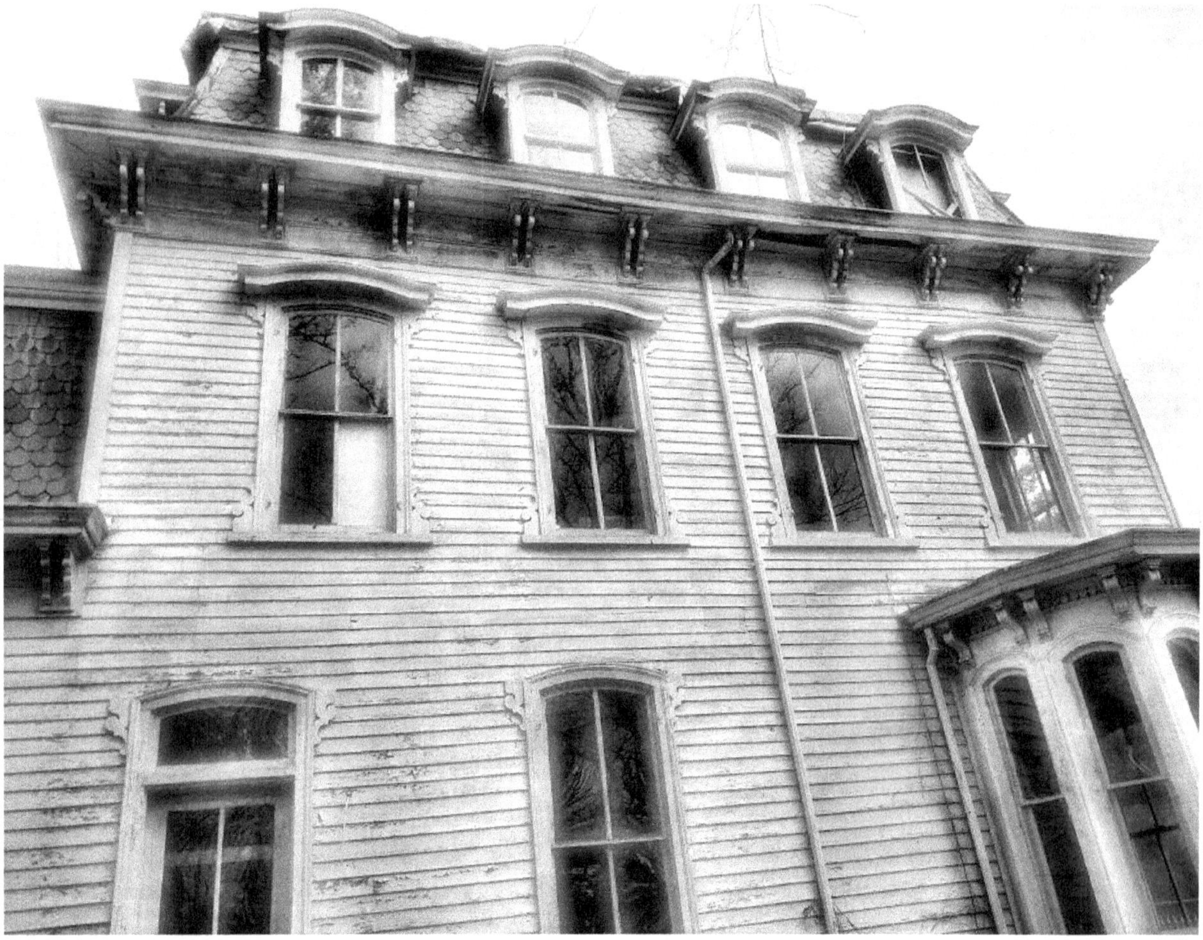

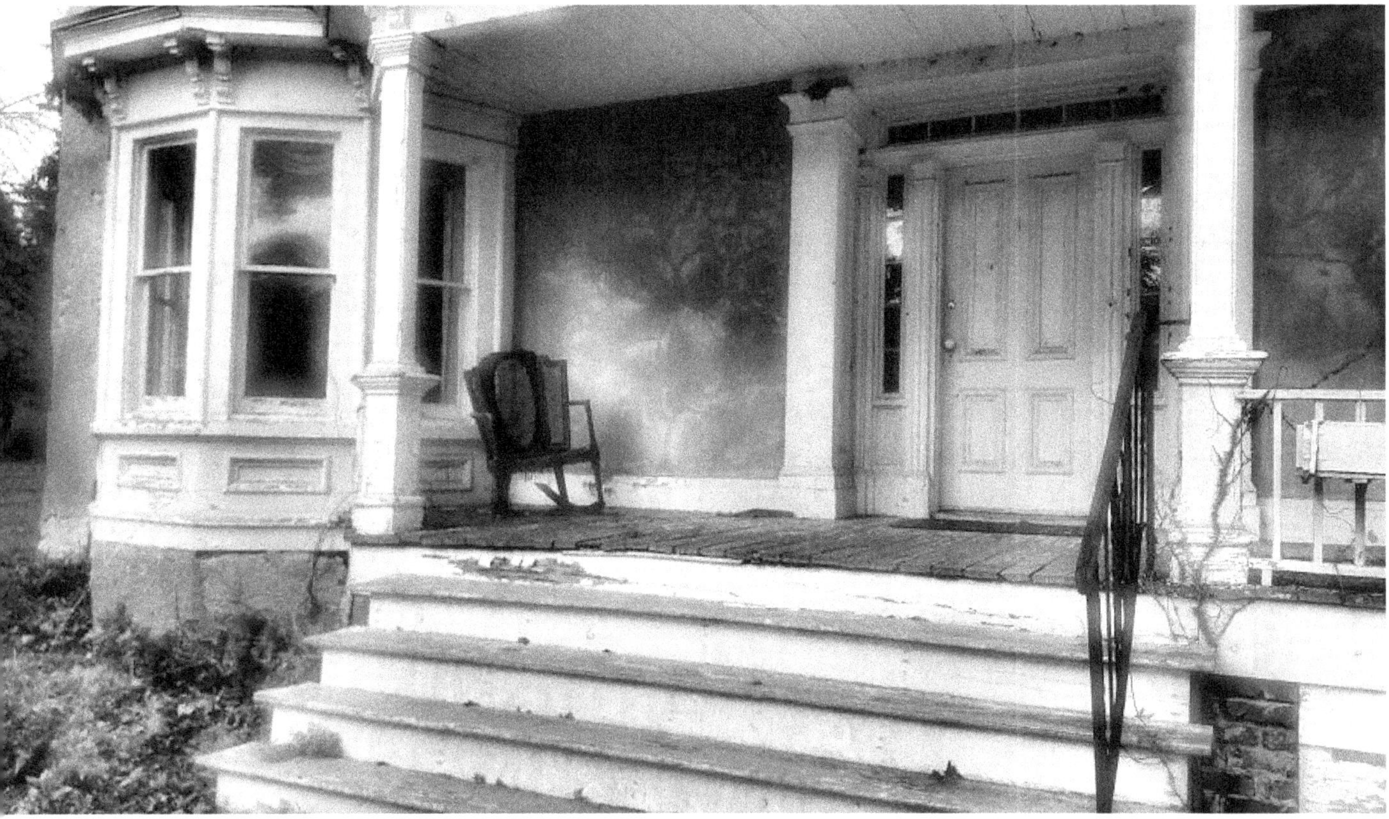

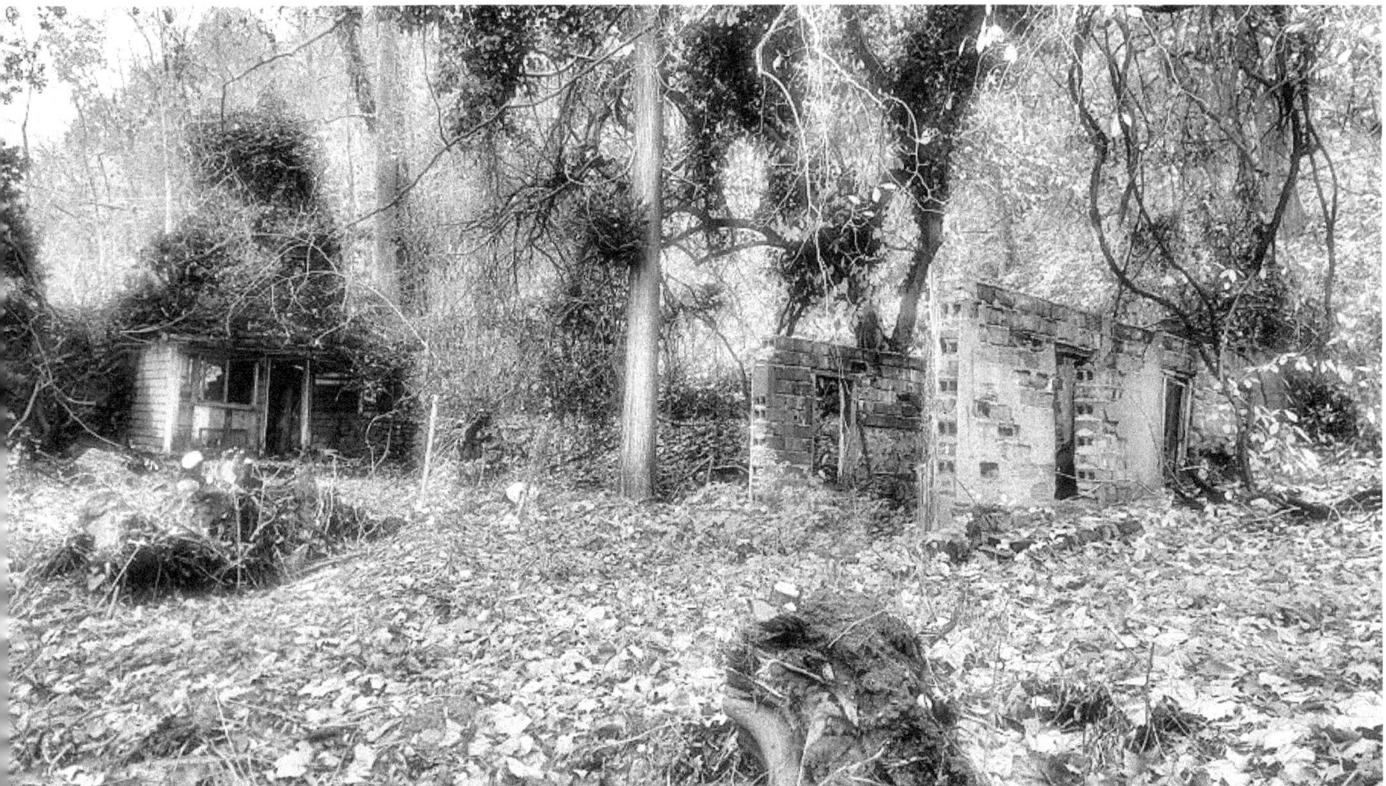

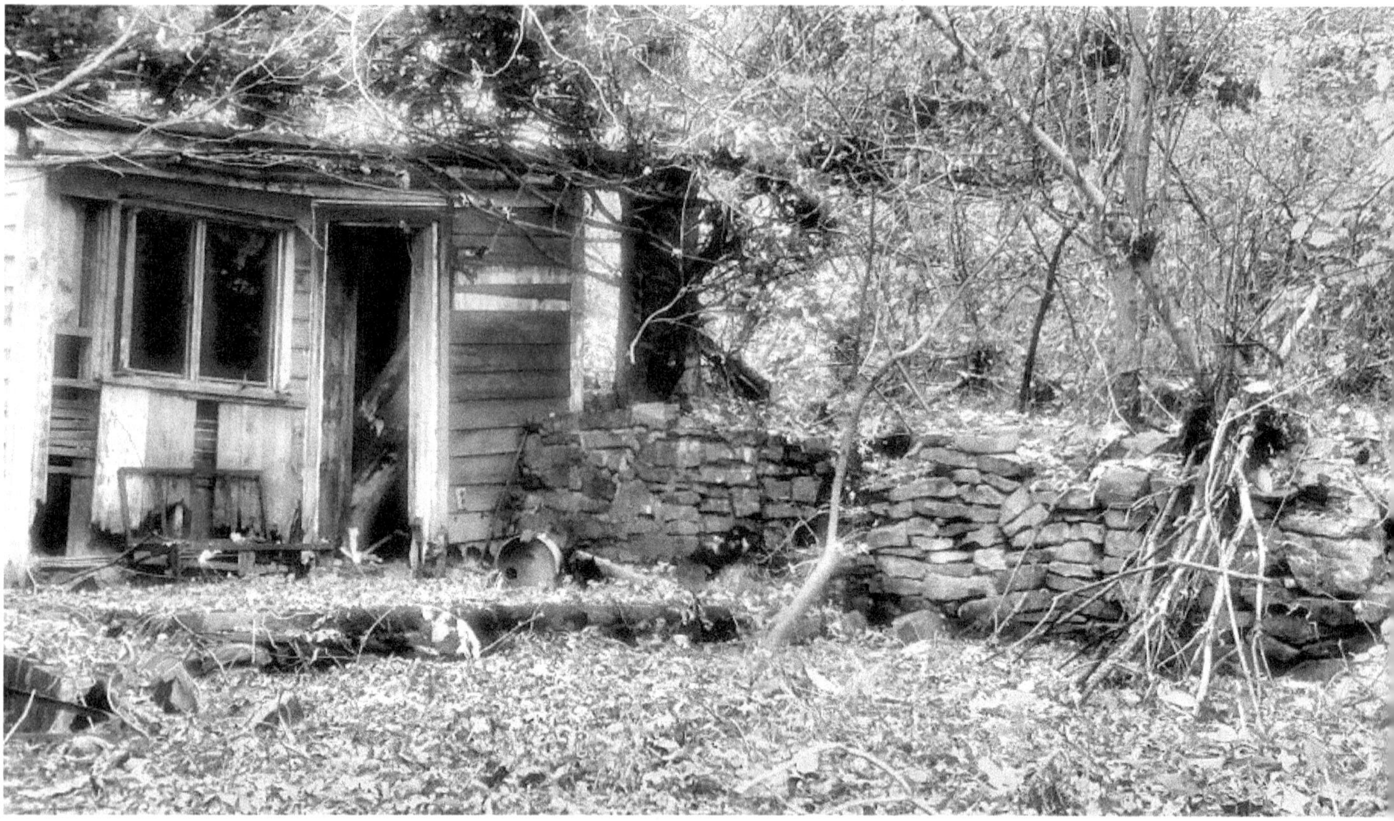

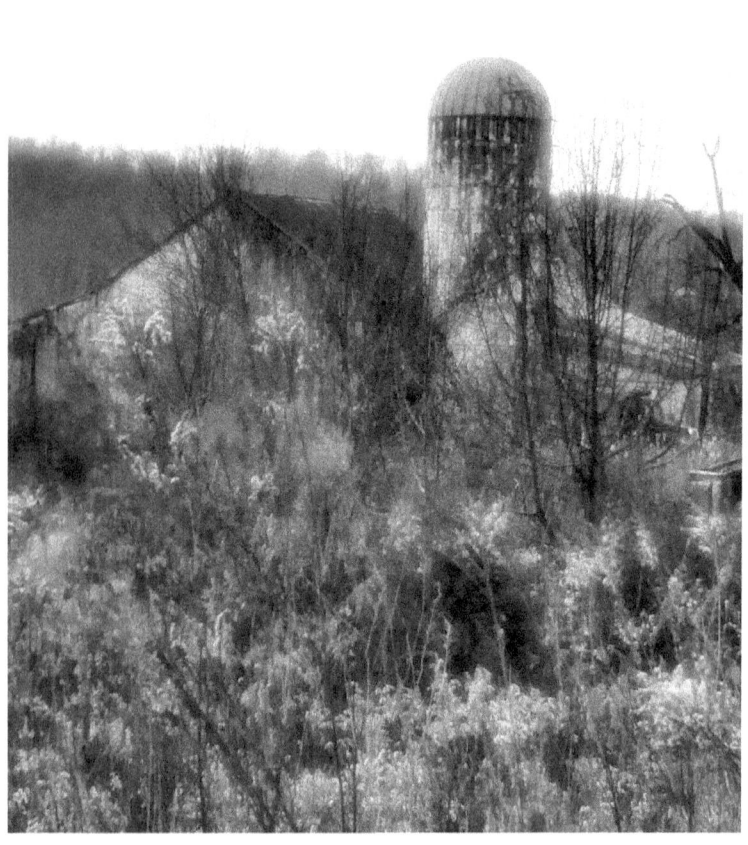

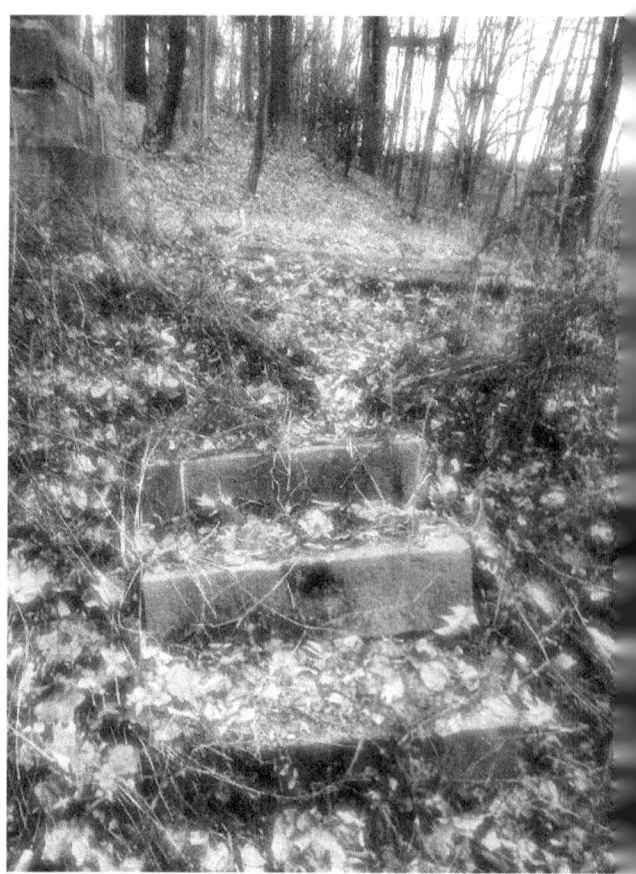

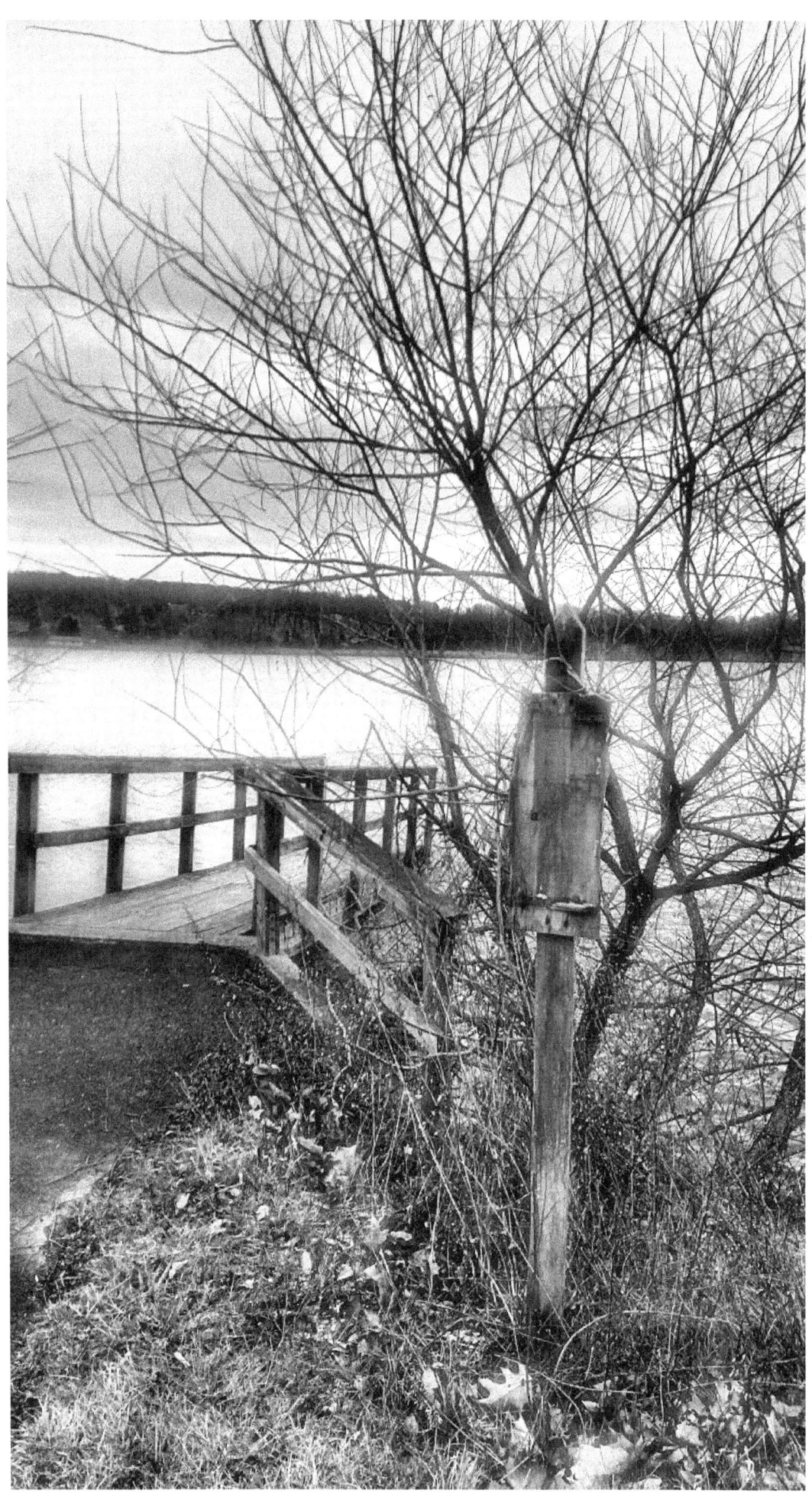

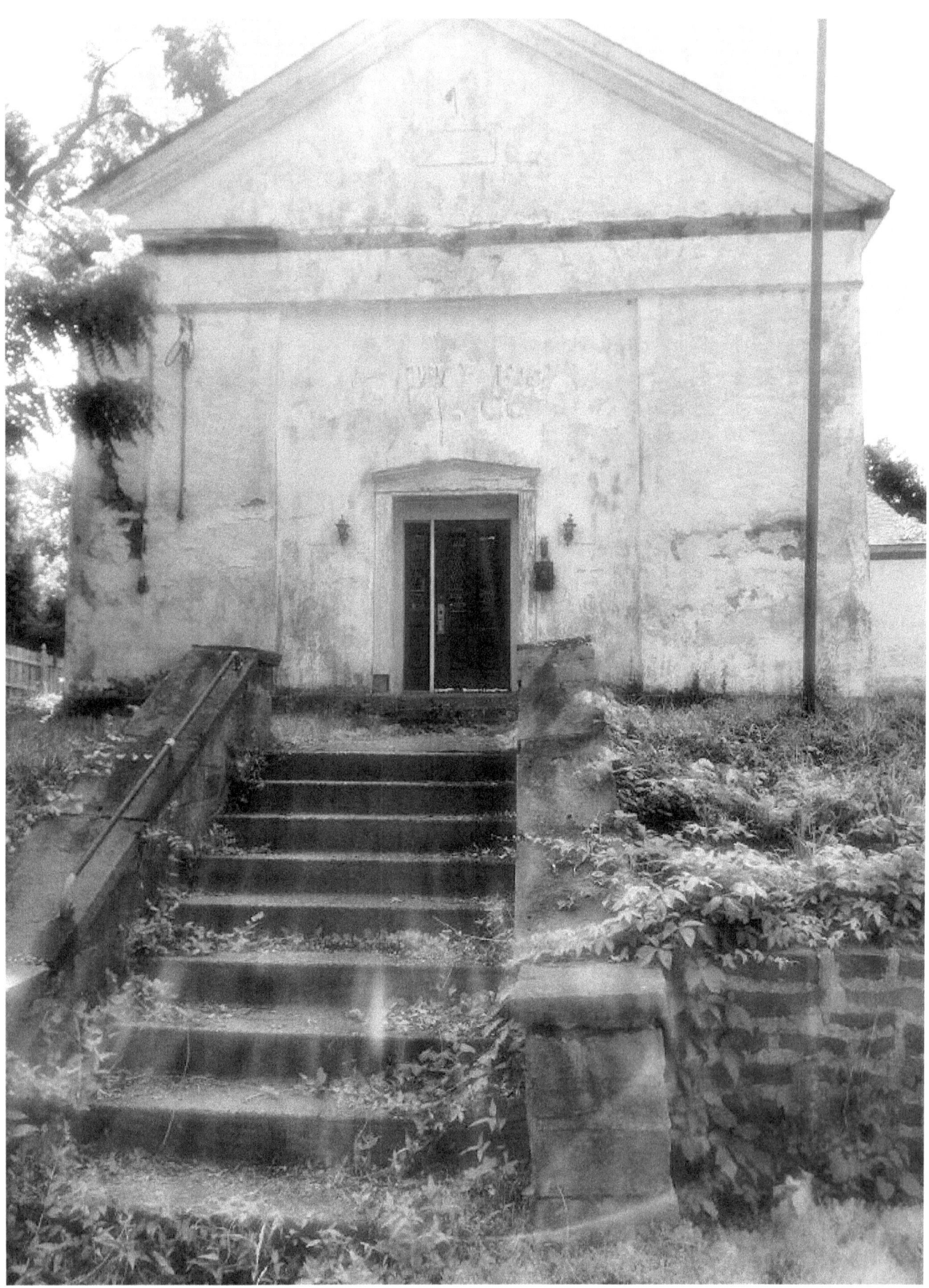

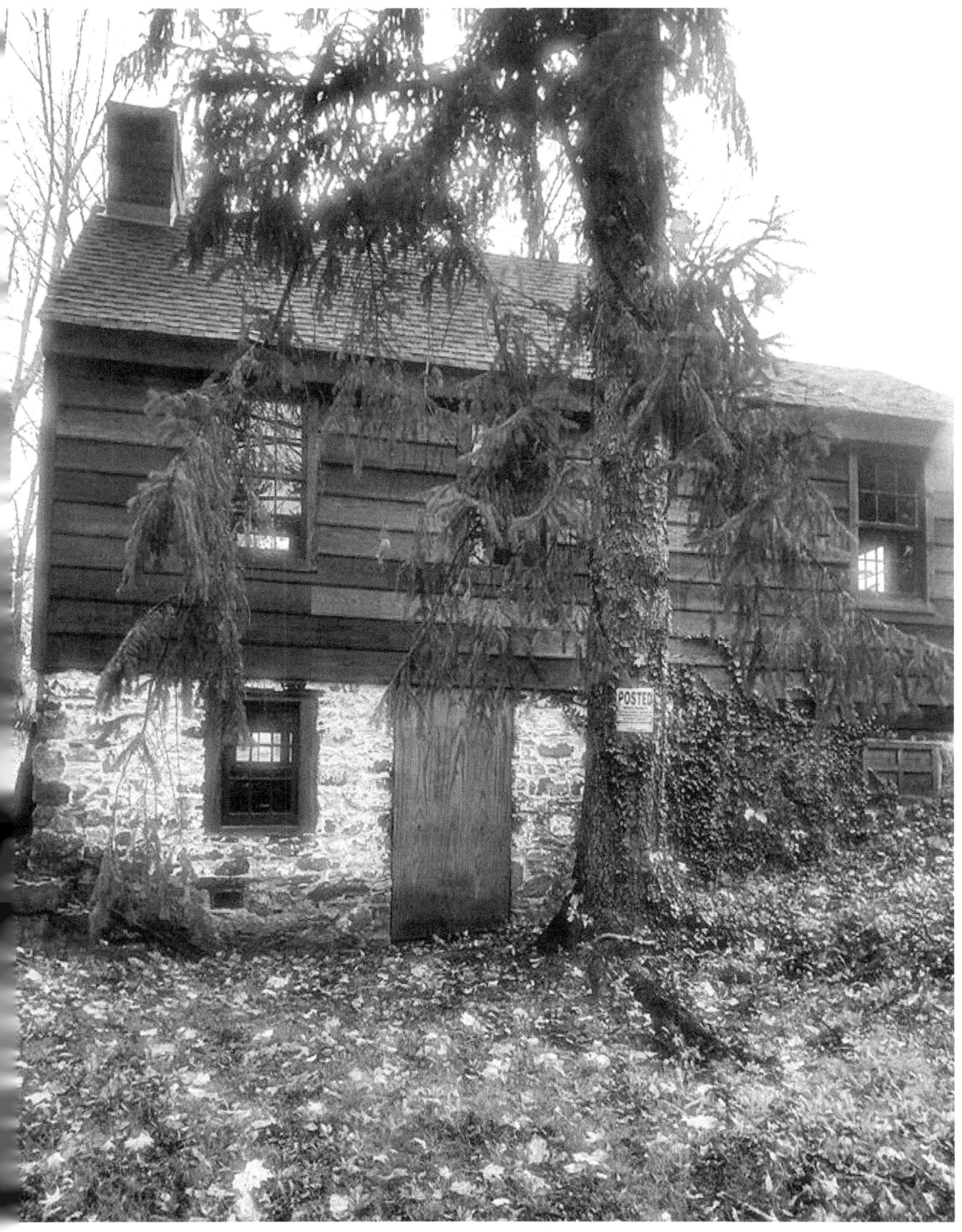

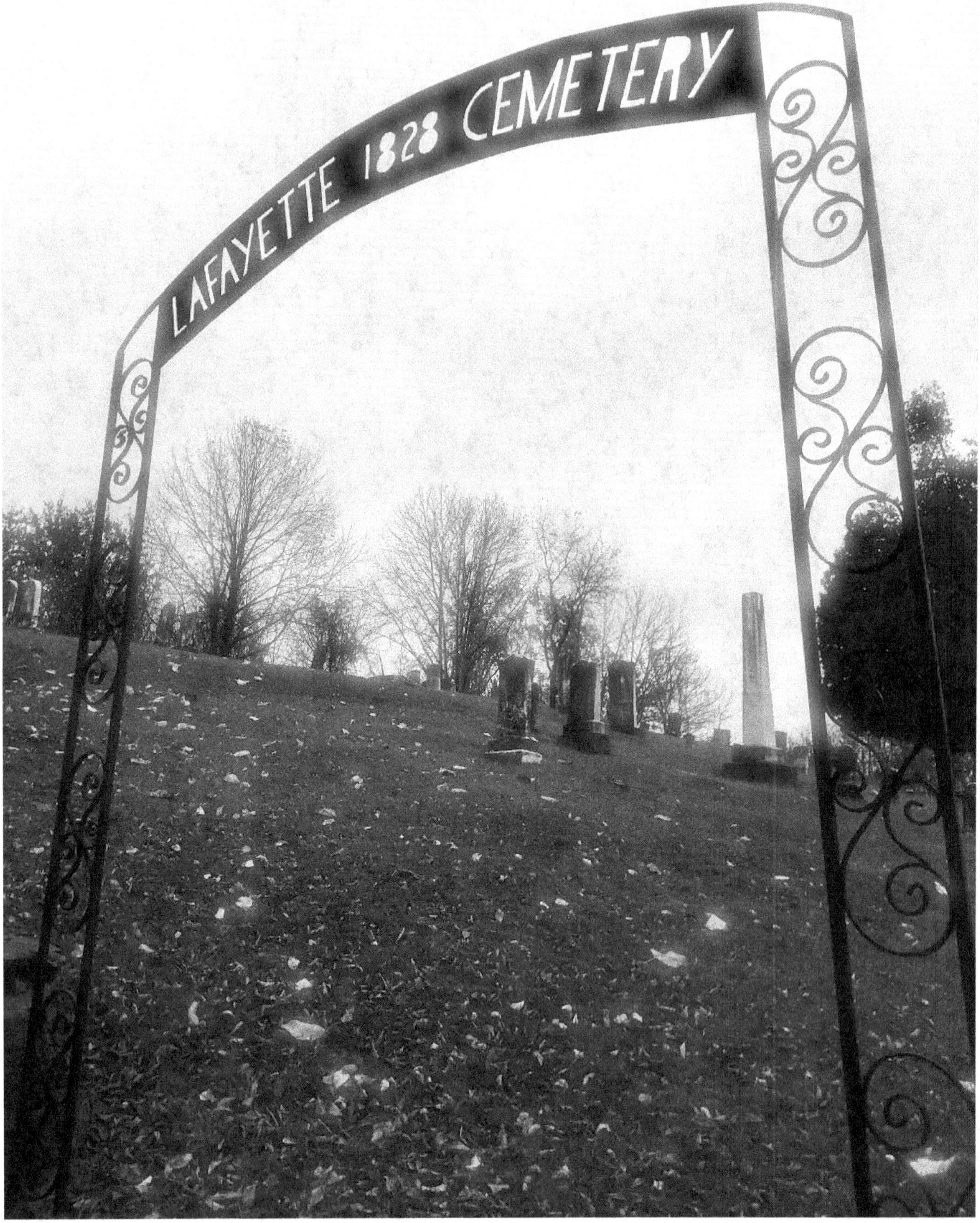
LAFAYETTE 1828 CEMETERY

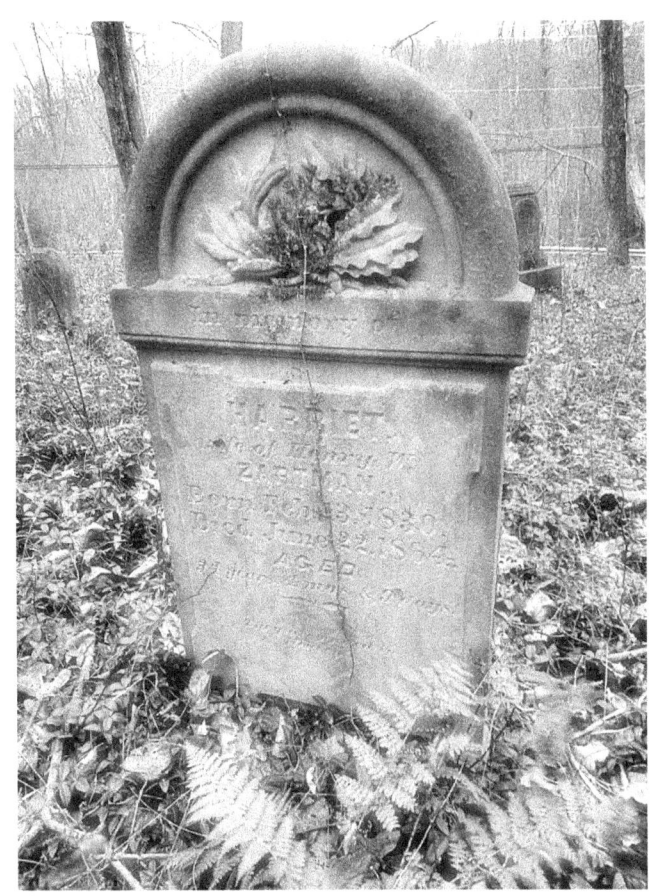

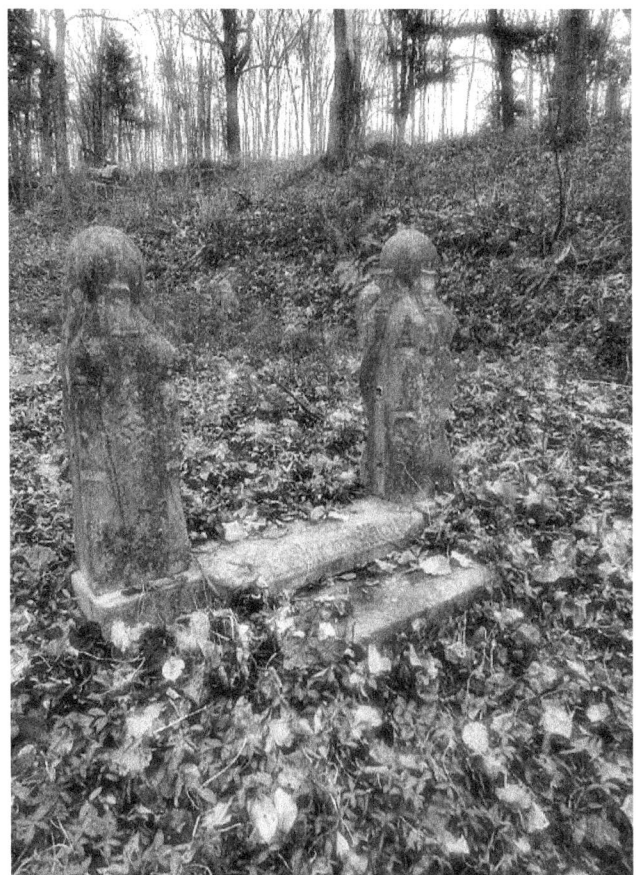

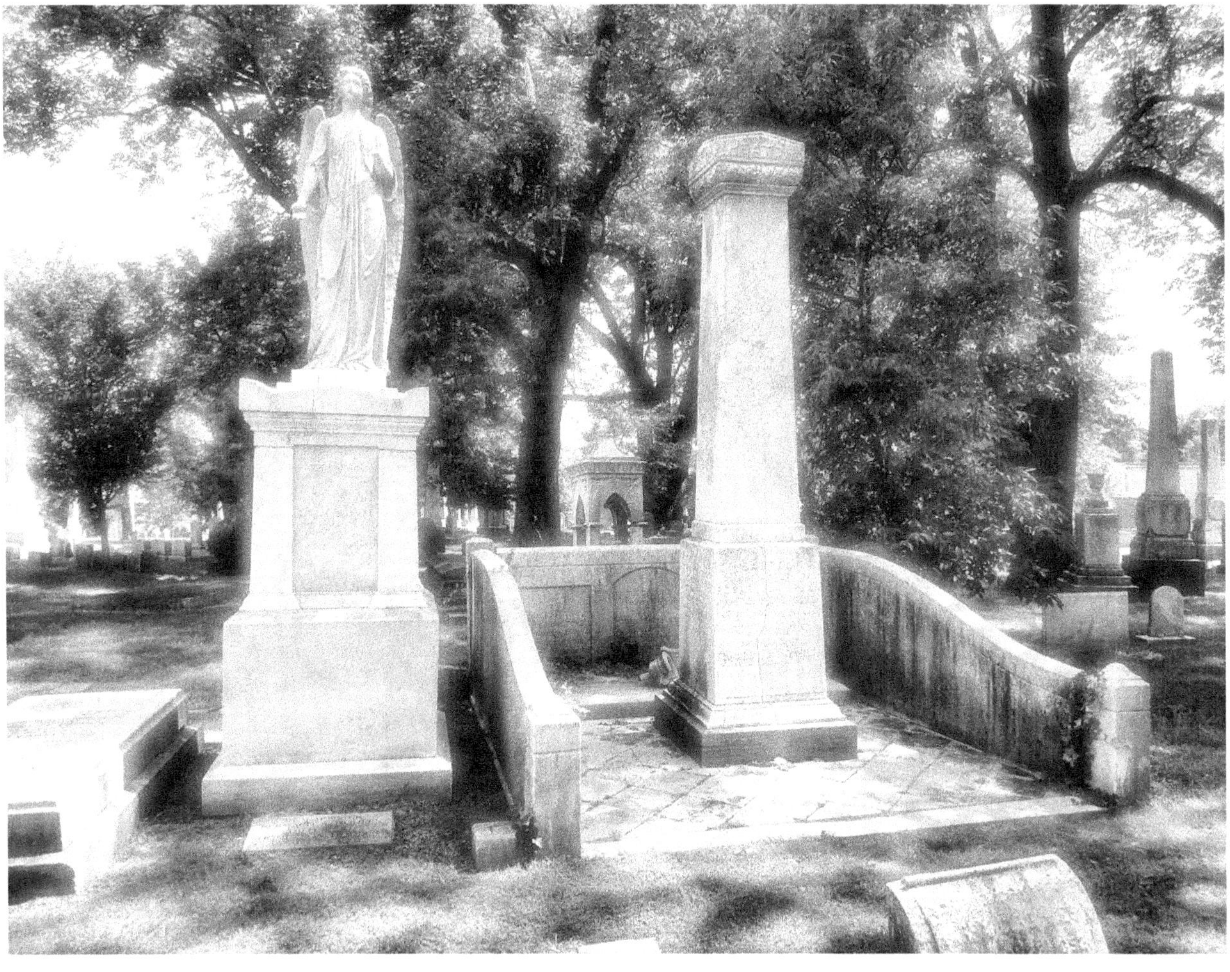

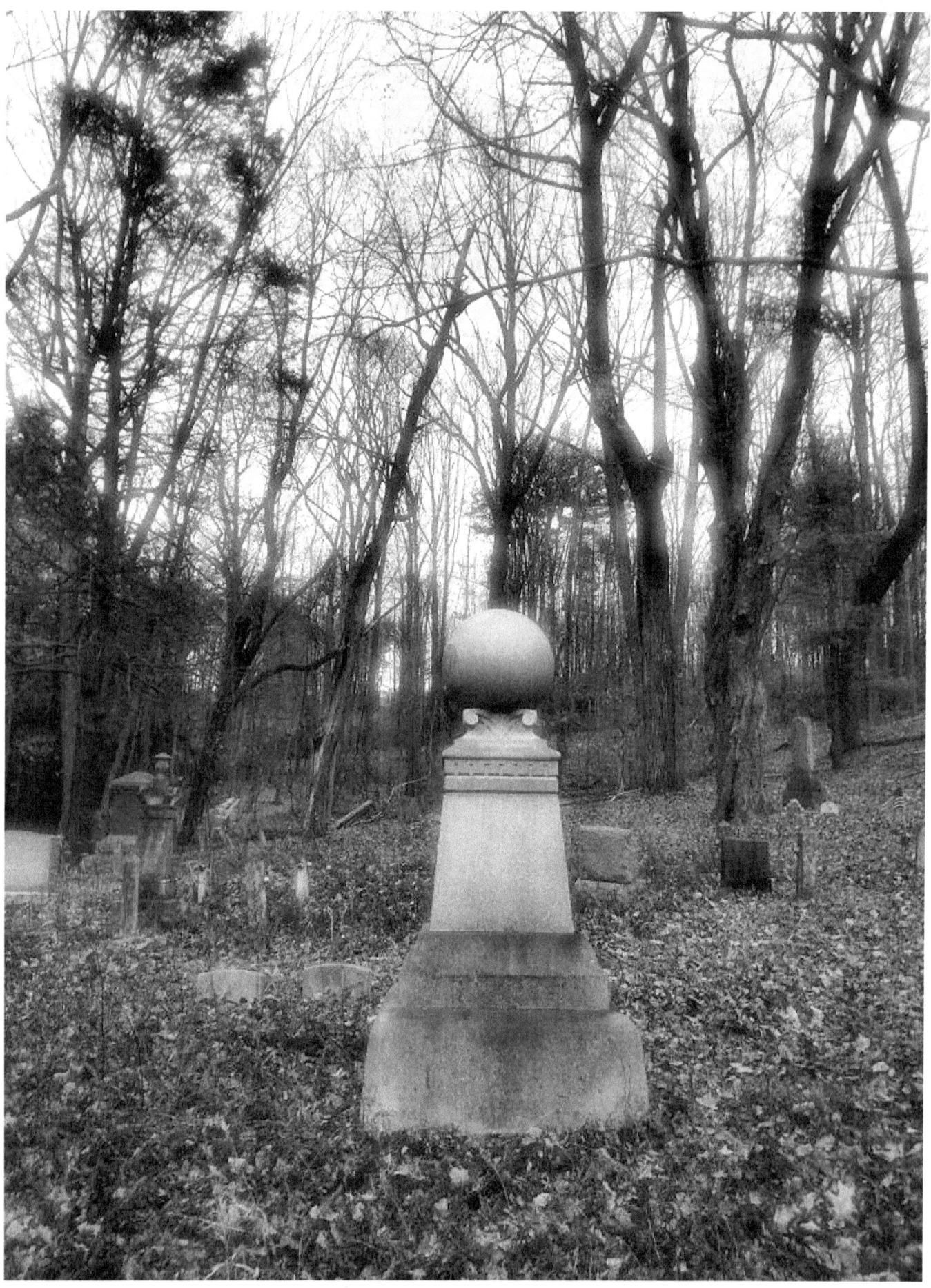

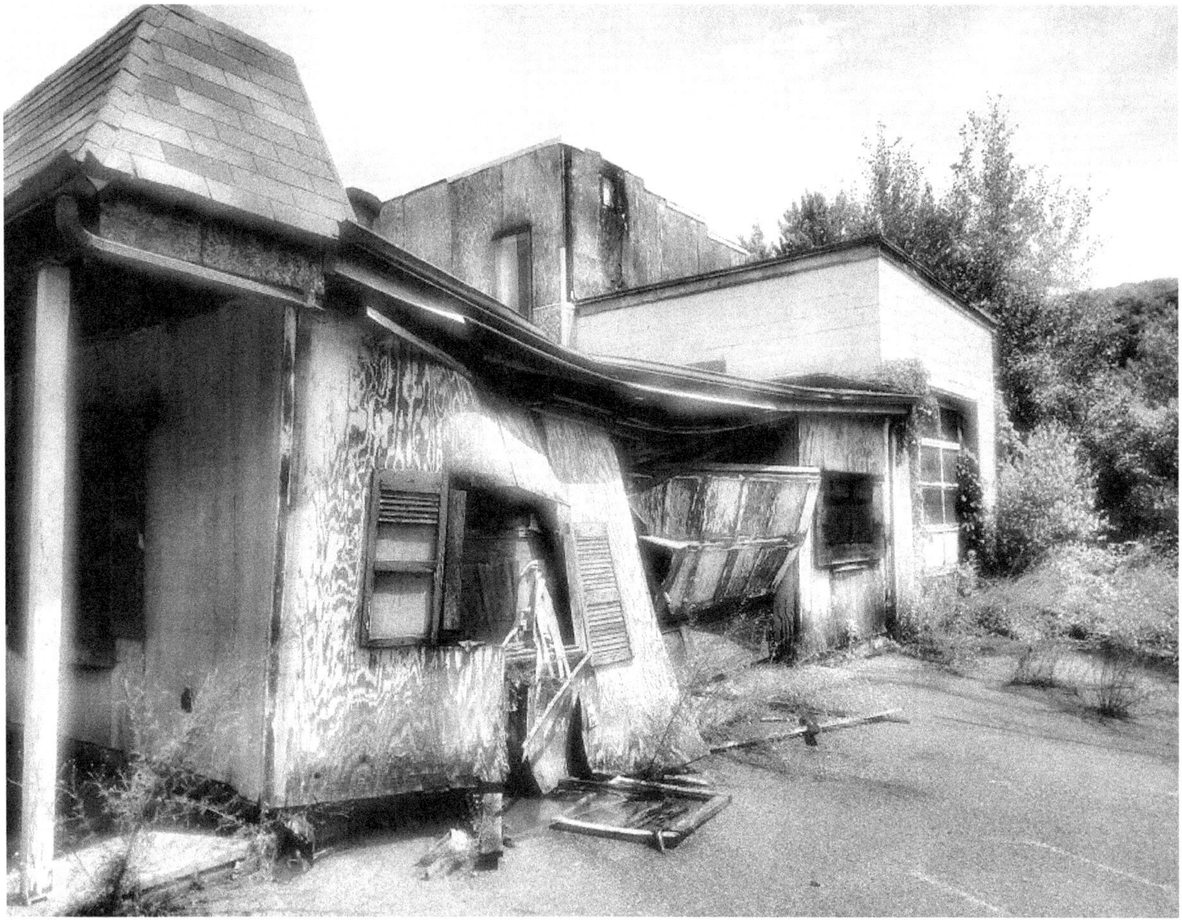

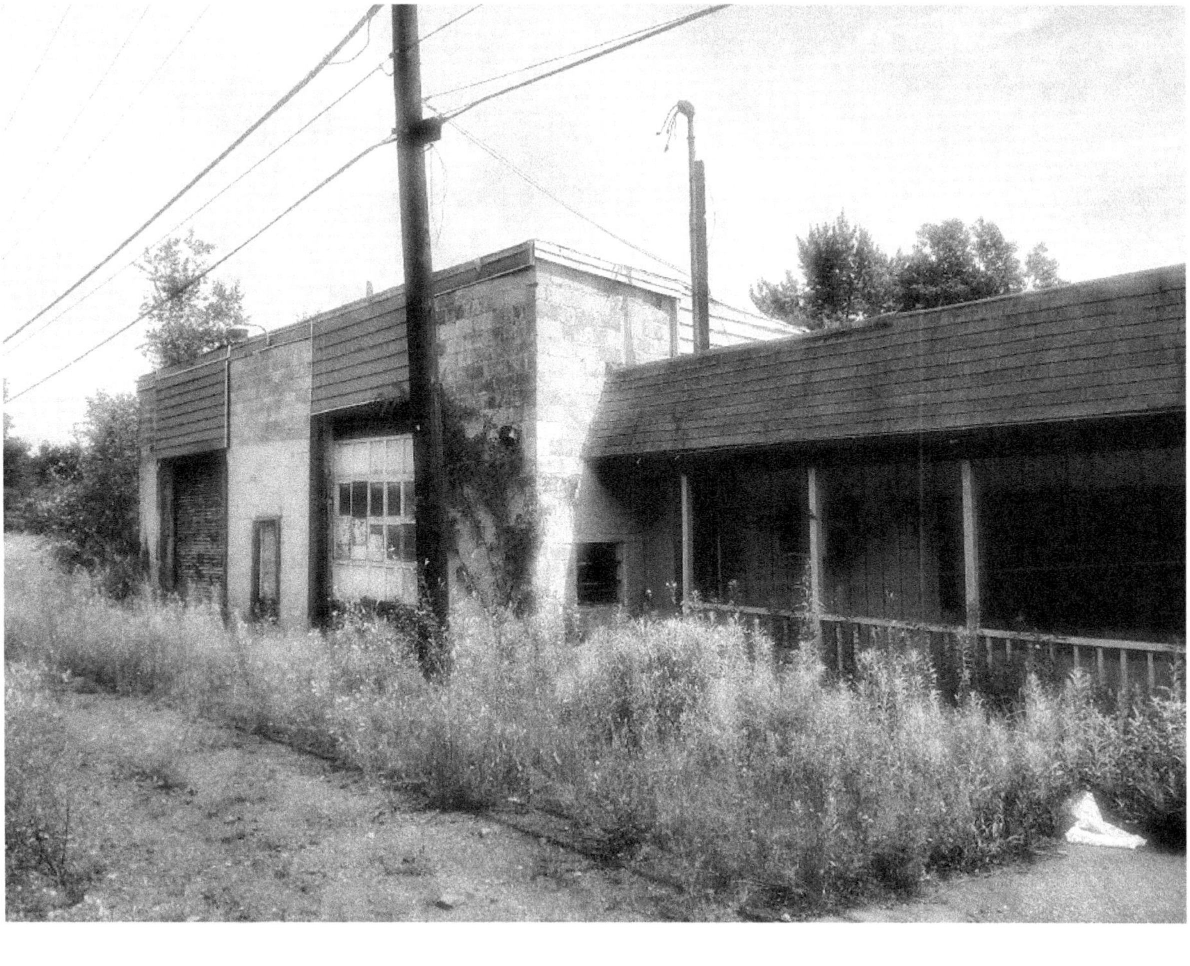

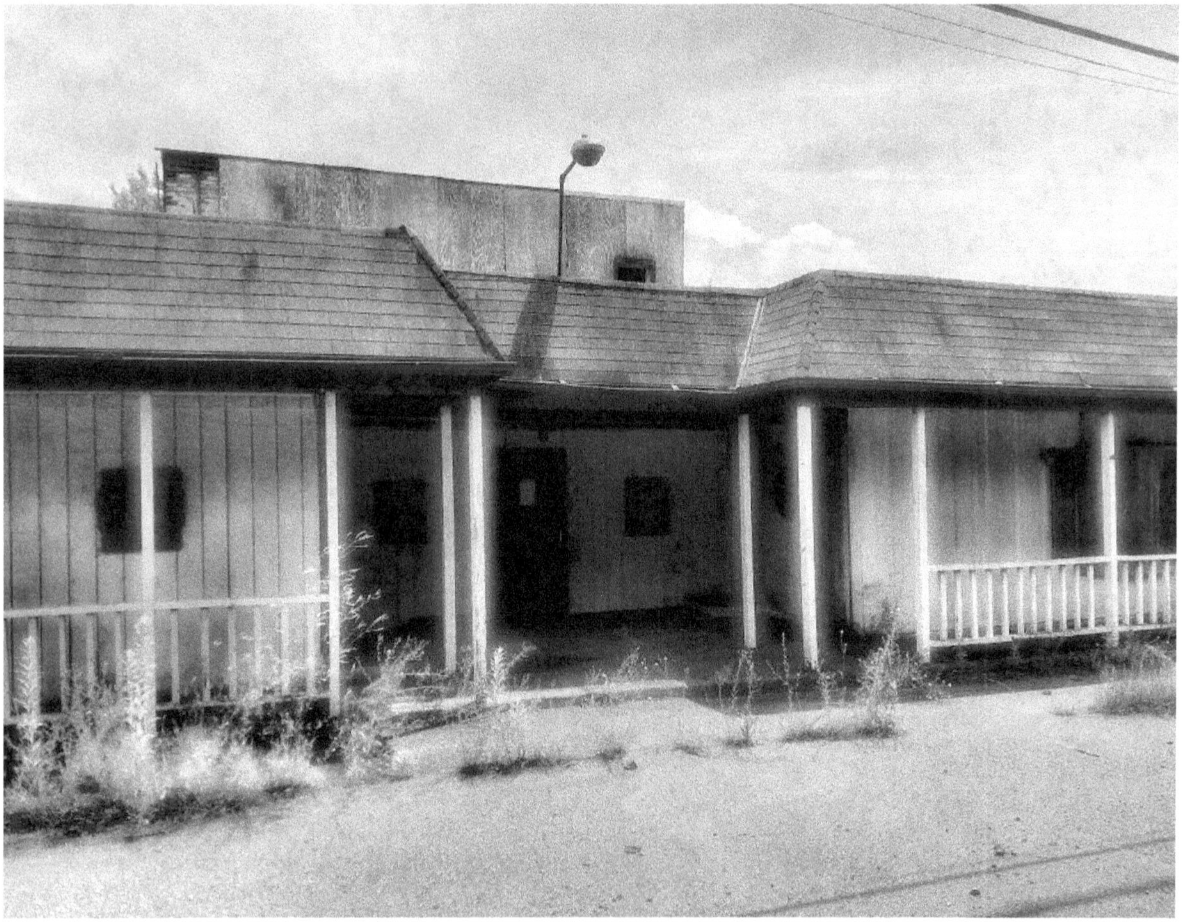

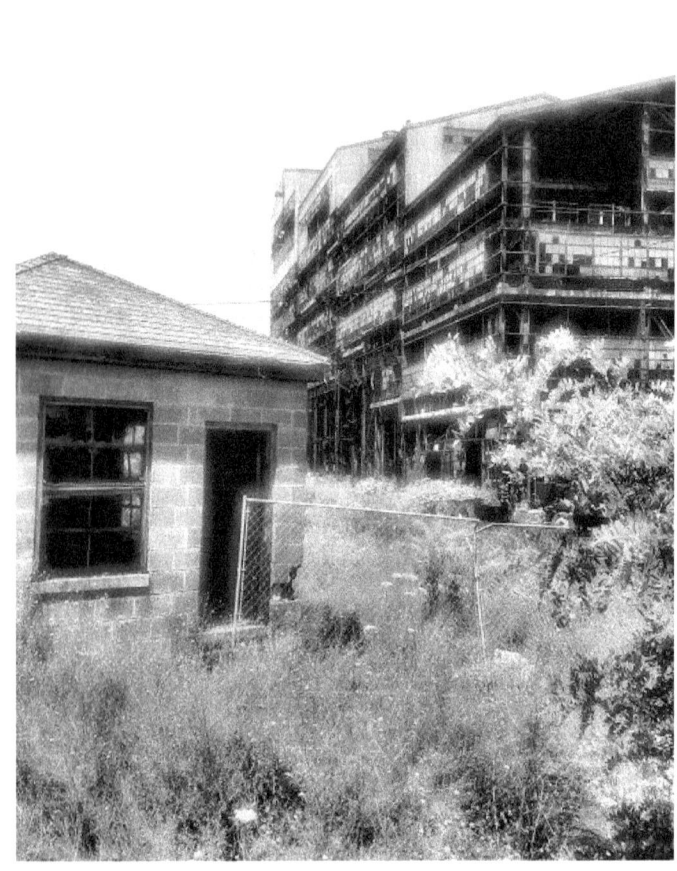

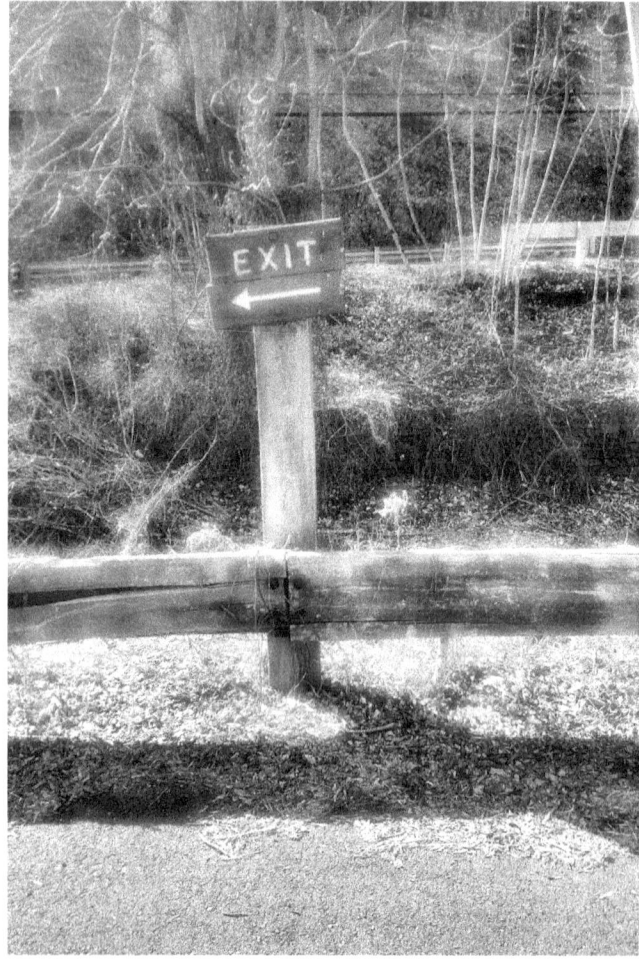

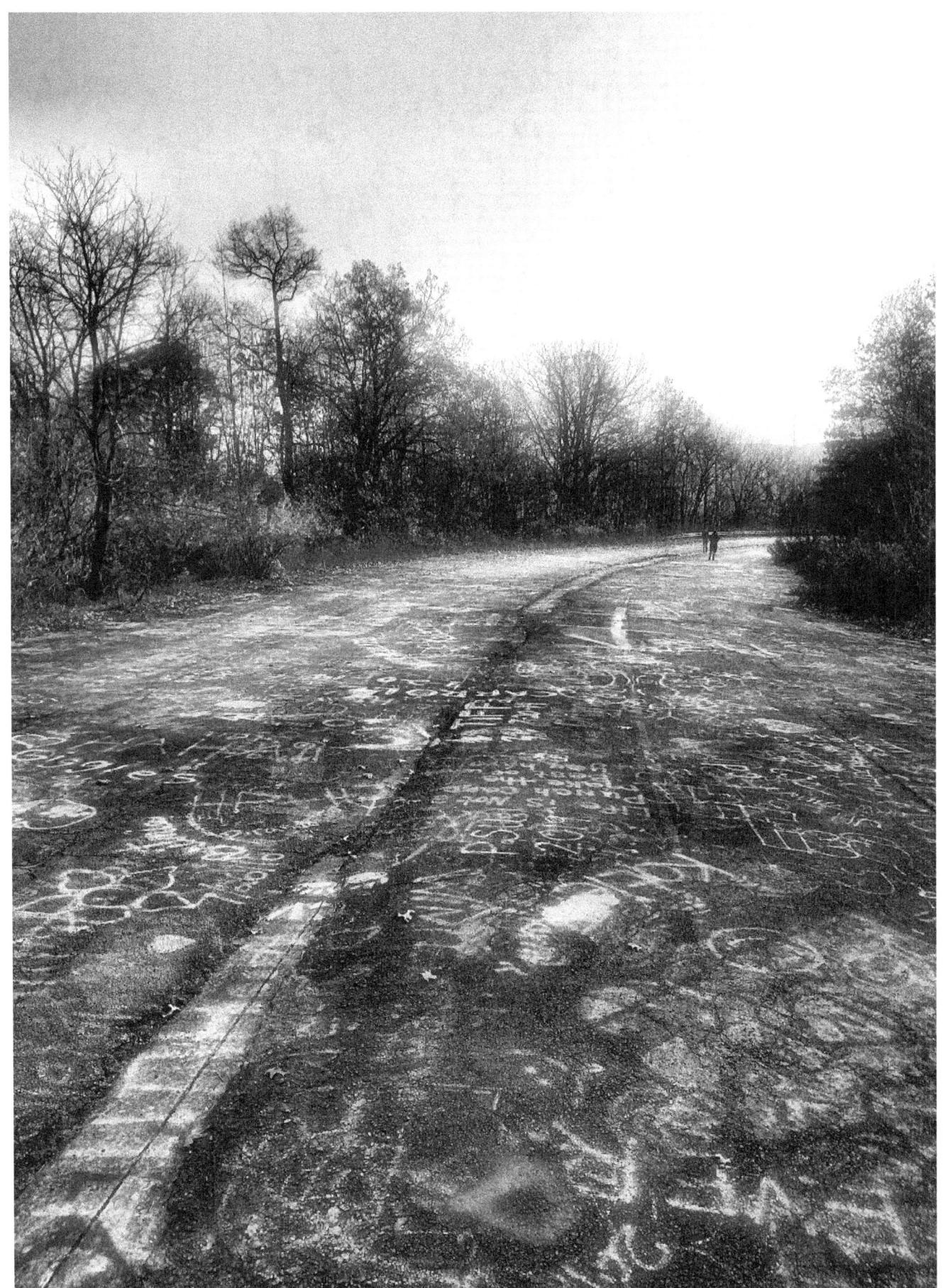

The seemingly endless, heavily-graffitied road of Centralia, PA

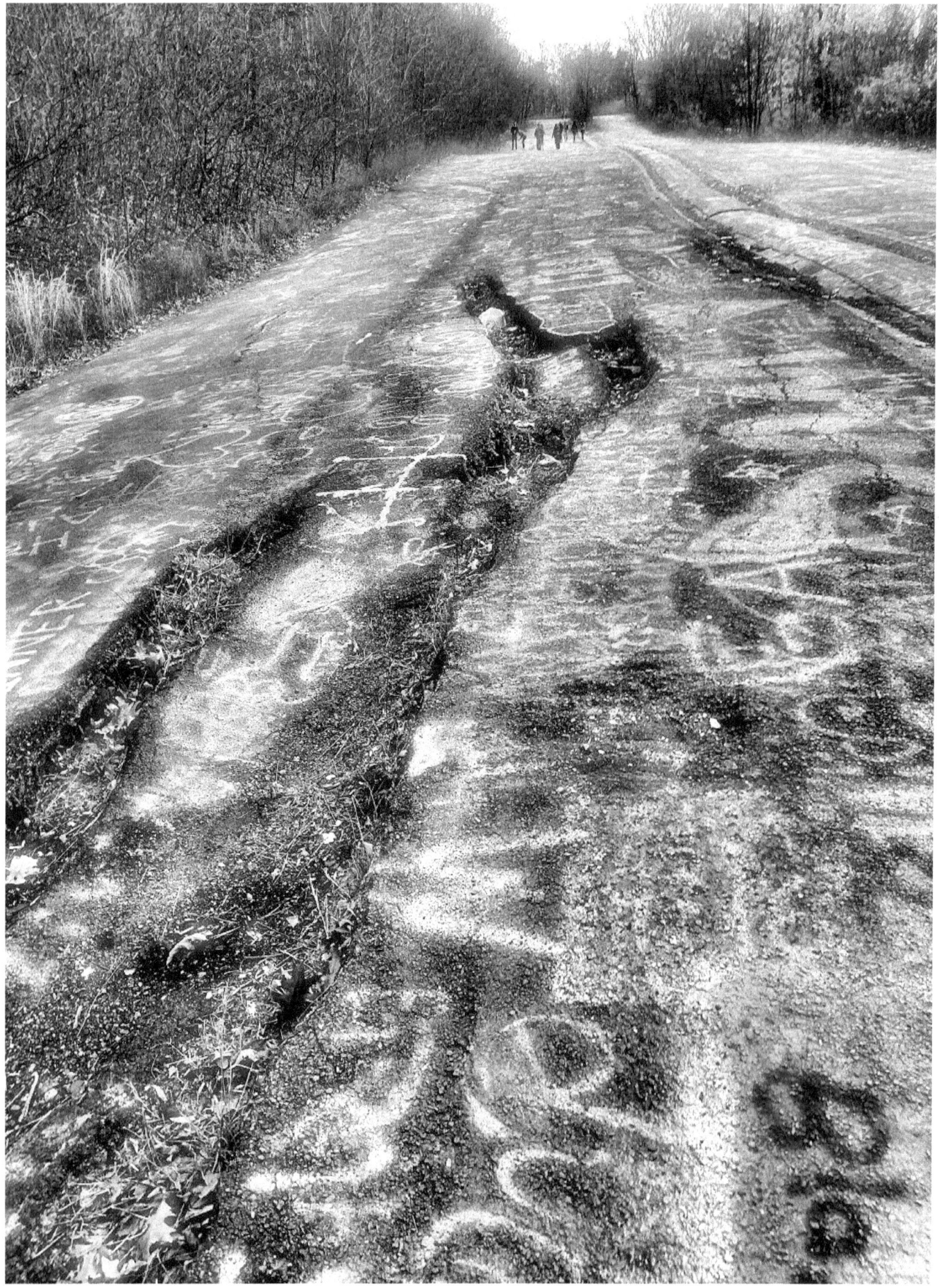

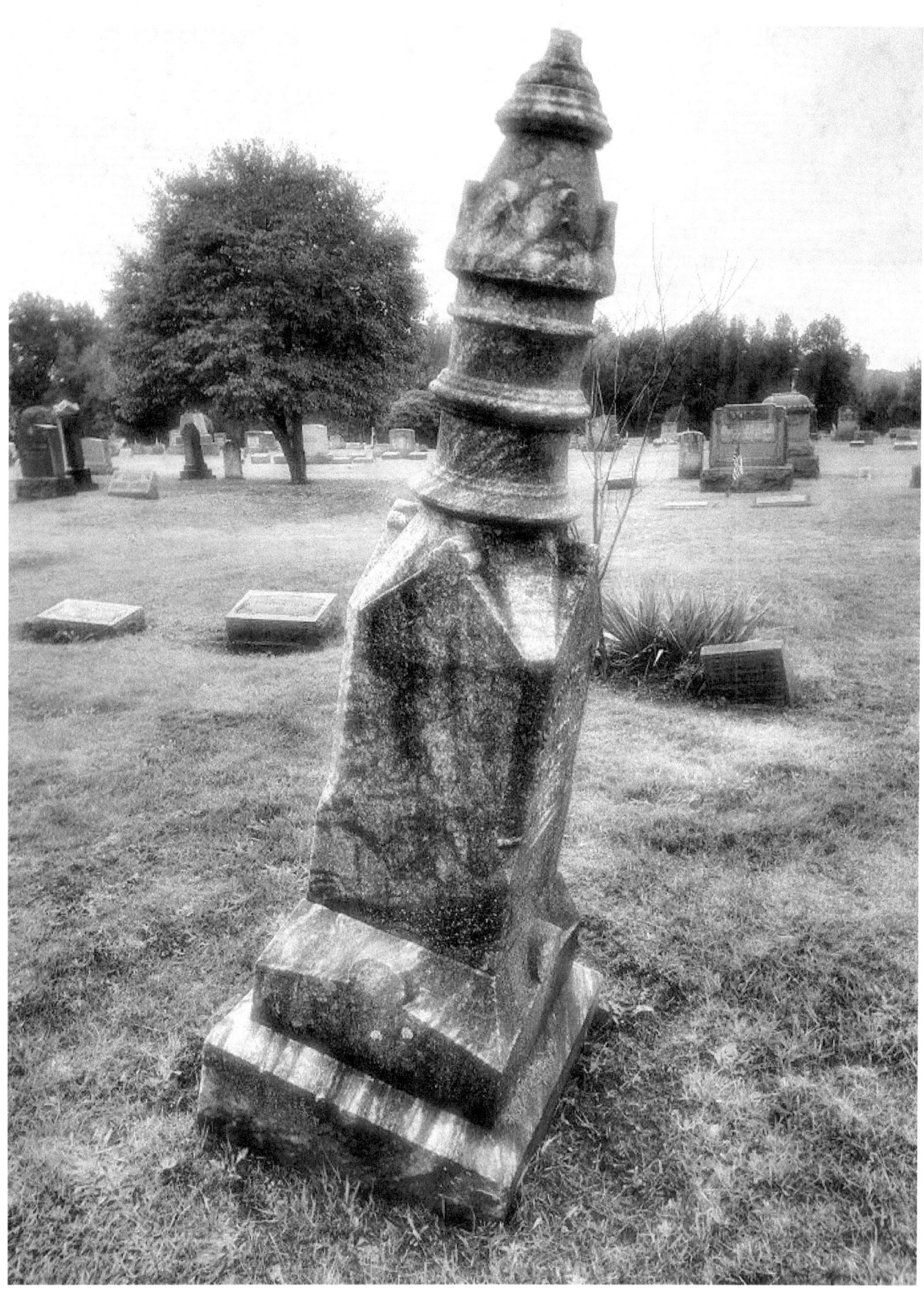

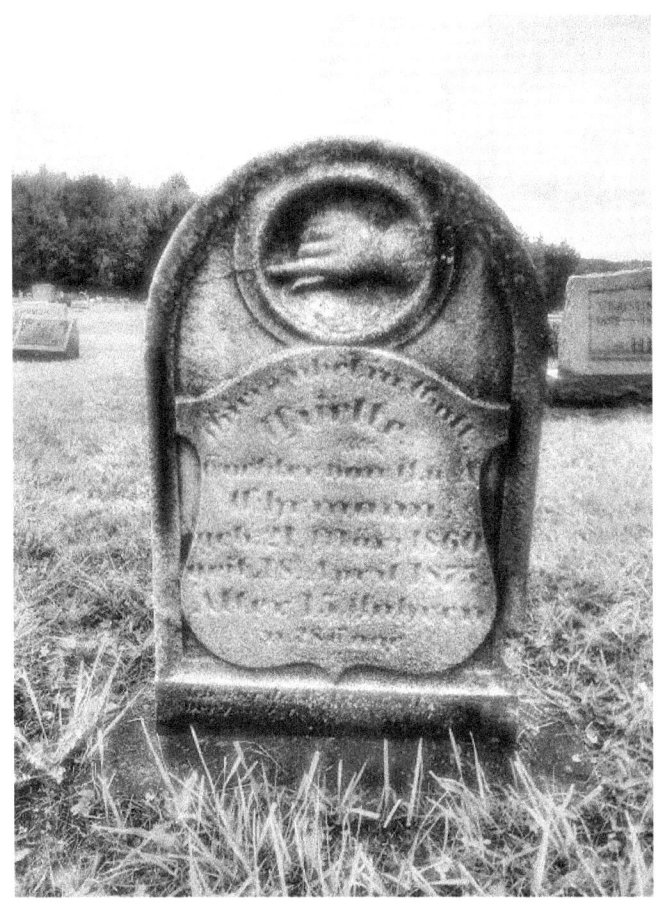
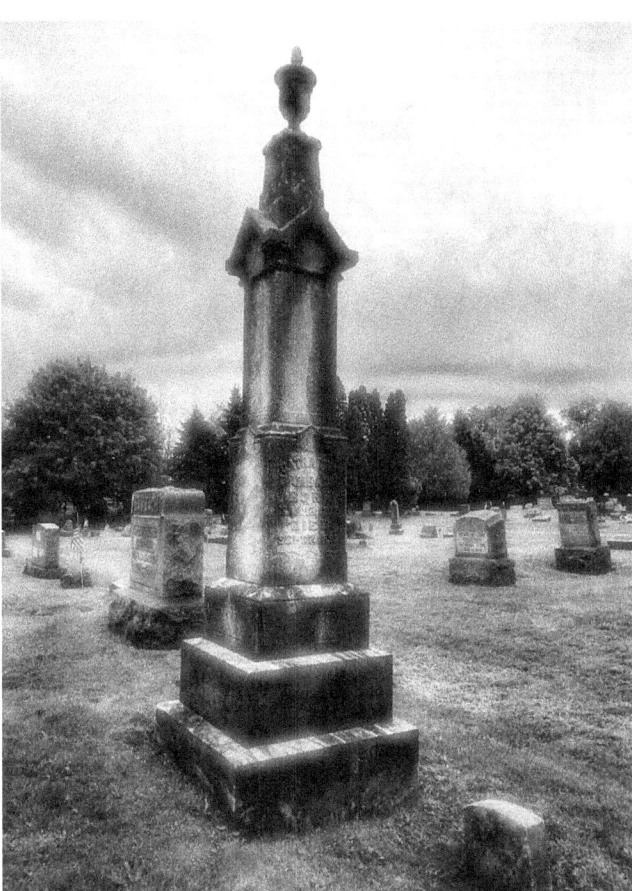

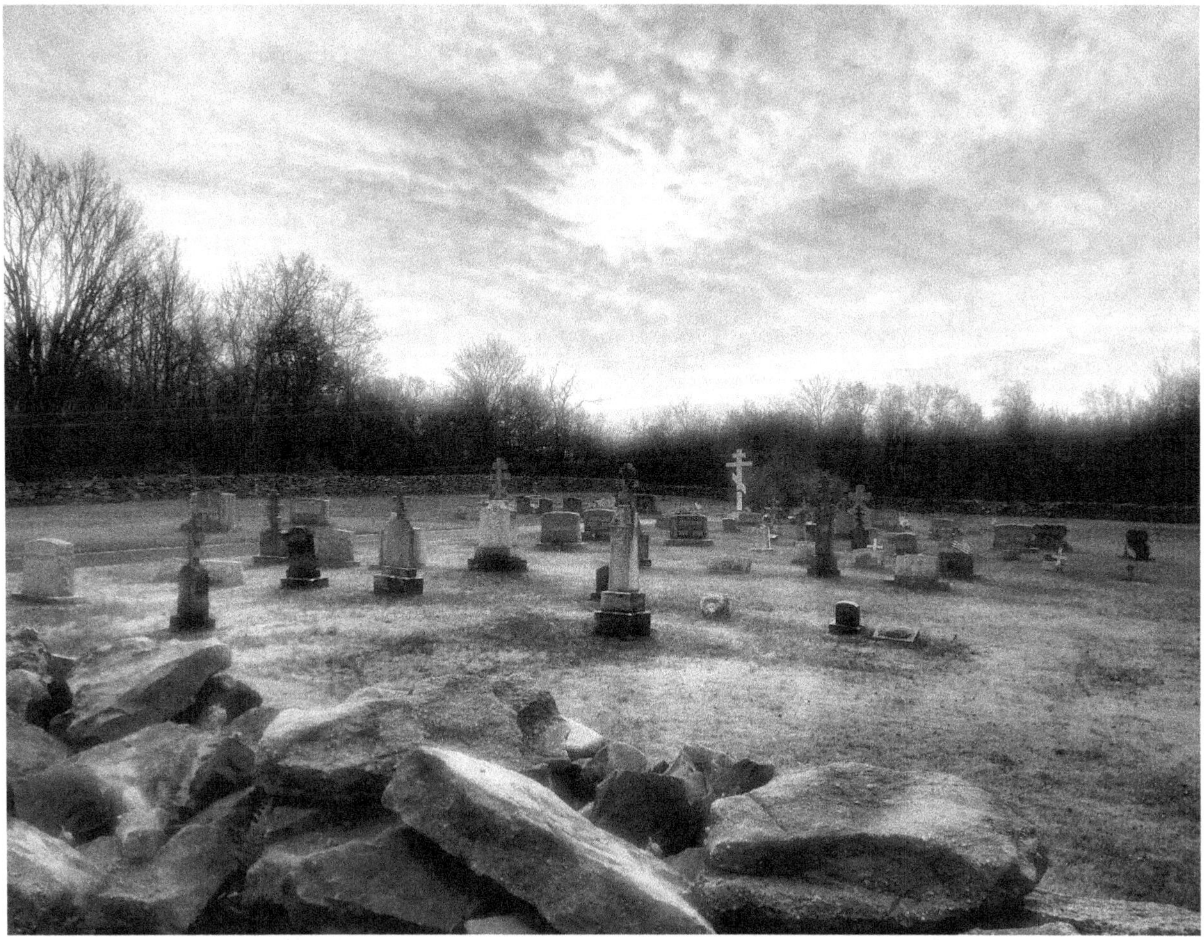

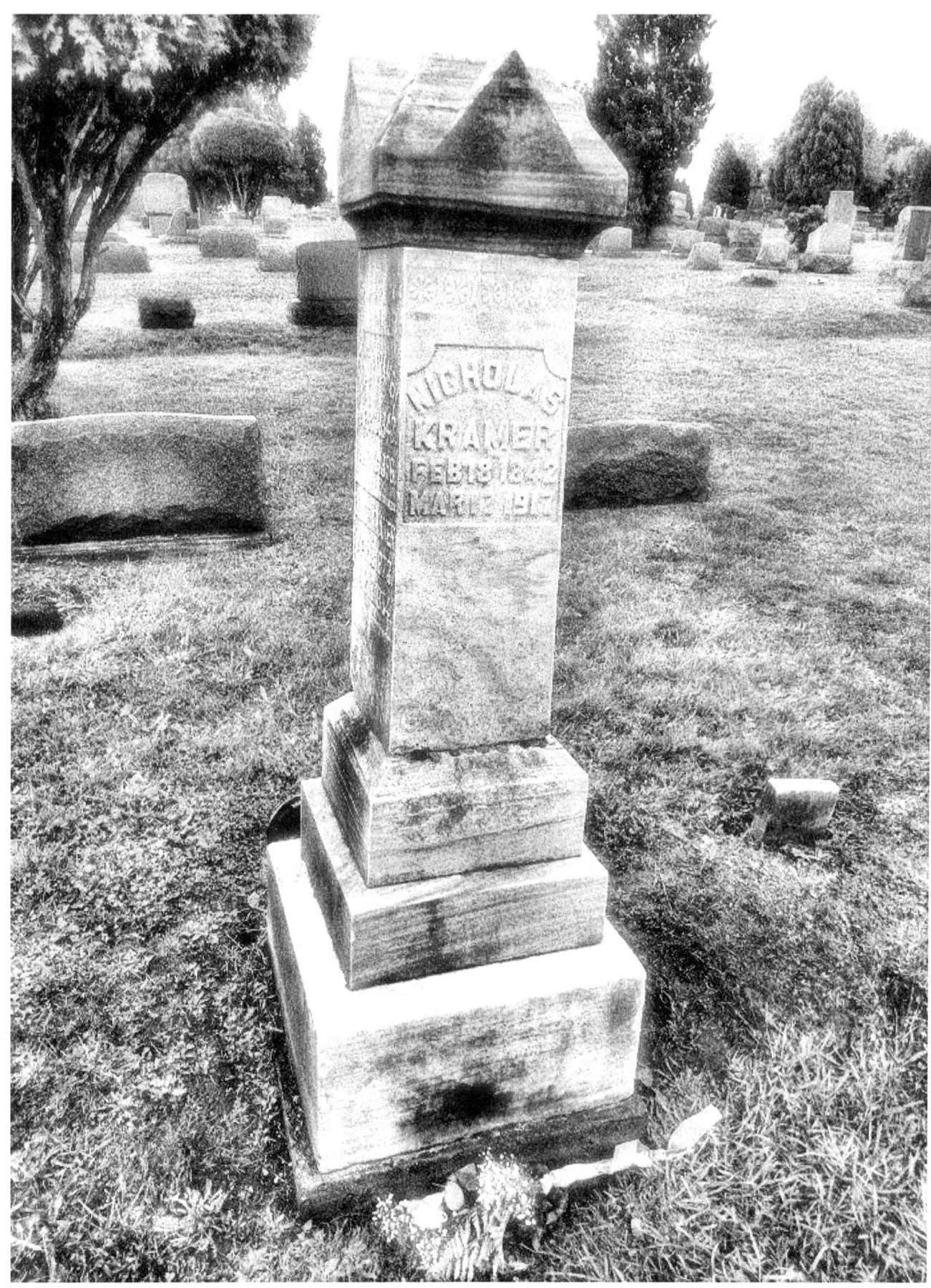

The headstone made popular by the original, "Night of the Living Dead".

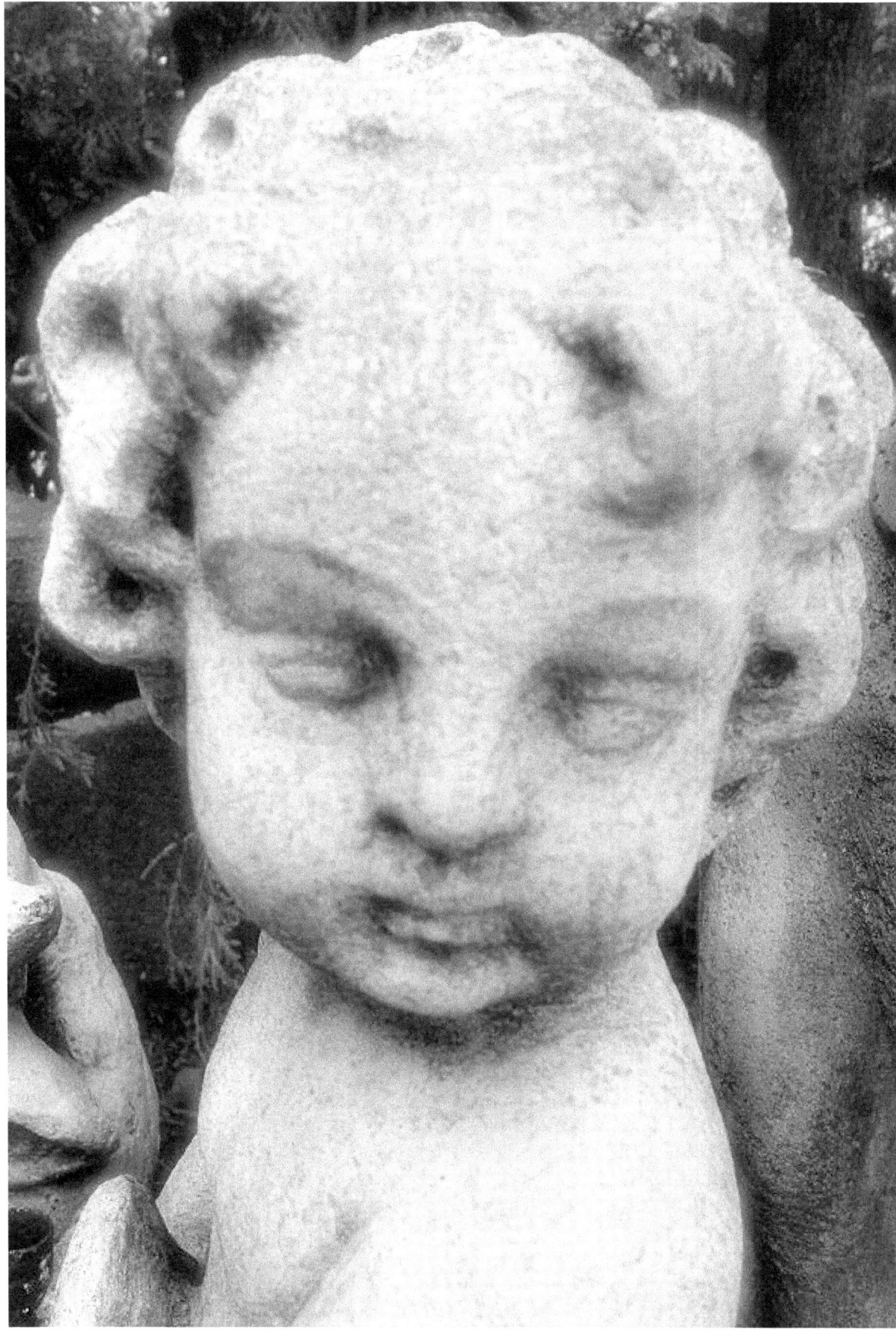

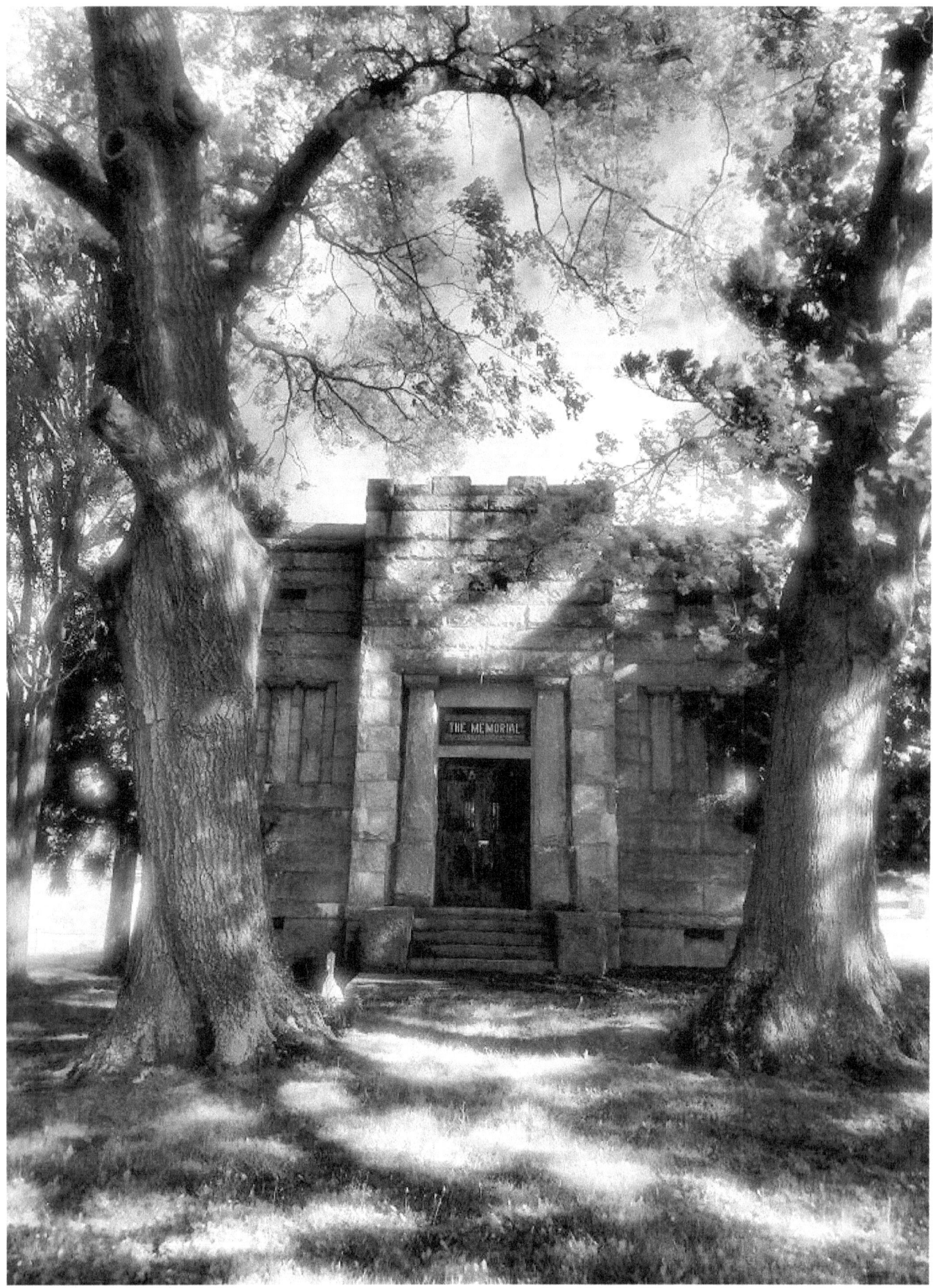

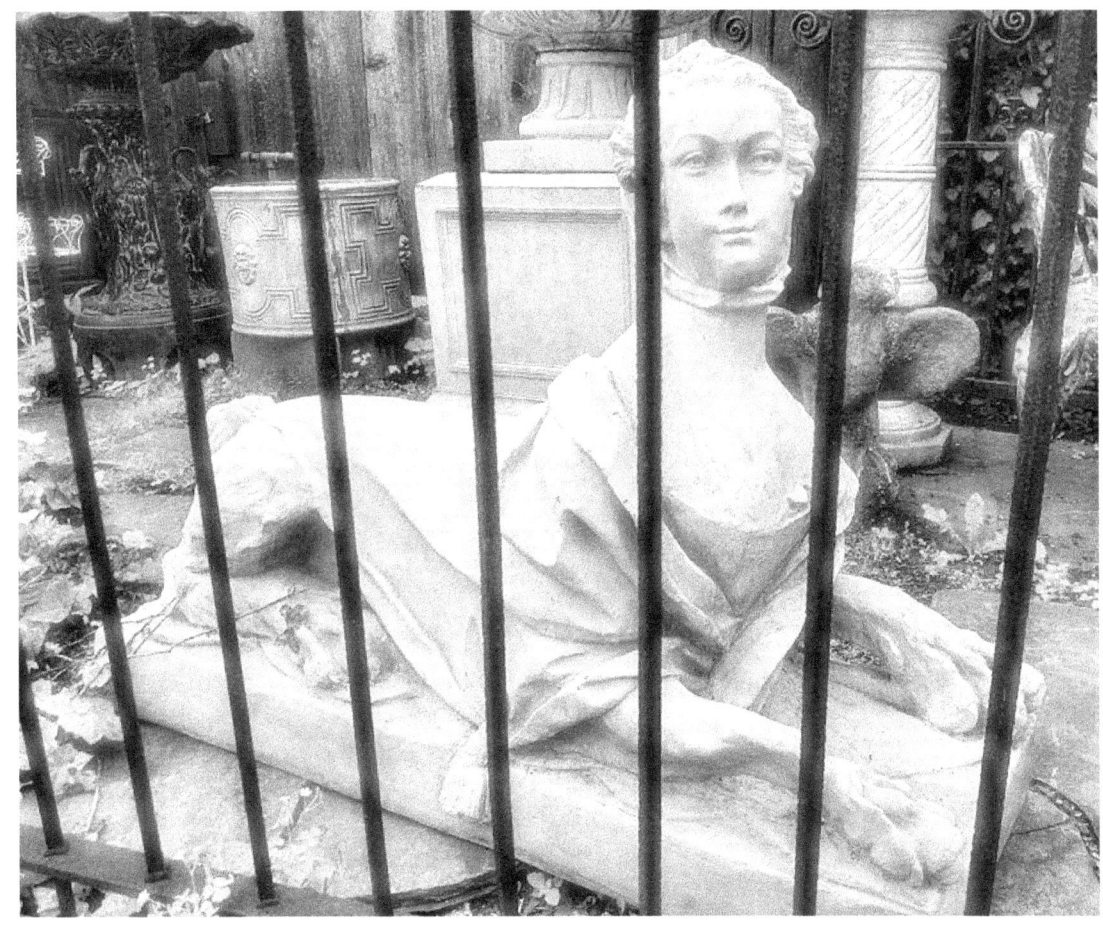

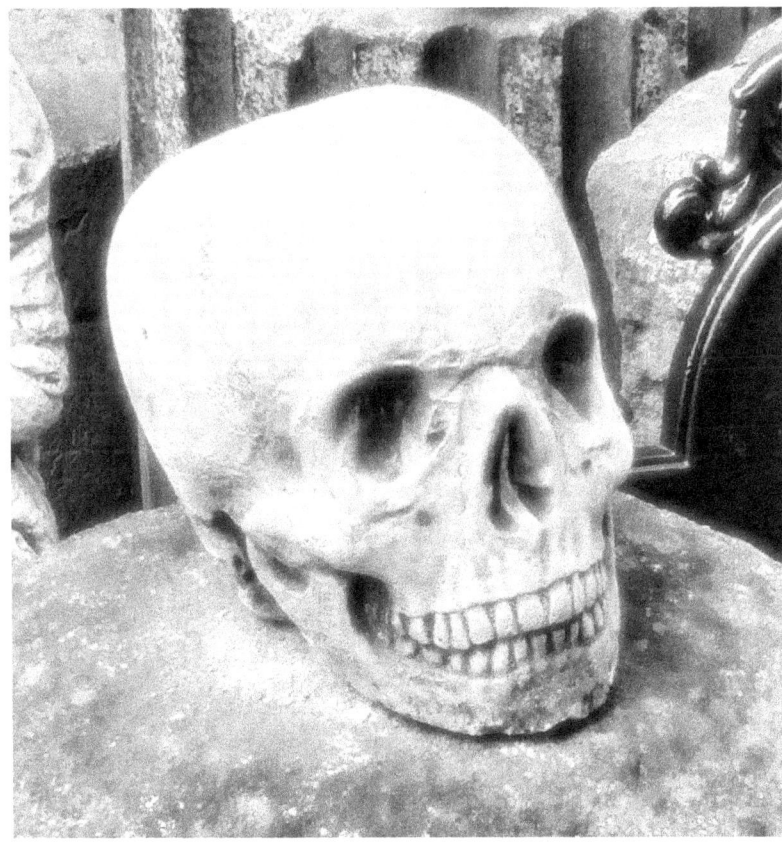

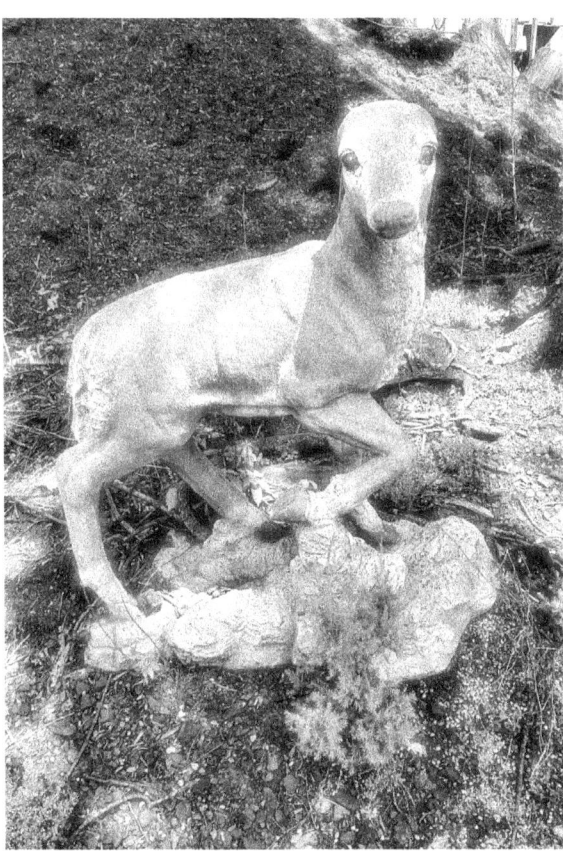

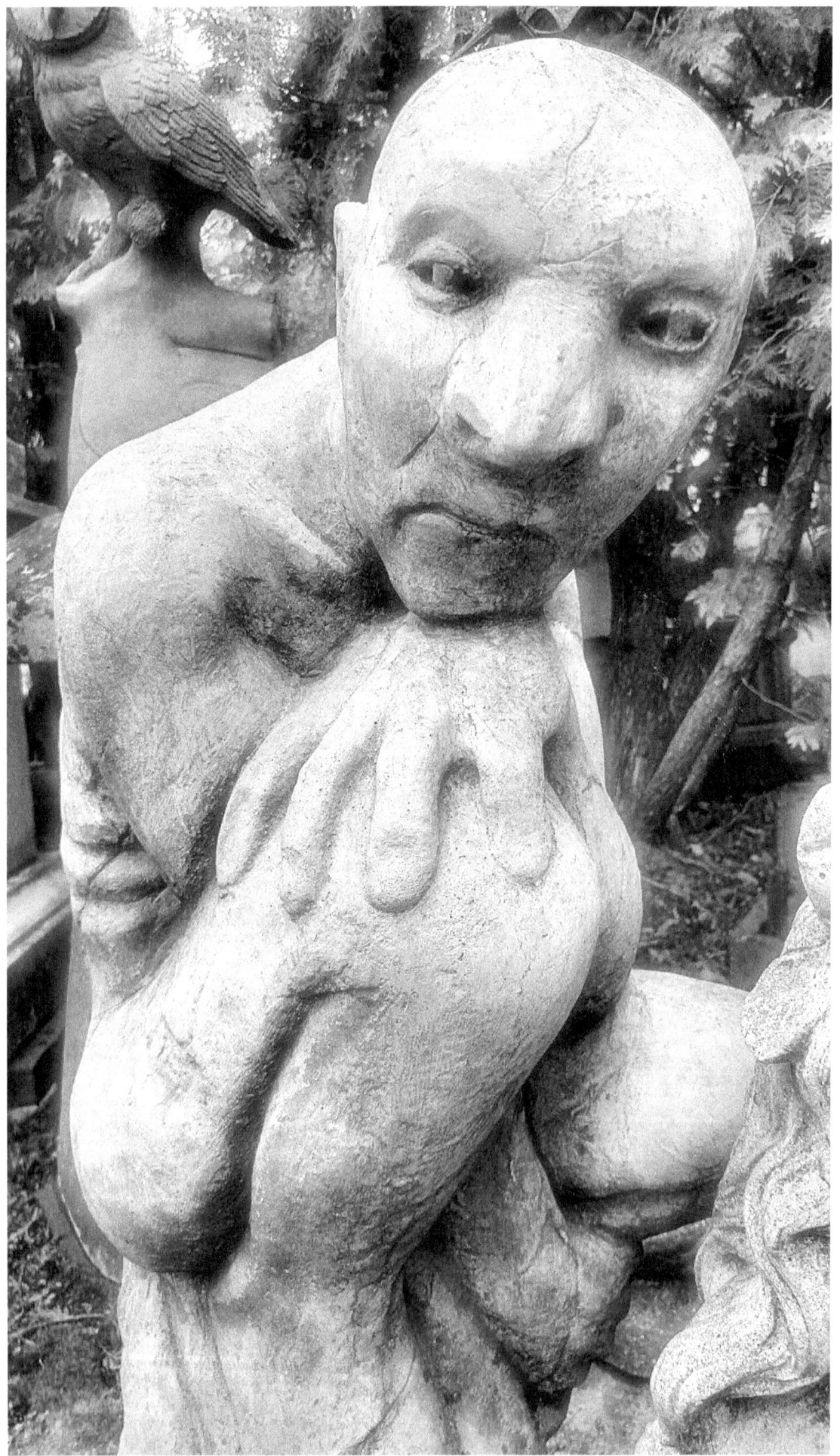

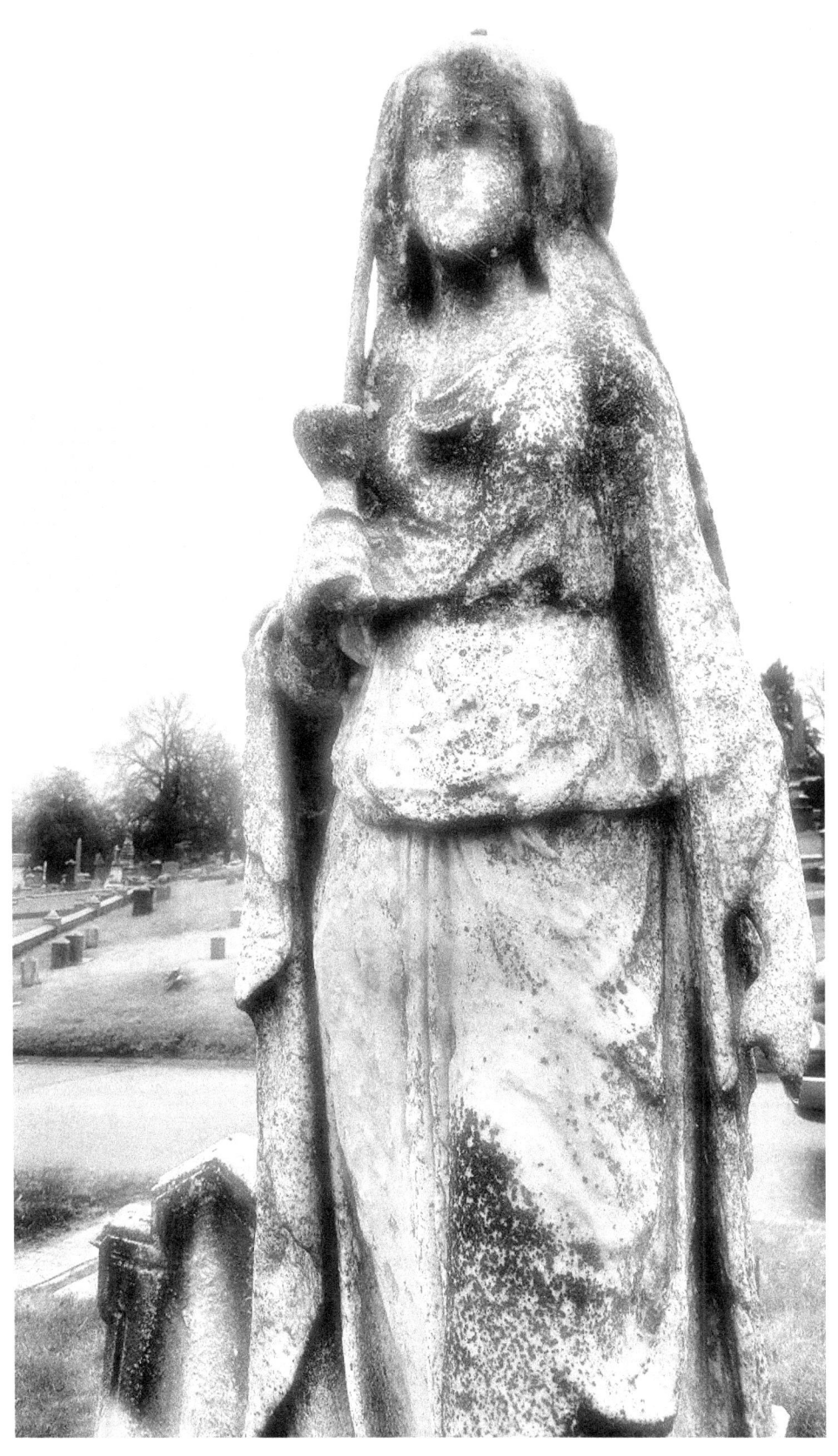

"The tragedy of life is not death, but what we let die inside of us while we live." ~ *Norman Cousins*

About the Author

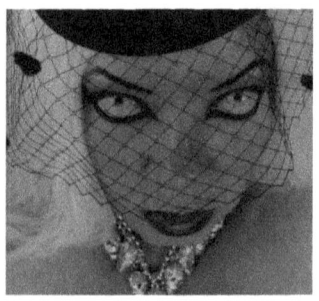

*A 2012 Fright Times Award Winner for Best Horror Collectible, Cinsearae started **Mistress Rae's Decadent Designs** as an extension for sharing her many creative endeavors, including one-of-a-kind eerie porcelain dolls, zombie babies, and Steampunk, Gothic, Fantasy and Comic Book-inspired jewelry and accessories.*

*She is also Editor/Publisher of award-winning **Dark Gothic Resurrected Magazine**, an author, and a graphic artist for Caliburn Press. She enjoys sketching, photography, atmospheric music (citing Nox Arcana and Midnight Syndicate), and frequently haunts local flea markets.*

You can find her virtual home at www.BloodTouch.Webs.com, and on the social media circuses of Facebook, Twitter, YouTube, Pinterest and Instagram @ Cinsearae.

**Some images from this book are available as postcards. For a list of items available (as well as limited edition, collectible ones) please inquire through www.MistressRae13.Etsy.com*

SEVERAL IMAGES FROM "TERRA MYSTERIA" CAN BE ALSO BE PURCHASED AS POSTCARDS, MINI POSTERS AND OTHER EPHEMERA. VISIT www.Zazzle.com/MirthfulMourning or www.Zazzle.com/Melodic_Mayhem FOR MORE DETAILS.

===========================

OTHER WORKS BY THE AUTHOR

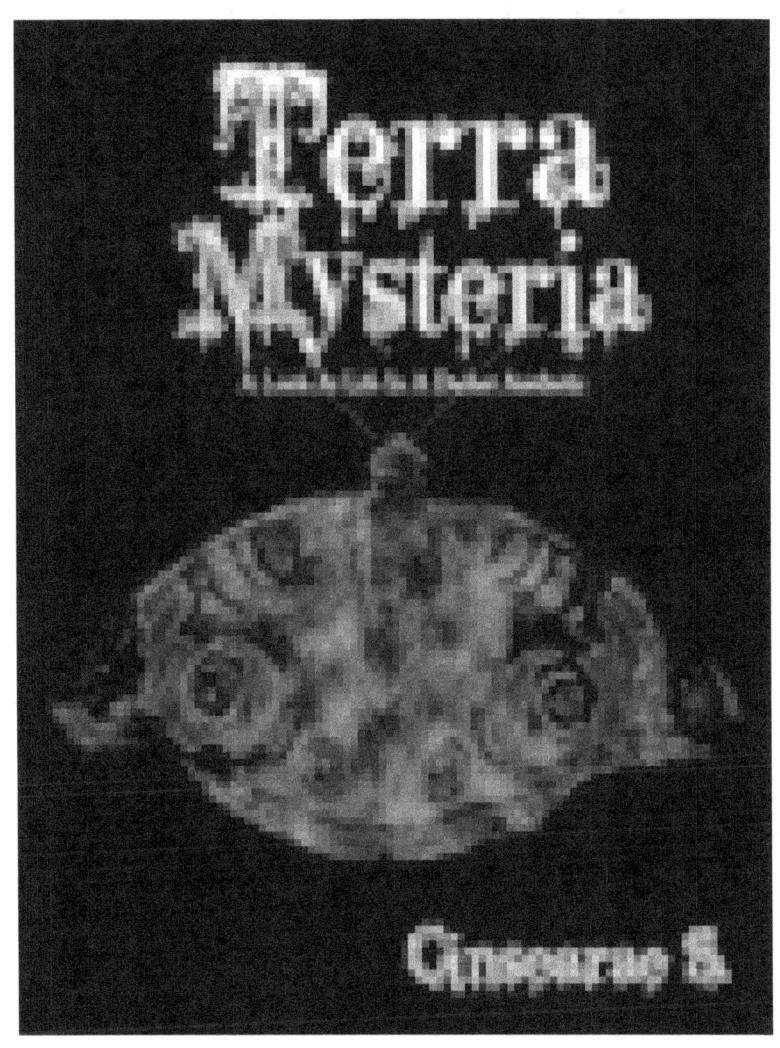

TERRA MYSTERIA: A Look at Life in a Darker Aesthetic
ISBN: 978-1-105-28566-0
Published with Lulu Press. (Search #12175621 at http://www.lulu.com.)

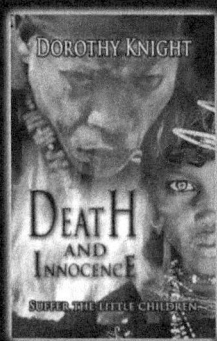 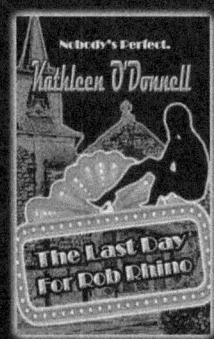 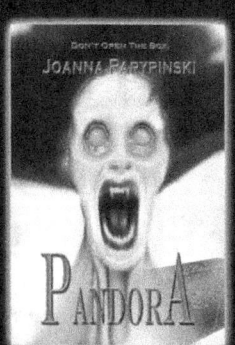 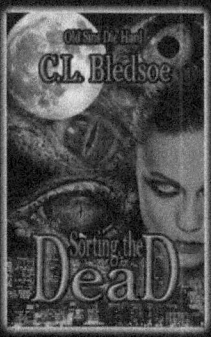 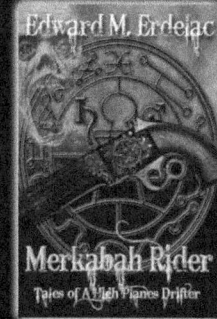
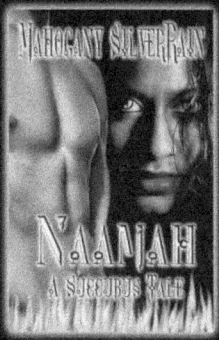 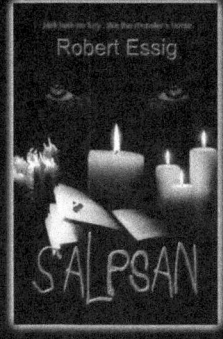 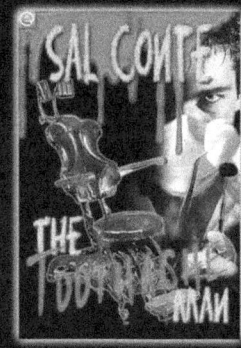 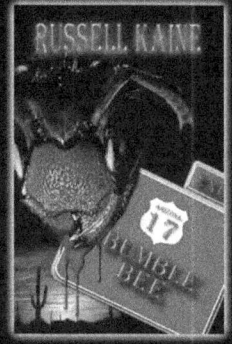 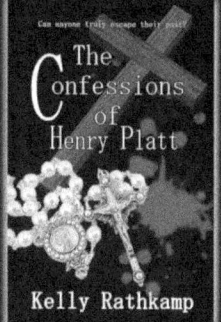
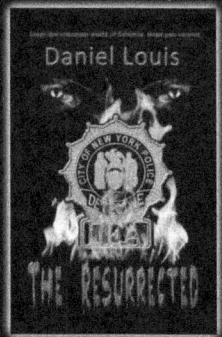
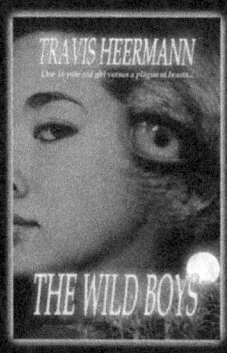
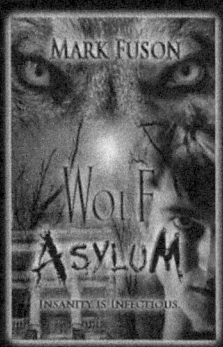 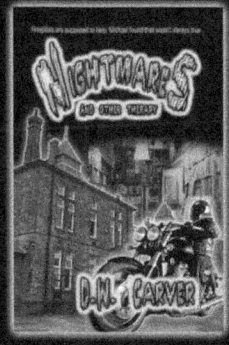 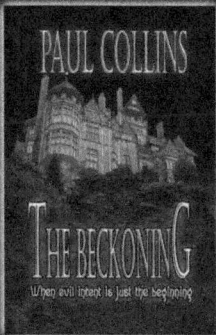 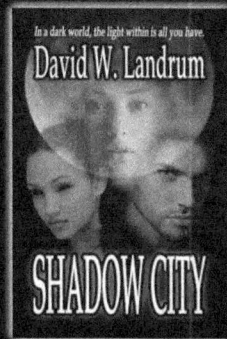 

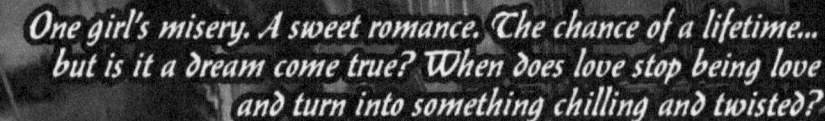

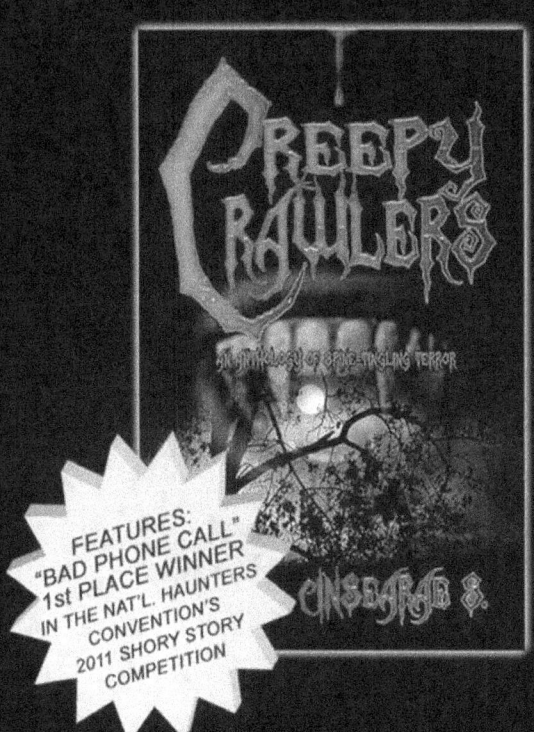
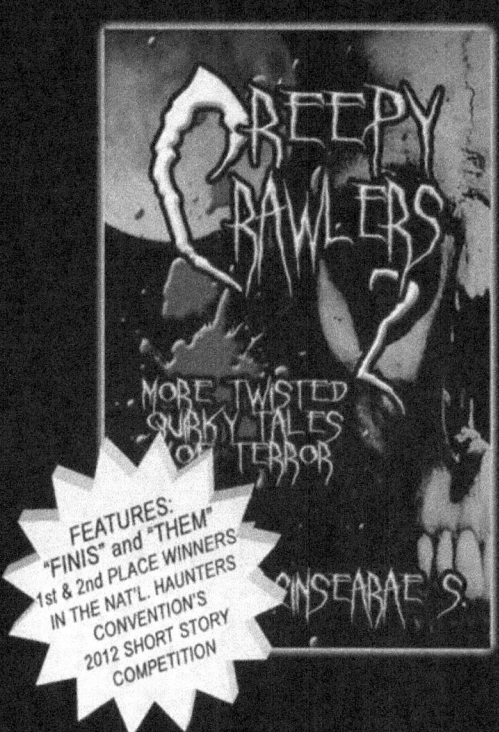

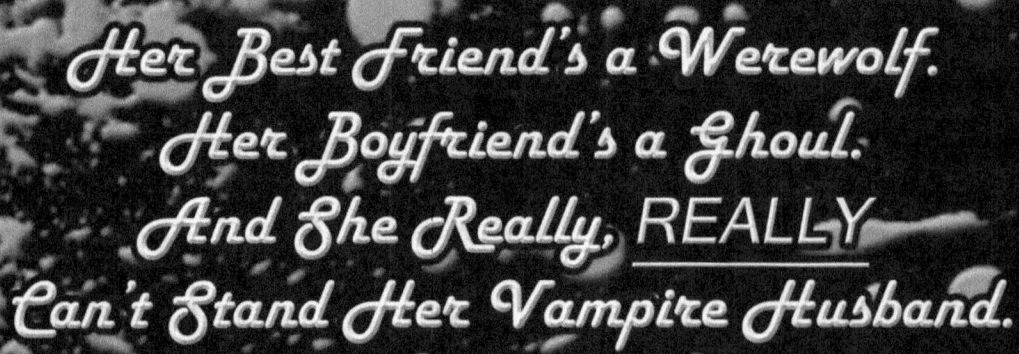
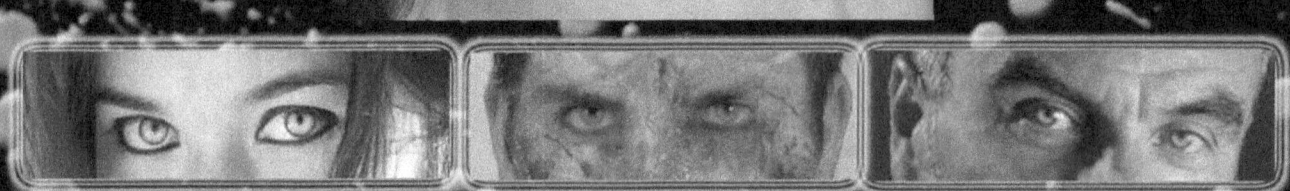
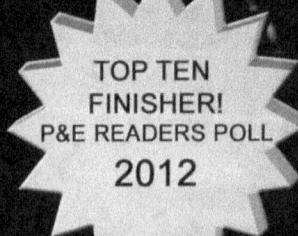

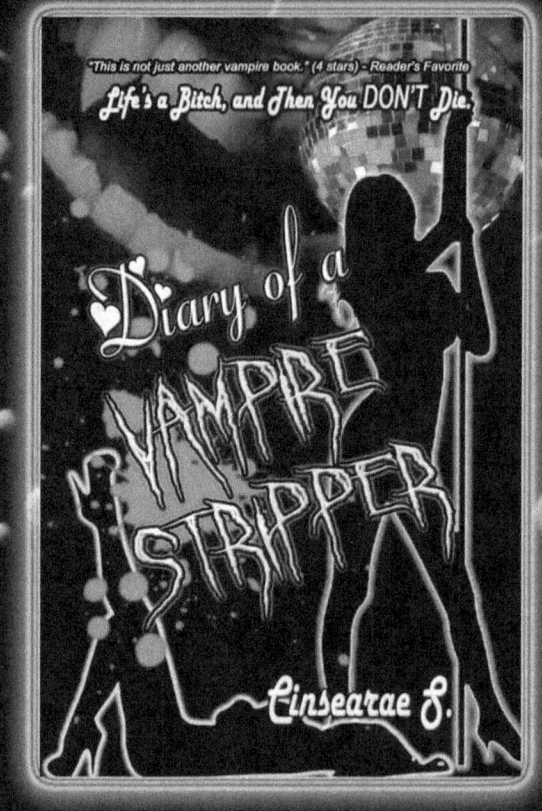

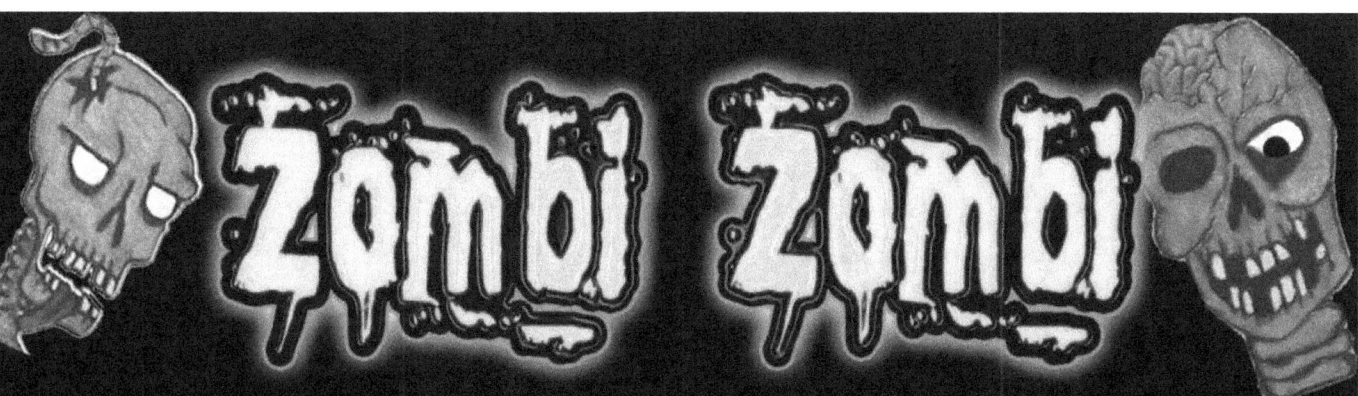
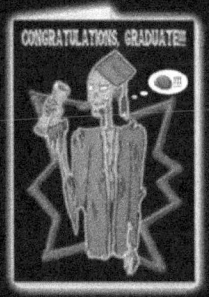 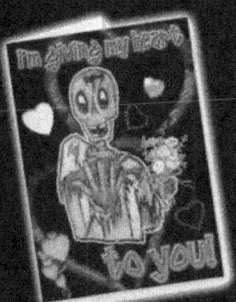 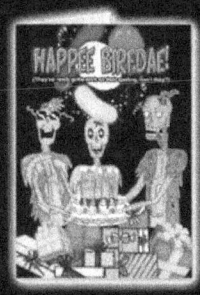 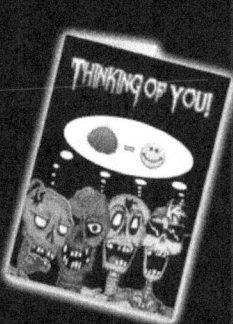 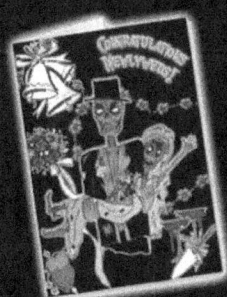
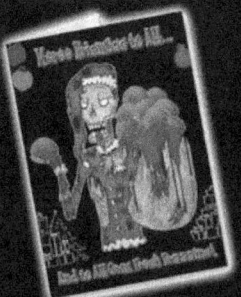 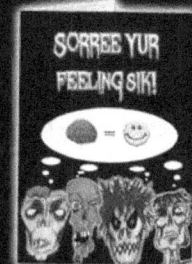  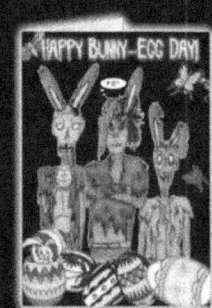 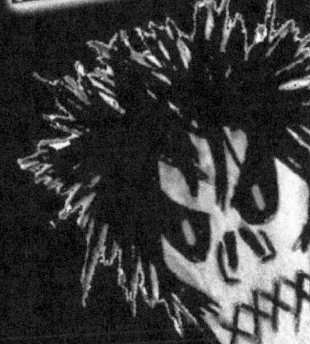

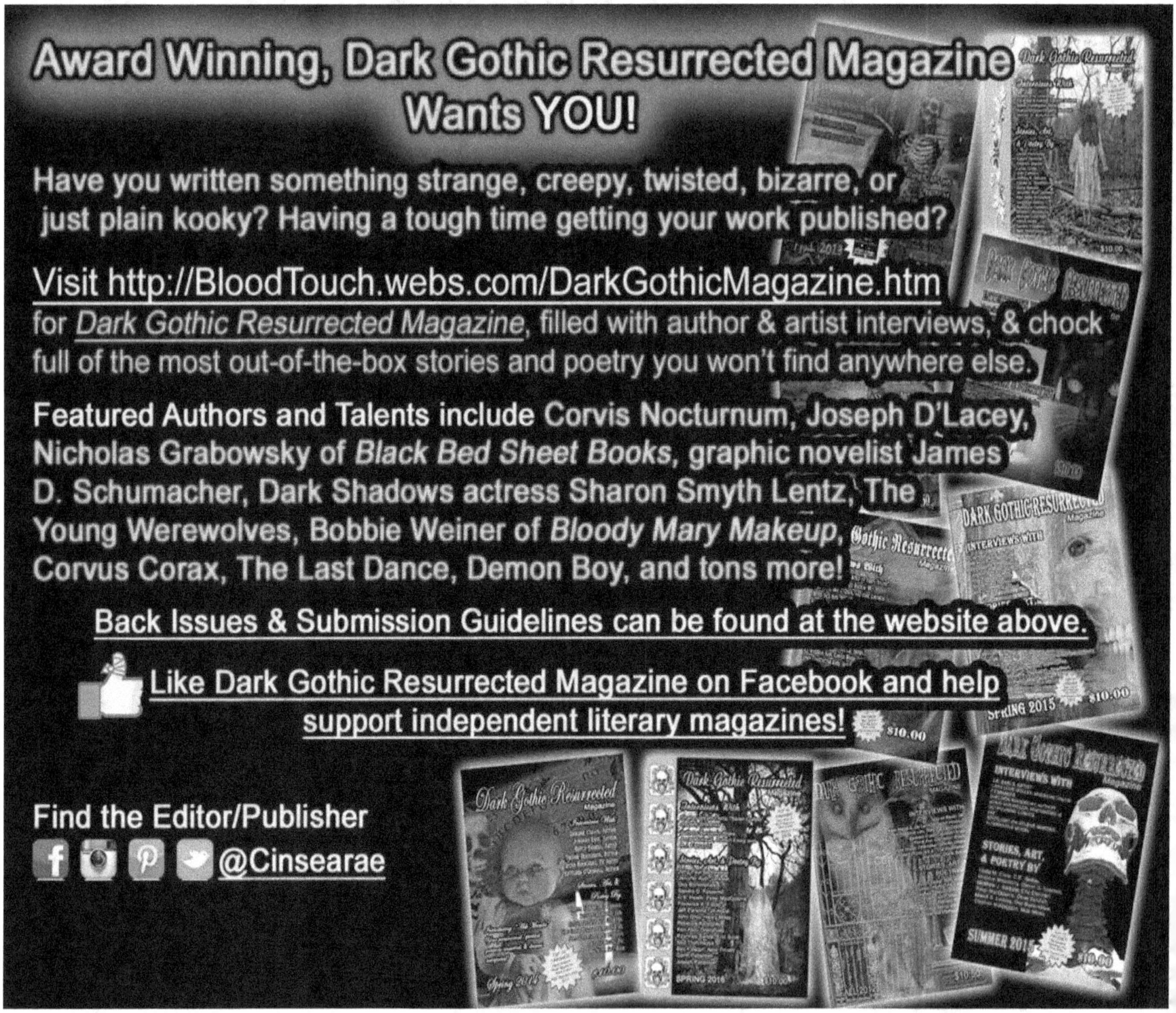

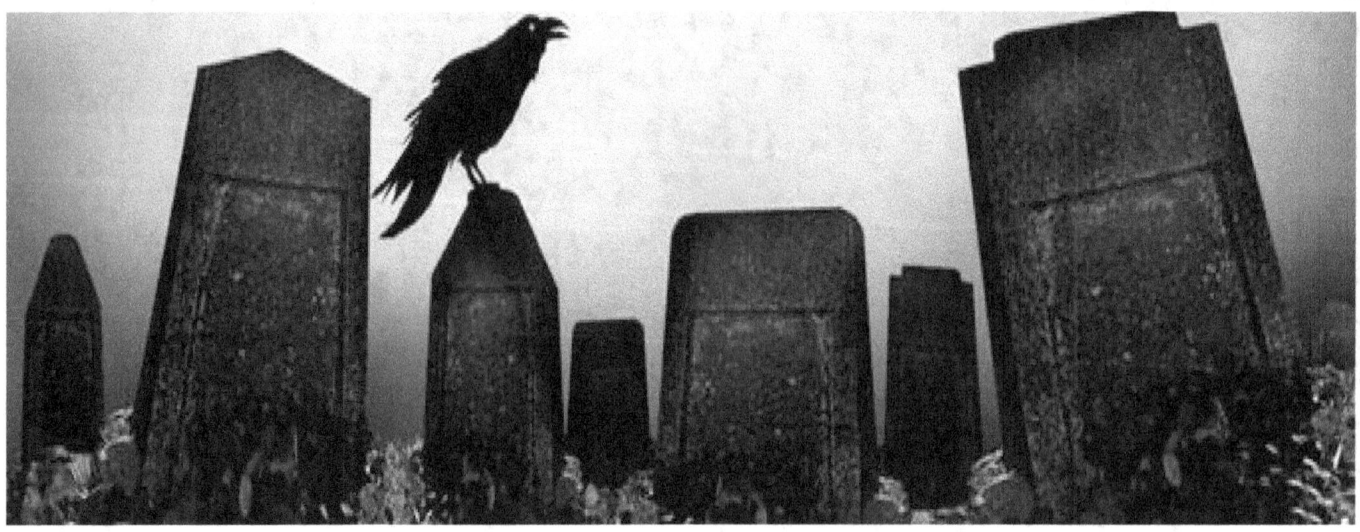